The Wisdom of Our Ancestors

THE WISDOM OF OUR ANCESTORS

*Conservative Humanism and
the Western Tradition*

Graham James McAleer

and

Alexander S. Rosenthal-Pubul

Foreword by Daniel J. Mahoney

University of Notre Dame Press
Notre Dame, Indiana

Library of Congress Control Number: 2023942034

ISBN: 978-0-268-20742-7 (Hardback)
ISBN: 978-0-268-20745-8 (WebPDF)
ISBN: 978-0-268-20741-0 (Epub)

DEDICATED TO JOS DECORTE (d. 2001),

professor of medieval philosophy,

and our teacher at Leuven

CONTENTS

Foreword, by Daniel J. Mahoney   ix

Preface   xv

INTRODUCTION   Conservatism: The Quest for a Quiddity   1

CHAPTER 1   Humanism: The Master Idea of
Western Civilization   23

CHAPTER 2   The Metaphysics of Conservatism   43

CHAPTER 3   Establishment   59

CHAPTER 4   Law   79

CHAPTER 5   Humanistic Enterprise   99

CHAPTER 6   The Conservative *via media:* Between Nationalism
and the Dream of Cosmopolis   121

CHAPTER 7   Liberty and History   143

CHAPTER 8   Conservatism without Reprimitivism   161

Concluding Remarks   175

Notes   199

Index   273

FOREWORD

Daniel J. Mahoney

A particularly discerning twentieth-century political philosopher, Leo Strauss, insisted that it is "better to understand the low in light of the high" rather than the other way around. That is the approach adopted by Graham James McAleer and Alexander S. Rosenthal-Pubul in this rich, learned, and invigorating book. Their aim is both high and serious: to establish the ennobling links between conservatism, Christian humanism, and classical wisdom at their wisest and most humane. In this laudable aim, in this welcome synthesis, they succeed admirably.

For a book on conservatism, McAleer and Rosenthal-Pubul are remarkably attentive to "what is going on"—to the debates that animate what is left of "the republic of letters" and public-spirited philosophy, theology, and political theory today. Theirs is a dialectical approach, first limned negatively by what they reject: not only a contemporary liberalism that reduces liberty to self-will and subjectivism but also a traditionalism that eschews the goods inherent in the liberal order. Nor do they reduce conservatism to classical liberalism, as many in the Anglo-American world do. Theirs, moreover, is a modern conservatism, addressing the moral crisis coextensive with late modernity but without rejecting modernity *tout court*. As conservatives and Christian humanists, they value the truth inherent in the liberal affirmation of human equality and common humanity. But for them, the goods of the liberal polity, not to mention the goods of the soul, will never be defined or maintained by freedom without purpose and self-limitation. Liberalism, for all its virtues, cannot begin to adequately answer the question of the nature of the human being, who is said to be free and equal. And in its decayed late-modern manifestations, progressive liberalism refuses to even ask the question. It is content—nay, it aggressively counters truth-seeking with negation and repudiation, rejecting "the perennial philosophy" and even the most minimal respect for "the wisdom of the ancestors." The original liberal promise of liberty and equality has thus to a large degree culminated in nihilism and moral debasement. This is the dire situation in which we find ourselves and that the authors of this book seek to address.

Our authors thus present conservatism—high conservatism, the conservatism of the larger Western tradition—as a *via media* between the late modern rejection of ordered freedom, of the natural moral law, of respect for family, tradition, and religion, and a hyper-traditionalist or reactionary turn to "privileged particular attachments." Too often, those who espouse the latter forget that, as our authors put it, the "the circle of sympathy ultimately extends universally" in the form of binding moral obligations that reach far beyond kinship and even the civic community. To be sure, the local—and the full array of particular—attachments have inherent dignity and must be defended against the levelling and homogenizing tendencies of doctrinaire egalitarianism. But salutary tradition is never an end-in-itself. It must respect the "moral consensus" of civilized human beings, a phrase taken from Aurel Kolnai, the Hungarian-born anti-totalitarian moral and political philosopher who is so admired by the authors of this book, and prudently navigate between the wisdom and dignity of the ancestral, of the tried and true, and the universal principles that ultimately ground common life. The cardinal virtues—courage, temperance, justice, and prudence (or practical wisdom)—belong to human beings as human beings, as does the humanizing quest, inherent in ordinary experience but pursued more systematically through philosophy, theology, and literature, for the simply true, good, and beautiful. High conservatism therefore refuses to succumb either to the exclusionary charm of the particular or to the tyrannizing allure of global cosmopolitanism. The latter, carried to its logical conclusion, leads to what Kant so suggestively called "soulless despotism" and that we today experience in manifold ways.

Following the lead of Roger Scruton, Pierre Manent, and older forms of Catholic thought, McAleer and Rosenthal-Pubul defend the nation as a just and legitimate political form without conflating nation-alism and conservatism. They are particularly critical of the neo-pagan Right with its preference for ethnonationalism and its disdain for prop-erly civic attachments. For them, there is no "end of history" with an unproblematic liberalism as the final form of the human adventure. At the same time, they will not abide the "illiberal" repudiation of repre-sentative government or commercial society either—the authors gener-ally side with Adam Smith and David Hume against those traditional-ists *and* Leftists who identify commercial society with luxury, moral corruption, injustice, and human degradation.

Most generally, the West has largely lost sight of "what it stands for or what it stands against," as McAleer and Rosenthal-Pubul state in their preface. The crucial nexus connecting territorial membership with rule of law and self-government, emphasized so well by the late, great English conservative political philosopher and man of letters Roger Scruton, is today under systematic assault. More deeply, we have largely lost an appreciation of our dependence on a natural order of things— and a beneficent Providence—above the human will. Our unfounded substitute faith in inexorable historical "progress" and in human per-fectibility played a major role in the genesis of totalitarian violence and mendacity on a mass scale in the twentieth century. As a civilization, however, we did not learn the lessons that the totalitarian episode should have taught us. Today, our smug and unphilosophical social science, with its deterministic emphasis on "social" causation, has next to no place for the civic and moral agency of human *persons*. McAleer and Rosenthal-Pubul are particularly good at articulating the intrinsic links between conservatism, Christian humanism, and the personalist affirmation of free will and a human soul that, while embodied, transcends material and social causation.

In its judicious mix of classical and Christian wisdom, humanism is, in the words of our authors, the "master idea of Western civilization." Such humanism is utterly realistic about the reality of human imperfec-tion and evil while simultaneously stressing human freedom, natural moral law, and conscience as both essential to human nature and in-forming human agency. In this connection, McAleer and Rosenthal-Pubul write incisively about the crucial role that classical humane let-ters and education in self-mastery play in ordering and elevating the human soul. Already in Xenophon's *Memorabilia*, Socrates had pointed out that a human being cannot be free or wise if he or she is a slave to the passions. Judaism and Christianity taught the great truth that every human being is made in "the image and likeness of God," a claim deepened by the very fact of the Incarnation, of God becoming flesh and blood. The great works of Greek and Latin wisdom—those of Plato, Aristotle, Seneca, Plutarch, and Cicero, among others—taught civilized human beings that dignity is also acquired or earned when we human beings live lives informed by moral and intellectual virtue. Classical Christianity would add that even free and virtuous human beings are "fallen" human beings, who must open themselves to the grace of God. Conversion, repentance, and forgiveness thus became invaluable treasures of the Western moral and spiritual patrimony. To jettison them is to jettison essential elements of our humanity. These themes luminously come together in what our authors call the "Benedict synthesis," the unforced melding of the deepest Christian insights about the "logos" at the heart of the created order, a "purified" Hellenism in search of wisdom about human nature and the nature of the "Whole," and modern liberty that refuses to bend to the positivistic and scientistic reduction of reason to narrow instrumental rationality. The late Pope Benedict XVI, the architect of this synthesis in its most satisfactory form, is thus one of the heroes of the book.

Avoiding angelism and reductive materialism, high conservatism has much to teach us about the meaning of what it means to be a human being worthy of civilized liberty. Authority should never be confused with authoritarianism, and liberty, equality, and human dignity must not lose sight of the nobility that allows human beings to achieve true "height" as well as "depth," in the words of Kolnai.

Drawing on the Russian philosopher Nicholas Berdyaev (who was not exactly a conservative but who was profoundly anti-totalitarian), the authors of this work brilliantly uncover the Achilles's heal of an *exclusively* modern humanism. As Berdyaev eloquently argued in *The Meaning of History*, if modern humanism initially exalts man, it ultimately debases him "by ceasing to regard him as a being of a higher and divine origin." Limiltess human self-affirmation leads inexorably to "self-enslavement," in Kolnai's phrase from his seminal 1949 essay "Privilege and Liberty." Divorced from the deeper insights of Christian civilization, it leads, in Berdyaev's words, to man's "own perdition." Liberalism proffers many legitimate aims and aspirations, including an enhanced concern for the weak and marginal (although this concern is presented in a more balanced and spiritually fulsome way in the Christian tradition). But liberalism fails miserably in providing "an adequate ontological ground for its humanism." It needs the salutary correction provided by conservatism, in no small part to prevent what is best in liberalism from perishing from this earth.

In the last lecture he delivered at the Collège de France in 1978, the great French anti-totalitarian political thinker Raymond Aron suggested that, while every human being should be free to find his or her own path in life, none have the right to invent their own tablets of good and evil. Such were the near final words of a liberal open to the best conservative thought. This wise and valuable book explains exactly why that is the case.

PREFACE

*It is a lack of confidence, more than anything else that
kills a civilisation. We can destroy ourselves by cynicism
and disillusion, just as effectively as by bombs.*

—Sir Kenneth Clark, *Civilisation*

It was about forty years ago that Sir Roger Scruton raised the question
of "the meaning of conservatism." It is a question we must ask again.
What is the meaning of conservatism for us, now well into the twenty-
first century? The answers in our present circumstances are by no
means self-evident. Our world is increasingly marked by the growing
opposition between *liberalism* and *nationalism*. More and more conservatives are themselves dividing along the line separating these two
camps.[1] Is there, however, a specifically *conservative* political philosophy that is not reducible to either liberal cosmopolitanism or nationalistic tribalism? Let us first examine the contenders before returning to
our main question.

Liberalism—the defense of the Enlightenment tradition—is a valorization of capitalism, libertarianism, cosmopolitanism, individualism, universal rights, and the idea of progress. After the brutal ideological struggles of the twentieth century, liberalism seemingly emerged
from the Cold War as the sole victor and remaining political doctrine
of global scope. The world order forged after the fall of the Iron Cur-
tain in 1989 was built on the pillar of *globalization*, defined as "the free
movement of goods, capital, and to a large degree labor (immigration)

across ever-more porous national borders." Globalization was reinforced by the development of supranational institutions and federations, such as the European Union (EU) (Treaty of Maastricht, 1992) and the World Trade Organization (WTO) (1995). And, of course, the whole edifice of the liberal world order took place under the aegis of the liberal superpower, the United States. In its "unipolar moment,"[2] the United States would shepherd the world toward a future based on liberalism, human rights, democracy, and free-market capitalism.[3]

This new world order was famously hailed by Francis Fukuyama as the "end of history": the idea that liberalism had vindicated its claim to be "the end point of mankind's ideological evolution"; that history would now move inexorably toward "the universalization of Western liberal democracy as the final form of human government."[4] In Fukuyama's conception, liberal commercialism has superseded all premodern iterations of the West, indeed, all forms of social variant, everywhere. We read Fukuyama as a liberal, therefore, and posit neoconservatism as a form of liberalism. For reasons we shall make clear in this book, we hold that progressivism is also a variant of liberal commercial civilization.[5]

Today, however, every aspect of this liberal world order has come into question. The U.S. "unipolar moment" and with it the post–Cold War paradigm of the liberal international order are giving way to an era of multipolarity,[6] neonationalism,[7] and great civilization rivalries.[8] Part of this is the fruit of liberalism's own success.[9] China, by entering into the global market economy, achieved decades of unprecedented economic growth. The British accountancy firm PwC projects that by 2050, China will have an economy roughly equal to the United States and Europe combined, with India in second place.[10] Attending this economic power is rising military muscle, with China's navy projected by some to be qualitatively equal, but larger, than the U.S. Navy by the 2030s.[11] Yet contrary to Fukuyama's early prognostications, China's economic liberalization (really a form of nationalistic mercantilism) has not led to political liberalization.[12]

To the rise of China, and other historic Asian civilizations, we may add the new assertiveness of Russia and political Islam.[13] Throughout the world, in a process Samuel Huntington called *indigenization*, civilizations are rejecting Western models and returning to their own roots. We do not know what the future holds, but the outlines of a polycentric, post-Western world are already coming into view.[14] Added to this, we may consider the West's own increasing doubts about serving as liberalism's missionary to the world. Fukuyama's optimism about liberal democracy's capacity to be universalized was battered and bruised by the war in Kosovo, and utterly deflated when the West, led by the United States, was basically defeated in Iraq,[15] and routed in Afghanistan,[16] by a stubborn political Islam and strident ethnic tribalism. The Russo-Ukraine War of 2022 has widely been perceived as the coup de grâce for the end of history thesis.[17]

In the long arc of history, what we may be seeing is the end of an era that began more than five centuries ago with the voyages of Columbus. We mean the era marked by the dominance of Europe, and latterly by the United States. What is more than anything else shifting power from West to East is the rising economic weight of the historically great Asian civilizations, whose vast populations are now augmented by rising economic growth and technical prowess.

These geopolitical considerations, epochal though they are, pale in significance to the internal evidence of cultural decay and demoralization. The modern West is no longer conscious of its identity: it no longer knows what it stands for or what it stands against.[18] The roots of this crisis have been a long time in coming; some of its contours, the sense of the loss of meaning, purpose, standards, and values in Western culture, were already sketched by nineteenth-century thinkers, such as Nietzsche and Dostoyevsky, and in the twentieth century by broadly conservative thinkers, such as Leo Strauss, Eric Voegelin, and José Ortega y Gasset. Without being exhaustive, some of the West's conundrums include (1) globalization as a suspension of territorial membership that roots rule of law and democracy (Scruton); (2) liberty ridding humans of an acceptance of dependency, a root condition of our humanity (Cardinal Robert Sarah); (3) a "culture of death" and sexual libertinism (Pope John Paul II); (4) a belief in human goodness that so minimizes evil that the ever-present possibility of war is ignored (Carl Schmitt); (5) the glamour of bourgeois life stunting the human spirit (Friedrich Nietzsche); (6) perfectionist ideals denying the splitness ritualized in religion (Eric Voegelin); and (7) sophisticated analysis of social causation obscuring the recalcitrant reality of human persons (Max Scheler).

Contemporary times have only seen an accelerating sense of tension and disorientation. In our cultural crisis, the ordinary guardians of our civilizational inheritance, the intelligentsia, have, in the aggregate, done little to sustain or transmit civilizational confidence. On the contrary, as Scruton noted, many intellectuals have fully embraced a "culture of repudiation."[19] A poignant example was furnished by one student's reaction to efforts to reintroduce a long-expunged[20] Western Civilization requirement at Stanford: "A Western Civ Requirement would necessitate that our education be centered on upholding white supremacy, capitalism, and colonialism, and all other oppressive systems that flow from Western civilizations."[21] The polemic against the Western heritage as irremediably evil has not remained contained within the academic world. The 2020s have, to date, witnessed a wave of iconoclastic fury against the traditional heroes and symbols of Anglo-American and Western civilization. In scenes reminiscent of the Puritan, French, and Maoist revolutions, statues of, among others, Christopher Columbus, St. Juniper Serra, George Washington, Thomas Jefferson, Ulysses S. Grant, David Hume, and Sir Winston Churchill were toppled or vandalized. Churches and synagogues were likewise attacked, and war memorials were not spared the culture of repudiation had for a generation steadily worn down the inherited reverence for the Founding Fathers of the United States, Christianity, and Western civilization. Now it had seemingly metastasized into a "revolutionary moment"[22] aiming to throw off the past and begin history anew from Year Zero. Here there was no calibrated judgment on defects within the Western patrimony, but a wholesale condemnation of it as fit only to be erased from human memory. Our cultural situation of disorder and decay has become searingly visible.

From the standpoint of the iconoclasts, the Western inheritance represents a burden of sin that its modern heirs must cast off or expiate lest they be implicated in the guilt of our ancestors.[23] It is little wonder, then, that once ubiquitous Western Civilization survey courses have been vanishing from universities in the United States. In some ways, "post-Westernism" is more an internal crisis than an external threat. It is a crisis of confidence. What is there to be proud of? Plenty, actually. We aim to recall what Edmund Burke called "the wisdom of our ancestors."

Our call to reclaim with reverence the spiritual and intellectual inheritance of the West comes in a time of transition in which the post-

Cold War order built around the premises of liberalism and globalization is challenged by the rise of a new nationalism. In this great contest between liberalism and nationalism, a central question is how conservatism is to be positioned between these forces. Russia was quicker to learn the lesson of Iraq than was the United States. Perhaps its historical alienation from the West allowed Russia to mobilize around a trend running counter to liberalism, that is, nationalism. Perhaps its own experiment with liberalism in the 1990s, which was experienced as a time of economic turmoil and political humiliation, triggered an antiliberal reaction. Whatever the cause,[24] the nationalist backlash against globalized liberalism ultimately arrived in the heartlands of the West. Disaffection with the EU following the prolonged economic crisis starting in 2008 and the migrant crisis of 2015–16 was followed by the Brexit referendum in the UK, and the rise of nationalist parties across the Continent who differed on many points but shared a common skepticism toward the EU's postnational vision and mass migration. Viktor Orban, Hungary's prime minister, put the matter starkly by declaring that the era of "liberal babble" was now over.[25] Meanwhile, the election of an avowed American nationalist[26] in Donald Trump signaled to the world the country's doubts about bearing the continued costs of maintaining the liberal world order. A renewed emphasis on sovereignty and borders in trade and immigration policy, combined with skepticism toward international institutions, were to characterize a new course of the United States. The roots of this nationalist resurgence are partially economic. The winners of globalization were largely those businesses that benefit from a globalized labor market and supply chains, but also middle-class consumers who benefit from a cheaper and greater variety of goods. Yet there were also losers of the globalization process in terms of the manufacturing working class in the developed countries who felt threats to jobs and wages from outsourcing and immigration. But equally or more so, the new nationalism was driven by cultural fears. Even in European nations where declining birth rates might argue for accepting high levels of immigration based on a purely economic logic, fears about the loss of national and cultural identity drove more and more Europeans to nationalist parties.

The new nationalism, though largely "populist" in temper, has not had a shortage of formidable intellectual defenders. Yoram Hazony's widely acclaimed *The Virtue of Nationalism* makes the case for the sovereign nation-state as the available alternative to some form of universalistic imperialism, including, as he sees it, the imperialism of modern liberalism. More radical thinkers, such as those on the French New Right (*Nouvelle Droite*), argue for "ethnopluralism," that is, the right of each ethnos to maintain its own character and culture against the homogenizing, universalist claims of liberalism and globalized capitalism. These Nouvelle Droite thinkers oppose mass migration and valorize particularism, pluriversality, cultural relativism, the primacy of tribal identity or ethnos, rooted community, antiglobalization, economic protectionism, borders, and bounded communities. These two value orientations—liberal cosmopolitanism and nationalism[27]—are in fact emerging as the main contenders to shape events more generally in the twenty-first century.

In Russia, a similar trend of exalting ethnos and particularism is found in the writings of Aleksandr Dugin.[28] Dugin is quick to point out that postmodernism has long been critical of liberal optimism and, at least since the Romantic movement going back to the German Counter-Enlightenment of Herder and Fichte, there have been all manner of literary, artistic, and musical works celebrating regions and peoples throughout Europe's hinterland.

Dugin is one of the most controversial thinkers of our time. Vilified as "the most dangerous philosopher in the world"[29] and "Putin's brain,"[30] he has been sanctioned by the U.S. government, and his daughter was recently murdered in a possible assassination attempt against Dugin himself. Some may question why a thinker like Dugin, who is sometimes cursorily dismissed in the West as a crank, if not a neofascist, would occupy a place in our work as an important interlocutor worth debating. Indubitably controversial and provocative, Dugin's place as the preeminent political philosopher in Russia supplies a part of the answer. Just as Putin presents Russia as a geopolitical alternative to the West (tensions with which have been recently exacerbated with the Russo-Ukrainian war), so Dugin's Fourth Political Theory presents itself as an ideological alternative to Western liberalism.[31] Understanding the ideologies that motivate a great power rival has self-evident value. But there are deeper philosophical reasons related to our project. Dugin represents a continuation of Heidegger's critique of humanism, and we present a defense of Western humanism, if rightly understood on the basis of its classical and Christian foundations. The liberal universalism of Fukuyama and the antiliberal particularism of Dugin represent two extreme poles, between which our own work aims to navigate. We aim, in short, to reconcile universal moral values with particularist loyalties. Because Dugin is still less well known than other thinkers we discuss, an overview of some of his core tenets will be of value. In his antimodernism and in his work of trying to dismantle liberal universalism and progressivism, Dugin draws crucially upon the work of René Guénon (1886–1951), and on the philosophy of Heidegger, the German conservative revolutionaries (as Schmitt, Junger, Spengler, and others), and the traditions of geopolitics (Ratzel, Mackinder, Haushofer, and others). We will say more about Dugin's ideas and sources in chapters 2 and 6.

Dugin may perhaps be approached as the continuation of an interrupted nineteenth-century Russian Slavophile tradition of philosophy that included Aleksey Khomyakov (1804–60) and Ivan Kireyevsky (1806–56). Whereas the Westernizers (Belinsky, Herzen) disparaged the Russian past and saw Russia's future in the embrace of the European Enlightenment and continuing the "turn to the West" that began with Peter the Great, Slavophiles rejected this interpretation of Russian history and destiny. Instead, they saw Russia as a great civilization in its own right, and they attacked Europe's Enlightenment for its one-sided rationalism and scientism, arguing instead for a Russian idea of "integral knowledge" (Kireyevsky), which includes mysticism, passion, and intuition. Slavophile themes find clear contemporary echoes in Dugin's Eurasianism (insisting on Russia's separate, non-Western civilizational course), his communitarianism (as against liberal individualism), and his romantic refusal to subordinate faith, mythos, and mysticism to scientific rationality. And much as the Slavophiles drew on German romanticism and idealism (Hegel, Schelling), Dugin draws above all on the German romantic Martin Heidegger.

Dugin sees liberalism as both the first and the last of the Western ideologies that characterize "modernity." The liberal concept of the autonomous individual for Dugin is born out of Cartesian subjectivity. Dugin presents liberalism's aim, as a political and cultural project, as the emancipation of the individual from all involuntary collective identities—religious, ethnic, and, finally, with the emergence of gender theory, even natural sexual identity. For Dugin, liberalism, by negating religion and ethnos, has an inherent tendency toward secular cosmopolitanism as the ideal. Once religious and ethnic differences among human beings are overcome, there will be only an undifferentiated universal humanity of free individuals. As with a related economic system, capitalism, liberalism has a similar tendency toward universalism that we today call "globalization" (a concept already foreseen in some ways by Kant and Marx). In the twentieth century, liberalism triumphed over the two modern alternative Western ideologies, fascism/Nazism and communism, vanquished in 1945 and 1989, respectively. The post–Cold War world is characterized by U.S. unipolarity, and the effort to universalize liberalism as the end of history that all nations and civilizations must ultimately accept. Liberalism for Dugin thus brooks no rivals and is fundamentally a universal imperium.

Dugin however proposes a fourth political theory. Postmodernism for Dugin is the final stage in the decadence of Western modernity and its metaphysics. But it is also an opportunity to transcend modernity and restore sacral order. The suspicion of universalist grand narratives, and the Heideggerian critique of Cartesian subjectivity, allows for the emergence of plurivocity—a diversity of discourses other than the Enlightenment project. The postmodern situation is therefore for Dugin an intellectual door that opens the space to reclaim the legitimacy of premodern traditionalism. It is the fact that Dugin turns to the sacral orders that preceded the Enlightenment and liberal modernity that establishes Dugin as a figure of "the Right." And just as plurivocity characterizes the intellectual landscape, so he sees multipolarity and the diversity of civilizations with their own worldviews characterizing the emerging postliberal era. There is no question that Dugin is a right-wing critic of Western liberalism with a hard geopolitical edge in favor of an assertive if not imperial Russian foreign policy. Dugin has at his worst been given to intemperate and indefensible outbursts replete with expressions of Russian expansionism, sympathy for violent actions, and militant anti-Americanism, anti-Westernism, and anti-Catholicism.[32] Whatever our ultimate view on the relation between Dugin and fascism, on his own terms he would see nationalism and its extreme apotheosis of fascism as the *third* political philosophy still caught up in the logic of late modernity, and thus he is proposing a fourth. Though

Dugin exalts the ethnos and broader categories of "the people" (drawing on the specifically Russian tradition of the *narod*), he overtly rejects the identification of ethnos and race or the idea of a race hierarchy[33] that was prominent in European extreme-right movements of the 1930s. Like the French Nouvelle Droite, he seems to embrace ethnopluralism and the coequality of distinct ethnically based communities, each with their own diverse value structures, but he differs in his more positive appraisal of Christianity. But it is not clear how Dugin's account can avoid cultural relativism and the rejection of universal moral principles. It seems that for him each ethnos generates its monadic moral universe without any apparent need for its moral values to logically cohere with those of others. Our own understanding of traditionalist conservatism differs from this, for although we recognize the value of particularity and attachment to the localities of place, custom, and culture, we also affirm the universal validity of natural law as articulated by some of the best classical and Christian thinkers of the Western tradition. We believe conservative humanism is a *via media*, an essential correction—and no mere aesthetic preference—of these value orientations. Traditional conservatism has a lineage distinct from both liberalism and nationalism (or ethnopluralism): it is neither cosmopolitan nor tribal. There is a throughline that runs from the social forms of the Middle Ages, to Burke, Ruskin, Scheler, Berdyaev, Tolkien, Kolnai, Scruton, and papal reflections on politics, known as Catholic social thought (CST). This Anglo-Continental political reflection defends ancestral traditions and accepts privileged particularistic attachments (to family, religion, hearth and home), but its circle of sympathy ultimately extends universally (natural law). It emphasizes personal virtue, tradition, family, and solidarity more than liberalism does, but it sees establishment, hierarchy, and natural law as counterweights to a straightforward celebration of the local and autonomous. It does not decry the state, but in affirming varieties of privilege it wants to forestall the collapse of the religious, familial, educational, and civil into statism.

Conservatism, distinct from both liberalism and nationalism,[34] is not necessarily opposed to all that issues from them. There are also hybrid forms (liberal-conservatism, nationalist-conservatism), and thus we will argue that there is a place for aspects of the Scottish Enlightenment in the thought-world of conservative humanism. In chapter 5, we argue that a humanist political economy requires this.[35] Put otherwise, there are elements of the Fukuyama and Dugin positions that need to be retained.

Central to the contemporary role of conservatism is to act as the guardian[36] of Western civilization's confidence. It is a difficult time for the West.

With the passing of Roger Scruton in 2020, now seems the right time to take stock of conservative thought, which has always had the defense of civilization as a guiding star. It is a massive field, and any avenue taken is likely to seem to others a bit eccentric. In describing his journey to conservatism, Scruton observed: "Leo Strauss, Eric Voegelin, and others have grafted the metaphysical conservatism of Central Europe on to American roots, forming effective and durable schools of political thought."[37] Throughout, we talk about contemporary events and figures, but our orientation is like Voegelin's—and he figures a good deal in the book—in developing an account of political humanism backed by the "metaphysical conservatism of Central Europe."

We are both graduates of the Catholic University of Leuven, Belgium, and we propose that conservatism in the twenty-first century must be a defense of humanism, the best lens by which to understand Western civilizational identity. A guidepost to Western humanism is found in Pope Benedict XVI's Regensburg Address: the West is a capacious synthesis of Christianity, "critically purified" Hellenism, and Latin culture. Because humanism has existed in classical, Christian, and modern secular forms, it provides us with a narrative of continuity that can best make sense of the West as an integral whole and explain the relation of its historic phases to one another. We believe that conservatism is the philosophy of politics that, for the foreseeable future, best secures the conditions making humanism possible.

Conservatism is a defense of tradition—but which tradition? Humanism broadly conceived has a legitimate claim to be *the* Western idea; indeed, it is an ancient tradition.

There are three historical iterations of humanism, which we detail far more in the introduction.

First, *classical humanism*—this is the Greek παιδεία and Roman *humanitas*—was a conscious cultivation of human excellence, striving for the full development of human faculties, particularly the moral, intellectual, and aesthetic. This is the central Greek ideal of culture (Jaeger) running through its poetry, art, rhetoric, philosophy, and political conceptions. Fully revived in the Renaissance, it became the basis of Western liberal education in the modern era up to the twentieth century.

Second, *Christian humanism* stems from the fact that Christianity can claim to be the most anthropological of all faiths. Christianity claims that God became man in the Incarnation. All human beings have intrinsic and transcendent dignity: created in the divine image, redeemed by the God-man, given freedom, and called to eternal life. In the Middle Ages, the West became a Christocentric culture, neither theocentric (like Islam) nor anthropocentric (like modern secular culture), but incarnational. As a value, the Incarnation addresses suffering and offers tenderness as a balm. In this consists Christianity's essential correction of the ancients. Embracing the divine and the human, Latin culture posits a harmony between body and soul, nature and grace, faith and reason, and church and state. This explains its openness to humanist culture: the Renaissance arose from medieval Catholic Italy.

Third is *modern humanism*. Often called *secular humanism* — which might not really be true[38] — it dates to the Enlightenment. It is a very complex phenomenon,[39] and to one of its varieties we are steadfastly opposed: the reduction of nature to biology; science conceived as conquest, the "relief of man's estate" (Bacon) through technoscience;[40] a critique of tradition, boasting liberation of man from nature[41] and inheritance;[42] a denunciation of religion as intolerance and superstition; and thus anthropocentrism, twined with an ethics of humanitarianism,[43] being an entitlement, nonreciprocal vision of rights and individual liberties. These elements make up atheistic liberal humanism.[44]

Russian theorist Berdyaev made the point that modern humanism reductively strips us to mere biological beings, its vitalism undermining transcendent dignity. Vitalist accounts emphasize scarcity, nakedness, necessity, materialism, positivism, and disenchantment. Berdyaev argued such bleakness would collapse into antihumanism,[45] the upshot being a spiritual deadening, a technocratic loneliness. Nineteenth-century vitalism imploded spectacularly with Nazism, its atrocities stemming from "the rupture of species" (Rolf Zimmermann),[46] racism its reigning ideology (Dugin, *FPT*, 44). Contemporary vitalism retains the old materialism and partibility, but offers a fresh blend, mixing in digital tech.

In a review of the best-selling proponent of transhumanism, Yuval Harari, Scruton finds him saying that modern life is "a constant pursuit of power within a universe devoid of meaning," and yet thrilling to the idea that "once the Internet-of-All-Things is up and running, humans might be reduced from engineers to chips, then to data, and eventually we might dissolve within the torrent of data like a clump of earth within a gushing river."[47] Here, we see vitalism slipping into angelism.

Though influenced by Berdyaev, the Jesuit Erich Przywara was prescient to observe that in a weird way we moderns are an unstable hybrid flopping between vitalism and angelism.[48] Cardinal Sarah elaborates. Contemporary innovation in communication "gives us the impression of generating space and time, of being gods capable of communicating without being stopped by any obstacle." At the same time, our angelism has a supplement: "genetics is a new god." Assured that we are solely "the result of the development of matter over the course of history," we can say that technologically elevating the genome can raise no serious questions—it's just matter, right?[49] Philosopher of science Jean-Pierre Dupuy concurs: "In this telling, the prokaryotic and eukaryotic cells that formed the basis of life have been converted into products of the human mind, genetic algorithms, even though these algorithms first appeared only toward the end of the twentieth century. Life is regarded as a digest, or summary, of *information*—the blueprint for the *fabrication* of living beings themselves. The materialist monism of modern science has suddenly become a spiritual monism: if the mind is identical with nature, it is because nature is interpreted as if it were a creation of the mind."[50]

On the one hand, liberalism's break with ideas of natural constraint includes what Pierre Manent calls "the dream-life of the angels."[51] For this reason, technoscience holds out the promise of suspending our shared history, overcoming that oppressive idea, the family.[52] Hegel's angelism broached the possibility. In Fukuyama's telling of Hegel, history can make us free because we have always been free of the earth: "The distinction between human and non-human is fully rational: only human beings are free, that is, able to struggle for recognition in a battle of pure prestige. This distinction is based on nature, or rather, on the radical disjunction between the realm of nature and the realm of freedom. The distinction between one human group and another, on the other hand, is an accidental and arbitrary by-product of human history."[53]

The "universal and homogeneous" state of Absolute Spirit is possible, it turns out, because we are angels, surfing above nature. This explains Schopenhauer's quip that in modernity the person becomes "a winged cherub without a body."[54] And yet, on the other hand, "man is materially obese" (Sarah), hoping "to clothe himself in silicon and steel."[55] On vitalism, princes of the Catholic Church agree with East Coast aesthetes: "For postmodern capitalism, man is a resource like any other,"[56] the electronic devices we use to enhance our personal brands making us "data-cows," the term used by the massive industry that mines, fragments, and monetizes our deepest secrets and desires.[57] The test of the political worth of conservative humanism is that it can thread its way between angelism (Hegel's "raising the Logos to complete clarity in consciousness"[58]) and vitalism[59] (materialism's "shrunken self").[60]

Berdyaev argued that it was the idea of divine beauty that decorated mortal life.[61] Conservative humanism affirms an obedience to a moral order transcending our will. From the ancients, it draws on the idea of human intellectual and aesthetic cultivation and the development of the natural virtues. From Christianity it draws upon a transcendent vision of the human being rooted in the Incarnation, which provides the foundation for a transfigured and universal form of natural law, and so emerges as a critical corrective of the moral particularism of the ancient city (in spite of certain ancient precedents in Stoicism)—and also a new cast of gentle virtues. The Christian doctrine of sin moreover tempers humanism with a sense of sobriety.[62] Conservative humanism must also be modern, not reactionary. Modern liberty—a consequence of massive changes in the thoughtscape of Europe: the Renaissance, the Reformation, the discovery of the New World, and the Industrial Revolution—is salutary. The astonishing refinements in the arts and sciences have granted opportunities for personal development far outstripping what was previously possible for ordinary folk. Despite its profound problems in modernity, conservative humanism draws on modern personalism and finds worth in some of its moral formulations and commercial logic.

What follows is a road map to the book's argument. Each chapter can be seen as a commentary on themes addressed in Scruton's *The Meaning of Conservatism*. We run far afield from Scruton, but his book is indispensable to conservative reflection. In launching off from Scruton, here we show how some of his analysis dovetails with our own.

ROAD MAP

Our introduction chapter will clarify the thought-world of conservatism. To some, even Fukuyama is a conservative, others, especially in the United States, think conservatism is libertarianism, or the policies of Reagan and Thatcher. Leftists view conservatism with horror as just a dog whistle for atavistic nationalism. In other chapters (2, 6–8) we work to distinguish conservatism from liberalism and nationalism. Here we suggest what conservatism means in a positive sense. Political conservatism only achieves self-consciousness when there is a crisis of tradition, as occurred in the West following the French Revolution. In that sense, conservatism is a modern movement, but one that strives to preserve continuity with the past. At the broadest level, conservatism is the defense of the ancestral. In the Western context, this largely means the "defense of humanism." This definition is more capacious than it seems at first, since it necessarily means also the "defense of the organs of tradition," how "establishment" (meaning "the institutions bearing values and offices"; see chapter 3) transmits the character and inheritance of a civilization to future generations. These organs are principally three: the institutions of religion, family, and education. However, against the atomic individualism of contemporary liberalism, libertarianism, and Thatcherism, we credit the state as part of establishment facilitating the sympathetic sociality of human nature. We affirm a balance sought by Scruton.[63] Scruton rejected Lady Thatcher's "liberal economics" because it wrongly stated the scope of establishment. Scruton defended the welfare state as necessary to modern conservatism— pointing out that it was Bismarck who established the German variant—and he argues in *Meaning of Conservatism* that where political and social goals warrant it, state ownership of something like a nation's railway system is an appropriately conservative policy. However, Scruton was at pains to point out that conservatism does not embrace the state as radically as socialists and nationalists.[64] Following Aurel Kolnai (1900–1973), we argue that conservatism is a justification of privilege, part of which is maintaining and expanding the scope of autonomous partnerships—family, church, guilds, trusts, small business, corporations, private schools, sports associations, townships, apprenticeships, and craft, among others. Self-organization is one of the pillars of conservative humanism (subsidiarity).

Chapter 1 is primarily historical. In contrast to Fukuyama's claim that liberalism is "the Western idea" superseding all that came before, we present humanism as the master idea of our civilization. Present in each of the West's great phases—classical antiquity, the Middle Ages, the Renaissance, and modernity—humanism is the arching value conservatism seeks to preserve. For the ancient Greeks and Romans, humanism signified an ideal of education focused on the full development of human intellectual, moral, and aesthetic faculties through philosophy, poetry, rhetoric, and other studies. Christianity, the religion of the God-man, supplied an egalitarian note affirming the singularity and unrepeatable value of each and every human being. Against certain dark strains in medieval thought, Aquinas championed nature, arguing that human persons have an integrity of their own and are able to shape their natural powers by a responsible freedom. In the Renaissance, Christian dignity combined with a revival of classical intellectual and aesthetic ideals, leading to an astonishing development of the arts and educational reform. We show in chapter 5 that modernity consolidated these gains by means of commerce and its facilitation of the "refinement of the arts and sciences" (Hume). However, modernity also sees the rise of secular humanism, with its advocates hoping to supplant God with science and technology. But as Berdyaev observes, at this very moment of maximum human self-assertion, humanism undermines itself. Without God, man has no transcendent dignity and becomes a merely physical, natural creature. As a result, argues Berdyaev, inhuman and antihumanistic forces that worship impersonal things such as race (Nazism) or economics (Marxism) come to the fore to threaten the human image. Even after the political defeats of these totalitarian systems, we contend that the secular-liberal West remains under threat of *reprimitivism*, devolving into "transhumanism"[65] or the "culture of death."[66] The role of conservatism is the defense of a Western humanism that affirms what John Paul II labeled "the transcendent dignity of the human person."

Chapter 2 examines the metaphysical situation to which conservatism is a response. Politics is about the relationship of the individual to the group. Metaphysically, Fukuyama takes up what we call the *univocal position*: all peoples are of one mind—the glamour and ease of liberal commercialism has universal appeal. Dugin's is the *equivocal position*. He, along with thinkers such as Seyyed Hossein Nasr,[67] René Guénon, and Zhang Wewei, defends capital "T" Traditionalism—all traditional civilizations are good and lead to truth; modern Western civilization, heavily inflected by liberal commercial universalism, is false and perverting. The middle ground is the *analogical position*, which aims to hold in tension the univocal and equivocal.[68] From Voegelin and Przywara, we derive a tensional metaphysics that grounds natural law and allows a judicious adoption of insights from liberal commercialism. Against Dugin, therefore, we defend the universalist claims of the West. However, against Fukuyama, this metaphysics also affirms the singularity and particularism of land and establishment. We take seriously Dugin's worry about futurism in politics and share the worries about technoscience expressed by Pope Francis.

Chapter 3 stakes out the political salience of establishment. We rely on Kolnai's treatment of privilege. As Scruton argues, conservatism is not a cynically "realist" politics but is rather oriented around ideals: a society has a self-image; laws are built around salutary fictions and myths; people understand themselves and others as agents, assuming both freedom and responsibility, pillars of rule of law.[69] It is the object of conservative politics to sustain this "surface of social consciousness" (Scruton). Pope Francis has recently made Scruton's point as to "the distinctive features of human life, which we are committed to safeguarding and promoting, not only in its constitutive biological dimension but also in its irreducible biographical aspect."[70] Kolnai argues that privilege—the professions, officer corps, professoriate, the bench, aristocracy, fashion houses, heralded sports clubs, and so on—embodies a hierarchy of values. The state is another such embodiment. Against some populism, privilege, we contend, is one of the pegs of a worthy humanism. A shorthand of this idea is Harvard Square, or a visit to any elite university. Our universities sit at the heart of power—training the next generation of leaders—and the buildings look the part. Because they are repositories of the refinement of the arts and sciences (Hume), graduating from a university means one is more sophisticated than when first attending. This sophistication—a competency around the order of values—comes with the trappings of worldly success. This latter is one meaning of privilege, but not the core meaning. The core of privilege are the porticos of University College London or the library at Coimbra, vehicles for accessing a value order transcending human will.[71]

Chapter 4 concerns rule of law and is a discussion of natural law. Central to Scruton's thinking is Burke's claim at the end of his address "Conciliation with the Colonies" (1775) that "English privileges have made [America] all that it is; English privileges alone will make it all it can be." Scruton rejects theories of natural right and sees liberty as a privilege in the gift of the state. If one takes the natural law tradition to span the efforts of Aquinas, Grotius, and Locke, he notes, one sees that there is barely any agreement on what the relationship is between nature and ethics, or any consensus about what makes for good politics. The natural law tradition cannot be the basis for a conservative politics.[72] We disagree, arguing that natural law is a necessary corrective of the irrationalities that can flare inside technoscience[73] and a critical control of the irrationalism of biocentrism.[74] A positive law position such as Scruton's[75] is all too easily buffeted by both these irrationalisms. They mangle rule of law, which, as Hume points out, is basic for the refinement of the arts and sciences.[76]

Chapter 5 is a conservative assessment of the worth of the Industrial Enlightenment and its postliberal critics. We borrow the term *humanistic enterprise* from Italian fashion designer Brunello Cucinelli and argue that the division of labor, despite its problems, is a worthy vehicle of humanism. The last forty years have seen a mountain of scholarship on Adam Smith that has significantly altered our understanding of his writings on the division of labor. We show that these writings have the bona fides of conservatism. We do so by showing that they match the ideal of differentiation set as a measure of healthy politics by a conservative of unimpeachable standing, Voegelin.

Chapter 6 details the growing divide in our time between liberal cosmopolitanism and nationalism. Where does conservatism fit? Liberalism of the Kantian variety argues for the transcendence of all national and particular loyalties in favor of a global federation embracing universal humanity. With the end of the Cold War, this "dream of cosmopolis" appeared closer to realization, and with the watchword of "globalization," where goods, capital, and people move across porous borders presided over by supranational institutions (WTO, WHO, the EU). More recently there has been a resurgence of nationalism insisting on the primacy of sovereignty, borders, and ethnic communities as the primary loyalty. The Anglo-Continental tradition[77] in this respect represents a middle ground valorizing particularist loyalties to family and nation but situates these loyalties within an *ordo amoris* that ultimately embraces all human beings. As such we argue that conservatism stands as a *via media* between nationalism and liberalism, rejecting both an undifferentiated cosmopolitanism and a narrowly tribal nationalism.

Chapter 7 addresses the central idea of liberalism, liberty. But what does "liberty" mean? And is there a specifically conservative form of liberty with which it contrasts? In proclaiming the universal victory of liberalism as "the end of history," Fukuyama understands the historical process as one of emancipation, the liberation of the autonomous individual in political, economic, and religious life. Setting Burke against Fukuyama (and their intellectual progenitors) allows us to compare and contrast liberal and conservative conceptions of freedom. Liberalism, in the well-known formulation of Isaiah Berlin, posits *negative* freedom, meaning that one is free to the degree one's actions are not externally obstructed. This notion of liberty underlies the familiar "freedoms" of Western states (speech, religion, press, etc.). Within moral limits, expanding the zone of personal negative freedom is an important modern achievement. Freedom in this sense is not, however, the only conservative value. Scruton challenges the primacy of liberty and emphasizes instead the authority of establishment as the source of other important conservative values, such as order, inheritance, property, solidarity, trust, and care. Burke argued that for negative liberty not to degenerate into libertinism it must be circumscribed within a framework of inherited and established political, religious, and social institutions that supply to it moral order. Burke's own idea of this order was a summation of the classical and Christian humanistic traditions. Socrates argued that one can be unfree not only when one's desires are externally obstructed, but also when one is enslaved by one's own passions. From this emerges an opposing conception of liberty not as unencumbered action but as virtuous self-mastery. Christianity in a somewhat similar vein speaks of persons laboring under the slavery of sin and requiring Christ's liberation. For Aristotle, the life of reason and virtue becomes the very end of politics. Christian humanism added that persons are freer once they have attained control over the enslaving passions. Burke develops these ideas into a critique of the Enlightenment and the French Revolution. At the same time, he champions the traditional liberties of the English and of religious tolerance, therewith integrating the best aspects of liberalism with the humanistic legacy of freedom and virtue.

Chapter 8 addresses *reprimitivism*—the motif of a falling away from civilization into barbarism—and it is found on the right (Voegelin) and on the left (Marx). This motif is no mere nostalgia, of which conservatives are so often accused. Civilizations are delicate, and reprimitivism, as thoroughly demonstrated by the Western totalitarianisms of the twentieth century, is always a real possibility.[78] In the case of the Nazis, reversion to primordialism was consciously embraced. Kolnai's *The War against the West* is our guide. We thus think Dugin's toying with biocentrism—the animating metaphysics of National Socialism—pernicious. However, there is another danger for conservatism. It must be owned that personalist philosophers of the twentieth century have edged toward angelism.[79] By this, we mean something specific. Personalism—a critical contributor to conservative humanism in the twentieth century—has reflected at length on our embodiment.[80] It has examined far less the character of our desire, yet desire is basic to politics. Thinkers such as Plato, Aquinas, Hobbes, and Nietzsche, to name only a few, have long appreciated this. We think there is another tool: conservatism needs to take psychoanalysis more seriously,[81] and not leave its inquiries exclusively in the hands of leftist thinkers.[82] Psychoanalysis has identified all manner of ruses by which the mind camouflages its most elaborate, and dark, strategies. It can thus help conservatives understand why civilization is stalked by primitivism. Early in all of Scruton's political works is a discussion of rule of law. Famously, conservatism is a law-and-order politics,[83] but our twist is to look at detective fiction as a conceit (Scruton) by which many in the contemporary West digest the theme of law in conservative politics. Lacan was convinced that psychoanalysis could help with the forensic assessment of a crime scene, but to see the value of thinking about law and psychoanalysis, consider only that the two highest grossing categories of the publishing industry are romance and crime novels.

METHOD OF OUR WORK

This book is genuinely a joint work that involved collaboration on all parts, but the two authors evenly divided their contributions based upon their primary intellectual interests and past work. Graham James McAleer is the principal author of chapters 2 (metaphysics), 3 (privilege and establishment), 4 (natural law), 5 (geography), and 8 (the danger of primitivism). Alexander Rosenthal-Pubul is the primary author of the introduction (defining conservatism), and chapters 1 (Western humanism), 6 (nationalism) and 7 (freedom). Both authors worked closely together on the preface and concluding remarks.

ACKNOWLEDGMENTS

It remains to thank friends Christopher Wojtulewicz, Paul Seaton, Jim Buckley, Brian Murray, Fr. John Peck, S.J., Miles Smit, John Hymers, Ted Roedel, and Biagio Tassone for years of kind support and fertilizing discussion. Thanks to George Owers for suggesting some important additional topics and directions. And we also want to thank Michael Millerman for generously sharing his expertise on Dugin. Particular thanks to the team at *Law & Liberty*—Brian Smith, John Grove, Lee Trepanier, Rachel Lu, Richard Reinsch (now at Heritage)—and Amy Willis at Liberty Fund. We are also grateful for the encouragement of Rachel Kinder throughout the publishing process and the staff at University Notre Dame Press for their fine work. Last, we thank Dan Mahoney for supporting this book from the very start and his kindness in writing a foreword to the volume.

Conservatism

The Quest for a Quiddity

We have discovered, it seems . . . the boasted wisdom of our ancestors.
— Edmund Burke, *Letters on a Regicide Peace*

Moribus antiquis res stat Romana virisque
[The Roman Republic stands on ancient customs and ancient men.]
— Ennius, *Annales*; quoted in Cicero, *De re publica* 5.1

The principal terms of our political discourse have become tangled. In particular, the effort to understand *conservatism* has been muddled by the tendency to identify it with other doctrines. The two most common candidates for capturing the meaning of conservatism are *commercial liberalism* and *nationalism*. By "liberalism," to be clear, we do not mean the liberalism of American vernacular, represented, for example, by the platform of the Democratic Party. Rather we speak of the liberalism of political philosophy described by Samuel Huntington: "Liberalism—the ideology of individualism, free markets, the rule of law, limited government and the rights to life, liberty and property—is associated with John Locke, Adam Smith, Thomas Jefferson, Immanuel Kant, John Stuart Mill and other eighteenth and nineteenth-century European and American thinkers."[1]

This is the liberal doctrine that Fukuyama presents as the final and universal ideology. It is also one many self-described American conservatives would recognize as their own. This is true even as Dugin—who also claims the mantle of conservatism—regards liberalism as the very antithesis of his beliefs. To be certain, traditionalist conservatism does not necessarily repudiate every idea in either liberalism or nationalism. Moreover, there are hybrid forms possible, such as liberal-conservatism and national-conservatism. Nonetheless, central to our contention is that conservatism has its own identity as a political philosophy. We aim here to distinguish conservatism from liberalism and nationalism more clearly. We isolate the principal elements of conservatism in a *positive* sense, saying first what conservatism *is.* In later chapters (6–8) we intend to explore what conservatism *is not.* As the argument unfolds, it will be clear that Western conservatism is an allegiance to the humanist tradition rightly conceived. Let us begin, however, with some preliminary and general considerations.

THE ESSENCE OF TRADITIONAL CONSERVATISM—REVERENCE FOR THE ANCESTRAL

Let us also not detain ourselves—conservatism is the defense of the ancestral tradition. The concept of tradition comes from the Latin verb *trado, tradere, tradi, traditus,*[2] which expresses the idea of "transmitting" or "handing over." Conservatism defends what has been "handed over" from one's ancestors. It understands this as an inheritance held in trust to be jealously guarded and preserved intact so that it may in turn be passed on to heirs. In this most general sense, conservatism may be said to be the default posture of most historic human cultures since ancient times.

To be clear, the conservative argument is not that any practice is legitimate simply because it is an inherited tradition. This is not conservatism, but cultural relativism. Obviously, a Western conservative informed, for example, by Christian conviction about human dignity will not approve of practices such as forced marriages, human sacrifice, cannibalism, abortion/infanticide, euthanasia, ritual suicide, or widow-burning simply because in certain times and places these practices have been inherited traditions. Actions that offend human dignity can be re-

jected on substantive grounds even where they are time-honored customs. Conservatism is not an excuse for blind, unreflective compliance
to past praxis. A conservative, however, will not lightly succumb to the
pride and folly of rejecting the resources of tradition on the premise
that his own generation is better and wiser than all that came before.
The conservative's default attitude is one of reverence for the past on
the assumption that there is a collective and accumulated wisdom in
history. Just as the memory of past personal experiences provides wisdom for individual life, so the collective memory of the past provides
wisdom for social existence. Cicero put it this way, "Not to know what
occurred before one was born, is to remain forever a child. For what is
the age of a man, unless it be woven with the memory of ancient things
from the age of our ancestors?" (Nescire autem quid ante quam natus
sis acciderit, id est semper esse puerum. Quid enim est aetas hominis,
nisi ea memoria rerum veterum cum superiorum aetate contexitur?).[3]
This disposition is seen, for instance, in the pious deference of the Romans to the *mos maiorum* ("custom of the ancestors"). Cicero in his
speech *De imperio* admonishes the Romans to "let indeed no novelty
be done contrary to the example and instruction of our ancestors" (at
enim ne quid novi fiat contra exempla atque instituta maiorum).[4] This
well expresses a classical conservative's first instinct of reverence for
ancestral traditions and ancestral figures. In China, where the veneration of ancestral ways was particularly developed, Confucius, its greatest sage, self-consciously disclaimed any novelty in his teaching: "I am
a transmitter, rather than an original thinker. I trust and enjoy the
teachings of the ancients."[5] The classical conservatism of modern Europe is associated, among other figures, with Edmund Burke. He opposed the modernist critiques of tradition by adherents of the Enlightenment and the French Revolution to the superior example and wisdom
of the ancestral: "Under a pious predilection for those ancestors, your
imaginations would have realized in them a standard of virtue and wisdom, beyond the vulgar practice of the hour: and you would have risen
with the example to whose imitation you aspired. Respecting your
forefathers, you would have been taught to respect yourselves."[6] The
continuity of culture itself depends on treasuring its tradition as a sacred patrimony from the ancestral past. Burke said that society is "a
partnership not only between those who are living, but between those
who are living, those who are dead, and those who are to be born."[7]

The modern European conservatism represented by Burke, however, differs in an important particular from the default traditionalism of all cultures at all times. Burke's conservatism is a doctrine of crisis. It replies to modernity, central to which is the critique of tradition. Immanuel Kant described the matter in the late eighteenth century: "Our age is the genuine age of criticism to which everything must submit."[8] Hence all claims based on authority, religion, and inherited traditions came under scrutiny during the Enlightenment. Moreover, liberalism was based around the idea of universal progress toward the single model of the liberal society (what we call "Averroism" in chapter 2). This progressivism tended to denigrate the whole inheritance of the past in favor of a monovision of the future. Thomas Paine said that "we have it in our power to begin the world over again. A situation, similar to the present, hath not happened since the days of Noah until now. The birthday of a new world is at hand."[9] Movements of "the Left" and of "progress" have always tried to begin the world anew in one manner or another.

This peculiarly modern desire to erase history and tradition becomes a concrete political project in the great event that divided conservatism and liberalism.[10] Leo Strauss aptly characterized the event around which the schism first developed: "The great watershed was the French Revolution, and the French Revolution led to the formation of two parties in Europe, the conservatives and the liberals . . . the conservatives stood for throne and altar, and the liberals stood for democracy (or something approaching democracy) and religion as a strictly private affair."[11]

Under the aegis of the French Revolutionaries, Christian time itself was abolished; the Christian calendar was replaced by a Revolutionary calendar, in which 1792 (*Anno Domini*) became Year One of the Revolution. The seven-day week, with its biblical associations, was replaced by the ten-day Decade. The aim was to build a wholly new modern civilization on the ruins of the old. The world was being made new. As a unique response to the revolutionary character of political modernity, Western conservatism was compelled to become politically self-conscious and to develop arguments and programs of political action to defend the traditional order. The default traditionalism outside the West was not seriously challenged (except later under Western influence). Hence, conservatism in the proper sense is a modern Western political movement arising from the need to conserve what came under threat.

THE CONSERVATIVE TRINITY OF TRADITION: RELIGION, FAMILY, EDUCATION

Unlike liberalism (or, for instance, Marxism), conservatism does not propose a single theoretical and universal political form to which all actual societies ought to conform. It focuses, rather, on the concretely given societies whose inherited political structures may differ widely. Given that ancestral traditions differ from one culture to another, conservatives might well defend different particular traditions in different contexts. Dugin is right this far. We need not be shocked that whereas Count Klemens von Metternich aimed to protect Europe's traditional order from liberalism (and nationalism!), American conservatives have been defenders of the moderate liberalism represented by the Founding Fathers. At least if we extend the notion of "ancestral" to include the spiritual and not just the physical progenitors of culture (as in the sense the Founding Fathers are "fathers" to Americans of many backgrounds), this definition of conservatism would seem to cover all traditional forms of conservatism. There are nonetheless certain elements of tradition that, albeit in varied forms, all traditionalist conservatives across time and place have sought to uphold.

So, which inherited traditions do conservatives wish to conserve? Conservatism has defended first and foremost those institutions and social practices that are most vital for preserving and passing on a given cultural inheritance. These are principally three—*religion*, *family*, and *education*. More accurately, it values the traditional forms of religion, family, and education. Any sudden or radical modification of these three great organs of tradition puts in peril the continuity of the culture, so conservatives are very wary of efforts to radically revise them. Let us take each of these in turn.

Religion

Conservatives from the start positioned themselves as the defenders of traditional religion. Roger Scruton explained that "the core of common culture is religion."[12] Nothing caused Burke more consternation about the Enlightenment and the French Revolution than their attacks on the "Christian religion which has hitherto been our boast and comfort, and one great source of civilization amongst us."[13] The antireligious element in Continental liberalism was perhaps more than anything that led to more than a century of conflict between liberalism and conservatism. Simply noting the association between religion and conservatism is not to say that all religious persons are conservative, nor that all conservatives are religious.

To be sure, there have been efforts to establish conservatism on a purely secular basis without any appeal to absolute religious or even metaphysical reference points.[14] It is unclear, however, how to escape what Strauss phrased "the necessity to which every thinking being is subject: to take a final stand, an absolute stand."[15] Even pluralists acknowledge some absolutes.[16] Of course, admission of the need for some moral absolutes for an adequately grounded system of philosophical ethics does not in itself provide an account for the social need for a religious system of ethics. For believers, this is a matter of truth, but there are more pragmatic reasons to explain the importance of religion for social morality. George Washington said in his Farewell Address: "And let us with caution indulge the supposition that morality can be maintained without religion. Whatever may be conceded to the influence of refined education on minds of peculiar structure, reason and experience both forbid us to expect that national morality."[17]

Though there are obviously nonreligious individuals who exercise moral excellences, the historical record of whole societies basing their moral code on nonreligious systems lacking the sanctions and sacralizing functions of religious belief has been inauspicious. In our own time, the decline of religious belief has also seen confusion around gender, the destabilizing of marriage and family, and an increasing loss of the sense of the sanctity of human life (reflected in activism around abortion and euthanasia). Efforts to replace religion with secular ideologies in the twentieth century produced the most murderous regimes in history. Turning to ancient times, the examples are few. Confucianism was for centuries the governing doctrine of China and began arguably more as a philosophy than a religion. Yet soon it acquired a religious character—replete with temples, rituals, and sacrifices. Stoicism for a time was a dominant doctrine among Roman elites (most famously Marcus Aurelius), and though a philosophy, it served some of the religious function of providing moral guidance. But it never replaced Roman religion at the popular level, and it eventually gave way to Christianity.

The reasons for the failure of nonreligious moral systems to act as adequate social traditions may relate ultimately to human nature as *homo religiosus*. Burke put it thus:

> We know, and it is our pride to know, that man is by his constitution a religious animal; that atheism is against, not only our reason, but our instincts; and that it cannot prevail long. But if, in the moment of riot, and in a drunken delirium from the hot spirit drawn out of the alembick of hell, which in France is now so furiously boiling, we should uncover our nakedness by throwing off that Christian religion which has hitherto been our boast and comfort, and one great source of civilization amongst us, and among many other nations, we are apprehensive (being well aware that the mind will not endure a void) that some uncouth, pernicious, and degrading superstition, might take place of it.[18]

A thoughtful effort to vindicate the viability of secular forms of conservatism is found in the work of Anthony Quinton's *The Politics of Imperfection*. Quinton sees the core of conservatism as a belief in the moral and intellectual imperfectability of human nature. This pessimism concerning human nature is for Quinton the taproot of three other core conservative tenets—(1) traditionalism, (2) an organic conception of society (as against contract theory), and (3) political skepticism.[19] These tenets all follow naturally: because a conservative mistrusts human nature, he affirms tradition because of his default skepticism of the notion that revolutionary changes will perfect society and not simply bring greater evils than those they seek to replace. This skepticism about man's moral and intellectual capacities likewise prompts suspicion of efforts to force society into the mold of abstract political theories. Conservatives rely instead on long historical experience and the accumulated wisdom of many generations. For Quinton, even though this core conservative belief in human imperfection may be derived from religious conviction—as with the Christian belief in original sin—it may also be equally derived from secular doctrines.[20] Quinton certainly is incisive about the conservative rejection of human perfectibility. Conservatism understands the complexity of the human soul. However much the conservative humanist may affirm the dignity of human nature, and rejoice in the possibilities of its cultivation, conservatism is not an "innocent" doctrine. On the contrary, its humanist affirmations are balanced with a profound realism about human limitations and capacity for evil. Both Christianity with its doctrine of original sin and the study of human history justify this sobriety. The conservative therefore is skeptical of that unqualified faith in progress that emerged during the Enlightenment; that very modern faith that has in its different degrees and iterations powered both liberal progressivism and the ill-fated utopian projects of modern revolutionaries. Indeed, the horrors unleashed by the modern secular utopian ideologues, from Jacobins to the communists, would seem to vindicate conservative skepticism of rapid change on the utopian premise of human perfectibility. Yet Quinton, in spite of his efforts to vindicate the idea of secular conservatism, actually helps provide an account for the necessarily religious tincture of conservatism. Judged even on utilitarian criteria, no secular ideology has yet proved equal to the task constraining the wayward impulses of human nature in the way of religion with its divinely sanctioned moral code, nor is there any reason to expect it will in the future. Quinton says an understanding of imperfectability leads the conservative to defend tradition. But we must also reckon with the historical reality that the concrete traditions of all known human cultures have been religious. Religion is indeed the fundamental tradition of a culture. Christopher Dawson states that "the world religions have been the keystones of the world cultures, so that when they are removed the arch falls and the building is destroyed."[21] To subvert religion is therefore to subvert traditional values. Hence, even though a conservative might be personally nonreligious, in practical terms, to properly value tradition and social order, a conservative must at least be a fellow traveler of religious faith,[22] understanding its importance and value for the culture, and the dangers of subverting or undermining its religious beliefs.

Most of the world civilizations are derived from the world religions. Whether one looks at Judaism in the history of ancient and modern Israel, at Christianity in the story of Europe, at Islam in the Middle East, at Hinduism in India, or Confucianism in China, religion has ever been the central animating force on all aspects of a culture from its traditional art, education, and law. These religions often persist in unchanged essentials generation after generation, binding a people to their forebears. A culture's traditional forms of artistic and intellectual life are typically derived from its religion. Religion is also characterized by rituals of communal belonging that mark the cycle of life, such as rites of birth, sacrifice, worship, initiation, marriage, and burial.

A religion such as Roman Catholicism, which played so large a role in the development of European civilization, speaks of Tradition with a capital "T." This is the apostolic tradition that the Church sees, together with the canonical scripture, as forming part of divine revelation: a revelation passed on from Jesus Christ to the apostles and thence to every generation in unbroken succession as the *depositum fidei* ("deposit of faith") the Church must guard and preserve but may not alter. Doctrines are often affirmed as part of this deposit by showing their connection with the apostolic tradition, locating them, for example, in the writings of early Church fathers. It is this idea of an unbroken tradition from a divine origin on which the Church rests its claims. Where reformist or modernist Christians articulate religion inside modern categories, hoping thereby to update the religion for relevance, the Catholic Church takes an "aristocratic distance" (Przywara) from shifting culture; relying instead on immutable principles of divine and natural law (see chapter 4 herein). Also, we contend in chapter 1 that Christianity makes a central contribution to what we take to be the guiding tradition of the West, humanism. This contribution includes among its religious elements the belief in humans as created in God's image; its doctrine of the Incarnation, which links the divine to the human story; its affirmation of the infinite value of every human soul; its moral teaching of universal benevolence; and its openness to human culture in many forms.

Traditional religion provides conservatism with a moral core, a set of absolute and immutable principles without which conservatism risks devolving into mere standpattism. Conservatives, moreover, generally see such a traditional religious form as serving social stability by liberating culture from the transient and unstable whims of the present and providing an enduring standard by which changes can be judged. The weakening or radical change in a culture's religion invariably produces corresponding weakening or radical change in a society's traditional values and institutions. For this reason, Western conservatives look at the tendencies toward the secularization and de-Christianization of the West as the gravest possible crisis. T. S. Eliot put the matter succinctly: "If Christianity goes, the whole of our culture goes."[23]

Family

The second institution conservatives seek to safeguard is the traditional family. Scruton says of the family, "The support and protection of this institution must be central to the conservative outlook."[24] This is because the family, being the early school of life, is what assures both the physical and the cultural continuance of society. To turn again to Eliot: "The primary channel of transmission of culture is the family: no man wholly escapes from the kind, or wholly surpasses the degree, of culture which he acquired from his early environment."[25]

Where liberalism has generally focused on the value of the individual rather than the family, the nineteenth-century Spanish conservative thinker Juan Donoso Cortés took note of a law of solidarity by which the individual is linked across time to his ancestors and descendants: "Through his ancestors he is in solidarious union with times past, and by the succession of his own actions, and through his descendants, he enters into communion with the future."[26] Traditional cultures have generally seen the family as the basis of all politics and social relations, and thereby an organic theory of politics is formed based on the family distinct from the more modern, liberal contractarianism. The Confucian social order, for example, is built upon the "five relationships," each of which (with the exceptions of friendship) aims to promote social harmony based on familial hierarchy, according to Mencius.[27] Aristotle adopts a similar view, pointing to the family and its various relations as the very basis upon which the political order rests.[28]

The foundation of the family is, of course, the institution of marriage. Although this institution has assumed different forms in different cultures, a principal end of marriage in traditional societies is invariably the procreation and rearing of children in the context of a stable and sanctified union between the sexes.[29] Of course, marriage ideally harmonizes the personal interest in love and companionship with the social interest. But liberals, being individualists, tend to emphasize the former value, traditionalist conservatives the latter. The liberal view sees marriage as principally about giving public expression to the feelings of love between two partners. In this view, it tends to be readily dissoluble when either or both partners have changed feelings. Conservatives would emphasize that marriage is the institution that secures the stable procreation and rearing of children through the union of the sexes. Hence conservatives are more apt to emphasize the need for stability in the marriage bond, and to associate marriage with social duties. This bond surrounded by venerable sacred religious rituals and vows serves to ensure the most basic biological and social continuity of culture. In some traditional cultures, the duty to marry and procreate is understood as a strict obligation.

The traditionalist emphasis on the stability of marriage and the procreation and rearing of children has been true cross-culturally. All the traditional world civilizations have laid emphasis on the essential role of marriage in the stable procreation and education of children for the physical and cultural continuance of the family and society. To turn again to Confucian China, which considered breaches of filial piety (reverence for parents) the most serious, we have the words of Mencius again: "There are three ways to be unfilial. To have no heir is the most serious."[30] According to Confucian doctrine, by threatening the continuation of a parent's line, children who refuse to procreate sin against their parents. Western conservatives have not generally taken things quite so far. Nonetheless, concern with "family values," that is, with the sanctity and stability of the marriage bond and its vital relation to the family, procreation, and child-rearing, has been a constant of Western conservatism. Thus, Burke's charge that the French Revolutionaries "gave a license to divorce at the mere pleasure of either party, and at a month's notice." And: "Their law of divorce, like all their laws, had not for its object the relief of domestick uneasiness, but the total corruption of all morals, the total disconnection of social life."[31]

Of course, it is true anthropologically that marriage and the family have taken different forms in different cultures and religions (e.g., monogamy, polygamy, and different understandings of kin groups). Dawson points out further the humanizing character of the specifically Christian view of marriage and family as it comes to the fore at the end of the Roman Empire. At the center of the Christian view was a new emphasis on the dignity of women: "The reconstitution of Western civilization was due to the coming of Christianity and the re-establishment of the family on a new basis. . . . the Church insisted for the first time on the mutual and bilateral character of sexual obligations. The husband belonged to the wife as exclusively as the wife to the husband. This rendered marriage a more personal and individual relation than it had been under the patriarchal system."[32]

Given the antiprocreative trajectory of contemporary culture, culminating in the sanctioning of abortion and same-sex marriage, the Roman Catholic Church for its part has stood firm in a countercultural way, defending an intrinsically procreative dimension of sexuality oriented to the gift of the child. It defends also the institution of marriage as the sole proper locus of sexuality.[33] The contemporary tendency to deny or play down the fundamental distinction of the sexes on which their union in marriage is predicated raises alarms for the traditionalist sensibility. Contemporary gender theory regards the distinction between masculine and feminine as an oppressive social construction and distinguishes this construction from biological sex. The Christian, by contrast, would emphasize the importance and sacredness of the human body in personal identity, which includes biological sex. One of the first affirmations of the Hebrew Bible is that "God created man in his own image, in the image of God he created him; male and female he created them" (Gen. 1:27), a distinction under increasing assault.

The Catholic Church on these topics does not stand alone. The *Dobbs v. Jackson Women's Health Organization* (2022) decision of the U.S. Supreme Court testifies to the strength and vitality of the pro-life cause in the predominantly non-Catholic nation. To varying degrees, most traditional conservatives of many faiths and cultures would agree with many of Catholicism's concerns in defense of the sacredness of human life and of the bond between sexuality, marriage, and the human family as a vital pillar of social continuity and flourishing.

Education

After religion and the family, next in importance is a culture's educational tradition. Just as a human community ensures its physical continuance through biological reproduction and the institutions of marriage and family, so it ensures its cultural continuance through its educational tradition, which replicates and transmits its cultural form from generation to generation. The German classicist Werner Jaeger defined education succinctly: "Education is the process by which the community preserves and transmits its physical and intellectual character. For the individual passes away, but the type remains."[34]

From its system of education, a people learns its culture's values and preserves the memory of its heroes and great stories that form its particular identity. For this reason, Dawson argues that culture is not only constituted by its educational tradition, but it also cannot survive its destruction: "A common educational tradition creates a common world of thought with common moral and intellectual values and a common inheritance of knowledge, and these are the conditions which make a culture conscious of its identity and give it a common memory and common past."[35] Preliterate tribes educate their children and initiate them into their way of life with oral stories about their gods and ancestors, which gives the members of the tribe a sense of connection, identity, and belonging. Patriots of every nation will, of course, celebrate the national heroes who give pride and identity to the nation. More broadly, such education will include the "canonical" literature, music, and art of more recent times.

But is there a general European tradition of education that has served the function of transmitting the Western way of thought and culture from classical antiquity, through the Middle Ages, until today? "For the system of classical studies, or 'humane letters' . . . had its origins some twenty-four centuries ago in ancient Athens and was handed down from the Greek sophists to the Latin rhetoricians and grammarians and from these to the monks and clerks of the Middle Ages. These in turn handed it on to the humanists and school-masters of the Renaissance from whom it finally passed to the schools and universities of modern Europe and America," states Dawson.[36]

In chapter 1, we argue that the Greco-Roman concern for the cultivation of the arts and sciences was the platform for the rise of a distinctive tradition of education that has generated Western humanism. This Western classically humanist tradition of education differs from other educational traditions in that its aim was not focused on the mastery of sacred texts, as can be found for in the educational traditions of ancient Egypt, India, Islam, and Judaism, among others.[37] Nor was it pragmatic in function, as in the learning of the arts of agriculture and industry or the vocational education of today. Its closest analogy perhaps is the Confucian tradition of China, which also focused on human development and the cultivation of moral virtue through the study of an ancient classical canon. But the European classical tradition differed from Confucianism in that it was originally the training of the free, self-governing citizen of the Greek *polis*[38] (hence the emphasis on rhetoric), later augmented by the study of philosophy, which involved learning habits of critical inquiry as much as mastering the authoritative words of the ancient sages.

The roots of the Western tradition of the liberal arts go back to ancient Greece, but it was primarily through the Latin tradition in its Roman and medieval Catholic forms that classicism was transmitted to the peoples of Western Europe. The long history of Latin letters has thus played a central role in forging the Western mind. Dawson states, "The great classical writers of the first century, B.C., above all Cicero, Virgil, Livy, and Horace, have an importance that far outweighs their intrinsic literary value, great as this is, for they are the fathers of the whole Western tradition of literature and the foundations of the edifice of European culture."[39]

This occurred first through the Roman rhetorical tradition (which we discuss in detail in chapter 1). Christianity amplified it with its own spiritual doctrines while making basic to the West the Bible with its Hebrew roots (addressed in chapter 4 and our concluding remarks chapter). The classical tradition was not jettisoned by the Catholic Church but rather given a central role in the intellectual formation of the Church fathers and later the monks and clergy. About St. Jerome, Dawson writes: "In him the two great traditions of the classics and the Bible meet together, and from him they flow out again in a single stream to fertilize the culture of the Middle Ages."[40]

The Roman classical education, systematized as the seven *artes liberales* by Martianus Capella,[41] became the basis of the trivium (grammar, logic/dialectic, rhetoric) and quadrivium (arithmetic, geometry, astronomy, music) syllabi of medieval school, monastic, and university education, capped by philosophy and theology. The Renaissance was a full resurgence of classical education, including the return to the original Greek texts, and the study of the best Greek and Roman authors became axiomatic to the best Western education well into the twentieth century.

These texts served as both a standard of excellence and fuel for new achievements. It is here where we can first see the importance of the classics for any project of Western conservative renewal. The classical languages and cultures inculcate some values—duty toward one's community, the primacy of virtue, the pursuit of excellence—which are central to traditionalism. Hence, we may note the central role of the classics in the great conservative thinkers. In his survey of the library of Burke, Carl B. Cone notes that "the veneration for classical antiquity is revealed by Burke's library, where numerous books by classical authors and about ancient times reflect the spirit of the age."[42] Burke's passion for ancient Greek and Latin letters, fostered no doubt by his education at Trinity College in Dublin, tells us that the great conservative thinker's political philosophy was intellectually nourished in the wellsprings of classical antiquity. To learn this tradition was to be initiated into the European way of thought and culture. It is still learned today to share the same intellectual formation that nurtured the European geniuses of art and science through the centuries—Petrarch, Michelangelo, Shakespeare, Newton, Cervantes, Goethe, Ruskin, Heisenberg. The Latin language was for more than a millennium the language not only of education, literature, and science, but also of diplomacy, religion, and liturgy. Our crisis of education is thus another factor that threatens to disrupt the basic continuity of Western civilization.

THE STATE, THE INDIVIDUAL, AND AUTONOMOUS COMMUNITIES

Traditional conservatism occupies a middle ground between the liberal theory of the state and that proffered by hypernationalism or totalitarianism. Despite the heavy reliance on the state in progressive or woke liberalism, classical liberalism's core is the affirmation of the individual as the start and endpoint of politics. Even if inconsistently sought, individual autonomy is the supreme value of classical liberalism, and protecting the autonomy and rights of the individual is the purpose of the liberal state. Conservatism, however, generally rejects the liberal view of the community as merely a collection of atomistic individuals. It would broadly agree with Aristotle that man is a political animal in the sense that humans are inherently social, seek fellowship with other human beings in community, and think of their identity in terms of community.

But even less would conservatives agree with the totalitarian view where the state absorbs all human activities. An infamous example is found in Mussolini's fascist manifesto:

Anti-individualistic, the Fascist conception of life stresses the importance of the State and accepts the individual only in so far as his interests coincide with those of the State. . . . The Fascist conception of the State is all embracing; outside of it no human or spiritual values can exist, much less have value. Thus understood, Fascism, is totalitarian, and the Fascist State—a synthesis and a unit inclusive of all values—interprets, develops, and potentates the whole life of a people. No individuals or groups (political parties, cultural associations, economic unions, social classes) outside the State.[43]

Hence, in the fascist view, everything is subordinated to the state. In sharp contrast to both the radical individualism of liberalism and the totalitarianism of fascism, the traditional conservative *via media* gives great emphasis to the autonomous communities that lie between the individual and the state. We discuss these as examples of privilege in chapter 3. Scruton writes: "Our search, then, is for intermediate forms of social participation, those forms which intelligibly present to the citizen the fact of his public life, and to generate his values . . . they contain the intimation of value, and hence must be 'autonomous.'"[44]

What are these autonomous communities? The most fundamental, we have already touched on, such as religious associations and the family, have their own self-regulating role within the society that the state ought to foster and not interfere with. The traditional conservative position on autonomous communities' dovetails closely with Catholic social thought. Pope Leo XIII, in the founding document of the modern tradition of Catholic social thought, *Rerum novarum*, writes: "The family has, at least, equal rights with the State in the choice and pursuit of those things which are needful to its preservation and its just liberty. . . . The idea, then, that the civil government should, at its own discretion, penetrate and pervade the family and the household, is a great and pernicious mistake."

And of voluntary associations, Leo XIII writes:

But societies which are formed in the bosom of the commonwealth are styled *private*, and rightly so, since their immediate purpose is the private advantage of the associates. "Now, a private society," says St. Thomas again, "is one which is formed for the purpose of carrying out private objects; as when two or three enter into partnership with the view of trading in common." Private societies, then, although they exist within the body politic, and are severally part of the commonwealth, cannot nevertheless be absolutely, and as such, prohibited by public authority. For, to enter into a "society" of this kind is the natural right of man; and the State has for its office to protect natural rights, not to destroy them; and, if it forbid its citizens to form associations, it contradicts the very principle of its own existence, for both they and it exist in virtue of the like principle, namely, the natural tendency of man to dwell in society. (*Rerum novarum*, para. 51)

In short, the conservative defends the legitimate autonomy of institutions—family, church, judiciary, juries, and even, after a manner, a nation's regiments, but also myriad voluntary associations, such as guilds and unions, cricket and darts clubs, flower arranging and knitting circles, to give but a tiny fraction of the examples—from domination by the state, while affirming at the same time the social nature of the human being against the extremes of economic and political individualism.

CONSERVATISM AND THE ECONOMY

We now come to the vexed question of conservatism and political economy. One will notice that nowhere yet on this list of causes traditionalist conservatives champion is any particular economic system. Classical liberalism is closely associated with a particular form of political economy, free-market capitalism, but traditionalists generally see economics as a more instrumental value, subordinate to that of culture.[45]

To be sure, private property (part of establishment) is an important conservative value,[46] but beyond that affirmation various economic forms have been proposed by conservatives. Some are supporters of various forms of capitalism or the market economy, but many regard the economy of agrarianism and the countryside as important and worthy of protection. Some conservatives champion distributism, seeking widespread distribution of property to protect workers from exploitation, promote self-sufficiency, and protect the local economy. Broadly, any economic system that provides generously for human material well-being without subverting religion, family, and education or the basic rights of property can be supported in conservative humanism. Communism or Jacobinism, with their militant atheism and anticlericalism, posit totalitarian absorption, and their disrespect for establishment and property is inherently unconservative. However, conservatives have not been slow to critique forms of capitalism where these become subversive of traditional culture. "Conservative thinkers have on the whole praised the free market, but they do not think that market values are the only values there are," says Scruton. "Their primary concern is with the aspects of society in which markets have little or no part to play: education, culture, religion, marriage and the family."[47]

Scruton identifies an essential part of conservatism as a defense of noneconomic values against the primacy of economics. Conservatives value most what Burke famously called in his *Reflections* "the *unbought* grace of life" as against the "economists and sophisters." Since all modern thought, left and right, tends to privilege economic values over religious and cultural values,[48] Scruton's concern raises one of the most controverted questions among conservatives: What stance to take toward liberal-commercial society? In his *A Political Philosophy* (2006), Scruton, on balance, favors free markets.[49] In *Conservatism* (2017), Scruton's opinion is more decided. He speaks highly of Adam Smith, contending that Smith "gave intellectual conservatism its first real start in life."[50] He credits the invisible hand with generating beauty: "Invisible-hand effects are not observed only in the economic sphere. The beauty of traditional villages built with local materials is the unintended by-product of the desire for durable shelter at the lowest cost."[51] There is no question that the liberal market economy coextensive with the rise of the modern middle class has involved dramatic material improvement in economic and technical advancement manifest in rising standards of living and physical longevity. At the same time, loss of spiritual meaning consequent on modern secularization, together with the decline of traditional institutions of culture, religion, and family, can only be viewed by conservatives with disquiet. To what degree are these things precisely a consequence of the materialism with which liberal modernity has been historically coterminous, if not indeed inextricably intertwined?

Economic liberalism and traditionalist conservatism struck a *modus vivendi* during the Cold War (e.g., the "fusionism" of Frank Meyer) when both were menaced by the onslaught of atheistic Marxism, but the absence of the common enemy has seemed to highlight the tensions. Atheistic Marxism fought against the spiritual foundations of Western civilization openly, for materialism was part of Marxist dogma. But with its demise, many conservatives began to wonder if the pervasive consumerism of modern global capitalism was not in its own more implicit way offering itself as an impoverished and materialistic alternative to traditional religion aiming to fill the spiritual void of modern man with the constant provision of material pleasures, entertainments, and comforts. As the West under the aegis of liberalism has become more secular, as the traditional ethos in family and education has eroded, many conservatives are tempted to reject liberalism root and branch. Some postliberal conservatives see the modern market economy as inextricably tied to evils such as secularization, the loss of social solidarity, cultural liberalism, and economic materialism.[52] Is it not under the liberal regime that the decline of religion, marriage and the family, traditional morality and education has accelerated? Might this atomization of communal institutions and traditions not be in some way connected to the division of labor central to liberal political economy? Even Smith, never mind Marx, worried about this.

Nonetheless, many conservatives are understandably unwilling to simply jettison the conquests of disease and poverty, along with all the beneficial elements of modern technology the modern market economy has made possible. These conservatives would reject as a kind of Gnosticism the suggestion that human material well-being is locked in a necessary and ineluctable conflict with the soul. Furthermore, there is the question of the alternatives. Many conservatives also fear more what may come after liberalism—prefigured perhaps in the rising menace of woke antiliberalism that aims to "cancel" alternative perspective, reform thought, and limit freedom of expression.[53]

This debate speaks to the tension between the premodern and modern elements within conservatism. Looking at the classical tradition, there is clear evidence of an anticommercial tendency, a reflection of their "aristocratic" values. Plato, like Aristotle and Xenophon, places the arts that aim at wealth under the heading of the "mechanical" (βάναυσόν).[54] Commerce and industry are here considered vulgar and utilitarian activities that draw men away from true culture (παιδεία) and the pursuit of the noble. Seneca likewise saw commercial occupations as unsuited to the free-born gentleman: "I respect no study, and deem no study good, which results in money-making. Such studies are profit-bringing occupations, useful only in so far as they give the mind a preparation and do not engage it permanently. One should linger upon them only so long as the mind can occupy itself with nothing greater."[55] Besides the concerns of the classical philosophers for the pursuit of wisdom and virtue over wealth, the civic- and martial-minded Romans were convinced that material excess (*luxuria*) led to enervation and moral decadence. We need think only of Juvenal's pithy remarks about how Rome is being brought down by a "luxury more savage than arms" (*saeuior armis luxuria*).[56]

For different reasons, Christianity has also been a font for suspicion toward the love of lucre in Western thought. The Gospels powerfully declare the primacy of the Kingdom of Heaven over all worldly goods and warn frequently against lust for money and wealth: "Take heed, and beware of all covetousness; for a man's life does not consist in the abundance of his possessions" (Luke 12:15). The monastic ideal held up voluntary poverty and renunciation as exemplary. Hence, in the Christian Middle Ages both the classical-aristocratic and Christian-monastic themes seem to play into the prevalent attitude toward commerce. And so Thomas Aquinas writes: "Therefore business, considered in itself, has a certain turpitude, inasmuch as it does not concern in its own nature any honorable or necessary end."[57] Medieval commerce and economic activity hedged in by the strictures on usury, just price theory, and monastic-ascetic ideals could never assume the primacy it today enjoys.

In this sense, Enlightenment figures in the tradition of classical liberalism, such as Montesquieu, Hume, and Smith, effected an intellectual revolution of the greatest profundity by arguing for not only the material but also the civilizing and moral benefits of commercial society. "Commerce cures destructive prejudices, and it is almost a general rule that wherever there is benign behavior, there is commerce, and that everywhere there is commerce, there is benign behavior," says Montesquieu.[58] Later liberal thinkers, such as Herbert Spencer, celebrated commerce dethroning the classical honor ethos, a case of stolid risk management replacing the warlike and reckless aristocratic codes (for more, see chapter 6 for Kant's theory of commerce and peace). As for Christian hesitations about embracing commercial liberalism, the least pious of liberals have not hesitated to declare religion hostile to wealth and prosperity. Voicing a common libertarian take, Ludwig von Mises bluntly stated, "A living Christianity cannot, it seems, exist side by side with Capitalism."[59]

What stance ought to be taken by the modern conservative? It seems there are things to be said both for the modern political economy and for the classical and Christian concerns about commercial materialism. To be certain, prior to the modern era, the vast majority lived in highly impoverished and disease-prone conditions. The modern market economy has far excelled premodern agrarian societies—for all the attendant virtues of pastoral life conservatives have praised—at creating prosperity and raising living standards. The state command economies of Marxist regimes are far less auspicious, bringing both poverty and totalitarianism in their wake. Moreover, markets have been a dynamic engine of technological innovations, including the vast medical advances that have so raised health and longevity in the modern world. These are genuine goods to be conserved rather than jettisoned. The principles of modern political economy are worthy of study and attention. The question is how these principles can be successfully instrumentalized, integrated, and subordinated within a proper hierarchy of value. Using Eric Voegelin, in chapter 5 we make a long argument that the division of labor does properly serve conservatism.

Traditional conservatism is primarily about the preservation of the three organs of tradition in their perennial time-sanctified forms—religious, familial, and educational. One will notice that none of these things is properly political. In the ordinary case, the transmission of religious, familial, and educational values are normal processes effected by culture, not the state. Most cultures or civilizations are "conservative" in this sense by default. Political conservatism, then, is in some sense an anomaly; it is a symptom that the normal processes of cultural transmission have broken down and are threatened by revolutionary forces striving to transform the culture. Conservatism is fundamentally about the conservation of religion, family, and education and their institutional supports. As we shall demonstrate, in the West, conservatism is the defense of those traditions distinctively shaped and succored by humanism. We also contend that for this reason conservatism is a humanist rejection of all those forces in the modern world that tend to degrade the human being. It is no coincidence that the iconic conservative Burke, utterly steeped in Christian humanism, was also a tireless defender of human dignity wherever it was threatened.[60]

CHAPTER 1

Humanism

The Master Idea of Western Civilization

We see humanism destroying itself by its own dialectic,
for the putting up of man without God and against God,
the denial of the divine image and likeness of himself,
leads to his own negation and destruction.

—Nicholas Berdyaev, *The End of Our Time*

WHAT IS *THE* WESTERN IDEA?

In 1989, Francis Fukuyama[1] famously proclaimed the world-historical victory of liberal modernity:[2] "The triumph of the West, of the Western *idea*, is evident first of all in the total exhaustion of viable alternatives to Western liberalism . . . what we may be seeing is not just the end of the Cold War, or the passing of a particular period of post-war history, but the end of history as such, that is the end point of mankind's ideological evolution and the universalization of Western liberal democracy as the final form of human government."[3]

The language here is notable. Why does Fukuyama refer to liberalism not merely as *a* Western idea but rather as *the* Western idea? It is after all not only liberalism but also its two ideological competitors for

23

global dominance in the twentieth century—Marxism and fascism—that were born out of the belly of Western modernity.[4] More importantly, liberalism (whatever antecedents it may claim) arose only very late in the story of the West—no earlier than the seventeenth century.[5] If Fukuyama is correct—and *The End of History and the Last Man* is a brilliant work—that the *essence* of the West is modern liberalism, then what becomes of the long inheritance of Greece, Rome, and Christendom that presided over European civilization for millennia before the emergence of liberalism?

The answer, of course, is that Fukuyama's perspective is unintelligible apart from the progressivist philosophy of history, which is itself a presupposition of the Enlightenment. Fukuyama's argument stems from Hegel and, as Scruton points out, Hegel must be commended for clarifying the utter centrality of self-consciousness to the meaning of human dignity.[6] In Hegel and Fukuyama, history is viewed as an upward march in which liberalism is the culminating end point. If we posit that liberalism is the standard of universal progress, then whatever value the classical and Christian eras have is determined by their contributions to liberalism. Liberalism, in short, supersedes earlier and ostensibly more primitive epochs and discourses. Stefan Rossbach has insightfully noted that Fukuyama's thesis trades upon the apocalyptic strain in the West's political thinking: liberalism is nothing short of a *renovatio mundi*.[7] But, put differently, the argument is not as *sui generis* to modernity[8] as Fukuyama claimed.

The conservative looks upon history in another manner. As Edmund Burke put it in his *Reflections*, "People will not look forward to posterity, who never look backward to their ancestors."[9] Leaning on "social inheritance,"[10] without uncritically rejecting all that is "modern," conservatism wants to uphold the perennial relevance of the premodern tradition. The conservative, in short, defends what in other contexts has been called a "hermeneutic of continuity,"[11] linking the present to the past. The reduction of "the Western idea" to modern liberalism not only devalues all that came before liberalism, but it also removes any critical distance from the Enlightenment project.

There is another idea we believe has a better claim to be *the* Western idea—the idea of *humanism*. The special European concern with the problem of man, his inherent dignity and status as a rational and moral being, has been a continuous focus of Western civilization from its birth to the present.[12] This theme of humanism has therefore assumed different forms in different epochs, such that it is possible to elaborate a *classical*, *Christian*, and modern *secular* humanism. Between the contributions of these different forms of humanism, there are both tensions and possibilities of syntheses. The value of exploring *the* Western idea through the lens of humanism is that it is possible to apprehend the essential attributes of the different epochs and worldviews in their mutual relations. To be sure, not every trend emerging from the story of the West is "humanist." Nonetheless, the Western intellectual tradition can be understood synoptically in relation to this master idea.

This will be explained in several stages. First, we will give a brief history of the development of humanism. Second, we tie humanism to the principles of conservatism[13] illustrated in later chapters. This will help explain why humanism is a moral ideal. Third, we use this ideal as a yardstick to explain the sources of the contemporary crisis of modern Western humanism. In this crisis, the fate of liberalism no less than other aspects of modernity is implicated.

CLASSICAL HUMANISM

The Greek Educational Ideal (παιδεία)

Ancient Greece is the origin (ἀρχή) of Europe, both in the sense of being the historical beginning and as a cultural font to which European civilization has returned for renewal over and over again.[14] It is in Greece that the self-consciousness of Europe as a civilization distinct from Asia first arises. Herodotus in the very opening of his *Histories* remarks on the division between Europe represented by Greece and Asia represented by Persia, and reads this divide between "West" and "East" back further to the Trojan War.[15] In what did the cultural distinctiveness of the Greeks consist? Werner Jaeger aptly regarded the Greek ideal of education as the key to understanding all of Hellenism. Most educational traditions in the world's cultures were about the acquisition of practical, technical skills for earning one's bread, such as agriculture or artisanship. There was also the more formal religious education meant to train a priestly caste, as in ancient Egypt or India. The Greeks, however, had an entirely distinct concept of education (παιδεία), having nothing in common with technical or sacerdotal training. "The intellectual principle of the Greeks is not individualism but 'humanism,' to use the word in its original and classical sense . . . it meant *the process of educating man into his true form, the real and genuine human nature*," states Jaeger.[16]

This perfected "form of humanity" of the Greeks exists at first only as a potency that must be actualized by cultivation. One must *become* fully human. Such a fully developed human being will also generally be the most useful to his fellows, but it is not required that all the things with which humanist education is concerned should be useful in the ordinary sense. Man is, as Aristotle explained, the rational animal. Liberal or humanist studies[17] are meant to fulfill and perfect this rational nature through the development of the intellectual and moral virtues. Humanism aims at what is an end in itself—the excellence of man.[18]

It is this educational ideal of developing the whole range of human powers that would later lead the humanists of the European Renaissance back to the Greeks. "The humanists learned from Xenophon, and Plato, and Isocrates that education is an art which should aim at the harmonious development of every side of human nature, physical, moral, and intellectual," states Christopher Dawson. "Thus they gained an awareness of the unlimited possibilities for the enrichment of personal life by art and literature and social intercourse."[19]

The origins of the Greek ideal of human excellence (αρετή) go back to the very first figure of importance in the Hellenic tradition, Homer, whom Plato refers to as "the educator of Greece" (τὴν Ἑλλάδα πεπαίδευκεν), the inspired poet who formed the Greek soul.[20] And, indeed, in the archaic form of Greek education (ἡ ἀρχαία παιδεία),[21] the study and memorization of the Homeric epics trained the soul, just as the system of gymnastics (γυμνασία) trained the body. The combination of physical sports and Homeric poetry was to produce the virtues of the good and noble gentleman (καλὸς κἀγαθός). A later, philosophically tempered version of this aristocratic ethos is seen in Aristotle's description of the "great-souled man" (μεγαλόψυχος),[22] who is concerned with the achievement of great and noble deeds, fearless in the face of danger, generous out of abundance, and contemptuous of all that is base and petty. The central value of the Homeric ethic is displayed in the famous advice of the *Iliad* given to Glaucus, and again to Achilles, "to excel always and to surpass all others" (αἰὲν ἀριστεύειν καὶ ὑπειρείροχον ἔμμεναι ἄλλον).[23] The striving among the heroes for the highest prize of honor emerged from an archaic martial ethos, but its echo appears in the competitive striving that pervaded all of Greek culture from the Olympic games, whose prize-winning athletes are celebrated in the poetry of Pindar, to the competitions among the tragic dramatists at the Great Dionysia.

The next great development in the Greek concept of education arose from the new political ideas associated the Greek city-state (πόλις/*polis*). The empires of the ancient Middle East were cosmological empires (Voegelin) in which godlike kings and pharaohs reigned over polities with tightly fixed hierarchies. By contrast, the citizens of the Greek city-states—but obviously not their enormous number of slaves[24]—were participating authors of the very laws that bound them. Their conception of politics presupposed an active citizenry. As the Athenian statesman Pericles put the matter, "We alone regard a man who takes no interest in public affairs, not as a harmless, but as a useless character."[25]

The practices of deliberation and persuasion particular to this form of government required a particular kind of education in political arts. This need was filled by the itinerant teachers known as the Sophists. On account of Plato's famous polemic again them, the Sophists have suffered a reputation as cynical manipulators, hence the vulgar concept of "sophistry." Whatever kernel of truth there may be in this caricature among the worst of the Sophists, scholarship has vindicated the centrality of the Sophists as the pioneers of Western humanist education.[26] Discussing the famous Sophist Protagoras, Jaeger remarks: "Protagoras' claim that cultural education is the center of all human life indicates that his education was frankly aimed at *humanism*. He implies that by subordinating what we now call civilization—namely technical efficiency—to culture: the clear and fundamental distinction between technical knowledge and power on the one hand, and true culture on the other, is the very basis of humanism."[27]

The major concern of sophistic education was what is expressed with the word (i.e., λόγος). The Sophists had an almost mystical concept of what language could achieve. "Speech is a powerful lord, which by means of the most invisible body effects the divinest works: it can stop fear and banish grief, and create joy and nurture pity," says Gorgias.[28]

Naturally, rhetoric stood at the apex of sophistic education in the arts of statesmanship. However, the mastery of language and discourse in all of its forms was seen as requisite.[29] Hence the Sophists systematized the study of grammar, studied the informal logic of argumentation (dialectics), and they studied poets to understand how language arouses and inspires (rhetoric). Moreover, the great rhetor must be able to discourse on any theme, hence the need for a broad base of knowledge in politics and history, and sometimes even astronomy, music, and mathematics were included in the sophistic curriculum.[30] So far from being a specialized form of education, rhetorical education was the basis of a universal education.

The edifice of sophistic education, however, came under sustained critique as a result of Socrates, who turns Greek philosophy, hitherto focused on the cosmic order, toward the human question.[31] For Socrates it is only the good of the soul that has supreme worth, and how to perfect it through moral virtue is the important philosophical question. He exhorted the Athenians: "Most excellent man, are you who are a citizen of Athens, the greatest of cities and the most famous for wisdom and power, not ashamed to care for the acquisition of wealth and for reputation and honor, when you neither care nor take thought for wisdom and truth and the perfection of your soul?"[32]

The problem from this perspective with the sophistic training was that in the wrong hands it could easily degrade into a mere science of technique, using words to manipulate and persuade so that the politician-rhetor might gain such worldly goods as power, wealth, and fame. Such use of rhetoric would not for Socrates morally improve either the rhetor or the people and would be without value. Socrates claims it is he, and not the rhetors, who is the true statesman,[33] for it is he who seeks to lead the people to the life of virtue. The martyrdom of Socrates captivated the Greek mind, making him the exemplar of the philosophical life governed by reason and virtue and an alternative to the rhetorical ideal. Therewith, Athens turns to "the rivalry of philosophy and rhetoric each claiming to be the better form of culture."[34] In the long run, however, both tended to move toward convergence,[35] as seen, for example, in Aristotle's work on rhetoric and the educational program of Isocrates. The problem of humanism for the Greeks became how to combine the moral wisdom of philosophy with the eloquence of rhetoric. The answer, which was the special achievement of the Hellenistic age, was to combine philosophy, rhetoric, and poetry (and even mathematics and natural philosophy) into an integral system of humanist education (ἐγκύκλιος παιδεία)[36]

Roman Humanitas

Greek ideals of culture and education were absorbed by their Roman conquerors with zealous enthusiasm. The Roman poet Horace famously tells us that "captive Greece began herself to conquer and taught her arts to the rustic Latins" (Graecia capta ferum victorem cepit et artes intulit agresti Latio).[37] It is from the Romans that our very term "humanism" derives. Aulus Gellius in his *Noctes Atticae* explains that proper speakers of Latin "gave to humanitas about the force of the Greek παιδεία; that is, what we call *eruditionem institutionemque in bonas artes*, or 'education and training in the liberal arts.' Those who earnestly desire and seek after these are most highly humanized. For the pursuit of that kind of knowledge, and the training given by it, have been granted to man alone of all the animals, and for that reason it is termed 'humanitas,' or 'humanity.'"[38]

Romans such as Cicero called the goal of culture *humanitas* because arts and letters have a refining, civilizing effect on human nature,[39] with the aim to distinguish man from the animals. For the Romans, as for the Greeks, the ideal of humanism retained aristocratic associations. And thus Seneca, in defining the liberal arts, asserts that "these arts are called liberal because they are worthy of the free man" (Quare liberalia studia dicta sint vides: quia homine libero digna sunt).[40] The "free" man here means principally the free-born gentleman who owns his own time, such that he can engage in the most elevated pursuits rather than being absorbed in merely useful labors to secure necessities. From here derives the traditional distinction between the "liberal arts," which have their own nobility and excellence (such as poetry, philosophy, music), and the "servile arts," which are not done for their own sake (such as manual, agricultural, and commercial labor).[41]

The Romans displayed no proclivity for the metaphysical, scientific, and mathematical elements of Greek thought, but they wholly absorbed and even advanced upon the Greek conception of the highly cultivated, public-spirited rhetor who combined moral wisdom with eloquence. The aim of rhetorical education was laconically summarized by Cato as "a good man, expert in speaking" (vir bonus dicendi peritus).[42] The figure who both taught and best personally embodied this ideal was of course Cicero, who argues for the need to unite rhetoric with moral philosophy. The fully developed rhetor is one wholly versed in "all the arts which concern the civilizing and humanizing of men" (omnes artes quae ad humanitatem pertinent).[43] Perhaps the culminating and magisterial Roman work concerning such a humanist education of the rhetor is Quintilian's *Institutio oratoria*, written in the imperial period when the educational rather than practical importance of rhetoric became primary. Here Quintilian provides a complete curriculum[44] for the rhetor, who must be thoroughly versed in the most eminent authors, both in Greek and Latin. This includes the fields of poetry (Homer, Virgil, Ovid, and the Greek and Roman tragic, comic, and lyric poets), rhetoric (Cicero, Demosthenes, Aeschines), history (Thucydides, Herodotus, Livy, Sallust, Caesar), and the philosophers (Plato, Aristotle). A similar canon of exemplary Greek and Latin authors remained foundational for Western higher education until well into the twentieth century.[45]

CHRISTIAN HUMANISM

Dawson thought classical civilization "a humanism in search for a theology."[46] Polybius is illustrative. Ancient humanism had set a standard of human achievement in philosophy, art, literature, science, mathematics, and politics. Still, Polybius credited Roman religion with making Rome stable.[47] But steeped as he was in humanism, Polybius thought the funeral rites and pageantry of Roman polytheism a sop proffered to the people by the ruling elites.[48] The ignorant masses, who unlike the *aristoi* cannot be taught restraint by education and philosophy, must be restrained by wonder and the supernatural: "If it were possible to form a state wholly of philosophers, such a custom would perhaps be unnecessary. But seeing that every multitude is fickle, and full of lawless desires, unreasoning anger, and violent passion, the only resource is to keep them in check by mysterious terrors and scenic effects of this sort."[49]

Ultimately, the "magic cosmion" (Voegelin) of the ancient world failed, resulting in "ancosmion," and amidst a host of rival religious movements,[50] and hard-fought politicking, the classical world looked eastward to the star of Bethlehem. Providentially, the Greco-Roman culture, which gave birth to Western humanism, encountered the most anthropological of all faiths, the religion of the God-man.[51] "The theme of God-humanity is the fundamental theme of Christianity . . . Christianity alone teaches that God became man," says Nicholas Berdyaev. "The gulf between God and man was revealed, not only the divine in man, but also the human in God."[52]

The significance of Christology for Western humanism is that it imparted a transcendent foundation for human dignity.[53] Already in the Hebrew Bible of Israel, in the opening chapter of Genesis, we see a foundation for such a religious humanism in the idea of man as created in the image and likeness of God. However, the doctrine of the Incarnation, according to which God himself became man in the person of Jesus Christ and, by his cross, conferred on every human soul an infinite value,[54] was a profound accelerant to the idea of human dignity. As Voegelin points out, human beings became so elevated that Christianity brought with it a heavy dose of alienation and anxiety.[55] The complexity of Christian theological ideas, and the intricacy they introduced into the elements of the soul, meant that we could never understand ourselves thereafter as mere stolid parts of nature, but as something altogether exotic and febrile. Illustrative are the torments of the Christian explorers of our mental life, such as Pascal, Kierkegaard, and Dostoyevsky. In Voegelin's language, Christianity sparked an unparalleled differentiation inside human self-understanding, a differentiation that opened to consciousness the higher reaches of reason and morals.[56]

The greatness and royal dignity of the human being was a major theme in early Christianity. St. Gregory of Nyssa says, "Oh, man, scorn not what is admirable in you . . . consider your royal dignity! The heavens have not been made in God's image as you have, nor the moon, nor the sun, nor anything in creation . . . behold of all that exists there is nothing that can contain your greatness."[57]

For Gregory of Nyssa, one of the manifestations of this unique spiritual dignity of the human being to which Christianity gave special emphasis is its freedom from natural determinism: "For the soul immediately shows its royal and exalted character, far removed as it is from the lowliness of private station, in that it owns no lord, and is self-governed, swayed autocratically by its own will; for to whom else does this belong than to a king?"[58]

Christian anthropology, to be certain, is complex. In one sense, it exalted the human being above anything the classical world had conceived, but Christianity also brought with it a new consciousness of sin, which in the Christian view placed man under a certain kind of slavery. Yet even Nietzsche credited this consciousness with generating the high value of inwardness, a discerning power. St. Paul noted that it is impossible to become free of sin by one's own power (Rom. 7:15–19). Slavery to sin was a theme taken up by St. Augustine in his polemic against Pelagius, accounting for the weakness of natural man, the wounds of original sin, and the necessity of grace. No more searching investigation of the problem of human evil can be found than in the work of Paul and Augustine. Where the Greeks and Roman philosophers had identified the cause of evil primarily in the ignorance of the mind, or in the sensual passions generated by the body, Augustine finds the roots of sin in the evil will and the pride that expresses itself in the lust for domination (*libido dominandi*).[59] It is this condition of bondage which calls forth the need for the Redeemer.

Down the centuries, Augustinianism has sounded a recurrent note of salutary caution within the Western tradition against the utopianism to which an unrestrained humanist optimism can lead. If classicism emphasizes the possibilities of human nature, Augustine reminds us of the limits inherent to our sinful and creaturely condition. Yet Christianity's final view is one of hope and wonder. By the mystery of the Redemption, says Pope St. John Paul II, the message of the Gospels, "in a hidden and mysterious way vivifies every aspect of authentic humanism . . . the Church knows with all the certainty of faith that the Redemption has restored his dignity to man, and given back meaning to his life in the world."[60] Thus Christianity, though sounding prudential and cautionary notes about excessive optimism regarding human nature, became also a powerful fountain of humanism with its doctrine of "the transcendence of the human person."[61]

Christology and the Birth of Christocentric Culture

The doctrine of the Incarnation was theologically formulated by the Council of Chalcedon (451) to carefully balance the unity and distinction of the divine and human natures in the person of Jesus Christ: "The same Christ, only begotten Son, acknowledged in two natures, without mingling, without change, indivisibly, undividedly, the distinction of the natures nowhere removed on account of the union."[62] Christ is therefore the bridge between the divine and the human, embracing both. Theology and culture always have a vital connection. The great monotheistic civilization of ancient Israel was *theocentric*, based around a divine law that governs all aspects of human life. Something similar is seen in Islamic civilization. Modern Western secularism gives rise to an *anthropocentric* culture that places man and his concerns at the center (while tending to sideline the divine). The Christian culture that arose in medieval and renaissance Europe is *Christocentric*,[63] both uniting and distinguishing the divine and the human: faith and reason, nature and grace, church and state. The medieval figure who exemplifies this ideal is Thomas Aquinas. A striking example is in his commentary on the *De Trinitate* of Boethius, where he raises the question of whether the human mind requires divine grace to know the truth. Aquinas replies that "the mind by its natural light, without the superaddition of any other, can see the truth" (scilicet mens lumine naturali sine aliquo superaddito possit veritatem videre).[64] Likewise, in discussing the relation between faith and reason, he presents an image of both harmony and distinction: "The natural dictates of reason must certainly be quite true: it is impossible to think of their being otherwise. Nor again is it permissible to believe that the tenets of faith are false, being so evidently confirmed by God. Since therefore falsehood alone is contrary to truth, it is impossible for the truth of faith to be contrary to principles known by natural reason."[65]

What we see in these texts of Aquinas is an example of the "Christocentric" worldview in which divine activity (faith/grace) and human activity (reason/nature) are both harmoniously united and yet retain their own place and distinctive character. In referring to the idea of a "Christocentric" medieval settlement of faith and reason, we do not of course mean to deny that other faiths meaningfully confronted the questions raised by Greek rationalism—such great luminaries as Maimonides in Judaism and Averroes and Avicenna in Islam make that clear. Christianity's distinctiveness lies rather in its peculiarly *anthropological* emphasis, the idea that the all-transcendent God assumes a human nature in the person of Jesus Christ. The medieval Christian understanding of faith and reason, as of church and state, is Christological in the sense that it takes the Incarnation as its model for how the divine and human relate—to paraphrase Chalcedon, the divine and human spheres are like two natures without confusion, but also without separation. The divine principle stands above the human principle, yet the human retains its natural integrity and power. It is this that creates the opening to humanism. Interestingly, Quinton, a secular conservative, argues it is also what makes scientific method possible.[66]

RENAISSANCE HUMANISM

These two mighty streams of classical and Christian influence come together in the European Renaissance, the great flowering of humanism. Because of its veneration for classical letters, this latter Christian element of the Renaissance is still often forgotten in the stereotype of the great age of Michelangelo, Erasmus, and St. Thomas More as a simple "pagan revival."[67] Dawson notes that for the Renaissance humanist educators "liberal education was the education of a Christian gentleman," and he goes on to speak of them as "devout Christians who wished to unite the intellectual and aesthetic culture of Hellenism with the spiritual ideals of Christianity."[68]

We also sometimes consider Renaissance humanism the ancestor of modern progressivism, forgetting that its main focus was the veneration of the past. The Dutch humanist Erasmus provided the age with a motto: *Sed in primis ad fontes ipsos properandum, id est graecos et antiquos* ("But return at once to the sources themselves, that is the Greeks and the ancients").[69] This statement aptly sums up the period's deep veneration of classical antiquity and its intellectual, educational, and artistic ideals. Its beginning was in Catholic Italy in the late fourteenth and early fifteenth centuries, where the social order proved amenable to a complete rebirth of classical humanism. The feudal system had given way to urban citizen-republics, such as Florence and Venice, reminiscent as they were of the Greek *polis*;[70] in turn this gave a new practical importance to the study of Greco-Roman rhetoric. During the same period, Byzantines such as Gemistus Pleithon stimulated a revival of the Greek language, which contributed to the Florentine Academy's work under Marsilius Ficino translating Plato and other ancient authors. It was in Italy, too, that the sense of man's transcendent dignity gave rise to the idea of freedom shaping destiny. This repeated Gregory of Nyssa, but was freshly and eloquently expressed by Pico della Mirandola's *Oratio de hominis dignitate*. Speaking in the person of God to man, Pico writes:

> "We have made you a creature neither of heaven nor of earth, neither mortal nor immortal, in order that you may, as the free and proud shaper of your own being, fashion yourself in the form you may prefer. It will be in your power to descend to the lower, brutish forms of life; you will be able, through your own decision, to rise again to the superior orders whose life is divine." Oh unsurpassed generosity of God the Father, Oh wondrous and unsurpassable felicity of man, to whom it is granted to have what he chooses, to be what he wills to be![71]

The Christian idea of a divinely conferred human dignity here meets the classical idea of acquired dignity.[72] The Christian sense of transcendence and freedom encounters the classical humanist idea of man in the raw state as incomplete and barbarous, requiring the influence of humane letters (*literae humaniores*) to refine and complete his nature. The great humanist educator Cardinal Jacopo Sadoleto writes, "We receive from Nature what is central in ourselves . . . but in a rough and unfinished form; it is the function of letters to bring this to its highest perfection and to work out in it a beauty comparable to the divine original."[73]

This cycle of studies, *studia humanitatis*, consisted, according to a canon of Pope Nicholas V (r. 1447–55), of five disciplines—grammar, rhetoric, history, poetry, and moral philosophy.[74] The classics, in the hands of Renaissance humanist educators, such as Leonardo Bruni, Guarino of Verona, and Vergerio, became part of an effort to "unite the intellectual and aesthetic culture of Hellenism with the spiritual ideals of

Christianity."[75] When we think of the Italian Renaissance, we are perhaps most apt to think first of the great flowering of the visual arts. It was during the Renaissance, thanks to figures such as Leon Battista Alberti, that painting, sculpture, and architecture were elevated to the status of liberal arts. The Renaissance let loose the greatest burst of artistic creativity ever seen: Brunelleschi's great dome in Santa Maria del Fiore in Florence; the idealized beauty of the human form in the freestanding sculptures of Donatello and Michelangelo; the lyricism of Botticelli's paintings and the perfection of Raphael; and Leonardo's close study of nature, which conjoins art and science.[76] These astonishing achievements testify, Reinhold Niebuhr says, to "a tremendous affirmation of the limitless possibilities of human existence."[77] The relative optimism of the Renaissance—its focus on the dignity of man and the refinement of human capacities—drew sustenance from both the classical and Christian ideals of dignity.[78] Together, these power much of the Renaissance humanist project. The Renaissance educational model of formation in "humane letters" meanwhile became dominant in Western education in schools and universities up to the twentieth century.[79] It is only rather recently that this educational model has experienced a "deep crisis."[80] Looking back, it is fair to consider classical humanist education a potent fuel of modern Western achievement from the Renaissance to the development of modern science.[81] A related development, and one of enormous significance, was the School of Salamanca in sixteenth-century Spain. Drawing on the Hebrew biblical idea of man as the image of God and the classical idea of man as the rational animal,[82] this school, which includes figures such as Francisco de Vitoria, argued for rights based on the universal human capacity for rational self-governance (*dominium*).[83] Affirming *human* rights, the Renaissance School of Salamanca framed a jurisprudence that resonates in modern rights discourse.[84]

MODERN HUMANISM

The culture of modern humanism that undergirds all modernity first emerges in the seventeenth and eighteenth centuries, culminating in the Enlightenment. It naturally exhibits great complexity—and we engage with the Enlightenment's complexity throughout the following chapters—but it can be best understood through four principal themes:

the conquest of nature, the idea of progress, the rights of man, and secular humanism. Let´s take them each in turn.

The Conquest of Nature

The anthropocentrism of modern humanism is powered in part by the extraordinary human mastery of natural forces achieved as a result of the scientific revolution and the continuous innovations that followed. Modernity is fundamentally a technological project. Its aim is "the relief of man's estate,"[85] Sir Francis Bacon famously put it, the material uplift of the human condition through the practical development of technology and economics (Marx's means of production). To gain this technological power requires the knowledge of natural forces, and indeed bending nature to man's will. Descartes said that the new science would "render ourselves *the masters and possessors of nature.*"[86] The means of acquiring this knowledge are the methods of modern science developed by Bacon and Descartes—what Fukuyama dubs "the Mechanism."[87] Baconianism builds on the resources of Greek mathematics and Aristotelian induction, but unlike the ancients, who valued theoretical understanding, the aim would be the augmentation of human power, studying nature to master it. Bacon put it concisely: "Human knowledge and human power meet in one; for where the cause is not known the effect cannot be produced; nature to be commanded must be obeyed, and that which in contemplation is as the cause is in operation as the rule."[88]

And, indeed, if one looks at the scientific revolution, the Industrial Revolution, and the digital revolution of our time we should have to say the Baconian-Cartesian project casts a long, powerful, and above all distinctively modern legacy. "And yet the principles of organization that are supposed to be common to everything existing in the universe are mechanistic principles; in other words, a machine that processes information according to fixed rules (an algorithm, in mathematical parlance) is taken to be the sole model for all the things there are in the world," says Jean-Pierre Dupuy.[89]

The Idea of Progress

The scientific and technological advances of the modern era fueled confidence and optimism concerning human capacities. The Enlightenment faith in man was strengthened by the hope that the same potency that had unlocked the secrets of nature and made technological achievements possible could do similar things for the social and moral life. "The sole foundation for the natural sciences is this idea, that the general laws directing the phenomena of the universe . . . are necessary and constant," states the Marquis de Condorcet. "Why should this principle be any less true for the development of the intellectual and moral faculties of man that for other operations of nature?"[90]

Where most cultures in history have reverenced the ancestral past, a new form of culture developed during the Enlightenment, which looks instead to the future, and regards the present as morally and intellectually superior to the primitive past. Moral and technological progress would proceed apace, leading to "the abolition of inequality among nations, the progress of equality within each nation, and the true perfection of mankind."[91] Ironically, Reinhold Niebuhr noted, the idea of progress also drew on the Christian sense of a linear, meaningful history, but without the qualification of the Christian doctrine of human sin, and thus Enlightenment humanist optimism ran riot.[92] It is this idea of progress, still all-pervasive in Western modernity,[93] that brings about the sense of discontinuity and revolutionary discontent. It is little surprise that the French Revolution strove to literally begin history anew at Year One of the Revolution.

The Rights of Man

Liberalism may be understood as the effort to give political form to modern humanism. The idiom of liberalism is the idiom of rights. The idea of subjective, personal rights has Catholic origins going back to the medieval and early modern scholastic debates,[94] but with the rise of liberalism, rights become the center of all political thinking. The American Revolution's Declaration of Independence (1776) and the French Revolution's Declaration of the Rights of Man (1789) are predicated on the idea that the purpose of politics is to protect the rights and freedoms of the individual. These rights are conceived as inalienable and universal, furnishing the argument for revolution. The idea of universal human rights is the mode by which the idea of human dignity is understood by the contemporary West. This idea of natural rights is originally an inheritance of Christianity, as can be seen, for instance, in the ideas of Vitoria and other Salamancans who developed the classical and medieval conceptions of natural law in the direction of a universal rights doctrine. If these universal rights are not merely human conventions (as the logic of modern atheism would seem required to suppose), theology (even if in an attenuated Deist form) still seemed necessary for most nascent liberal thinkers of the Enlightenment (Locke, Voltaire, Jefferson). God for early liberalism becomes first and foremost the author and granter of rights and freedoms the state cannot take away. The Enlightenment movement, it should be said, also sought to reform the legal system away from once widespread cruelty and executions and in favor of toleration and humanitarianism. One might think of Enlightenment figures such as Cesare Beccaria, who worked to abolish torture and the promiscuous use of the death penalty; of Emperor Joseph II's emancipation of the Jews in the Austrian Empire with the Patent of Toleration (1781), which helped promote religious tolerance and the end of the Jewish ghettos throughout much of Europe; and of the U.S. Bill of Rights, or the birth of antislavery societies.

Secular Humanism

Meanwhile, however, the theological underpinnings of Christian humanism were being undermined. The most revolutionary aspect of modern humanism is the emergence of a secular form of humanism. It draws from the Renaissance idea (Pico) of man as the "free and proud shaper" of his being and shares that confident Renaissance optimism in man's rational and moral faculties. Where it differs is that it asserts not only the dignity and freedom of man but human self-sufficiency. At first aligned with liberal Christianity (Locke) or Deism (Voltaire), the Enlightenment grew over time more hostile to theology. Some religious thinkers[95] have argued cogently that the distant God of the scientific mechanism and Deism—which tends to remove the divine *Logos* from a continuous and active role in the creation—paved the way to the complete materialism of today.[96] The more radical Enlightenment thinkers taking materialism to its logical conclusion veered toward atheism and saw God and Christianity as an obstacle to the free development of human faculties. An early example is Baron d'Holbach: "The human mind confused with its theological opinions, forgot itself, doubted its own powers, mistrusted experience, feared truth, and abandoned her direction blindly in order to follow authority."[97]

In fairness, d'Holbach was a radical at the time even for the French Enlightenment, but the secularizing tendency was toward anthropocentrism, making man rather than God the central theme of modern culture. Progressively, the various cultural activities—politics, economics, art, law, literature, and such—have become secularized and autonomous from religious concerns.[98]

The Crisis and Contradictions of Modern Humanism

Yet, ironically, by dethroning God, the modern dialectic of humanism also dethroned man, and this is why we argue that the true defender of the gains of Western humanism is conservatism. Berdyaev sees a "self-destructive dialectic" within modern humanism: "Humanism not only affirmed man's self-confidence and exalted him, but it also debased him by ceasing to regard him as a being of a higher and divine origin . . . the result of man's self-affirmation once he had ceased to be conscious of his tie with the higher and Divine and Absolute nature . . . was to bring about his own perdition."[99]

The materialism of the Enlightenment's logic, however, ultimately fails to provide an adequate ontological ground for its humanism. Human self-assertion in modernity arrived at the point of displacing God and creating a human-centered culture. But if the human being is only a natural, material being, man has no transcendent origin, meaning, or dignity. Modern developments in science, such as heliocentrism and evolution, have tended to make humanity conscious of its smallness and insignificance within the material world of nature and to relegate man to the status of one more animal. And thus at the very moment of modern humanism's most audacious assertion of human supremacy, humanism gives way to the most profound antihumanistic biologism. In his review of Yuval Harari's bestsellers, Scruton puts the point this way: "Harari assumes that the biological science of human nature gives the true and full account of what we are. But I am something more, or something other, than the biological entity in which I am incarnate. I am also this 'I,' this subjectivity that is both the owner of all the states of mind that matter to me and also the target of those attitudes in others (love, friendship, respect) that endow my life with a meaning."[100]

The antihumanism in contemporary Western culture is not without practical consequence, as plainly evidenced by the rise of totalitarianism in the twentieth century. Contradicting the Enlightenment's optimistic faith in humanity and human progress, National Socialism and communism slaughtered millions without compunction at the altar of subhuman material forces, such as race or economics, which these ideologies worshipped (see chapter 8). Totalitarianism was made possible precisely by the powers unleashed by modern science and technology. Berdyaev warned in the 1930s: "What is taking place in the world today is not a crisis of humanism (that is a topic of secondary importance) but the crisis of humanity. We face the question, is that being to whom the future belongs to be called man, as previously, or something different? We are witnessing the process of dehumanization in all phases of culture and of social life. Above all, moral consciousness is being dehumanized. Man has ceased to be the supreme value: he has ceased to have any value at all."[101]

Berdyaev's suspicion that modernity has turned antihuman and is sweeping away human dignity continues to have salience today. We can see it in the discussions of "transhumanism" and what John Paul II called a "culture of death,"[102] which excuses callousness toward human life, such as with abortion and euthanasia, on the very ground of liberal autonomy and individualism.[103] The undermining of the moral foundations of human dignity can be seen dramatically in the contemporary fate of human rights discourse.[104] With a figure such as Vitoria or even Locke, rights are metaphysically grounded in a Christian anthropology in which man has an exceptional and transcendent dignity as a rational nature, an *imago Dei*. This dignity is universal to all human beings and transcends the particularities of race and culture, but if the human being is simply one more physical organism, then human rights lose their foundation and become merely the artifact of a particular historical culture—that of the West. In that case, rights claims have no greater truth value than any other set of historically conditioned human cultural conventions. The claim that human rights are universal cannot be sustained on the basis of either the secular materialism or the cultural-moral relativism prevalent in contemporary world. The ethnic identity politics of both the Left (critical race theory[105]) and the Right (Dugin, the French New Right) indeed explicitly challenges the claims of Western rights concepts to universality, which is denounced by Dugin and other ethnopluralists as Western imperialism. Secular humanism in the twenty-first century is therefore ending ironically in the self-negation of its universal rights claims and opening the path to a resurgence of primitivistic forms of identitarianism.

Modern humanism is in crisis because its commitment to human dignity is not self-sufficient but depends upon an older and richer inheritance. At the same time, the modern is constantly tempted to reject this inheritance on account of what Scruton called a "culture of repudiation." The resolution of the modern crisis of humanism depends on conservatives who understand the nature of this crisis and who know above all what must conserved. The indispensable role of the conservative is as the guardian of that great spiritual and intellectual inheritance that has fueled Western civilization's formidable past achievements, and on which the hope for its future revitalization depends.

CHAPTER 2

The Metaphysics of Conservatism

"Still, myth not only survives but, in our time, even revives in response to the perversion of immanence in the period of enlightenment and ideology," writes Eric Voegelin.[1] Aleksandr Dugin's apocalyptic conservative mythology is confirmation of this observation. A bit like Tolkien with respect to Englishness, Dugin is what Voegelin calls a "symbolist."[2] Just as Comte provided the symbol[3] of the progressive bureaucrat that structures our civilization's MBA programs, so Dugin is the symbolist of Eurasianism,[4] the geopolitical rival[5] of Western globalism penned by that other great contemporary symbolist, Fukuyama.

Dugin's geopolitics or symbolic geography[6] has a baroque metaphysical framework. Inspired by the work of the French theorist Gilbert Durand—who argues that the imagination is particularized in myth in varied cultures and that myth is the true driver of history,[7] a position that echoes in Scruton[8]—Dugin thinks nations and civilizations have angelic essences determining their fundamental character (*Fourth Political Theory* [*FPT*], 42, 48). In his apocalyptic thinking, angels are either algorithms or myths. Political health depends upon an *angelomorphosis*, myth gaining victory over algorithm. Human dignity requires living under myth, for only in such a political condition is a person what Dugin dubs a "radical subject" (*FPT*, 168, 203),[9] a person crushed by neither collectivism nor anomie.

Despite the Bible testifying that nations have guardian angels (Dan. 10:13), some might be puzzled by this talk of angels, but, as we will show, Dugin is contributing to an ongoing (secular!) European debate about politics and angelology that dates at least to Heidegger on the right and Benjamin on the left. Others might be puzzled by talk of apocalyptic politics, and this is hardly surprising. Even theologians today are embarrassed by eschatology, which some think an oddity of their faith.[10] Those theologians who do think about the end-times, as Voegelin observes, approach them so strained that they end up bewildered.[11] Voegelin would not be surprised by Dugin, who used to have a radio show called *Finis Mundi*.[12] After all, he famously argues that "immanentist apocalypses"[13] define the politics of modernity: progressivism, positivism, Marxism, communism, fascism, and National Socialism all stem from philosophies of history that transmuted[14] biblical apocalypticism.[15]

Perhaps the first encounter with Dugin is so strange because he has consciously set himself against the Enlightenment. It is a signature of the Enlightenment to flatten the queerness of the world. Consider only J. L. Mackie's famous argument from queerness against the existence of objective values: they cannot exist, he contends, because ontologically they would be just so queer; given our materialism and historicism, objective values would be metaphysical orphans, completely inexplicable. Scruton argues that conservatism dates to the Enlightenment; that conservatism is "a work of rescue" seeking to block new political movements designed "to destroy or destabilize customs, institutions and forms of life on which people in one way or another depended."[16] Dugin should be read in this light. After all, the great Renaissance Jesuit political theorist Francisco Suarez thought each nation had two guardian angels. Jean Bodin, intellectual mentor to Schmitt and Voegelin, thought angelic guardians basic to political analysis.[17] It is highly likely that Schmitt's idea of the *katechon*—an institution that resists apocalyptic forces, and an idea absolutely basic to contemporary European political philosophy[18]—derives from Bodin.

If conservatives such as Tolkien, Scruton, and Dugin believe peoples cohere around tales and myths, then matters are delicate. Benedict XVI argues that Christian theology is demythologizing, that it rightfully sees a positive role for reason in judging religion. He warns that down the ages most divinities have been cruel.[19] In *On the Eternal in Man*, Max Scheler proposes that you can replace Christ, but the idol arising in the emptiness will be much less nice. For example, it would be a brave person who hopes for the return of the Viking gods.[20] We do not think that Dugin's apocalyptic conservatism has the resources to avoid collapsing into an antihumanism, because he derives his conservatism from Heidegger's metaphysics of risk. It makes for an unstable brew of angelism and vitalism.[21] Theirs is an account of risk without risk management, so to say. We think conservative humanism is a defense of rational order.

WHAT'S WRONG WITH THE WEST?

What is the metaphysical foundation of conservatism? Some might think the question needless, but we do not think you can get too far without engaging metaphysics. It enters into the meaning of self, action, community, obligation, and law. The basic vocabulary of politics is inescapably metaphysical. About this, at least, we agree with Dugin. At the start of the twenty-first century, he thinks we are at an impasse, and that impasse is conceptual.

Asked in an interview about the most important area studies for international relations, he proposed philosophy and sociology. The reason is the contemporary scene. In Dugin's florid style, today "is the dusk of logos, the end of order, the last chord of masculine, exclusivist domination" (*FPT*, 207), a time when plenty of people think reason hostile to equity. Here is Derrida: "What is metaphysics? A white mythology which assembles and reflects Western culture: the white man takes his own mythology (that is, Indo-European mythology), his logos—that is, the mythos of his idiom, for the universal form of that which it is still his inescapable desire to call Reason."[22]

From the Frankfurt School to Derrida, from feminism to critical race theory, reason is judged by many to be a lie,[23] a mere cloak of capital and power.[24] As illustrated by the internet—as much a venue for conspiracy theories as sharing wisdom[25]—confidence in rationality has cratered,[26] and Dugin is not wrong to observe that logocentric philosophy is ending (*FPT*, 204). For a rightist, Dugin sounds a woke note: "Nowadays all this *logocentric* philosophy has come to an end, and we must consider another road for thought, not in the *logocentric*, phallocentric, hierarchical and exclusivist way" (*FPT*, 205). The other path he recommends is chaos, inspired by the metaphysics of Heidegger.

Politics is about the relationship of the individual to the group. Adam Smith describes the earliest criminal trials: "Intercession was therefore made betwixt the parties, either by some individual of eminent worth and consequently of authority, or by the whole society together, advising and exhorting the parties concerned to such and such measures."[27] In broad strokes, liberalism puts the accent on the individual and conservatism on the group, what Scruton calls "the first-person plural."[28] Broad strokes are, of course, inadequate. For example, people in the West might be thought to favor individualism, but many think their lives are governed by the stars (astrology) or bacteria in their stomachs,[29] some are fans of Jung (as is Dugin [FPT, 42]) and believe their lives governed by transcendental archetypes, and yet others, who like yoga and meditation, relish the ideal of absence of self. Metaphysics is needed because even the basic terms are unclear. For example, long before Descartes told us the *ego* is a thinking thing, the self was one of the most perplexing issues in all of philosophy. Aquinas was sure that you and your neighbor are discrete selves, but Averroes had argued that mind was a single universal. David Hume would later deny there was a self at all, Schopenhauer said it is an illusion, and Arnold Zuboff — originator of the Sleeping Beauty paradox in game theory — argues that you and your neighbor are one identical individual. And, for good measure, Darwin and Freud think we are our parents.

Fukayama's "triumphant liberalism" (Dugin) trades on the Averroist idea that we are all one mind.[30] Both he and Dugin agree that twenty-first-century politics is uniquely situated. The reason is that political theory is played out. Fukuyama takes Kojève's reading of Hegel on universal recognition to mean that liberalism is the summit of humanism (see chapter 7 herein). If the fundamental driver of political history is the desire for the recognition of one's dignity, then history is over: it is consummated in liberalism. The classical world was a master culture which granted recognition only to an aristocracy. Christianity was a slave culture that granted equal dignity to all in principle, but because it was otherworldly, it tolerated inequality. On this reading, liberalism is essentially secularized Christianity[31] and *in concreto* gives universal and equal recognition to all. There is no political development beyond liberalism;[32] it has abolished the master/slave distinction. Once liberalism is globalized there will be no political barriers to entry, and globalized markets will ensure the full bounty of the planet is available (*FPT*, 96–97, 112). There is now no need to spend time trying to think up new concepts; they have no work to do. What is required is just the practicalities for effectuating the universal mind: all free, all equal, all desiring luxury. Liberalism takes on the mien of destiny (*FPT*, 19), the only permissible "content of our extant social and technological existence" (*FPT*, 20).

Dugin agrees that Western thought is consummated in liberal commercialism, but he sees this simply as exhaustion (*FPT*, 204). He also thinks postmodernism has refuted the beneficence of Enlightenment rationality, and he agrees with critical race theory[33] that its purported "objectivity" is racist (*FPT*, 44–45).[34] For Dugin, globalization is just Anglo-Saxon ethnocentrism, "the purest manifestation of racist ideology" (*FPT*, 45). Western logos is racist, therefore, not despite, but precisely because of its universalism (*FPT*, 163). Dugin contends that Fukuyama's one mind is rancid, in fact, logos including its own decay (*FPT*, 208). Postmodernity, though clarifying in an important way, is itself emblematic of this decay: "The architecture of the postmodern world is completely fragmented, perverse and confused" (*FPT*, 209, 26). Nonetheless, Dugin believes we are postmoderns, hybrids of flesh and data engineering. For this reason, conservatism must reply to postmodernism, the frame of any possible viable politics today, a point with which Scruton concurs.[35]

ANGELS AND PRINCIPALITIES

Our postmodern politics is antihumanistic,[36] Dugin argues, but it is a problem we do not think he escapes. To make his point, Dugin directs us to Deleuze, for whom ours is an age bent on "the production of non-human forms of subjectivity" (*FPT*, 174).[37] In his review of Yuval Harari's *Home Sapiens* and *Homo Deus*—books that sold millions of copies and came highly recommended by President Barack Obama—Scruton quotes Harari: "Once the Internet-of-All-Things is up and running, humans might be reduced from engineers to chips, then to data, and eventually we might dissolve within the torrent of data like a clump of earth within a gushing river."[38] In the transhumanist "age of technology" (Huning), "neither man nor God is there" (*FPT*, 175). Instead, Dugin argues, the actors in our politics are angels. He is not the first.

Astounding as this might seem to some, angels are a topic in contemporary European thought. The legendary debate at Davos in 1929, which pitted Heidegger against Ernst Cassirer, the establishment philosopher of the Weimar Republic, crescendoed in a discussion of angels. Against Cassirer's neo-Kantianism, Heidegger argued that even if the categorical imperative has some manner of ahistorical objectivity, it is still finite: it is a "higher being," an angel, but still a creation.[39] Heidegger's accusation is that the apogee of Enlightenment humanism—the strict equality of persons before the moral law—is no more than medievalism, trading on the idea of magical beings untouched by grubby history. Nor is it just rightists invoking angels. Around 1940, Walter Benjamin wrote his classic *On the Concept of History*. The argument figures Paul Klee's painting *Angelus Novus*, which Benjamin owned. In the argument, the angel wants to make the shattered earth whole again, but a wind from paradise grips the wings of the angel and draws him back. History follows in his wake, but not a history of progress, just a wreckage.[40] God prohibits the angel from enacting an apocalypse (in Voegelin's terms, God prohibits the immanentizing of the eschaton; see chapter 5).[41]

Likely inspired by Benjamin,[42] Italian anarchist Giorgio Agamben contends that the administrative state is the secularization of the medieval government of angels.[43] Christian theology posited a God both immutable and providential: a transcendent sovereign who nonetheless has a care for every hair on every head (Luke 12:7). How is it possible to mediate these two poles of the divine? Angels: in the theology of providence, managing the domestic life of the household (*oikos*, whence "economy") was the task of angels, and, once secularized, the task of state administrators. The modern household—its income, sexuality, education, health, and welfare—is laid bare before the data-gathering of government management: "Having established the centrality of the notion of hierarchy, angels and bureaucrats tend to fuse, exactly as they do in Kafka's world. Not only are celestial messengers organized according to offices and ministries, but worldly functionaries in turn assume angelic qualities and, in the same way as angels, become capable of cleansing, enlightening, and perfecting. . . . What is decisive, however, is that long before the terminology of civil administration and government was developed and fixed, it was already firmly constituted in angelology."[44]

The modern history of the West has been the intensification of angelism,[45] the stripping away of all human-scale associations and institutions able to decentralize, diffuse, and resist power. On one side, the state, on the other, populations stripped bare—headless bodies, so to say, related to one another through management metrics. Agamben is fond of the famous frontispiece to Thomas Hobbes's *Leviathan*: the state, in the figure of a giant, hovers over a city, its streets empty of people; the city's residents, with only their backs visible, are embedded in the torso of the man-state.[46] If this infantilization were not enough, the problem is compounded "when the *polis* appears in the reassuring figure of the *oikos*." The state veils its power in images like "the Common European Home." Power inoculates itself from judgment as care of the family.[47]

Dugin agrees, and adds that contemporary politics is an *Angelpolitia*, because data, algorithms, networks, what he calls *the superhuman entities*, now have authority (*FPT*, 166). Once your dating life is directed by an algorithm, you are managed by an angel (*FPT*, 175), and love has become an instance of Deleuze's nonhuman subjectivity.[48] The ambition of the Internet of Things is to strengthen our sinews with biodigital micro cogs and elevate our minds with the cloud's code: as one transhumanist puts it, "nanosystems, designed by human minds, will bypass all this Darwinian wandering, and leap straight to design success."[49] Pope Francis observes: "Decisions, even the most important decisions, as for example in the medical, economic or social fields, are now the result of human will and a series of algorithmic inputs. A personal act is now the point of convergence between an input that is truly human and an automatic calculus."[50] Techno-ontology[51] is the horizon of our lives.[52] Massively funded by government, business, and the purchasing power of citizenries, it leaves little untouched.[53] Directing your phone toward a scanner to buy a bottle of milk triggers a digital cascade that moves data records in the central banks of multiple countries.[54] Like the barcodes of the globe's emporia, these digital exchanges are not designed to be read by human eyes.[55] Machines "talk" to one another, and our lives organize around their incessant chatter. Metaphysically, this is only possible because we are a micromanaged "mass of identical objects" (*FPT*, 20): our fusion with digital has made us all data-cows. "This then is the *first thing* that is truly new about the present era: a new sort of exploitation, in which human beings are not only exploited in the use of their labour for extraction of natural resources; rather, their lives are *themselves* the resource, and they are exploited in its extraction," says Justin Smith.[56] Fukuyama's fantasy of a one-mind liberal commercial cosmopolis has arrived. But, as Pope Francis points out, there is a marked political asymmetry in tow: "On the socio-economic level, users are often reduced to 'consumers,' prey to private interests concentrated in the hands of a few. From digital traces scattered on the internet, algorithms now extract data that enable mental and relational habits to be controlled, for commercial or political ends, frequently without our knowledge. This asymmetry, by which a select few know everything about us while we know nothing about them."[57]

Dugin: "Political angelology must be considered as a metaphor which is both scientific and rational" (*FPT* 176). He coins *political angelology* to express that super digital platforms, untethered from "historical or economic laws and patterns," are the return of the principalities of old (Eph. 6:12). This development is antihumanistic because the fate of persons in the liberal state is to be free, but only as little people.[58] Echoing Agamben, we can say ours is a postpolitics, because citizenries are suspended: Big Tech acts as a state of exception.[59] On offer is only a *minimal humanism*, atomized and aggregated in data (*FPT*, 172–73); the right of the small man is permitted, but the right of the great, the *homo maximus*, forbidden (*FPT*, 53).[60] Imagine only if a child, when asked by a teacher what she wished to be when she grows up, answered: "I want to be like Caesar, killing and enslaving the Gauls." The girl would be marched off to the school counselor and the parents called in for a talking-to ("Why on earth did you buy her the *Gallic Wars*?").

Shifting from a diagnosis of our politics to a cure, Dugin believes we are in the time of the *Endkampf*, the apocalyptic "war of angels" (*FPT* 176, 27, 31). He thinks of angels in two ways, the evil and the good. One type of angel, the bad kind, are the algorithms of super digital platforms but, the other, with Dugin blending Jung and the Bible, is the angel protecting an ethnos.[61] Dugin says that "the heroes of postmodernity are 'freaks' and 'monsters,' 'transvestites' and 'degenerates'—this is the law of style" (*FPT*, 26),[62] and thus, trading in oddities itself, theology is back in business.[63] Postmodernism has opened a space again for the release of repressed divinities from the ruins of Christianity. Countering the global spread of digital angels managing restive populations is a "new shield," the angels or messengers of "ancient archaic values." Dugin's conservatism is a case of rescuing suppressed ancestral rituals,[64] values, deities, and even "sciences," such as alchemy. Dugin was editor of the Russian journal *Cherished Angel*,[65] and for him angels[66] are exemplars of Plotinus's *nous*, the particularized ways of knowing or consciousness Dugin opposes to Fukuyama's Averroism (*FPT*, 197). Ours is a time in which the West's universal *logos* does spiritual battle with the particularist myths of other civilizations (*FPT*, 167, 183). Dugin thinks it is Heidegger who first made this clear.

THRILLING TO RISK

Dugin arrives at angelology but starts with Heideggerian metaphysics: "History, apparently, has ended, and post-history is only beginning, and one has to search in it for a space of struggle, to win back this space and expand it" (*FPT*, 198). This idea of "a space of struggle" is Greek in inspiration, but it is retrieved from Heidegger, who argues that to exist is to prevail, that reality is fully historically particularized, having no hidden inner universal architecture. This is the metaphysical picture supporting the pluriversum. What populates these singular prevailings—"the fate of a historical people"[67]—are a people's angels: "those irrational aspects of cults, rites, and legends that have perplexed theologians of earlier ages" (*FPT*, 27–28).

Heidegger was attracted to the violence endemic to Greece, and in this he does a great service. We hold to the ideals of modified classical humanism. We shall say more about the positive legacy of the ancients, but Heidegger shows why there can be no direct *moral* return to the ancients. Heidegger's language can be a bit gnomic, but here is the man himself, and we will immediately explain. To understand reality, Heidegger tells us to look at it in the "original way, and here this means in a Greek way. We know that Being opens itself up to the Greeks as *phusis*. The emerging-abiding sway is in itself at the same time the seeming appearing. The roots *phu-* and *pha-* name the same thing. *Phuein*, the emerging that reposes in itself, is *phainesthai*, lighting-up, self-showing, appearing."[68]

The key word here is *sway*. In German this is *walten*, which means *to prevail* or *to reign*. What Heidegger is arguing is that, for the Greeks, to be is to prevail in contest, the winner shining forth, dominant, and self-sufficient. He is not wrong. Here is historian Tom Holland: "Never had there been a poem as vivid with a sense of brightness as the *Iliad*. The play of light was everywhere in its verses. . . . The queen who dressed herself did so by putting on robes that dazzled the eye. The warrior preparing for battle sheathed himself in refulgence, 'brighter than gleaming fire.'"[69]

Holland documents that there is nothing in ancient sources that recommends caring for the poor and broken. Quite the opposite, in fact: "It was only by putting others in the shade that a man most fully became a man." To the ancients, the poor, weak, and sick were objects of contempt. Among many examples, he notes that women dreaded running into Roman legionnaires because it invariably meant rape. Ancient fascination with the exhibition of power meant a consecration of violence: "Beauty was everywhere—and invariably it hinted at violence. To blaze like a golden flame, and to attain a godlike pitch of strength and valour: this it was, in the *Iliad*, to be most fully a man. Physical perfection and moral superiority were indissoluble: this was the assumption."[70] "No ancient artist would have thought to honour a Caesar by representing him as Caravaggio represented Peter: tortured, humiliated, stripped almost bare."[71]

This sensibility explains the punishment of crucifixion. Holland observes that there is scant historical record about the practice. It is as though it were so shameful that the ancients themselves could barely bring themselves to discuss it. What evidence there is, is clear: crucifixion was a punishment designed, not merely to kill, but through its torture to inflict maximum ridicule and humiliation. The Athenians likely invented it, and they were keen to fob it off on the Persians. The upshot is that none of us should wish to return to the archaic Greeks, and certainly not in Heidegger's iteration of what the Greeks were about. Here is Heidegger, clearly enthralled: "For the Greeks, appearing belongs to Being, or, more sharply stated: that and how Being has its essence together *with* appearing. This was clarified through the highest possibility of human Being, as the Greeks formed it, through glory and glorifying. Glory means *doxa*. *Dokeo* means: I show myself, I appear, I step into the light. . . . Glory is the repute in which one stands. Heraclitus says . . . 'for the noblest choose one thing above all others: glory, which constantly persists, in contrast to what dies; but the many are sated like cattle.'"[72]

In the first part of the quote, Heidegger is rejecting Aquinas's argument—which appears again in Descartes's *Meditations*—that because it is conceptually possible to distinguish being and essence, it is metaphysically possible for the two to exist apart. On this rests Aquinas's most powerful argument for the existence of God. Heidegger rejects this: "Being essentially unfolds as appearing."[73] It is conceptual confusion to think there is being held in reserve (essence): being is always unfurling.[74] Note how the second part of the quote slides from appearing to appearing in glory. This fits what Holland said about the Greeks: "It was only by putting others in the shade that a man most fully became a man." And, sure enough, Heidegger confirms it is part of the idea of appearing, of showing up at all, that some show forth as noble and others as cattle. Heidegger's metaphysical talk of prevailing and risk is a struggle for recognition, and in Dugin's iteration, a geopolitical struggle.

Heidegger's collapsing the distinction between being and essence has implications for natural law. We discuss this in chapter 4, where we hope to show the importance of natural law for any viable humanism. Dugin makes clear the stakes. Following the Greeks, Heidegger identifies a "pre-ontological chaos" (*FPT*, 209): "We must grasp that form of Greek Dasein in which this Dasein's fundamental passion ventures into what is wildest and most far-flung."[75] Humanism is an accretion of historical thought, a cultural concept emerging from Western reflection, not an adequation to anything original in the world's furniture.[76] Fatally, humanism assumes the idea of human nature—the refinement of the passions through the arts and sciences—but nature originally is chaos. The West has misidentified reality. The West's idea of nature is a pacification, and this is a colossal error repeated from Plato, down through scholasticism, and right up to modern philosophy, according to Dugin. Glimpses of the error abound: "The point of origin that came before the human is parallel to him and will remain after him" (*FPT*, 203). There is always chaos, because what we call *nature* the

Greeks had better identified as *phusis*: "Now, what does the word *phusis* say?" asks Heidegger. "It says what emerges from itself (for example, the emergence, the blossoming, of a rose), the unfolding that opens itself up, the coming-into-appearance in such unfolding and persisting in appearance—in short, the emerging-abiding sway."[77] Everything in nature seeks to reign.

Phusis is risk because whether one holds sway depends upon prevailing. Dugin: "If we correctly decipher the logic behind the unfurling of Being, then thinking mankind can save itself with lightning speed at the very moment of its greatest risk" (*FPT*, 29). About chaos, Dugin thrills: "Now it is its turn to come into play." The problem here? Play is plenty structured! Reality for Heidegger and Dugin is a game of chance, a wager. It explains Dugin's highly doubtful claim that once racism is purged from National Socialism, the latter "becomes harmless and decontaminated" (*FPT*, 46). He says this because he thinks National Socialism is expressive of Heidegger's insight into the truth of metaphysics.[78] This metaphysics generates what Dugin calls *maximal humanism*, a freedom where "great risk and serious dangers emerge. Having left the limits of individuality, man can be crushed by the elements of life and by dangerous chaos" (*FPT*, 53).

This is not conservatism, but vitalism, exposure to a buffeting reality:[79] "Yet, only that which increases freedom will make the choice of authentic Being a reality—only then will the stakes be truly great, when the danger is infinite" (*FPT*, 54). Of course, a vision of reality as crushing elements is a metaphysical speculation, an invocation of Heraclitus, and one disputed in the long tradition of Western metaphysics. But there is another problem: invoking chance, Dugin is closer to Western logocentrism than he thinks (*FPT*, 209).

In an analysis of play, Caillois identifies four basic kinds: games of competition, chance, mimicry, and vertigo. These categories include boxing, roulette, dress-ups, and waltzing, respectively. Because we derive our moral and legal language from games—"that crosses the line," "level playing field," "take turns"—games build civilization. In light of anthropology, Caillois breaks play into two pairs: mimicry and vertigo, competition and chance.[80] The former characterizes original Australian and American societies: "ruled equally by masks and possession." The latter pair characterizes Assyrian, Inca, and Roman civilizations: "orderly societies with offices, careers, codes, and ready-reckoners."[81]

An example of the latter pair: Peter Thiel gives an analysis of American colleges as the playing of a game combining competition and chance.[82] Colleges are tournaments where students try to climb the GPA slippery pole. But they are also insurance policies, a degree is a ticket to bettering one's condition, or holding one's own, hedges in a society with little safety net. This, he contends, explains the popularity of colleges despite the shocking cost. Colleges are generators of officers, lawyers, and accountants. Specializing in the training of symmetry, balance, and regularity, colleges are Apollonian institutions, centers of risk management. Aboriginal societies are Dionysian: civilizations built from games marked by pantomime and ecstasy. These two kinds of civilization do not play well together: Caillois hints that games with too hefty a dose of vertigo are unsustainable in our Roman civilization. In dwelling on risk, Dugin is still firmly in the Apollonian. After all, ever since Pascal and Hume, the logic of risk and probability has been heavily investigated.[83] Dugin's radical subject, it turns out, is not all that. And that is a good thing, in fact.

Dugin explicitly embraces play, recommending a curious French movement from the first half of the twentieth century called the Simplists, whose journal, *Le Grand Jeu*, urged people "to live their lives without maturing to remain playing at being children" (*FPT*, 188–89). As Caillois argues, the kind of games we play matters. Humanism, we argue, supports rule of law facilitating the refinement of the arts and sciences, building a civilization wherein the prestige of mimicry and vertigo has been overtaken by norms of competition and chance.[84] Put differently, the unmasked policeman — rule of law — replaces the masked shaman: "The uniform is also a disguise, but it is official, permanent, regulated, and, above all, leaves the face exposed. It makes the individual a representative and a servant of an impartial and immutable rule, rather than the delirious prey of contagious vehemence."[85]

INDIVIDUALS NOT ANGELS

A significant problem with Heidegger is what he found attractive in the Greeks. We find attractive the modification of the ancient legacy in Christian humanism. For humanism, that modification is morally necessary and — the point of this book — defensible. However, we also think

Heidegger an unreliable narrator of Western metaphysics. The point is important because Dugin does not believe liberal commercialism is able any longer to convince; it is for this reason that he believes its endurance purely a function of imperialism, a global arrangement propped up by the heft of the United States (*FPT*, 155, 193). In chapter 4 we defend natural law, and in chapter 5 some aspects of commercial liberalism, so it is crucial that we show how Dugin has mangled metaphysics. Apart from the fact that Dugin has not loosed himself from Roman civilization (Caillois) as much as he thinks, is he otherwise right that if one does not want to be racist, one must accept his pluriversum? With less sophistication, certainly many in the West suspect humanism, reckoning it as a shorthand for the dead white privileged cis male, in woke vocabulary.

We defend conservative humanism as a political middle between individualism and nationalism. It is also an ontological middle between Fukuyama's angelism (Averroism) and Dugin's (household gods). In its metaphysics, Western humanism has strongly affirmed personal individuality. Liberals are right to point to this emphasis. However, the tradition has also been at pains to account for the coordination among individuals. At its most abstract, this has resulted in intense metaphysical speculation over natures and species (Aquinas), preestablished harmony (Leibniz), and, in warmer hues, sympathy (Smith). Humanism has wanted to affirm the autonomy of persons but also resist atomic individualism: affirm belonging, and its obligations, without state or nation swallowing individuals. Catholic social thought has preferred the terms "solidarity" and "subsidiarity" to try to capture the respectful envelopment of the two poles of value.

Let us give two examples of how the metaphysical tradition has thoroughly affirmed the individual. A conservatism built on Western humanism must affirm the individual as much as liberalism, therefore. Here is Aquinas thinking through the relationship between individual and species. The language is technical, but just pick out the remarkable focus on the individual:

> It remains, then, that human nature happens to have the character of a species only through the being it has in the intellect. Human nature has being in the intellect abstracted from all individuating

factors, and thus it has a uniform character with regard to all individual men outside the soul, being equally the likeness of all and leading to a knowledge of all insofar as they are men.[86]

This nature has a twofold being: one in individual things and the other in the soul, and accidents follow upon the nature because of both beings. In individuals, moreover, the nature has a multiple being corresponding to the diversity of individuals; but none of these beings belongs to the nature from the first point of view, that is to say, when it is considered absolutely.[87]

Aquinas is arguing that metaphysically (the furniture of the world) there are only individuals. However, patterns can be discerned among them, so a species or nature is the analogy that runs between individuals.[88] It is this analogy that registers in the mind and harmonizes what otherwise has "multiple being" in discrete individuals that conform to the pattern. Individuals belong to a species because they display rather like attributes ("equally the likeness of all").[89] We discuss it more formally in chapter 4, but Aquinas's natural law picks out these common patterns ("uniform character"). What do people hope for? The world over it is the same: a home, with family fed, healthy, and competent, and friendship among the generations. Belonging: a place that requires work but also gives membership; a rich identity, those belonging dressed decoratively in the markers of that membership. And a relationship with the divine: globally, people participate in stylized rituals in honor of their gods, some in hope of continuity for the community, others in hope of personal continuity. Thus, a common pattern: individuals want to express a bit of singularity and flair (decoration and fashion) and also want solidarity (home).

Leibniz also valorizes the individual, arguing that each individual is a singularity whose logic can be distilled into an algorithm.[90] Dugin is right to see this angelism (what he thinks of as digital microscopization [*FPT*, 199]) incipient inside the Western tradition.[91] However, it is crucial to appreciate that Leibniz also rather beautifully thinks of each and every individual as a garden replete with gardens within. Here is not the place to explore the intelligibility of this idea (but it is more intelligible than you might think). The point to take away is that a garden (a person) is a pattern of color, shape, and motion in a place. Reality is harmony, not fronting off against crushing elements. Leibniz: "There is, therefore, nothing uncultivated, or sterile or dead in the universe, no chaos, no confusion, save in appearance."[92] Effectively, Leibniz would remind Heidegger that *phusis* originally means "rosebud," of which the latter was well aware. Leibniz is perhaps recalling Dante? "Into the yellow of the eternal Rose that slopes and stretches and diffuses fragrance of praise unto the Sun of endless spring" (*Paradiso* 30:124–26). Dugin's angels are not lifted in love about the Rose Eternal but amped by the rock, soils, and tributaries of land masses and thrill to the risk of glory and catastrophe.

Like Aquinas, Leibniz affirms the individual and places each in a pattern. Flair and symmetry, we might say, are the great motifs of these two representatives of the Western metaphysical tradition. The upshot: we are not free-floating atomic individuals, nor are we simply absorbed into a collective. Securing our singularity, in fact, is establishment. Conservativism is a defense of privilege, social formations that populate our world with values. Establishment secures both rule of law and refinement of the arts and sciences to assist the adoption of flair by the individual. Persons refine through proximity to the high values housed in establishment. We explore this pillar of humanism next.

CHAPTER 3

Establishment

Roger Scruton observes that conservatives are not inclined to criticize inherited institutions and laws. Conservatism is a defense of "establishment," he argued, "an affirmation of the values of hierarchy and privilege."[1] With this affirmation, as Voegelin points out, conservatism speaks to a metaphysical problem. The human is positioned between the transitory and lasting, "the ephemeral lowliness of man to the everlastingness of the gods."[2] Establishment helps minimize the anxiety of existence, the "horror of losing, with the passing of existence, the slender foothold in the partnership of being."[3]

The papacy is the oldest continuously occupied governing office, a vivid embodiment of hierarchy and privilege. Its legitimacy rests on the claim that it has a privileged partnership with Being, with the One Who says, "I Am." Unsurprisingly, the teaching office of the papacy, the magisterium, invokes a realist, objective, and universal moral theory, natural law. Natural law is not a product of history, but expresses the abiding character of being: "Some restraint is necessary for man considered either as an individual or in society. Even the barbaric peoples had this inner check in the natural law written by God in the heart of every man. And where this natural law was held in higher esteem, ancient nations rose to a grandeur that still fascinates — more than it should — certain superficial students of human history" (Pius XI, *Divini redemptoris* [1937], para. 21).

Though the papacy adopted elements of ancient aristocracy, Pius XI makes explicit a Christian correction of classical humanism. Nietzsche thrilled to antique ideals of nobility, but Christianity announced a fresh, egalitarian emphasis: "Whereas all noble morality grows out of a triumphant yes-saying to oneself, [slave morality is low], only an after-birth, a pale contrast-image in relation to its positive basic concept, saturated through and through with life and passion: 'we noble ones, we good ones, we beautiful ones, we happy ones!'"[4] By contrast, St. Paul writes, "Not many of you were wise according to worldly standards . . . but God chose what is foolish in the world to shame the wise, God chose what is weak in the world to shame the strong" (1 Cor. 2: 26–27). Where the ancient world tended to think in terms of hard divisions of caste, in which slaves exist to serve masters, hierarchy for Christianity becomes a hierarchy of function among human beings of equal dignity, in which the higher ought to serve the lower. One might compare Aristotle's account of slavery in the *Politics* with the Gospels — "He that is greatest among you shall be your servant" (Matt. 23:11). For this reason, Tom Holland has argued recently that St. Paul is the engine of the West's reformism (think of the uniquely Christian achievement of abolishing slavery). Christianity is woke, contends Holland. He is not exactly wrong; Christianity does have progressive, reformist, but also conservative accents. Mindful of the potential for moral subversion in the progressive accent, Przywara speaks of the magisterium taking an "aristocratic distance" from schismatic enthusiasm.[5]

However, if progressivism subverts, establishment corrupts. We are all beneficiaries of political reforms that have torn down malign establishment. Conservative humanism must needs wonder: In what consists a genuinely moral "aristocratic distance"? This chapter argues that Max Scheler's account of the hierarchy of values is a sure guide to a moral "aristocratic distance." Like natural law (which is the topic of chapter 4), Scheler's theory of value is realist, objective, and universal. The principal modern authors we rely upon — Voegelin, Scruton, John Paul II, Benedict XVI, and Przywara — all express his importance to their thought. In our moral accounting of establishment, we rely on Scheler, and most particularly, his greatest conservative commentator, Aurel Kolnai.

MODERN IRRITABILITY

Liberalism is not inclined to obey either nature or grace, which explains, as Manent points out, the "extraordinary irritability" of the modern mind.[6] Evil for a stock Kantian liberal is that someone or something—an institution, a law, a custom, or nature—might serve as the basis of a person's action. Acting on the basis of what is inherited or passively encountered is a moral evil, a diminishment of autonomy, and thus a diminishment of personhood. Persons have dignity when they are self-legislators, constructing a life from the purity of a rationally accessed moral law.[7] Kant gives the image of a courtroom where the self is judged but is also the judge.[8] For this reason, as explained by Scruton, Kantian liberalism "is essentially revisionary of existing institutions, seeking always to align them with the universal requirements of the first-person perspective."[9] But for the conservative, it is precisely social order—the expectations of others and the standards of institutions—that makes any human action possible. For the Kantian, state laws governing the age of consent are inevitably transgressive, an always-suspect restriction of self-determination and an affront to an emerging adult's freedom-centered dignity. But, as Scruton points out, such laws stem less from considerations of freedom and more from recognizing the salience of moral phenomena, such as innocence. It is in light of a moral value such as innocence that humans make sense of their actions, themselves, and their liberty.[10]

Conservatives do not think the world and its objects are morally neutral. Progressive thinkers disagree. In Benthamism, the world and its objects have no moral specificity until lifted into the moral calculus of the greatest happiness of the greatest number. In Kantianism, the world and its objects have no original moral character. They only attain moral bearing once clarified in the rationality of the pure will. Scheler says that, for Kant, the natural world is a "porridge." This idea is fully on display in a standard-issue liberal university professor, such as Richard Rorty: "The old story was about how human beings might manage to get back in touch with something from which they had somehow become estranged—something that is not itself a human creation but stands over and against all such creations. The new story is about how human beings continually strive to overcome the human past in order to create a better human future."[11]

Rorty mocks the "really real," the putative order of metaphysical truths to which we ought to defer. Romanticism, imagination, absolute freedom, utility, innovation, and human beneficence—utopia—are his watchwords. The richness of life is always a human accomplishment, for there is no "magnetic attraction exerted on the human mind by the really real." Rorty's university progressivism is a rejection of obedience to establishment, tied to liberal individualism and self-creationism. It expresses the belief that experience is a projection of human categories, but it also exemplifies Charles Krauthammer's "holiday from history" thesis: the proposition that after the Cold War, the West stopped thinking about the world. The world, that is, that hitherto had existed: a world of scarcity, geography, tribes, nations, ideology, establishment, and power; Dugin's world, in other words. Instead, there is an open, unencumbered, and unrestricted utopia of imaginative possibilities for human development, the Fukuyama thesis. The "wise intellectual," Rorty tell us, has a "desirable openness to novel proposals with familiarity with the fates that have overtaken many past proposals. Such people recognize that although the only hope for the future lies in the human imagination, novelty alone is never a sufficient recommendation. A combination of romanticism and pragmatism lets them see the relation between the human present and the human past as analogous to the relation between earlier and later stages of individual development: there is no immanent teleology in either case."[12]

Though writing at the turn of the millennium, nowhere does Rorty take seriously the darker layers of our human makeup. The events of 9/11 cast no shadow. A major voice in universities in the United States at the time, Rorty seemed oblivious that political Catholicism was making a return in the papacies of John Paul II and Benedict XVI or that the rise of political Islam might shape the West's imagination. French theorist Jean-Pierre Dupuy believes that American intellectuals could not digest 9/11 because the dramatic reemergence of the sacred—that politics remains what it always was, the problem of murder and sacrifice—beggars contemporary university belief.[13]

Nor did Rorty give thought to thinkers more aware of Augustine's reflections on original sin. Rorty certainly knew of psychoanalyst Jacques Lacan, but Lacan argues that imagination is antiprogressive. Imagination is the psyche's tool for allowing human desire's most catastrophic fantasies indulgence, without getting caught, so to say. Cultural productions and mores skirt close to what is taboo and allow space for cunning, but ultimately controlled, aggressions: think only of the barely controlled rage of spectators in a European football stadium, the slayings in computer games, and the murders at the opera.[14] Lacan, whom we discuss more in chapter 8, ranges across games, plays, art, and historical events to make his point. And then there is Darwin. For all his desire to be novel and contemporary, Rorty seems not to take Darwin seriously. Rorty is a modern-day Marquis de Condorcet, the Pollyannaish booster of the Enlightenment. Darwin pointedly defers to his fellow countryman, the demographer and killjoy Reverend Thomas Malthus. Darwin adopted his population principle. Malthus posits a conflict between fecundity and scarcity, to which Darwin added a tribalism endemic to the biological as the driver of history.

The Counter-Enlightenment, which Schmitt did much to popularize, is tied primarily to three Cassandras: the Frenchmen Joseph de Maistre (d. 1821) and Louis de Bonald (d. 1840), and the Spaniard Juan Donoso Cortés (d. 1853). They argue that civilizations are fragile. History, they contend, does not bend toward justice; it can just as well devolve into reprimitivism (see our chapter 8). This triad probed what excesses might result when progressivism subverts establishment, when embodiments of learning, sanctity, modesty, service, political, diplomatic, and industrial expertise are openly mocked.[15] They questioned whether civilizations can survive the decline of religion, the weakening of tribal bonds, an indifference to bookishness, and skepticism toward high art. Can the obligations that a people owe to its past and future members be isolated from the laws of inheritance and the privileging of family? Why are hierarchies so stubborn and why do they reassert themselves even after the most violent leveling? Why do ideals of nobility resurface in ages addicted to the transvaluation of values? Is the fascination with the knight—fully on display today in *Star Wars*, *Harry Potter*, *Hunger Games*, *Game of Thrones*, and *Lord of the Rings*—of no real political and cultural significance?

In *Political Romanticism* (1919), Schmitt argues that the Counter-Enlightenment theorists owe something to Edmund Burke. Averse to "political geometricians" (Schmitt), Burke argues that a polity is best thought of as "the original plant." Subversion, he argued, always involves calculating minds who foolishly replace tradition with schemes they believe adequate to the nuances of governance. His gardening motif counters that politics is a tending to, a careful cultivation of an inheritance. Revolution, Burke warned, was no great drama to be celebrated, but a wrecking of institutions that leave the people exposed to raw government power. For example, revolutionary attacks on religion are inevitably also attacks on property: church property is managed for the ages, a physical reminder to government of its limitation, and it serves a social bond transcending immediate pressures, a bond of the dead, living, and yet born. Gardening, not revolution, is the best way to think of political change. Retaining their identity, plants nonetheless change to suit the season, and so must politics: conservatism is not the same as an embalming rigidity, nor does it experiment with fundamental, sweeping change. This would be to treat "the original plant" as no better than a weed. Does Burke's idea that government requires constant reminding about its limitation explain why George Washington instructed that each regiment build a garden?[16] It is no surprise then that progressives such as Bentham, Kant, and Rorty thin out the world to rid it not only of its recalcitrance but also its controlling richness and glamour.

VALUE TONES

The idea of reality saturated with values was made famous by Scheler.[17] He is part of a select club of philosophers credited with developing far-ranging ethical systems. Scheler argues that persons in their judgments and acts defer to "the mysterious laws of the interresonance of love and hate" (die geheimen Gesetze des Echos von Liebe und Hass). Ordering our primary orientation to the world through love and hate is the ready access we have to discrete, extramental value tones. A civilization's moral history is the relationship between the acts of persons and this "invisible Order."[18] Scheler's innovation depended on phenomenology; a method of inquiry marked by an acute focus on experience. A case of discerning with precision the contents of our consciousness is our experience of the extensive and intensive qualities of values.

We have only to write the word *peach* and readers immediately have the value in mind: you might remember the taste of the fruit, but may just as well remember the scent of a perfume, a bar of soap, or its hint in the smell of a rose. Values are part of the furniture of the world, and the qualities of objects and persons are constellations of values. For example, if I tell you a story about how I met a benefactor, or if I tell you about a civil chat with a man on a train whose conversation suddenly flashed with malice, you have clear to mind value tones that make these encounters comprehensible. The ontological standing of values also loosens the grip of the state: values ground the independence of social relations; they make possible original collective responses open to all humans for shared experience.

In addition to Scheler, something like this account of the world and its objects[19] is defended by Shaftesbury, Hume, Smith, Ruskin, Kolnai, and Tolkien, and other names could be added.[20] Scheler speaks of "the beautiful structure of the world of values." Here is Ruskin describing the particular beauty of English country towns: "They are not so often merely warm scarlet as they are warm purple;—a more beautiful colour still: and they owe this colour to a mingling with the vermilion of the deep grayish or purple hue of our fine Welsh slates on the more respectable roofs, made more blue still by the colour of intervening atmosphere. If you examine one of these Welsh slates freshly broken, you will find its purple colour clear and vivid."[21]

It might be thought this value discernment hoity-toity, but it is, in fact, utterly everyday and common. If you go into a paint shop and ask for a can of white paint, the clerk, besides looking over at his pal and grinning, will ask, "White paint? Would that be magnolia, antique, off-white, or brilliant white, perhaps?" Having had a bit of sport, the clerk will then offer you a paint chart with twenty or more shades of "white." Our oft-criticized youth can talk for literally hours about fine distinctions in the shape, padding, and decoration of sneakers. Fine distinctions are not just for Diaghilev and the Ballets Russes adding flexed wrists and abrupt shifts of weight to the *grand jeté* and *développé*.[22] Discrete unities, value tones are extensive. Returning to our paint chart: *extensive* means the way indigo takes up a specific value space on a mapping of blue colors. The extension of the value can also be hyperized, so to say, as an historical space, for example, a shade known as *Jaguar indigo*, a car paint specific to Jaguars of a certain age.[23] Values also have a tonal intensity. Kolnai argues that human acts are not all equally localizable under a simple rational rubric, as suggested by utilitarianism, for example. Rather, acts have varied moral emphasis: objects of the will's choice are laden with values, and some of these exhibit "a tone of warning, urging, vetoing, and commanding."[24] The most imperious tones underlie negative, rather than positive precepts. Some value tones intrude upon our daily lives most forcefully as prohibitions: "Do not kill," "Do not steal," and so on. For the value tones composing the negative prohibition "Do not kill," consider Smith's description of a murder:

> To the man who first saw an inhuman murder, committed from avarice, envy, or unjust resentment, and upon one too that loved and trusted the murderer, who beheld the last agonies of the dying person, who heard him, with his expiring breath, complain more of the perfidy and ingratitude of his false friend, than of the violence that had been done to him, there could be no occasion, in order to conceive how horrible such an action was, that he should reflect. . . . His detestation of this crime, it is evident, would arise instantaneously and antecedent to his having formed to himself any such general rule.[25]

Negative claims of justice, in other words, have strong emphasis: they literally make their presence felt,[26] and impose the strictest duties.[27] By contrast, a positive precept, such as "Defend the widow and protect the lowly," certainly makes a claim upon us, but less forcefully than "Do not kill," and this is evident from our daily practice. Positive precepts are built on higher and more admirable values, but values with less emphasis. To fail in these duties diminishes our moral standing but does not (straightforwardly) make us morally corrupt.[28]

So much for the extensive and intensive character of value tones. How do they fit in a hierarchy and what are the implications for a conservative politics?

VALUE HIERARCHY

Our access to the value texture of the world is through "value-ception," the work of sympathy. Sympathy has an a priori character, namely, being alert "to worth of others in general."[29] This is because sympathy registers the grand mimicry running throughout the natural world. "The relationships between expression and experience have a *fundamental* basis of connection, which is independent of our specifically human gestures of expression," states Scheler. "We have here, as it were, a *universal grammar*, valid for all languages of expression, and the ultimate basis of understanding for all forms of mime and pantomime among living creatures."[30] As an opening onto the world, emotion is like a web relaying value information. Sympathy—and here Scheler departs from the Scottish tradition—does not exhaust what it is to be human. Sympathy is a feature of our vitality, linking all in natural community, but humans are also persons. Humans are composite, having levels in our identity.[31] The human body is only identifiable as a discrete individual, argues Scheler, because bearing a person.[32] Rather like Aquinas and Leibniz, Scheler thinks persons have an "intrinsically individual character," our "own ideal value-essence,"[33] such that each of us is aware of our character as a "pattern of personality" before our persons are filled out by concrete, determinate acts in history.[34]

As a conduit of value-ception, it is also part of the a priori character of sympathy that it is a preferring and places some values after others. Ranking is inescapably part of value-ception.[35] Inquiring into "the height of values," Scheler observes that values which are less transitory, less dependent, and less relative rank higher. Love is a high value—as art from pop songs to opera testify—because it is absurd to say, "I love you, for now." It is part of the value essence of love to be *sub specie quadam aeterni*.[36] It would be a value confusion to expect to be literally loved at your place of work, which is merely expressive of a lower value, a bond of common interests. Work is a place of dependency, therefore, whereas marriage is how two become one flesh. This logic is universal. For example, a bespoke wedding dress is a value higher than the bolt of fabric from which it was made—the former is less relative than the partibility of the bolt from which it was cut.[37]

Scheler identifies four basic categories, each of which includes a myriad of discrete values. The value categories form a hierarchy and, in order from highest to lowest, they are (1) spiritual and personal, (2) intellectual and cultural, (3) vital, and (4) pleasurable or pragmatic.[38] Human beings work (pragmatic), have family and national connections (vital), enjoy hobbies, games, and reading (intellectual), and praise (spiritual). Persons relate to one another via these four basic categories of value, but a person pronouncedly appears only "wherever we meet with *signs* or *traces* of its spiritual activity, in a work of art, for instance, or in the felt unity of a voluntary action, we immediately encounter in this an active individual self."[39] Persons have a unique, perduring, disclosive standing.[40] Should a civilization's symbol or organization invert the rankings, occluding persons' disclosive standing, such a civilization must be reformed. Much of Scheler's writing put this ranking to work identifying philosophical and political ideals that engage in value reversal.

Among many examples,[41] Scheler identifies the fashion victim. Fashion might bring people together, but, argues Scheler, its core value, vanity, can easily trip the abandonment of the self. Ever sensitive to how he is received by others, the "abnormally vain man" lives out a social self, leaving his personal, individual essence untended. The *spiritual vampire*, as Scheler terms the fashion victim, is the human type mired in vanity. Aquinas identified a leading characteristic of vanity as exhilaration in novelty. The spiritual vampire, writes Scheler, "does not fasten on a single individual, but always on one after another, so as to live a life of his own in their experiences, and fill the void within." In fashion terms, such a man lacks a style signature. There is a reversal of value here, one typical of the modern world, according to Scheler: the high value of personal discrimination is forsaken for lower generic values of assimilation. That which is highest, persons, and that which is finest, the life of the mind, hobbies, and praise, play second fiddle to what is least inspiring, routinization. Scheler compares this reversal to the idea of hypnotic usurpation.[42] This image captures nicely the person falling away from disclosive standing. Fashion is a precarious value, therefore, but more about that in chapter 5.

What can we make of the following example from Pierre Manent? About the Soviet empire, he states: "The most casual and least observant traveler, in seeing the sadness of housing and clothing, the stiffness and brutality of physiognomies, the difficulty of obtaining the most elementary services from one's neighbor—even the most naïve and favourably disposed traveler, I say, was forced to notice that the communist regime granted only the most meager share of the useful and the pleasant and that it frustrated cruelly and incomprehensibly these two fundamental springs of human life."[43]

Even the lowest values in the ranking are values and thus basic to human cultivation. The Soviet Union was a catastrophic failure[44] because it could not secure even pragmatic and vital values for its people. The West's problem, as Scheler never tired of showing, was more that value confusion had seeped into its self-understanding. During Iraq War II, it was commonplace to see on the rear of the same car both these bumper stickers: "No blood for oil" and "If you don't like the traffic, stop breeding." The first affirms that economic value cannot trump persons, but the second rejects the personal and spiritual aspects of family life for a sterile contemplation of nature. Ours is an age that has lost "emotional community with the living cosmos and an organic outlook upon the world."[45] Had we this emotional community, argues Scheler, we would intuitively appreciate that our vitality aims to realize "*more-than*-vital" values.[46]

Value theory aims to safeguard the standing of persons, and as such it is a critical plank in conservative humanism. Persons resist reduction to Dugin's vitalism, but also, contra Fukuyama, they are firmly rooted in the pantomime of nature. It is hierarchy that prevents reductive—and primitivizing—characterizations of persons. For this reason, conservatives are right about the positive moral character of privilege, the establishment of hierarchy.

PRIVILEGE

Values, says Kolnai, are an "autonomous, impersonal code of objective norms": they are universals discerned as qualities inherent in persons, objects, and actions. These universals are "the timeless moral order which genuine Conservative statecraft recognizes as the irremovable measure of its designs and acts."[47] When discerning behavior, we are, in fact, "bowing to the intrinsic evidence of Moral Cognition." In other words, values compel our attention. However, Kolnai believes their appeal is not unaided. He added significantly to value theory when arguing that recognition of, and support for, values requires privilege.

His signature contribution is the analytical precision with which he pursues the connection between values and their support in social reality, institutions of privilege. Kolnai: "Civilization signifies and demands mastery over nature and self-mastery of mankind, noble distance, objectivity, nobility, obligingness, tolerance, uprightness, readiness to come to an understanding and to community with what is alien, refusal to give the precedence to the drives for validation and struggle, acceptance of the multiplicity of values and needs."[48]

Civilization, "noble distance" from raw appetite, is housed in the offices of the peerage, the bench, ambassadorial staffs, officers on quarterdeck and NCOs, curators, management and stewardship, trustees, football coaches and captains, and artisans and their tools, to name a tiny fraction. These offices are structured by discrete value tones, and though a simple intuition of each is possible, in the normal course of things, values make their appeal in and through establishment. Moral perception is only rudimentary without the mediation of the ties expressed in associations: hearth and home, the village (with its civic hall and church), farms, schools, guilds and unions, workshops, and the like. An early reader of Kolnai, Scruton writes:

> Every arrangement that allows people to value an activity for its own sake will also provide them with a paradigm through which to understand the ends of life. The working-man's club, the businessman's marina, the institutes and societies of urban and rural life—however remote these may seem from some snobbish ideal of fellowship—are in fact the stuff of human society. Through them men and women are able to define themselves, and to discover the language in which to express their common essence. . . . An autonomous institution provides language, custom, tradition, fellowship: a member may transport that mental framework to the rest of life, and so make sense of himself as a political being.[49]

"Privilege" is Kolnai's word for value-bearing social formations. These formations are vantage points on value order, but their role is more than aiding value-ception. They have a political role. Privilege, a manifold of memberships and belonging, breaks up power,[50] Kolnai writes:

> Privilege means the social projection, the institutional recognition, the traditional embodiment of the essentially insurmountable dividedness [among persons] . . . the fact that a few or rather, very

many men in different ways transcend the "common level" of mankind, as though that in man which points beyond man took shape
in them, in this or that limited respect, so that through their instru-
mentality others reach beyond their own immediate possession or
proper nature, and enrich themselves by a contact with higher values primarily alien from them and not properly theirs, according
to the mode of Participation.[51]

There are myriad centers of privilege, spanning the liberal and
mechanical arts: the car mechanic's garage, as much as the university,
is value-bearing. It is the job of government to assist, and build upon,
these autonomous institutions. Of course, Kolnai does not think there
is some one-to-one relationship, say, that a lord's privilege assures that
the aristocrat is gallant or that all car mechanics are ingeniously adap-
tive. However, value-bearing social formations do have an affirmational tendency: the trappings of aristocratic privilege, for example, do
encourage gallantry.

There is, today, no more dirty word than "privilege."[52] What re-
silience it has is drawn from moral consensus, patterns of sensibility
and manners diffused through settled communities. As in Scheler, for
Kolnai the stress in moral consensus is upon *sensus*, that is, the percep-
tual-emotive register of human life. Ideology can corrupt sensibility,
but, of its own, sensibility, a bit like coral, gathers round social nodes,
which fix in view the immovable lure of values. We are all alert to the
content of moral *sensus*, which consists of

> highly general dimensions of right-doing and wrong-doing, which
> I would quote here in the language of values rather than of obliga-
> tions: that benevolence is good and malice, bad; that veracity is
> right and mendacity, wrong; and similarly with the contrast-pairs
> of courage and cowardice, self-control and intemperance, respect
> for others and arrogant self-assertion, yet on the other hand self-
> respect and servile self-surrender, adulation or pliancy, dignity and
> meretricious cynicism, magnanimity and cruelty, chastity and lust,
> self-control and intemperance, honesty and dishonesty, fidelity and
> treachery, loyalty and treason . . . what we are facing here is a con-
> sensual perspective of feelings, insights, views and codifications.[53]

Kolnai was Austro-Hungarian, a Jewish convert to Catholicism. Fleeing the Nazis, he settled in England and loved a particular English expression: "I knows a gentleman when I sees im." Simultaneously, the expression speaks to moral consensus, privilege, and that establishment is tone-setting. For the latter claim, he offers a compelling phenomenological observation. Imagine, he asks, climbing a hill. On the flat, before climbing, various aspects of the landscape stand out. Even a little elevation, however, adds richness to what one sees. In particular, with the climb underway, one can come to see behind the buildings and copses that previously had blocked one's sight. In making the climb, "our horizon has *widened*; our perspective has become *enriched* and more *articulated*. The enhanced verticality of our position implies a more adequate, a more graded and more *comprehensive* vision of things and their connection in space."[54] The phenomenology of height shows that civilizational values, "noble distance," are acquired atop elevated social positions or establishment.

This modifies populism. Kolnai grants that egalitarianism is a value, but care is required. Kolnai identifies egalitarianism as a low value, tending toward a disvalue: for it tends to restrict our very capacity to recognize value, rejecting, as it does, raised positions (this is why progressive humanitarianism is pernicious). Constellations of words and social concepts in all cultures set the refined, dignified, and noble at a height. If populism is fostered by modernity, and before it, by a certain strain within Christianity, then a politics of privilege is necessary to shore up institutions of height, the importance of which phenomenology, ordinary language, and social practice confirm. Unless shored up, populism will eat away at privilege, and therewith "noble distance," and even dignity.

Therefore, establishment is one necessary feature of a society with a healthy politics: "Positions of authority, power, rank, prestige, wealth, etc., deserve being respected and honored not because they warrant personal excellence but because they stand for a vital necessity of social order and are conducive to the recognition by and in society of the hierarchical distinction of values. . . . So far, an 'aristocratic' society is both possible and desirable."[55]

It is an implication of the consensus expressed in "I knows a gentleman when I sees im" that these value-bearing sites of privilege sit atop a broader reservoir of value-ladenness. Kolnai thought the eighteenth-century Scottish development of the idea of the moral spectator a critical improvement in moral analysis. The standards of institutions are a spectator over the people, but, equally, all have expectations of others, and "the people" monitor their governing institutions. Wondering about the origins of genius, Hume[56] argues that the individuals celebrated in history books emerge from a spirit of genius pervading a people, and essential to this common spirit are conditions fostering law, mastery of mechanical arts, learning, and commerce. And so Hume: "Can we expect, that a government will be well modelled by a people, who know not how to make a spinning-wheel, or to employ a loom to advantage?"[57] We explore evidence of this diffusion more in chapter 5, but an illustration of the Hume and Kolnai point is industrial design. It is not museum curators who are the primary conduit by which the world has been made beautiful: artists and engineers, builders and draughtsmen have given us elegant bridges, houses, tower blocks, cars, watches, aeroplanes, kitchens, and bathrooms. Hume and Smith were the first to discern the intimate relationship between commerce and the refinement of the arts and sciences. They would be unsurprised that the signature beautiful object of our age is the iPhone: utility combined with design, the iPhone graces the lives of the hundreds of millions who use it to register the teeming hieroglyphs of places and peoples: "The nobleness *of* society depends, not merely on the nobleness (in the widest sense of the word) of its *leading* members," says Kolnai, "but also on the nobleness of its members in general, as a whole, and the possibilities it affords for the unfolding of the nobleness virtually present in its average, I would venture to say in its *humblest* members."[58]

Establishment relies on, consolidates, but refines the original value experience and dignity of the people. Put another way, establishment is the *vox populi*. A constellation of moral and aesthetic values, nobility, embodied in privilege, makes prominent the desirability of distance and independence; it teaches the importance of being dominant, or at least, being self-contained and not put upon. With these attributes, nobility affirms the urgency of dignity to human life: "In my own surmise, nobleness is not so much a special value modality besides vital, moral and aesthetic value as the mark of a specially intimate *compenetration* between a concrete being (notably, a person) and some salient modality of vital, aesthetical, intellectual or moral values," says Kolnai.

"We would call a man 'noble' whom we could not as it were *imagine* to act or behave in any situation otherwise than with intensity, grace, genius, originality, grandeur, justice, generosity or high-mindedness."[59]

Moral insight is, in any rich sense, social, and will be vulnerable should privilege be destroyed. Luckily, moral hierarchy has a potent illustrator, who has cemented his place in popular culture: J. R. R. Tolkien.

ESTABLISHMENT'S POPULARIZER

Despite the Right's complaining about liberal bias in Hollywood, there are a great many conservative films. High up the list must be *Master and Commander*, a detailed study of character and command aboard a British naval ship in the period of Nelson. One can hardly imagine a more hierarchical setting. It was nominated for ten Academy Awards in 2004, but lost out, almost all going to the archconservative *The Return of the King*, which was the last in a trilogy of films dramatizing Tolkien's *The Lord of the Rings* (*LOTR*) and won eleven Academy Awards—and it ranks among the very top all-time for box office receipts. Oddly, it is remarkably common to meet liberal, humanitarian, globalist, secular people who love, absolutely love *LOTR*, which is worlds apart from the Fukuyama worldview.

Tolkien was a conservative, which he explains in an interesting way in this important, somewhat long, passage reflecting on *LOTR*:

> The story is cast in terms of a good side, and a bad side, beauty against ruthless ugliness, tyranny against kinship, moderated freedom with consent against compulsion that has long lost any object save mere power, and so on; but both sides in some degree, conservative or destructive, want a measure of control. But if you have, as it were taken "a vow of poverty," renounced control, and take your delight in things for themselves without reference to yourself, watching, observing, and to some extent knowing, then the question of the rights and wrongs of power and control might become utterly meaningless to you, and the means of power quite valueless. It is a natural pacifist view . . . but the view of Rivendell seems to be that it is an excellent thing to have represented, but that there are in fact things with which it cannot cope.[60]

The Elves and hobbits both share this contemplative attitude toward value tones, "delight in things for themselves." For Tolkien, elvish craft[61] traces the contours of values structuring nature, and most especially the values exhibited by wood, and hobbits tend to the seeds of the garden, potencies of color, texture, movement, dimension, structure, and scent. The vow of poverty, as Tolkien uses the expression,[62] is an abandonment of the power to manipulate objects contrary to their nature. It is a deferential or obedient attitude to establishment (the return of the king!). It is, to follow Kolnai, a bow to the sovereignty of objects.[63]

Tolkien saw harrowing things at the Somme, but he was not a metaphysical pessimist, like Schopenhauer. Certainly, as befits a conservative, he was sober-minded: "I fear it must be admitted that there are human creatures that seem irredeemable short of a special miracle."[64] Skewering a worldview such as Rorty's, Tolkien says that "the presence of the terrible" is essential to fairy stories, for "a safe fairyland is untrue to all worlds."[65] He admired the refinement and manners evoked by Jane Austen—but was no real fan of the literature—for they "cloaked or indeed held in check . . . the everlasting cat, wolf, and dog that lurk at no great depth under our social skin."[66] Like Burke, Tolkien thinks gardens hold in check "the everlasting cat."

The Shire is the embodiment of this politics, because the hobbits are gardeners. Tolkien was a Burkean. The Shire is an autonomous, agricultural region of self-sufficient communities, where beer-drinking and pipe-smoking are primary activities, and though the king's law is acknowledged, the king also seems far away.[67] Tolkien had a dear love of gardening,[68] and that love clearly shapes *Lord of the Rings*. Think only of the setting of the story: as happiness turns to bitter struggle, so the land changes from the fields of the Shire, to the savannah of Rohan, and finally to the rank sterility of heaven as a yellow rose—gardening is constitutive to being human. "A man is both a seed and in some degree also a gardener," says Tolkien.[69] Samwise Gamgee is the hero of *LOTR*. He is Frodo's gardener, and it is he who drags Frodo, the ring bearer, across the finish line and saves Middle-earth from Lord Sauron's evil: "I think the simple 'rustic' love of Sam and his Rosie (nowhere elaborated) is absolutely essential to the study of his (the chief hero's) character, and to the theme of the relation of ordinary life (breathing, eating, working, begetting) and quests, sacrifice, causes, and the 'longing for Elves,' and sheer beauty."[70]

Gardening is an ennobling of the land, and self. The following is a value thesis: "There are of course certain things and themes that move me specially. The inter-relations between the 'noble' and the 'simple' (or common, vulgar) for instance. The ennoblement of the ignoble I find specially moving. I am (obviously) much in love with plants and above all trees, and always have been; and I find human maltreatment of them as hard to bear as some find ill-treatment of animals."[71]

What is it about gardening that makes it conservative? Samwise, the "chief hero," clarifies. Sam's heroism is a corrective of the heroics of the Elves in Tolkien's *magnum opus*, *The Silmarillion*. Lust for the Silmarils—jewels embalming the light of the trees of Valinor—destroys solidarity among the Elves. Tales of remarkable heroism fill the pages of *Silmarillion*, but the bravery of the Elves is always a rearguard action: it cannot repair the ever-renewing fracturing provoked by lust for the jewels.

What is the difference between gardens and jewels? Unlike the incorruptible, but corrupting, Silmarils, gardens must be tended. Gardens and gardening make you tenderer. The gardener armed with hoe and shears is a tough-minded protector, controlling, but ultimately obeying the logic of plants, humbly attuning craft to the seeds of life. Sam is a true knight, for he combines toughness with tenderness. He is a figure not of glory, but solidarity, or, to use Tolkien's preferred term, fellowship. Gardens are his tutor.

Sam is a good example of "I knows a gentleman when I sees im." The principals in *LOTR* are all aristocrats, except Sam, who is an ordinary hobbit. Gandalf is an angel, Galadriel and Elrond are of ancient lineage, Gimli and Legolas are highborn, Boromir is the son of the Steward of Gondor, Aragorn is a king, Bilbo and the rest of the hobbits in the story are members of families linked to The Thain. As the story unfolds, Sam rises in stature, and others fail: the highborn Boromir falls, caught in the madness of desire for the ring, and he betrays the fellowship. Others, such as the hobbits Merry and Pippin, are fools. Galadriel, though a hero in *LOTR*, has had to reestablish her standing over many ages: she participated in the primal rebellion against God's governance, as described in *Silmarillion*. Saruman, another angel, falls, utterly. Tolkien agrees with Kolnai. Hierarchy does not guarantee noble acts, but it does encourage them. Sam loves Elves and admires them. Lowborn he might be, but at a critical moment he lives up to the ideal of the knight, ably illustrated for him by Aragorn. At the critical moment, it is establishment that helps Sam save Frodo, and Middle-earth. Indeed, as Saruman notes toward the end of the book, moments before his death, all the hobbits have come back from the war as knights.

Sam does what only three others are ever known to have done: once holding the ring, he gives it back freely. As Frodo starts to fail, slowly destroyed by the lure of the ring, it is Sam who literally carries him to the fires of Mount Doom so the ring can be consumed in the flames. Frodo spent and prostrate, Sam could take the precious as his own. He does not, because he is schooled by gardening. Tolkien explains the ontology of a plant thusly: "a helpless passive sufferer."[72] About trees, he says: "Every tree has its enemy, few have an advocate."[73] By the end, Frodo is like a plant, and Sam's service to the Shire and Frodo never falters.

Though there are austere gardens, the English cottage garden is whimsical. Hobbits are somewhat childlike. As Shaftesbury points out, all gardening is about geometry, but ludic, too:[74] the playful is amplified in the cottage garden. Sam matches Kolnai's beautiful lines: "Children, though compelled to obey, are kings because they are enticed away, enchanted, into the fairyland of idealized mankind, into the innocent sphere of pure mathematics, into the abstract and leisurely world of eternal forms."[75] By contrast, Sauron and Saruman have no gardens, and, as Tolkien explains, they introduce a false theology — "worship of the Dark,"[76] a "Satanist religion."[77] They replace fertility with sterility. Mordor is akin to a rank lunarscape, a twisted nursling of Sauron's resentment: Isengard begins with a destruction of the forests, an act that provokes the last march of the Ents, the retribution of the trees.

In *LOTR*, Elves are all glamour and charm, but in *Silmarillion* this is very far from the case (much like *The Hobbit*). Though contemplatives, Elves are not gardeners. Tolkien takes a critical distance from them: "[Elves] wanted to have their cake and eat it: to live in the mortal historical Middle-earth because they had become fond of it (and perhaps because they there had the advantages of a superior caste), and so tried to stop its change and history, stop its growth, keep it as a pleasaunce, even largely a desert, where they could be 'artists' — and they were overburdened with sadness and nostalgic regret. In their way, the Men of Gondor were similar: a withering people whose only 'hallows' were their tombs."[78]

Elves are not destroyers, nor do they tend. Elves have something of a tree's aloofness, and on account of their detachment leave Middle-earth something like a desert, its potencies left untilled. They have something of a cavalier quality about them. By contrast, Sam fusses over Frodo's gardens, and this service prepares him for the greater service to Frodo and to Middle-earth itself. It would not cross Sam's mind to embalm the light of the trees of Valinor (the Silmarils): not out of a lack of imagination but because his value preference forbids it. Sam is like Tolkien, who tells us of his "passionate love of growing things."[79]

In Tolkien, conservative humanism has a popularizer. Sam is a perfect illustration of establishment because he hits all the marks of the value hierarchy. He loves herbs for his cooking (pragmatic), he is a gardener, marries Rosie, and has a family (vital), adores the harmony of gardens and the elegance of the Elves (contemplative), and, unlike Merry and Pippin, has a sharp awareness of the awesome standing of Gandalf (spiritual). Sam is Tolkien's moral and political exemplar because gardens relate to place, home, beauty, life, obedience, and service. They touch upon Dugin's concerns. However, seasonal and daily tending to a garden is to commit afresh each day to solidarity and balance. Gardening links the legacy of geography and the heritage of craft to symmetry and geometry (Fukuyama). It spans vitalism and angelism: a garden is a combination of the ancestral and a conceit, a story composed in a design of values tones.

Gardening is conservative, because it injects high worth into the world without embracing militarism (fascism) or dismissing bourgeois suavity (communism) or subverting historically settled patterns of life (progressive humanitarianism). Like Burke, Tolkien believes gardening is humanizing. It is emblematic of that civilizing, "aristocratic distance" (Przywara), that depends on the rank of value tones.

CHAPTER 4

Law

Chapter 3 introduced a Schelerian theory of value: a realist moral theory that discerns value tones exhibited by the world and its objects. It is a theory well suited to conservatism. The examples offered there show that values saturate experience and deliver order, place, richness, deference, and guidance. In a word, establishment. By contrast, liberal theory is linked to the proposition that values are not found in nature but projected into bare materiality by human will. We saw that Richard Rorty is a typical example of this idea. His position had long percolated in the West. Sundry Anabaptists and Puritans judged human nature untrustworthy. Nature was a hindrance in getting to God, a distraction from scripture and grace. God's law was promulgated in the texts of the Bible, not in a sacral universe. The materialists of the scientific revolution saw in nature only matter in motion. Not for them was St. Francis's Sister Moon and Brother Sun. Theology and science both made a casualty of natural law.

Natural law is another realist moral theory. It claims that right and wrong do not change because what it means to be human does not change. Life, sex, pride, and veneration are immovable fascinations for us. The theory purports that reason discerns and elaborates upon the ordered promptings of our most pronounced and consistent desires. Oriented by these appetites, reason determines certain things must be avoided, and others done. Originating basic obligations and liberties, natural law is the measure of the rationality of the law.[1] It monitors human developments of law (positive law). Tastes, mores, and circumstances change, and deliberative bodies and judiciaries of varied polities craft, revise, and dispense with myriad laws as sensibility and national conditions alter. Sometimes, on account of faction, ideology, and corruption, human formulations of law conflict with the unchanging core of rational human nature. If a positive law clashes with the few, but socially foundational, obligations and liberties stemming from our fixed appetitive core, that law is unjust. Natural law trumps human law, when push comes to shove.

Though basic to moral, legal, and political reflection until the end of the eighteenth century, natural law today is largely ignored. It seldom figures in law school education, textbooks on philosophy of law give it a cursory mention, and in the great publication machine of modern university research it is judged "unappealing." In these venues, natural law is a marginal presence at very best. Catholic moral theology is the exception and a critical resource for conservatism.

In the twentieth century, Catholic moral theology innovated by twinning its long-standing guardianship of natural law with a phenomenological personalism responsive to value ethics. Innovation was necessary to acknowledge the moral gains of modern liberty. In a seminal 1965 document, *Dignitatis humanae*, the Catholic Church at Vatican II made the acknowledgment: "A sense of the dignity of the human person has been impressing itself more and more deeply on the consciousness of contemporary man, and the demand is increasingly made that men should act on their own judgment. . . . This demand for freedom in human society chiefly regards the quest for the values proper to the human spirit."[2]

As though making up for lost time, a flurry of subsequent Church documents has examined this quest. At the same time, those documents have articulated anew the abiding significance of natural law. If persons are to flourish, the Church contends, it is critical to appreciate that desire is under law.

Contemporary humanism cannot rely either on utilitarianism or Kantianism. These are the two favored moral systems of liberalism, but neither takes desire seriously enough. Utilitarianism reduces us to pleasure-seekers and naïvely thinks the appetite for pleasure immediately responsive to our calculated preferences. It ignores our appetite for noble action; that our desire for recognition is more than willing to sacrifice pleasure for grandeur. Kant grasped this and made a basic contribution to human dignity by dwelling on our capacity for high-minded rational action.

However, both theories share the same premise: our appetites are bare materiality, pliable and readily molded to human agency. For just how weak a premise this is, consider *jouissance*. An idea derived from psychoanalytical practice, jouissance describes the activity of desire and its starkly perverse manipulations. Lacan observes that "the naturalist liberation of desire has failed historically." That, despite the best efforts of the Enlightenment, "we do not find ourselves in the presence of a man less weighed down with laws and duties than before the great critical experience of so-called libertine thought."[3] Part of the reason is that psychopathology has discerned in infantile appetite "an obscure agency there, a blind and tyrannical agency."[4] This is not Kant's Radical Evil, the idea that we oppose the moral law from self-conceit. Rather, jouissance is the claim that we desire to hurt ourselves: "the mutilation that is proper to man."[5] Kant thinks self-conceit needs to be humbled by the law; Lacan thinks we take pleasure from the law doing so. We make of humility humiliation and we like it. Lacan quotes at length Kant's example of a man who claims his appetite for his favorite woman irresistible. Kant imagines a scenario where outside her chamber there is a gallows. If the cost of an "irresistible" night of pleasure was execution on the morrow, Kant argues the fellow would soon find himself well able to moderate his impulses (Kant: "he cognizes freedom within himself").[6] To think that no man is perverse enough to enjoy a woman today and enjoy his execution on the morrow is naïve. It was the Marquis de Sade's great contribution, contends Lacan, to help make clear that in fact very many "a partisan of passion" (Lacan) would make that choice eagerly.[7] Desire is not like prime matter or mere matter in motion.[8] Desire, so to say, has its appetites, and they are not all pretty, coherent, or high-minded.[9] For this reason, and as do natural law theorists, Lacan argues desire must be under law ("law and repressed desire are one and the same thing").[10] This is his theory of the phallus,[11] to which we return at the end of the book. It is one of the goals of chapter 8 to show that psychoanalysis is an overlooked resource for conservativism.

Keenly aware of the problematic character of appetite, natural law is an accounting of desire under law. To be fair, the original architects of liberalism were equally fly to appetite. Pierre Manent identifies the architects as Machiavelli and Hobbes. He argues they are most responsible for discrediting natural law, but even so it would figure prominently for a couple more centuries, and not least in the Scottish Enlightenment. It is no coincidence that Thomistic natural law was developed around topics of homicide and war. Basic to human experience, sex, power, and pride feature prominently in killing (in Viking myth humans are born out of a homicide).[12] Aquinas hoped to moderate these dynamics. Machiavelli's criticism of natural law is that it moderates too much, robbing the politician of the violent intimidation essential to statecraft, and Hobbes contends it does not moderate enough: killing must be off the population's menu entirely.[13]

Expressed theologically, natural law is a participation in eternal law, the life of Christ.[14] Expressed intuitionally, the first formal principle of natural law—do good and avoid evil—is derived from a metaphysical axiom "that the good is diffusive."[15] Though natural law offers insight into the precarious nature of desire, it is also fundamentally affirmational or optimistic about human nature. In Thomistic natural law,[16] four core appetites are discerned: desire for life, family, solidarity, and religious encounter.[17] The inclinations prompt us to seek these domains of good. The priority of these appetites is derived from observation; they represent a shorthand anthropology. Observation, twinned with the metaphysical axiom, means natural law is not a deliverance of divine revelation. Scripture refines, certainly, but the core holding of Thomistic natural law is that we can know the good, true, and beautiful in varied domains of life independently of divine assistance,

The Jesuit theologian Karl Rahner speaks of the "luminosity of being," and natural law offers itself as the sure way that rule of law reflects this luminosity. Human nature is prepackaged with an original justice that sustains, and sometimes controls, later elaborations of just order. It is by law that humans are most tightly bound in community. The primary inclinations root humanism because each is an attachment to a good: life, fertility, communication, and veneration. Human life consolidates around this core of goods, which reason articulates. For example, the desire for life leads directly to reflection on the rules adjudicating just and unjust killings. Given the appetite, self-defense is rationally warranted, but the precise contours of the rules of self-defense require significant reflection. Can a person stand her ground or is she obligated to run and only turn and fight back once her back is against the wall? Are the rules the same for all? If there is something demeaning about having to run when arbitrarily attacked, must someone of high standing run like a regular person? Can a nun or monk fight back at all?

Natural law does not purport to manage all the demands placed upon us by the intricacies of communal life. It cannot, for example, discern the niceties involved in the proper exercise of gratitude or discretion. Virtue is required, as is the supplement of custom. Nonetheless, the framework that is natural law is critical to rule of law. Our core inclinations are law-bound—they have always already promulgated rules—prior to any exercise of human ingenuity. Though civilizational and national variety about this core is found, no communities begin as a *tabula rasa*. There are no communities that do not have rules concerning these domains, such as courtship rituals, regulations for games and festivals,[18] standards for war, or religious rites. Difference the world over is found, but so is continuity—throw a ball anywhere in the world and humans run after it, albeit in a varied assortment of games.

However, rule of law collapses quickly under two dynamics found in liberalism that feed off one another. Liberalism's promise is that humanity produces its form of life without deference to a rule or criterion set by nature or reason.[19] The liberal conception of dignity surreptitiously reduces to vitalism: the human stripped of all original order, ductile drives putting into question any ideal of obedience. Law depends on obedience, yet liberalism rejects the latter as a worthy value. The goal of liberalism is to fuse freedom and power, to annul the political relation of command and obedience. Unconstrained, liberalism, as Manent puts it, thinks the human a transformer toy, able to shape-shift as whim or technoscience requires.[20] The biocentrism stemming from liberalism's program of disenchantment (materialism and equivocity) flips suddenly, the human not really terrestrial at all; liberal dignity is radically transcendent (angelism and univocity). Natural law, by contrast, is an embodied personalism that avoids this weird destructive oscillation.[21]

There is no humanism without rule of law, and natural law is a necessary corrective to liberalism's subversion. However, perhaps a more serious problem for conservatism than liberal dislike of natural law are the conservative reservations about its worth. Even the popes have wobbled.[22] The typical liberal complaint—that natural law is too conservative a morality—we take as a recommendation, obviously. Nonetheless, we want to show that natural law is well founded. In the remainder of this chapter, we discuss five criticisms of natural law from the right. In answering these challenges, we isolate five further positives recommending natural law to conservative humanism. Complaints against natural law from the right include the following: it is unnecessary (Scruton), abstract (Schmitt), theological (Strauss), unnatural (Heidegger), and not specific enough (Hibbs). Let's take each in turn.

Unnecessary

Burke argues that a vigorous defense of rights depends on upholding establishment. Rights, he believed, were historically earned, not "natural rights": rights are birthed with institutions of law. Scruton takes this to mean that liberty and property are matters of positive law, bound to the legal traditions and histories of particular peoples. By this, he did not mean democracy. He did not link positive law to the outcome of majoritarianism—indeed, in the third edition of *The Meaning of Conservatism* he was scathing about the majoritarian distortions of traditional British politics introduced by the Labour prime minister Tony Blair. After Blair's "reforms," from a Burkean vantage, Britain's House of Lords exists in name only,[23] so Scruton strongly affirmed the judiciary as a last bastion of privilege against majoritarian rule. He recognized that the modern state must have some rule by statute or legislation. However, he insisted on the autonomy of the common law as an inheritance, refined over a thousand years, of an English sensibility about how best for English life to cohere. Scruton was, of course, hostile to the administrative law increasingly encroaching upon the UK through its membership in the EU. This new legal order eroded the privilege of an autonomous English judiciary, which, in the past, its eye ever on the common law inheritance, had been a bulwark of conservatism in Britain.[24] Western humanism, like every myth, is a composite of values, which are always local and regional values, a point made by Scruton.[25]

There are reasons to pause and take stock of Scruton's position. Brexit only happened because a deep sense of fair play undergirds British democracy. When the 2016 referendum went against those wanting to remain in the EU, they did not simply accept the democratic decision. They fought hard to have the referendum voided. It took a long, painful time in British life, but ultimately this ploy was repudiated at the ballot box as unfair. The Remainers, as they were called, got their second referendum,[26] which is already against the rules of the game, but widespread disgust at the shenanigans saw the original decision reaffirmed, and massively so.[27] The 2019 decision was a populist reaffirmation that the rules of games matter.[28]

Scruton perhaps had an overintellectualized view of how peoples bond. Certainly, he is right to note the critical role law plays in cementing community, but he oversells the law as an intellectual, elite phenomenon.[29] Establishment and populism are part of our ordinary experience of the value hierarchy. Games, and what is out of bounds, illustrate. The law has the attributes of a game.[30] Its membership guards the rules of procedure, court rituals, and dress-ups[31] as jealously as the members of the local darts league. Huizinga profoundly observed play as the form of civilization.[32] Caillois has provided a classification of the types and rules of games that enables an analytically rich sociology of cultures.[33] The bewilderment greeting the cancellation of national sports with the Covid-19 pandemic in 2020 highlights the social centrality of games.

Furthermore, common law is not perhaps as conservative as Scruton believed. The justices of the U.S. Supreme Court used common law to set the stage for the most divisive Court judgment in recent U.S. history: the *Roe v. Wade* (1972) decision generating a federal right to abortion, annulling the localism of the states.[34] Sixty-three million abortions later, *Dobbs* corrected the historical record on the common law in the United States, but common law has offered no refuge for the unborn in the UK.[35] It is at least plausible to argue that a society that has institutionalized homicide at the heart of family is neither healthy nor dedicated to rule of law.[36] Natural law theory grants ample room to positive law and custom, but it is ultimately not the law of the (particular) land, rather of nature that must prevail: natural law is opposed to relativism[37] and to any idea of justice reducible to national will and its history.[38] The English tradition of common law is rightly celebrated — evident in

the number of countries whose legal systems make ample use of it—
but it trades on a deeper ideal of fair play. This ideal has its own rules,
and they are not country-specific. They make use of the trust implicit in
the inclination to solidarity[39] and are sometimes formalized rationally
(e.g., as much in the rules of international sports federations as in war).

Typically, the rules are left unspoken: as Manent puts it, ours is "a
world essentially albeit potentially ordered."[40] Operating silently, they
nonetheless shape our actions. Manent's point evokes Scheler's "invisible Order," and a good example are collectors. Found all over the
world, collectors shape and present their collections along the same
lines. Whether patchwork quilts, stamps, tobacco, handbags, watches,
soccer shirts, Starbucks cups, hi-fi, sneakers, or stones,[41] collectors literally display their inclination to the order of the good, true, and beautiful.[42] Think of the handbags on display in a cloffice (a woman's closet/
office) and the mortification if someone at the Zoom meeting should
question the authenticity of the Lady Dior on display. On occasion, it
is necessary to explicitly bring to bear this subterranean order. As Dr.
Martin Luther King Jr. observes, order is not enough, there must be
just order. Sometimes the referee blows the whistle. King made his
point by relying on Thomistic natural law, and on Christian personalism.[43] Kolnai explains great moral reformers: "The 'dissentient conscience' that in fact is moral conscience, far from challenging or derid-
ing moral consensus, strives to lift it from the abyss of oblivion and
indifference, to reawaken it in men's minds and to place it once more in
the focus of their attention. It endeavours, not to abolish the Law but to
restore it. It appeals to moral consensus as against the layer of amoral
interests which hides it from sight and the sway of immoral idols
which overshadow it."[44]

It is to make this essential corrective of positive law that we think
natural law necessary to conservative thought. Humanism requires
that sometimes the global (Fukuyama, so to say) trumps the particular
(Dugin).

After 9/11, the English judiciary has been consistently hostile to
detention of terror suspects in the United States.[45] Perhaps they have
been in the right, but regardless, their common law sensibility raises
another problem for Scruton's linkage of settled law and sovereignty.
After 9/11, the U.S. government adopted Carl Schmitt's decisionism,

innovation in law required by extraordinary circumstances.[46] Put differently, Scruton was outflanked on his right by Schmitt's postliberalism.[47] We touched upon Schmitt in chapter 3 and do so in chapter 5. Now let us look at Schmitt's criticism of natural law.

ABSTRACT

Spanish jurist Francisco de Vitoria (1485–1546) offers one of the most complete elaborations of Thomistic natural law. Much of his work is a reflection on the legal implications of the New World. His most consequential application of Aquinas is coining "humanitarian intervention."[48] It is also why Schmitt rejects natural law. Schmitt repudiates any notion of law trading upon "the inhuman/humanitarian distinction," believing it generates a new ferocious kind of enemy. Disgusted at the practice of cannibalism, Vitoria argued the Spanish could overthrow the Aztec rulers and transform Aztec culture (regime change), even if people themselves consented to the gory sacrifices. Schmitt argues this natural law branding of the inhuman subverts rule of law, for it makes some into enemies of mankind. Law becomes discriminatory: a ruse to generate targets so that killing efforts can be intensified. Natural law cloaks cruelty.

The discovery of the New World is one of the signature events marking modernity, and Vitoria's reaction to it reveals, Schmitt thinks, that the spirit of humanitarianism[49] incubates inside natural law.[50] Natural law is a theory of personal embodiment,[51] for Schmitt an abstraction at odds with rule of law, which is a function of geography. He means this quite literally.[52] "Law and peace originally rested on enclosures in the spatial sense. . . . *Nomos* means dwelling place, district, pasturage; the word *nemus* has the same root and can have ritual significance as forest, grove, woods."[53] Detached from land, natural law makes rule of law precarious.[54] Its formalism obscures the geographical elements of law, which are restraining.[55] Schmitt is famous for the claim that politics is rooted in the friend/enemy distinction, and even though this sounds belligerent, Schmitt thought the distinction tracked the boundaries of a place and decreased the likelihood of killing. If nations are tied to land, nations cannot go abroad lawfully looking to mix it up with others: those lands are beyond the reach of a sovereign observing rule of law.[56] By contrast, the formalism of natural law is expansionistic, facilitating empire, a point Dugin gets from Schmitt (*FPT*, 74–75).

Unsurprisingly, when modern rationalism appropriates Aquinas, it intensifies any tendency in the theory to abstraction.[57] Schmitt argues that natural law in Aquinas is concrete. In the Middle Ages, just war theory had an institutional setting: evolving from a feudal and estate-based consciousness, war was bound to a spiritual power, whose canon lawyers functioned as spiritual directors of sovereigns. Medieval spirituality was geographical: "Thus, for Vitoria, Christian Europe was still the center of the earth, both historically and concretely oriented to Jerusalem and to Rome."[58] This meant that natural law was originally keyed to a place and for the people of that land. Around World War I, however, when the work of Vitoria was reintroduced into international law, this peculiar lived context of the medieval use of natural law jurisprudence was ignored. Natural law thinking now operates, as Schmitt puts it, in an "empty space" isolated from the geographical spiritual consciousness of Catholic Christianity.[59] It is this detachment that thoroughly cements its cruelty. Schmitt turns natural law round on itself: it is infected by angelism.

Is natural law an enemy of humanism, as Schmitt contends? He is right to emphasize geography, and in chapter 5 we show that land has a historical place in Anglo-Continental conservatism. We argue there that place figures prominently in a humanistic political economy. It is a delicate matter, however. Schmitt links not only land and law but what the law protects, the venerations of a people: "Neither can one speak of the *noos* of "many people," since *noos* is universally human—common not just to many, but to all thinking people—whereas something walled or enclosed, or a sacred place, all of which are contained in the word *nomos*, expresses precisely the divisional and distinguishing orders whose particularity . . . [means *nomos*] is a primeval form of ritual, legal, and political cohabitation."[60]

Dugin draws from Schmitt his polycentric postliberalism (*FPT*, 99) with its emphasis on the fates of peoples (*ethnoi*).[61] In Dugin, the fusion of land and ethnos tips into organicism. Ethnopluralism gets mereology wrong: it folds persons too completely into the whole.[62] There is too much solidarity and not enough subsidiarity. This is flagged by Dugin's claim that good politics derives from a metaphysics of occasionalism (*FPT*, 69). Occasionalist metaphysics treats the operations of concrete objects as epiphenomena of an underlying cause.[63] Typically, the cause is God, but in modernity, some offer the state as a candidate or social forces,[64] and in Dugin, it is the identity of a people. Vitoria gives an interesting thought experiment, and I do not think there is much doubt about Dugin's answer to it.

A city is under siege and the besiegers offer a deal. Rather than raze the city to the ground, the attackers will leave the city alone if the city picks and kills one innocent resident, man, woman, or child. The fate of the people appears to require the city to pick someone and dispatch that innocent. Vitoria argues this would be a tyrannical act, for no person is simply a part of a whole. Rejecting organicism, he states, "For a member cannot suffer injury, since it does not have its own proper good to which it has a right. But a man can suffer an injury, since a man has a proper good to which he has a right. . . . But an innocent person is his very own good and alone he suffers, and therefore it is not lawful to kill him."[65] The point of the thought experiment is to show that persons are wholes with juridical standing underived from claims of the city (terrestrial or divine). Vitoria uses this reasoning to condemn political rites of human sacrifice. The juridical completeness of discrete persons is the peg upon which Vitoria hangs his innovation of humanitarian intervention and, in this light, the innovation carries more moral worth than Schmitt thinks.

Dugin would decide the example differently, and the reason is metaphysical. His occasionalism means the fate of a people trumps discrete persons: in Vitoria the independent juridical standing of persons is a consequence of Thomistic metaphysics, wherein persons are genuine secondary causes.[66] Occasionalism does not accept secondary causality. Aquinas captures the significance of persons as secondary causes in his pages on natural law: "subject to divine Providence in a more excellent way, in that it [human nature] is itself made a participant in this Providence, by providing for itself and for others" (*ST* I-II, q. 91, a. 2). Vitoria argues that homicide is an offense against God, who is master of life and death, but also an offense against the individual killed, as each of us is a bearer of rights on account of our lordship over self (*dominium*).[67]

Not folding into angelism, in fact, the abstraction of natural law is salutary, for it is a block on organicism (vitalism). Natural law is essential to conservative humanism because it enables us to think rightly about the juridical completeness of discrete persons.

THEOLOGICAL

We thus cannot agree with Leo Strauss, who thinks natural law offers no metaphysics, only a theology. Natural law, he claims, is not what it purports.

Strauss argues that philosophy is the exercise of autonomous understanding, but natural law cannot be a philosophical discernment of natural justice. At least, if it is agreed that Aquinas offers the classic formulation, then natural law is inescapably theological. Ernest Fortin, a Catholic Straussian, argues that this is so, because law requires promulgation; it needs a lawgiver to make the law publicly known. Aquinas has smuggled God into his supposedly rational account of law, just as Strauss contends. Natural law is really piety. This particular charge is not especially powerful in our opinion because Aquinas says promulgation is original to reason:[68] "The first common precepts of the law of nature are self-evident to one who possesses natural reason, and do not need to be promulgated" (*ST* I-II, q. 100, a. 4, ad 1).[69]

Aquinas argued that "no reality lacks its specific operation."[70] Quarks, gluons, and proteins all display a logic. Our species, *Homo sapiens*, has its "specific operation," the rational articulation of appetites. Strauss on the Thomistic position: "Man is by nature inclined toward a variety of ends which possess a natural order; they ascend from self-preservation and procreation via life in society toward knowledge of God."[71] The first two inclinations have had confirmation from Darwin, being the fundamental principles of natural selection, and primatology confirms the third.[72] Put otherwise, reason identifies in human animal appetite a legal framework: prohibitions against suicide, child abuse, and hatred, and obligations to self-care, family, and rule of law. Legislators in all countries mull over laws respecting these themes all the time. Aquinas says, "Law is nothing else than an ordinance of reason for the common good" (*ST* I-II, q. 90, a. 2).

In a letter to Voegelin, Strauss writes that the Greeks show "that truly human life is a life dedicated to science, knowledge, and the search for it," not deference to divine revelation.[73] Fatefully, contends Strauss, Aquinas inherited both Greek philosophical tradition and a legacy of biblical ethics. This blending of Athens and Jerusalem is disastrous, for it not only weds law to "theology and its controversies," but also obscures the difficulty of moral knowledge and the fraught decisions inevitable in politics. The problem with Thomistic natural law is that it does not take politics seriously enough. For Strauss, the relationship between reason and law is a delicate one: reason must not collapse into national passions, but it is still tasked with pragmatic judgments to defend the polity.

Strauss prefers the Greeks because they understood that there are no "universally valid rules of action" dictated to politics. This is just as well, for events sometimes require political leaders to make harsh decisions, incompatible with rules derivable from natural law. For example, Aquinas and Vitoria elaborated a theory of just war with protections for innocents. Natural law, counters Strauss, makes nations vulnerable, tying the hands of leaders confronting acute, even, existential, events. Decisions, not laws, are sometimes basic. Echoes of Machiavelli and Schmitt are clearly heard.

However, Strauss overstates the place of God in Thomas's natural law reasoning. The obligation respecting a knowledge of God merely posits that the question of God must needs be addressed at law. Archaeology favors Aquinas.[74] An ivory figurine known as the Lion-Man found in Germany and dating to 35,000 years ago is the earliest indisputable work of art so far found. It is also thought to be the first known religious artifact.[75] The earliest human burial sites include extremely expensive grave goods, pointing to some idea of an afterlife and perhaps gifts for the gods.[76]

Conservatism can use the metaphysical framework of natural law to advance public reasons for shaping politics. Furthermore, proponents can also insist that the theologico-political problem is inescapable. Natural law does not entail integralism, never mind theocracy, but nor does it default to laicism. This means, against Strauss, a moral-political pressure always weighs on the statesman, curbing the scope of action. The gods will have a say, too.[77]

A signature of contemporary politics is the rise of political forms of Islam, Catholicism, Hinduism, and, in Russia, Orthodoxy. The liberal establishment in the United States was caught napping on 9/11. Another casualty of political Islam was Fukuyama.[78] Conservative humanism makes a resource of Christianity rather than running from it. The trick is to do so without embracing what the New Right finds so attractive about political Hinduism[79] and Russian Orthodoxy.[80] Dugin: "Not only the highest supra-mental symbols of faith can be taken on board once again as a new shield, but so can those irrational aspects of cults, rites, and legends that have perplexed theologians in earlier ages . . . all that is ancient gains value and credibility for us simply by virtue of the fact that it is ancient. "'Ancient' means good, and the more ancient—the better" (FPT, 28).

Theology—the analytical assessment of religious experience—has an essential role to play in politics because veneration is an inescapable part of nations. An expression of theology and jurisprudence, natural law is a rational elucidation of animal appetite and, as Thomas puts it, a participation in the Eternal Law, in Christ, the Logos. Unlike Dugin's ancestralism, natural law is not simple piety. As our arguments show, it makes a critical contribution to conservatism for it operates as a demythologizing of political reason and religion.

UNNATURAL

In a recent work on Thomistic natural law, James Carey isolates an important argument against natural law in Heidegger. This argument helps clarify certain nonnegotiables in conservative humanism.

Through his novel approach to experience, Heidegger claims careful attention shows that natural law is not remotely natural. That is, it is no part of original human experience. Like Strauss, Heidegger returned to the Greeks. Only, for him, the world of the Greeks was a harsh battle for recognition: life a competition for glory.[81] Strauss returned to Greece to torpedo Aquinas only to find himself outflanked by Heidegger. Nature, as discussed by the Greeks, was thoroughly rational, believed Strauss. However, Heidegger used the Greeks to show that the world is intrinsically nonrational. Strauss, under no illusions about his teacher, granted that Heidegger's version of the Greeks fore-closed the possibility of ethics and politics.[82]

The ideals of nature that Aquinas and Strauss held dear, were, Heidegger argued, a picturesque abstraction crafted by Western phi-losophy.[83] Importantly, Heidegger even argues that ideals of logic are formulated in light of prevailing metaphysical theories.[84] Logic is his-torical, not a transcendental criterion of thought. In fact, what made possible philosophy (Strauss) and law (Aquinas) was a decline,[85] an ideal of nature born of theology, obscuring man's "elemental field" (Carey) where "doing violence in the midst of beings" (Heidegger), humans, bereft of any preexisting order, encounter the challenge of authenticity.[86] Nature and humans are both uncanny, but we, "the violence-doer" (his term), are the uncanniest, able to discipline nature.[87] Being, for Heidegger, is utterly intimate to us and decidedly not our friend: with audacity, we must wrest from it what we can (ridden with anxiety we work to discipline what can overwhelm us at any moment). Przywara argues that Heidegger's elimination of any background order to existence expresses a Romantic fascination with disintegration[88] and thus Heideggerian heroism is, as Strauss puts it, "a being at home be-yond the most extreme homelessness."[89]

Dugin's polycentric conservatism, rooted in national risk, is an ap-plication of Heidegger and retrieves from his thought a workable geopolitical position.[90] Nonetheless, it is marred by what mars Heideg-ger's thought itself. Conservative humanism contends that rule of law is unsustainable if persons are reduced to risk and the drive to prevail. Putting matters succinctly, there is a choice to be made: taut authen-ticity or nature kindly displaying a logic discernible by reason and sci-ence? There is only one option able to sustain rule of law.[91] We think Przywara is right to see in Heidegger a negative eschatology:[92] a vision of civilization as decadent, bent on a reprimitivism.

INDETERMINATE

Comparable to human rights activism today, natural law historically has been used to cancel ancient cruelties, and its just war tradition re-mains nimble around modern strife. However, the final complaint from the right we will consider is that natural law reasoning cannot deliver specific policy. The American Thomist Tom Hibbs argues that natural law was designed by Thomas to have fundamental support from the virtues. He downplays Thomas as inheriting a long medieval legal tradition and argues that Aquinas's core ethical ideas are Aristotelian, the life of the prudent sustained by a community practiced in virtue.[93] *Pace* Hibbs, natural law can deliver policy. Let us consider a postmodern phenomenon: the retreat of the state and the problem of violence it raises.

After World War II, the West's grand strategy was peace through prosperity, the means including international institutions, open seas for commerce, and a state monopoly on violence for the common good. Across the world today, this neoliberal order is in retreat.[94] A cantonization is afoot[95] as nation-states cede internal authority,[96] with power leeching to partisans, mafias,[97] indigenous police,[98] and breakaway provinces.[99] It is also in retreat within the United States. Unlike most countries, even European ones, universities in the United States occupy one of the commanding heights of the culture. At the start of April 2020, Johns Hopkins University (JHU) gained permission from the state of Maryland to create a private police force of one hundred armed officers. The risk assessment[100] of the university is that Baltimore's security situation is not sustainable.[101] Can natural law help shape a modern university's police policy?

Crime in Baltimore is high by national standards, and student calls to the city police have sometimes gone unanswered. Two of Baltimore's last three mayors have committed crimes, and the reach of city authority is dwindling. There is a perception that since the 2015 Freddie Gray riots, Baltimore police have disengaged. Police morale is known to be low, and less than one-third of the city's more than 300 murders a year see an arrest, never mind conviction.

Baltimore has come full circle. The city rose to prominence during the War of 1812. To augment the fledgling U.S. Navy, Congress issued letters of marque, allowing private shipping companies to arm and roam the seas to capture British merchantmen and booty. Investing in privateering proved lucrative for Baltimore. Two hundred years later, the state of Maryland has abandoned its monopoly on violence and granted jurisdiction and arrest powers to a private entity, also the state's single largest employer.

Baltimore is a bastion of the Democratic Party, the party of secular liberal humanism in the United States, and, unsurprisingly, some city residents have complained about the "militarization" of JHU, expressing concern about accountability and racial profiling. One state senator has likened JHU to the Vatican City inside Italy. This analogy is not as silly as it might sound.

Thomas Hobbes devoted *Leviathan* to "the mutual relation between Protection and Obedience." Who protects, governs. Commenting on Hobbes, Schmitt puts the point pithily, "The *protego ergo obligo* is the *cogito ergo sum* of the state." The state of Maryland has diluted its sovereignty. Split sovereignty is thoroughly explored in the natural law tradition.

The natural law tradition examines norms and mores analytically prior to civil law. A hundred years before Hobbes, Vitoria explored the licit use of violence in the absence of civil law. His prompt was Spain's encounter with the New World and the legal puzzles that arose over contested jurisdictions and mores. A lurid question posed to Vitoria was whether the Spanish could stop the Aztec practice of cannibalism. This question led to Vitoria's work on the *ius gentium*—the binding laws of all peoples—which is viewed as a milestone in the development of international law. He argued thus: Granted that the Spanish have no civil jurisdiction in the Aztec kingdom, and they are not themselves being eaten, still natural law permits the Spanish to intervene, depose the rulers, and change mores. Vitoria's analysis bequeathed the innovation of the legal grounds for humanitarian intervention.

For Vitoria, it is morally unproblematic that JHU intends in certain circumstances to use violence to protect its staff, students, and property. A private person has, he argues, "the right to defend himself and his property, but does not have the right to avenge injury, nor even, indeed, to seize back property which has been taken from him in the past." How he defends this thesis is startling.

His *On the Law of War* (1539) begins boldly: "Any person, even a private citizen, may declare and wage defensive war [*bellum defensivum*]."[102] Our democratic and humanitarian sensibility has schooled us to believe that only states wage war, but Aquinas (d. 1274) would be just as startled as we are by Vitoria's formulation. Vitoria was a Thomist, certainly, but one who knowingly departed from Thomas's theory of homicide.

In *Summa theologica*, II-II, q. 64, Aquinas insisted that only a public authority charged with upholding the common good can intentionally kill and wage war. By contrast, Vitoria thinks split sovereignty is the original condition of communal life. Invoking an axiom of Roman law—force may repel force—each of us, along with the state, has the right of war. The axiom assumes a prior harm, so war undertaken by a private person is a *bellum defensivum*. States, however, have an added rationale for war: "The commonwealth cannot sufficiently guard the public good and its own stability unless it is able to avenge injuries and teach its enemies a lesson, since wrongdoers become bolder and readier to attack when they can do so without fear of punishment."[103] The right to avenge is tied exclusively to public authority.

Aquinas restricts the deployment of violence to public authority, but, observes Vitoria, "the nub of the problem is to define the commonwealth, and say who is properly its prince."[104] The problem of split sovereignty poses the question of where to draw the line between a private entity and a public authority.

Vitoria wrote before the concentration of power in the nation-state, when dukedoms, cities, and enclaves abounded, all laying claim to the rightful use of violence. He proposed that a private entity becomes a public authority once attaining self-sufficiency. He defines the standard: "A perfect community or commonwealth is therefore one which is complete in itself; that is, one which is not part of another commonwealth, but has its own laws, its own independent policy, and its own magistrates."[105]

Google—and there are other companies, such as Walmart—is edging toward this standard.[106] *Fortune* relays the scope of its recent lobbying: "The massive company said it lobbied on dozens of issues, reflecting how integral its services have become to American lives and commerce. The filing cited privacy, data security, antitrust, taxes, tariffs, trade, the opioid crisis, artificial intelligence, cloud computing, autonomous vehicles, immigration, the future of work, encryption, and national security."[107]

JHU is not far behind. Set firmly under the view of Baltimore's citizen police review board, the university has declared its ambition to be a leader in twenty-first-century policing, effectively making review redundant. Its police force is restricted to defined areas around its three urban campuses. However, an agreement with the city is already in place that should residents ultimately feel comfortable around its police, the boundaries of the university's police jurisdiction can expand. Natural law is able to determine specific policy matters, and Vitoria would conclude that it could be moral for a modern university to share a state's sovereignty, even to the point of deploying violence.

This chapter has sought to show the importance of natural law to humanism. More than other ethical theories, it squarely confronts the problematic character of human desire and is unembarrassed to insist that inclination requires rational articulation. Replying to rightist skepticism about the tradition, we saw that nativist wisdom is rarely enough to sustain rule of law. Against Scruton, positive law needs grounding in natural law just as much as natural law needs supplementing by positive law. Furthermore, we think nativist traditions of law rely on a deeper accounting of order, as found in games. Moral reformers can effectively be viewed as not offering new insight but lifting from oblivion moral consensus long present but muted. Against Schmitt, conservative humanism argues that a critical part of just order is the conviction that persons have a juridical completeness in their own right. This insight is crucial to resist political rites of sacrifice. It is bad legal mereology to think that persons are derivative of an organic whole. Natural law is an answer to the question of veneration, but in assessing this inescapable political problem, it does not collapse into being essentially a theology (*pace* Strauss). However, natural law is committed to a sacral universe, that is, a metaphysics of cosmos, wherein natural harmony sustains moral judgment. Conservative humanism does not think rule of law sustainable when persons are reduced to an existentialism of risk (as seen in Heidegger). Rather, communities are surrounded by nature dense with value, and from which they derive universal moral orientation. We do accept Hibbs's overall point that natural law needs supplementing. Though agile around concrete policy, the tradition has always said as much itself. We now turn to political economy. Eric Voegelin will be our guide.

CHAPTER 5

Humanistic Enterprise

Humanistic enterprise is a term we borrow from fashion designer Brunello Cucinelli. His eponymous label, with annual revenues in the region of $450 million, is explicitly built on principles of fair profit, dignity at work, and tending the land. In the company manifesto, dignity at work includes "an amiable workplace that enables workers to look up at the sky and the landscape, perhaps spotting the home they are going back to after work, to their family." The ideal of the monastery inspires fair work: "Outside the working hours one should never be online for business reasons: Saint Benedict often reminded his monks that there is a time for work and a time for the soul."[1] But the nub of the issue, not addressed in the company's manifesto, is the division of labor.

It is well documented that natural law thinking in Renaissance Spain made valuable contributions to economic theory.[2] It is less well known that Spanish theology had an even greater influence. Replying to Reformation ideas of predestination, Spain's theologians sought to balance God's causal power with ideals of human liberty. Leibniz modified the Spanish Jesuit theology of freedom in his *Theodicy*. Famously declaring ours the best of all possible worlds, Leibniz describes the *Theodicy* as a work of theology and natural jurisprudence.[3] As Agamben observes, Leibniz's effort to blend causation and liberty resounds in Adam Smith.[4] It is important to recall that the *Wealth of Nations* has for its full title *An Inquiry into the Nature and Causes of the Wealth of Nations*. What's natural in Smith's account of business as "natural liberty" are the legal, intellectual, moral, and passional necessary causes that must be in place to access the land's bounty. Dugin is very astute when he says that Smith wrote "the political and economic Bible of the modern epoch."[5] At the heart of the "economic Bible" is the grace of the division of labor,[6] Smith contending that persons are united in moral sympathy through its operations.

DIVISION OF LABOR SUBVERTS DIGNITY?

The cogency of twinning morality with the division of labor is hotly contested by postliberal thinkers. Postliberalism is a grab bag of right-ists and leftists, who no longer believe that the Enlightenment delivers the ideals of humanism.

From the right, John Gray argues that surveillance capitalism is our fate because the division of labor has broken up communities. Smith argued that increased specialization at work would generate greater abundance. Specialization requires special buildings housing special machines. Factories generate social atomization, argues Gray, and this explains why we install porch cameras in our houses, and other record-ing devices, such as Furbo (to watch our dogs), Alexa, Cayla (a doll Germany has outlawed for spying on children), and LawMate, a popu-lar nanny cam. Everyone is working in special buildings, and there are no longer neighbors to monitor homes or to ask to bring in our packages left at the door.[7] Atomization, argues Dugin, has foisted transhumanism upon us. Human life has morphed into numerical code: our iPhones, iPads, and nanny cams have transformed us into cyborgs. The intimacy of screens we carry in our hands immerse us in a spectacle society, and our lives play out in a venue that is someone else's private property.[8]

From the left, Walter Benjamin argues that Marxism examines the economic law of the "motion of modern society."[9] Mathematical ideas of friction, argued Marx,[10] generated the perverse idea that sympathy is funneled through the division of labor. "The clock was the first auto-matic device applied to practical purposes; the whole theory of the production of regular motion was developed through it," wrote Marx. "Its nature is such that it is based on a combination of semiartistic handicraft and direct theory."[11] Marx argued that Jacques de Vaucanson's experiments—he made watches and automata[12]—had "a tremendous influence on the imagination of English inventors."[13] With the motion of humans at work mimicking the motion of machines,[14] the division of labor changes the concrete efforts of human bodies and minds into abstract mathematical relations[15] and generates a mystification: abstraction cloaks the real value added by human efforts, and commodities become like manna from heaven: miracles rather than sweat, tiredness, and worker ingenuity.[16] Behind this mystification hides the inequality of the owner's profit and the pay given for the worker's production. This is the core holding of Marxism, contends Benjamin.[17] Agamben adds that the cloak of this mystification is the fashion industry.[18] In love with brands, we venerate objects sporting logos and are blind to the crippling inequalities in property lying behind the mask of glamour. Marxists call this mask the "fetish." Occluded by the fetish relation to objects is the human person. Hence, alienation: only if my work is my property, says Marx, can my production act as a mirror in which you can see my peculiar human essence.[19] Mystification triggers alienation, which is dehumanization. The division of labor makes us monsters.

Must the conservative's attitude toward the Industrial Enlightenment (Joel Mokyr) be postliberal? Certain alternatives are closed off. Only libertarians can still take comfort in Lady Thatcher's famous comment, "Who is society? There is no such thing! There are individual men and women." Rome is no help: Cicero would not have known one end of a hoe from the other, but his slaves would. It took the humility of the cross to first suggest to monks to dirty their hands in the monastery garden, and it took Christian humanism to complement the *artes liberales* with the *artes mechanicae*. Is a turn to neomedievalism an option?[20] Mainstreamed by thinkers such as Ruskin and Tolkien,[21] it is a criticism of industrialism, lamenting the replacement of religious faith with economic materialism, the exchange of rootedness for anomie, and the collapse of craft with mechanism taking over.[22] For the neomedievalist, the Industrial Enlightenment is the callous destruction of urban (gentrification and suburbanization)[23] and rural landscapes.[24]

What are we to make of the neomedieval critique of the effects of the Industrial Revolution and its supporting idea-world? On the one hand, among many depredations,[25] modernity gave us extractive agriculture, under which the slaves of the U.S. South—the engines of the extraction being their bodies—suffered.[26] On the other, Fukuyama would no doubt point out, and with considerable justice, that neo-medievalism dramatically undersells "the Great Enrichment" (Deidre McCloskey) wrought by the Industrial Enlightenment. The liberal capitalist order has proved demonstrably better at creating and distributing more wealth to more people than either its predecessor (the agrarian and guild system) or proposed successors, such as communism, which is responsible for some of the very worst kind of abject horrors of the twentieth century. A defender of the Industrial Enlightenment, Virginia Postrel makes this observation: down the ages, billions of women's lives have been spent spinning. In 1770, out of an English workforce of 4 million, somewhere in the region of 1.5 million married women were spinning (oddly enough, known as *spinsters*). The machine age would put those 1.5 million married women mostly out of work, but in revolutionizing cloth production, people such as Richard Arkwright freed women from spinning for the first time since the dawn of civilization.[27]

We propose that Eric Voegelin shows conservatives how to steer between neomedievalism and postliberalism. In doing so, we contend that the division of labor makes a significant contribution to humanism. The classical formulation of the division of labor belongs to Smith. Critically, this formulation gives a starring role to the land, and in an unusual way. A way that opens out onto some values affirmed by neomedievalism. This means the division of labor does not automatically collapse into Fukuyama's Averroism (global angelism) and, as a corollary, space is opened for an ideal of nation that nods toward what is legitimate in Dugin's postliberalism.

The rest of this chapter has three basic parts. In the first two, Voegelin is used to elucidate Smith's philosophy of history. The third part takes on the postliberal challenge to a conservative humanism affirming the Industrial Enlightenment.

THE VOEGELIN STANDARD

The Wealth of Nations is a philosophy of history.[28] A challenge to every philosophy of history is Voegelin, famous for coining the phrase *imma-*

nentizing the eschaton, or *do not immanentize the eschaton*.[29] Modern philosophies of history, he argues, are secularizations of biblical apocalyptic thinking.[30] What's wrong with apocalyptic politics? Voegelin proposes these problems: a lack of pragmatism, the correction of the world sought by the apocalyptic drive is so divergent from the pragmatic needs of people, political order is subverted; cancellation of our living in a cosmos, which twists our sense of embodiment, race, and natural home;[31] and thus a perverse accounting of our human standing in reality, with inevitable malformations of our mental health and moral solidarity (cf. John Paul II's "culture of death").

In his *The New Science of Politics* (*NSP*) (1952), Voegelin observed that modern politics keeps falling prey to utopian myth. This is why modern politics has been so ugly: "Anybody who wants to lead his own way of life, unmolested by the idealist, is a criminal."[32] He noted an eerie similarity between modern political movements—such as progressivism, communism, and fascism[33]—and the medieval apocalyptic theology of Joachim de Fiore (d. 1202). Joachim argued that history is a copy of the Trinity. Ancient history was the age of the Father, an age of law. Medieval history the age of the Son, the reign of the sacraments and Church. However, both law and sacraments are terminated in the age of the Holy Spirit. In this new age, state and church administration are suspended, a spirit of play and childlike freedom prevailing. This is the end of history. Joachim prophesied that a spiritual leader would usher in the new age of the Spirit and gave a date: 1260. Joachim echoes in Fukuyama, but does he also echo in *The Wealth of Nations*? What is interesting about Joachim, according to Voegelin, is that he is not actually a Christian theologian, he is a Gnostic.

Original to the ancient Mediterranean, Gnosticism was contemporary with the emergence of Christianity, a rival, contends Voegelin, not a Christian heresy.[34] However, the prevalence of Gnostic political movements is a consequence of Christianity, and for at least three reasons: apocalypticism, differentiation, and anxiety.

Gnosticism was given legs by Christ: "Considering the history of Gnosticism, with the great bulk of its manifestations belonging to, or deriving from, the Christian orbit, I am inclined to recognize in the epiphany of Christ the great catalyst that made eschatological consciousness an historical force both in forming and deforming humanity."[35]

Voegelin describes modern political movements as "immanentist apocalypses" because they ape, and seek to make real, the end-times in the here and now.[36] Modern politics is a mutation of St. Paul's great symbol, a "kingdom that is truly the end."[37] As to what is truly the end, on offer are "the modern apocalyptic visions of the perfect realm of reason, the perfect realm of positivist science in the Comtian sense, or the perfect realm of Marxist Communism."[38] These Gnostic movements seek to mimic the Apocalytpic promise: "And there shall be no more curse: but the throne of God and of the Lamb shall be in it; and his servants shall serve him. And they shall see his face; and his name shall be in their foreheads" (Rev. 22:3–4).

Differentiation is a critical Voegelian term of art and requires we spend a little time explaining.[39] He maintains that the tension between compactness and differentiation is native to consciousness as such. "The maximum of differentiation" is Greek philosophy and Christianity (*NSP*, 79, 164), where it culminates in ideals of personal liberty, being an evolution in the history of civilizations. Maria König, a research collaborator with Voegelin, argued that the transition from compactness to differentiation was discernible in Paleolithic artifacts. An example of compactness, ancient objects show an initial ritual use of spheroids. A symbol of the human—and our Neanderthal counterparts—enclosed in wholeness. Spheroids gave way to the ritual use of cups and skulls. With their openings, the half-spheres of cups and skulls mimicked life under a vault, with heaven and earth distinguished. König also thought that the discovery of so many skulls around springs spoke to a notion of a netherworld, too, and thus another differentiation.[40] König's research into the tripartite consciousness of the Paleolithic confirms a Voegelin thesis: "The history of symbolization is a progression from compact to differentiated experiences and symbols."[41]

In his history of civilizations, Voegelin argues that early civilizations were gripped by an overwhelming sense of cosmos. He argued that the first political form was cosmological empire: polities keyed to the experience of celestial and seasonal change, their rulers standing at the center of geographical space.[42] For example, the Babylonian king was the axis through which ran the points of the compass. Of himself, Cyrus said, "I am Cyrus . . . King of the four quarters of the world."[43] This compactness gave way to a partial differentiation under pressure from ecumenic empires. With the extension of empire, more and more strangeness was encountered, and this eroded the surety of geographical consistency, introducing history as a way to explain differences in mores. Alexander the Great is an example of geography partly dislodged by history. He declared, "When you address yourself to me, address me as the King of Asia."[44] Alexander did not think of himself as at one with the cosmos, like Cyrus, but a portion only (Augustine's *civitas terrena*).[45] Alexander expresses an awareness of otherness: his was an ecumenic empire, reflecting a change in consciousness wherein historical understanding is prominent.

The compactness of cosmological empire means that freedom and individual flair were hamstrung.[46] Even more than the differentiation of ecumenic empire is required if personal identity is to come to the fore.[47] More intense symbols of differentiation arose in Greece and Israel. Greek letters describe the soul in dynamic relationship with transcendent values:[48] an experience consummated in Christianity,[49] with Jesus preaching that not a sparrow falls from the sky without God's grace-filled permission: "not one of them shall fall on the ground without your Father's care" (Matt. 10:29). In Judeo-Christianity, the lock of the cosmos on the human spirit is sprung: the prime value of persons becomes apparent to consciousness.

Differentiation finds completion in Christianity, however. Fused with Greek science and philosophy, Christianity is the consummate differentiation because it articulates human psychology beyond natural order, isolates elements, and compounds relations, within our psyche, and it takes hierarchy—or, differently put, alienation—to a fresh level, for example, modeling the psyche on the mind-bending idea of the Trinity. It is Christianity—"an increasingly self-conscious vision of the divine Beyond"[50]—that decisively breaks the social compactness of cosmological myth. Nonetheless, it is part of the strangeness of Christianity that a wholly other transcendence is not unconnected to the cosmos. Christianity is a soteriological doctrine but with strong cosmological motifs: combining nature, natural law, and the operation of supernaturally given grace. Recall Aquinas's famous formulation: *grace perfects nature.*

It is on the back of this differentiation as developed in Christian eschatology that Gnosticism finds its fuel. St. Paul: "On the question of the coming of our Lord Jesus Christ and our being gathered to him, we beg you, brothers, not to be so easily agitated or terrified, whether by an oracular utterance, or rumor, or a letter alleged to be ours, into believing that the day of the Lord is here. Let no one seduce you, no matter how" (2 Thess. 2:1–3). Begging will only get St. Paul so far, because Christianity brings with it waves of anxiety.

All politics, according to Voegelin, addresses a metaphysical vertigo.[51] In this sense, human nature is unchanging. Unchanging both because we cannot escape the anxiety that we are suspended over a metaphysical abyss (think of the whirlpool example at the start of Descartes's *Meditations*), and on account of our encounter with the transcendent, we live in an order not of human making: the stars, the verities of reason, or the grace of God.[52] On account of Judeo-Christianity, the problem is amped up: we now worry the cosmos is suspended over nothing (*creatio ex nihilo*). This generates a hallmark of Christian civilization, intense anxiety (see Pascal, Kierkegaard, and, the most anxious of all, Hume). It is anxiety that opens the door to Gnosticism.

Why was the West not consoled by Christianity? Voegelin argues that a key Gnostic driver is the high moral adventure required by Christian belief, which, for many, is insupportable, provoking debilitating anxiety. The Christian call to faith is to live in belief, and not certainty, to potentially experience the aridity of the dark night of the soul (*NSP*, 122). It is a humbling call. Our reason is offended by this call to incompleteness,[53] by the call to an obedience completed by grace. In explaining secularization in the West, Voegelin argues that many had not "the spiritual stamina for the heroic adventure of the soul that is Christianity." Exhausted, the modern Westerner falls "back on a less differentiated culture of spiritual experience," one that removes doubt (*NSP*, 123–24).[54] This is immanentization.

History is the chronicle of the human effort at order: imposed to stabilize, political symbolizations reply to metaphysical precariousness.[55] These "saving tales" include the king as compass, king and pope as two swords, Puritan commoners as saints of God (*NSP*, 146–47), and the workers of the general strike (Sorel). Symbols or "magic cosmions" manage anxiety, they are "the sedatives that keep it down."[56] The West's great political choice is between the Christian "saving tale"[57] proposing trust in the cosmos[58] (see Scruton on the myth of the Eucharist[59]) or symbols of Gnostic certitude,[60] such as the mechanism (Fukuyama), party, or führer. Voegelin: "There is no alternative to an eschatological extravaganza but to accept the mystery of the cosmos."[61]

Does our symbol "accept the mystery of the cosmos"? Luxury is the great symbol of commercial civilizations. How does it fare? An exemplar of luxury is the moon phase watch. This luxury watch has a little aperture on the dial inside of which is a moon—often playfully figuring a little face. Contemplating your watch, you observe how much of the moon shows in the window, then look at the night sky, and the waxing and waning ought to match. An ingenious mechanical system enclosed in a small space on your wrist is keyed to the heavens.[62] Watch enthusiasts call it romantic. Beautiful—it embodies transcendent values—the moon phase complication is not just an index of modernity's prowess, it is a continuation of celestial measurement made by our earliest human and Neanderthal ancestors.[63]

The complication is a symbol stretched between compactness and differentiation. It is made possible by the division of labor.[64] As we have seen, for Voegelin, differentiation is the emergence of "personal psyche."[65] Commercial, as opposed to pastoral, civilization is built on varied work specializations generating complex objects: iPhones, Kelly and Birkin bags, high-end audio (such as McIntosh), and watches that have minute repeaters and show moon phases. These refinements of the arts and sciences embellish human life and encourage hobbies, collecting, fascinations, and personal flair—differentiation. Differentiation is a requirement of a humanistic politics, argues Voegelin. We agree.

In Voegelin's terms, the division of labor is an Enlightenment symbol, and key is whether it holds open differentiation. Put differently, it is time to show that the moon phase complication is a symbol of the differentiation of consciousness, and not an immanentizing of the eschaton. Or, put differently again, it is time to show that Adam Smith is not Fukuyama.

IS LUXURY A SYMBOL OF DIFFERENTIATION?

In Scotland, Glasgow has the reputation of a tough town, a city for "hard men." Glaswegians love to poke fun at Edinburgh, a snotty city, they say, full of people who like opera. Times change. In his *Lectures on Jurisprudence*, Adam Smith comments that Glasgow suffers from fewer capital crimes than Edinburgh.[66] Glasgow is safer, he reasons, because it is a commercial city.

In an elegant formulation, Voegelin characterizes modernity as the moment "when the orientation toward a *summum bonum* was replaced by the flight from the *summum malum* of death in civil war."[67] Hobbes is pivotal.[68] For him, killing abates once a materialist philosophy is enthroned. Life reduced to quanta of energy, peace can prevail once violent power is centralized in the state, "crushing the proud by the Leviathan" (Voegelin). Voegelin argues that the embrace of materialism was basic to the Enlightenment. Materialism, with its exclusive emphasis on vitalism, removes the experience of the "ground of existence." A good politics must be tensional:[69] Voegelin was fond of the Catholic concept of *analogia entis*. Just as games include tension, the heights of victory and the abyss of defeat, so a good politics is an ever-fragile reconciliation of the compact and the differentiated. Gnostics seek "absolute coordinates" for their lives,[70] but critical to humanistic politics is combining "saving tales" and flair: "Without the ordering of the whole personality by the truth of the myth the secondary intellectual and moral powers would lose direction. It is, on principle, the insight that has found its classic expression in the Anselmian *credo ut intelligam*."

Through disenchantment, Hobbes rids his politics of tension. Smith is not a materialist.[71] Smith agrees with Voegelin: "We move in a charmed community."[72] Smith's is an enchantment theory of history. Linking land, capital, and fantasy, Smith writes:

> The capital of the landlord, on the contrary, which is fixed in the improvement of his land, seems to be as well secured as the nature of human affairs can admit of. The beauty of the country besides, the pleasures of a country life, the tranquility of mind which it promises, and wherever the injustice of human laws does not disturb it, the independency which it really affords, *have charms that more or less attract every body*; and as to cultivate the ground was the original destination of man, so in every stage of his existence he seems to retain a predilection for this primitive employment. (*Wealth of Nations* [*WN*] III.i.3, 378; emphasis added)[73]

The deeper reason for enchantment is play. Smith thinks you and I are "lovers of toys." The first page of Voegelin's massive *Order and History* (*OH*) is a rumination on the idea that play is basic to history. Basic because play is part of nature. Play is the substratum from which "the differentiated human creations like rites, myth, law, speculation, etc., have to grow" (*OH*, 3:185–86). Play is "the counterpressure of reality," reality itself suggesting mutual analogies of man and gods, society and celestial, "consubstantial partners in the community of being" (*OH* 4:76). In play, we experience the *analogia entis*.

Consider the cell phone. Youth carry phones in their dominant hand, only passing it to the less dominant when about to use the phone. What is strange about that?

Why in the past was the dominant hand left free? For 35,000 years, the dominant hand was never obscured, because security required it. Swords, dirks, and pistols have been a part of dress for millennia.[74] What is the meaning of our changing a weapon for a phone? What anthropological revolution does it signify?

Smartphones are vehicles for playing games, or watching games (TikTok), curating collections of photos and followers, indulging hobbies and daydreaming of purchases—differentiation. Smith's providential invisible hand describes the implications of our interest in toys, games, and collections. In a counterfactual to our natural sociability, Smith imagines the owner of a large estate who is utterly indifferent to others but who, despite himself, builds up the life of others. The indifferent landowner's house and gardens are complex systems; so many toys to entertain. The gardens are arranged in artful patterns, the productive fields likewise, the house is decorated—containing fanciful clocks, stylized furniture, and whimsical hobby collections—and the dinner table is set for the play of taste, scent, and vision.

Because the landlord cannot manage all these moving parts himself, he must empower a staff. He needs to spend money on gardeners, clockmakers, a sommelier, a chef, and liveried staff to serve at table. Putting it crudely, if the selfish landlord wants to enjoy the playfulness of chef's cooking, it is essential that the servers not be grubby and smelly. Enchantment makes him generous. Despite his rapacity, he must share his food, his plumbing, his wine, and the produce of his gardens. Abundance, though owned, is shared. Property (compactness), and its sustaining powers, is shared, facilitating broader decoration (differentiation). Since morality is mimicry for Smith (*TMS* I.i.4.8), parity of sorts eventuates between landowner and staff, and this symmetry *is* sympathy (*TMS* I.iii.2.2, I.iii.2.8). As lovers of toys, we are also made moral. Your phone is the invisible hand, and it makes you moral, too.[75] The utility of the phone—messaging—is far outstripped by its role as a fantasy-deliver system. More than 5 billion people have cell phones and, with them, do nearly $4 trillion of mobile commerce annually.[76]

Discussing the transition from feudalism to capitalism, Smith argues that to afford "expensive vanity," landowners needed to increase the productivity of their lands. The sure way to do this is leasing land to tenant farmers.[77] Rule of law assures tenants a continuity in their holding, and thus they can improve the land: their innovations are paying the "tax" of the lease but also supplying a profit, so the farmers, too, might participate in "expensive vanity" (*WN* III.iv.11–15, 419–21). The invisible hand is a distribution of resources made at the behest of beauty. Commercial societies deliver vanity because they intensify the division of labor. Cultures of enchantment, these societies are ever renewed by fantasy. The history of opulence is a function of the relationship between countryside and town, or food and fancies, we might say. The countryside provides utilities necessary to survival, but, in addition, materials for the craft of towns. The desire for food is limited, the appetite of the imagination, unbounded: "The desire of the stomach is limited in every man by the narrow capacity of the human stomach; but the desire of the conveniences and ornaments of building, dress, equipage, and household furniture, seems to have no limit or certain boundary. . . . What is over and above satisfying the limited desire, is given for the amusement of those desires which cannot be satisfied, but seem to be altogether endless" (*WN*, I.xi.c, 181).

After food on the table, all seek the "elegancies of life," and an example is a moon phase watch. It is an accomplishment of the specialization that prompts increases in dexterity, time-saving, and the invention of a great number of machines (*WN* I.i.5, 17).[78] These increases result in greater efficiencies, therewith more production, and in consequence are the causes of the wealth of nations: populations fed and decorated.

REPLIES TO OBJECTIONS

Voegelin's philosophy of history illuminates the conservative character of Smith's treatment of the division of labor. Let us return to the postliberal criticism to better see how the division of labor builds humanism.

Gray argues that commercial society has no solidarity. If the moon phase is an adequate symbol of our order, then commercial society has compactness, a common, enchanting myth. We are not as atomistic as many believe. This is what Smith conveys through his turn to sympathy. Smith does not deny our self-absorption, but our self-love always contends with the alacrity with which we give sympathy. Adornments prompt that sympathy. Collectors of handbags gather on discussion boards, sneakerheads report spending about 40 percent of the day thinking about and discussing their beloved shoes,[79] and petrolheads fix one another's classic cars at the distance of thousands of miles.

Certainly, sociability is not now going down to the Legion, or staffing the tombola at the Knights of Columbus dinner.[80] However, it is arguably Smith's greatest achievement to theorize how the division of labor coordinates a plenitude of contending—personal and collective—interests, vanities, and privileges. This point is conservative. Solidarity is a critical conservative value, but it is all too easy for the Left and the Right to slip into organicism. Smith gets the mereology right. In a passage that reads like many found in medieval treatises on natural law, Smith writes: "Among equals each individual is naturally, and antecedent to the institution of civil government, regarded as having a right both to defend himself from injuries, and to exact a certain degree of punishment for those which have been done to him" (*TMS*, II.ii.1.7). Continuing the antiorganicism of natural law, Smith makes the point that each individual is a whole and not a part of a whole: "So, by the wisdom of Nature, the happiness of every innocent man is, in the same manner, rendered holy, consecrated, and hedged round against the approach of every other man; not to be wantonly trod upon, not even to be, in any respect, ignorantly and involuntarily violated, without requiring some expiation" (*TMS*, II.iii.3.4).

Myriad discrete wholes—persons—are coordinated by the division of labor, which also coordinates the independent operations of nations: "We do not love our country merely as a part of the great society of mankind: we love it for its own sake, and independently of any such consideration" (*TMS*, VI.ii.2.4). Adding color to this ideal of national life, here is T. S. Eliot:

> Yet there is an aspect in which we can see a religion as the whole way of life of a people, from birth to the grave, from morning to night and even in sleep, and that way of life is also its culture. . . . It includes all the characteristic activities and interests of a people: Derby Day, Henley Regatta, Cowes, the twelfth of August, a cup final, the dog races, the pin table, the dart board, Wensleydale cheese, boiled cabbage cut into sections, beetroot in vinegar, nineteenth-century Gothic churches and the music of Elgar. The reader can make his own list. And then we have to face the strange idea that what is part of our culture is also part of our lived religion.[81]

Smith helps show that Eliot is not just a pretty version of Dugin, but a substantively different version of nationalism: "Every independent state is divided into many different orders and societies, each of which has its own particular powers, privileges, and immunities. Every individual is naturally more attached to his own particular order or society, than to any other. His own interest, his own vanity, the interest and vanity of many of his friends and companions, are commonly a good deal connected with it. He is ambitious to extend its privileges and immunities. He is zealous to defend them against the encroachments of every other order of society" (*TMS*, VI.ii.2.6).

The division of labor, which begins with relationship between country and town, culminates in the solidarity of the similarly placed, a seeking of privilege in a national setting without organicism. We discuss the role of nationalism in humanism in chapter 6.

Vitalism and angelism are metaphysical temptations, and we have argued that the division of labor steers between the two. Dugin argues transhumanism is our fate in an age of global technicism (*FPT*, 30). Does this match the phenomenology of commerce? The moon phase watch is not angelism, but enchanting and historical: it is an artful, timekeeping geometry. The same can be said of $1,000 jeans. There is a bespoke market for wealthy men who wear jeans to work. Wearing quality shoes and sweaters, these men want high-quality jeans to complete the costume of the relaxed, independent-minded, and highly successful man of business.[82] It might seem mere bragging, but a full ethnography includes boutique owners explaining that these men are serious hobbyists, typically fascinated by the whole process of jean and denim manufacturing. They are collectors.[83] The owners send swatches of rare and unusual denim in the post to aid client education, and these mailings act as invitations to step into the shop and add to the collection. In one boutique, seamstresses work inside a glass cube, so the enthusiast can see the craft—somewhat like the open kitchens so popular now. Insofar as these men truly are fascinated by denim, its various aesthetic and human qualities, they defer to something other than themselves, something high and admirable that arrests their will.

Highly sought after is denim made in Japan on centuries-old hand-looms.[84] This posture of submission to the ancestral is a kind of "sober service" (Przywara) owed to God: Jerry Muller summarizes Smith's providentialism: "Luxury facilitated increase in purchasing power of the working majority by keeping price of commodities low and wages high."[85]

Pope Francis is sharply critical of the inequalities in property and power introduced by digitization: one sharp commentator goes so far as to speak of a new serfdom gripping the West.[86] Digitization has stoked angelization: financialization of the economy,[87] a revolving door from bank to bureaucrat,[88] staffed by an isolated, proto-fascistic clerisy,[89] obsessing on Twitter. The clerisy is an internationalist managerial class, wanting identically the same furniture, bedsheets, and coffee houses when traveling across the globe.[90] Averse to belonging, with no experience of the land ("flyover country"), they are alienated from the folk their metrics govern. The revolving door fosters rent-seeking monopolies—even Fukuyama has soured on the clerisy for this reason. Catholic social thought (CST) holds that politics trumps economics,[91] and thus government administration of commerce is, sometimes, absolutely morally required. Vigorous enactment of rule of law is always necessary but by no means always sufficient. Direct engagement with business, directed by ideals of solidarity and distribution, is sometimes necessary.[92] Recently, under Pope Francis, the Vatican has called for curbs on the financialization of the economy[93] and greater government supervision of the work of corporations on robotics.[94] As Roger Scruton argued, libertarians might be against regulation, but conservatives are not.[95]

CST has always granted broad liberties to markets, but equally insisted that the economy requires judicious management; it is one of the reasons we have establishment.[96] However, the popes caution that all economic activity depends on a deeper reserve of trust, that is reaffirmed every day in billions of micro interactions across communities (what CST terms *distributive justice*).[97] Contract law (commutative justice) cannot capture the specificities of these interactions, nor can bureaucracy. For this reason, CST has always encouraged business and business schools to take seriously ethical reflection. Sometimes, business ethics is risible (the UK's largest biscuit maker supplies free kit to a local youth football team),[98] sometimes it is weighty and complex (Exxon's engagement with healthcare infrastructure in Angola),[99] and sometimes it reclaims the ancestral (Prada's preservation of craft, land, and high culture).[100] Francis asks us to admire the beauty of skyscrapers, but to remember that the business contracts that divide the labor of such towers has a political and moral foundation. In part, this is what CST means by "subsidiarity." Francis's *Laudato Si'* is, we believe, the first encyclical to explicitly state that it is a moral obligation of government to support small business. The point has always been implicit in the norm of subsidiarity, and Francis reaffirms the long-standing papal interest in distributivism, which aims at a proliferation of cottage industry and analogues: what it terms *differentiated production*.[101]

Turning to the left, Benjamin is clearly impressed by Marx's bleak descriptions of the division of labor as a mechanization of the human being. He is a hard thinker to place, however. Benjamin does not agree with Marx that private property is the "transcendence of all estrangement":[102] he was an avid collector of both books and toys.[103] Smith acknowledges significant problems inherent in the division of labor. The repetitions involved in some work narrow life, stripping reflection and invention, even making some "as stupid and ignorant as it is possible for a human creature to become" (*WN*, V.i.f, 782). The antidote, says Smith, is fashion (*TMS*, I.iii.2.1, 50), and Benjamin appears to agree. He quotes Eugène Montrue, who argues that fashion is "a witness to the history of the great world." Making cell phones accessible is critical to differentiation, for "the poor," contends Montrue, "have fashions as little as they have a history, and their ideas, their tastes, even their lives barely change."[104]

Leo Strauss summarizes the Marxist project: "The vision of a world society which presupposes and establishes forever the complete victory of the town over the country, of the mobile over the rooted, of the spirit of the Occident over the spirit of the Orient; the members of the world society which is no longer a political society are free and equal, and are so in the last analysis because all specialization, all division of labour, has given way to the full development of everyone."[105]

This is a fair summary, for here is Maurice Cornforth, the leading English Marxist theorist of the midcentury (and a former pupil of Wittgenstein): "The eventual and final abolition of shortages constitutes the economic condition for entering upon a communist society. When there is socialized production the products of which are socially appropriated, when science and scientific planning have resulted in the production of absolute abundance, and when labour has been so enlightened and organized that all can without sacrifice of personal inclinations contribute their working abilities to the common fund, everyone will receive a share according to his needs."[106]

The suspension of the human condition,[107] made possible by "absolute abundance," is the apocalyptic core of Marx's philosophy of history. His is a weird vitalistic angelism, triggering the immanentizing of the eschaton. Voegelin calls it a "paracletic immanentism" (*NSP*, 125), a summoning, through which "the bleakness of annihilation creeps over a society" (*OH*, 2:163) in a *Blutrausch*.[108] The Marxist "realm of freedom" — ably described by Cornforth — proffers the "active mysticism of a state of perfection, to be achieved through a revolutionary transfiguration of the nature of man" (*NSP*, 121). There is little need for a luxe moon phase watch when your world is modeled on an aping of the *nunc stans* Christ.[109]

Benjamin sees an upside to collecting and fashion, but Agamben does not. Fashion is a fetish that blocks the truth of production from surfacing. Agamben believes himself to have found a new field of study, the "choreography of power": the science of "acclamations, ceremonies, liturgies, and insignia."[110] Agamben argues that the imagistic character of contemporary politics is akin to the liturgy of the Catholic

Mass. In each, the true bearers of power are dolled up and masked.[111] Whether at Mass or sporting fashion,[112] we are all in thrall, declares Agamben, to "the society of the spectacle."[113] Agamben is fond of the monastery as a manner of organization: a way of life detached from power and vanity.[114] The basic drive of anarchist politics is toward collective solidarity without the state: not exactly desiring self-management, therefore, but certainly desiring micro groups to organize and manage themselves without government regulation and monitoring. Anarchists distinguish themselves from libertarians by stressing, not the self, but the group, and separate themselves from the Catholic ideal of subsidiarity by denying in principle that the state can worthily assist those in genuine need or deal justly in matters of the common good. On this view, the West must return to what it was not long ago: a patchwork of self-determining enclaves and "principalities." This is how the modern drive to the unified national provider state is eclipsed: with a fragmenting of the field of power, hence anarchist syndicates or municipal assemblies.[115]

Interestingly, Brunello Cucinelli's business plan invokes the monastic and is consciously a revival of the Italian "age of communes": an affirmation of the Italian social and physical landscape shaped in the Middle Ages by self-sufficient trading communes distant from the authority of the aggrandizing medieval papacy and Holy Roman emperor.[116] However, Agamben's compatriot shows there is no contradiction between the fashion spectator and submission to moral judgment. Cucinelli's is a neomedievalism blended with the fashion industry, a business version of the conservative humanism we are defending.

HUMANISTIC ENTERPRISE

From his fourteenth-century castle vantage, Cucinelli can look over the Umbrian hills that surround Solemeo, the once dilapidated Italian village restored to life through his fashion label. Fields that had gone to ruin are now home to sheep tended for his trademark knitwear, abandoned houses are now the workspaces and homes of seamstresses, and forlorn streets now bustle with young students leaving classes at the school for *artes mechanicae* recently established by Cucinelli.

Humanist enterprise is Cucinelli's term for his brand of capitalism, and his business is evidence that profit and dignity can be drawn from the ancestral. Cucinelli is not alone. Heritage, the idea of craft and place, is as good as gold in the marketplace. Prada, Louis Vuitton, Chanel, Cartier, Hermès, Jaguar, and Ferrari, all explicitly draw on heritage, the two car companies even beginning vintage divisions. Cucinelli is the benchmark. He reads Cicero, prays with the Benedictines, and has great solicitude for the land and its people. He and his company are an enterprising embodiment of Christian humanism.

Theoretical support comes from Scheler, whose "Christian Love in the Twentieth Century" (1917) develops a model of business organization, the estate. The first thing one likely thinks of when hearing the idea of the estate is a country estate, a manor with surrounding lands, cultivated for food or sport. Scheler's idea does not exclude such estates — and a monastery brewing beer or tending a farm is another example — but an estate is any business organized around place, history, and self-sufficiency for itself and its workers. The estate — a place where knowledge is gained, innovation exercised, and a space that is also a web of sympathies — cements a person's dignity. The estate is a place of work, a property that fosters a standing in the community: it provides a role for self-regulating human effort. Linked to a community, it is a concern of families in a locality.

Here is how Scheler puts it: "An estate is something stable, a standing or status, something wherein a man is self-sufficient, but which he nevertheless does not freely choose like a profession, since he merely finds himself 'placed' there. But to know one's estate is to be truly at home in the State, at home in the consciousness of firmly defined and assured lawful rights on which no one may trespass."[117]

Note that Scheler's talk of status and trespass is close to Smith's: "His own interest, his own vanity, the interest and vanity of many of his friends and companions, are commonly a good deal connected with it. He is ambitious to extend its privileges and immunities. He is zealous to defend them against the encroachments of every other order of society" (*TMS*, VI.ii.2.6).

However, many of us will not recognize this vision of work. Basic images of modern work are anonymous office blocks, vast factories in China, and contract workers toiling in halls of cubicles. Such images convey the idea of a worker having a function but no role: a mere body able to be slotted into changing conditions of work and replaced rapidly if necessary.[118] By contrast, an estate is home to work that shapes a person's identity. Scheler is convinced that personalism makes the desire for estate irrepressible. It is striking to learn that 99.7 percent of all German companies are small or medium-size. These are typically family-owned and draw on local communities for workers even though their markets tend to be international niche exports.[119] Perhaps it is shocking to learn the situation is almost the same in the United States: 89 percent of all businesses have fewer than twenty employees (99 percent of all businesses have fewer than 500 workers).[120]

Design houses always depend on the liberal arts, but at Solemeo's "School of Craftmanship"—the costs of attending the school are borne by Cucinelli—the crafts of mending and linking, cutting and assembly, tailoring, masonry, and gardening, along with philosophy and ethics are taught. These mechanical arts are about history and place. They express and reinforce the long life of the village of Solemeo: they build upon the physical memory of the thousands of villagers who built and rebuilt their homes there. These arts also assert the independence of the village, its competency to shape full lives for its young and old. They make a place "dense," alerting others, and government, that deference is due to land and to lives organized around traditional skill and innovative work. The estate is an identity, a confidence.[121]

We have argued that Smith's identification of the division of labor as the cause of the wealth of nations is an essential conservative insight. Old European churches have Marian shrines where Mary is implored to save the locals from war, famine, and plague. COVID-19 gave us a hint of how quickly the food supply might shrivel if a truly debilitating disease across the whole population arises. It also showed how sophisticated systems of supply mostly did well and rode out the shock. Our resilient supply chains are an instance of the division of labor. On balance, and not without management by a judicious national political establishment, the Industrial Enlightenment complements our ancestral humanism, drawn from ancient, medieval, and Renaissance sources.

It has been argued that the West is a *pax consumptionis*, what is in fact just a collective of concupiscence (Larry Chapp). To the contrary, Cucinelli shows that fashion can be genuinely personalist. His business plan stretches between husbandry of land and flair. Indeed, his fashion is firmly in history. The neutral tones of his scarves, with one dyed strip running along, is a manner of decoration that dates to the earliest fabric found from the Neolithic. His business, solidaristic and personalist, committed to the land and style signatures, is contiguous with the moon phase.

In Voegelin's terms, the moon phase complication is a symbol of cosmos and differentiation. An exhibition that the human condition is an "In-Between of imperfection and perfection, time and timelessness, mortality and immortality."[122] The moon phase watch worn on the wrist indexes this In-Between. It prompts a playful look to the heavens (cosmos) as part of its enchantment. It retains myth, which is essential (*OH*, 4:10), but the watch displays a double differentiation:[123] the division of labor and a person's style signature. In Plato's theodicy, Voegelin tell us, forces of order have personality, forces of disorder do not (*OH*, 3:154). The tensional remains—neither vitalism nor angelism—and thus Smith's philosophy of history resists the temptation to immanentize the eschaton. Given the division of labor, the end-times will be orthodox: "For as lightning cometh out of the east, and appeareth even into the west: so shall the coming of the Son of man be" (Matt. 24:27).

CHAPTER 6

The Conservative *via media*

Between Nationalism and the Dream of Cosmopolis

LIBERAL COSMOPOLITANISM

After the Cold War and the defeat of communism, some conservatives (sometimes called neoconservatives) argued that the United States must assume a new role: maintain and spread "a liberal international order, the spread of freedom and democratic governance, an international economic system of free-market capitalism and free trade."[1] In this last view of conservatism, liberalism and conservatism are virtually identified. Liberalism is perceived here as the unifying doctrine of Americanism that must serve as its universal and missionary creed. This kind of universalism has precedents in Jefferson's exceptionalist discourse of America as an "empire of liberty"[2] and in the rhetoric and policies of Woodrow Wilson, an architect of the League of Nations, who famously sought to make the "world safe for democracy."[3] The United States is here indeed a particular nation, but with an exceptional mission of converting the world to liberalism. In essence, this is an American exceptionalist "spin" on the universalism inherent in liberalism since its Enlightenment origins. This universalism is immediately evident from the creedal statements of the two liberal revolutions, the American and the French. In an alternate history, the revolutionaries could have focused on merely particular historical grievances against

121

the British and French crowns. Instead, we find that Jefferson's Declaration of Independence affirms that "all men are created equal" and goes on to enumerate as universal rights those of "life, liberty, and the pursuit of happiness." The preamble to the French Revolutionaries' Declaration of the Rights of Man and of the Citizen refers to itself as affirming the "natural, unalienable, and sacred rights of man."[4] Both revolutions, therefore, appeal for justification to the rights of man as such, that is, to universal rights grounded in nature. The new philosophy of history posited a unilinear unfolding of progress toward liberal universalism. The French *philosophes* also saw this Enlightenment ideal as the measuring rod by which the relative development of different cultures and civilizations could be assessed. Some nations have approached that ideal more closely than others, but all would eventually follow the same path of progress and development. The Marquis de Condorcet, for example, asks rhetorically: "Will all nations one day attain the state of civilizations which the most enlightened, the freest, and the least burdened by prejudices such as the French and the Anglo-Americans, have attained already? Will the vast gulf that separates these people from the slavery of nations under the rule of monarchs, from the barbarism of African tribes, from the ignorance of savages, little by little disappear? Is there on the face of the earth a nation whose inhabitants have been debarred from the enjoyment of freedom and the exercise of reason?"[5]

Would the condition of Enlightenment inexorably unfold of its own, or were active measures required to give history a push? Marxists with their own vision of progress would later ask the same question. European powers of the nineteenth century saw themselves as active agents of modern progress, an advanced vanguard of history who would rescue the rest of mankind by bringing light to benighted "savages" still sunk in the darkness of slavery, despotism, and superstition. The end goal was to bring all of humanity to "civilization" in the singular—that is, to the one universal civilization. It is this monism that especially irks Dugin.

Liberal cosmopolitanism is most fully developed perhaps in the greatest of the Enlightenment philosophers, Immanuel Kant. In *Perpetual Peace: A Philosophical Sketch*,[6] Kant envisions the disorder of warring sovereign states supplanted by a pacific global federation of nations bound together by a system of international law and governance with free movement across borders. Kant affirms moreover that there is an inherent tendency in universal history to "progress" toward such a cosmopolitan world-society, speaking of "the hope that, after many revolutions, with all their transforming effects, a universal *cosmopolitan existence* will at last be realized as the matrix within which all the original capacities of the human race may develop."[7]

Central to the possibility of realization of such an international order for Kant would be universalizing "republicanism,"[8] the Enlightenment (or liberal) principles of individual freedom, universal equality, and representative government: "A *republican constitution* is founded upon three principles: firstly, the principle of *freedom* for all members of society (as men); secondly, the principle of the *dependence* of all members of society on a single common legislation (as subjects); and thirdly, the principle of legal *equality* for everyone (as citizens)."[9]

A key obstacle for Kant to the realization of the cosmopolitan ideal is the persistence of "*linguistic* and *religious* differences," which tend to "separate the nations and keep them from mingling," which "may certainly occasion mutual hatred and provide pretexts for wars."[10] Kant thus sounds in a moderate form what would later become an enduring concern of liberalism: the belief that religious and ethnic attachments are obstacles to the realization of universal humanity. We may thus call liberalism a *secular cosmopolitanism* that typically favors the attenuation of religious and ethnic identities and distinctions. But how would this come to pass?

For liberals, one of the great forces of history that will bring break down divisions among human beings is the spread of commercial civilization, which crosses borders and induces a state of global interdependency. As Kant put the matter: "Nature also unites nations which the concept of cosmopolitan right would not have protected from violence and war, and does so by means of their mutual self-interest. For the *spirit of commerce* sooner or later takes hold of every people, and it cannot exist side by side with war."[11]

This idea of the global commercial society fostering pacific and internationalist values is a staple of the liberal ideology. To one who defines politics in Schmitt's terms as "a zone of contention between friends and enemies," we would call liberalism *postpolitical* insofar as it looks forward to the replacement of politics by economics. Francis Fukuyama noted that Enlightenment thinkers regarded it as critical for the bourgeois ideal of commerce to eviscerate the martial ethos of the aristocracy. For Fukuyama, the basic value system of aristocracy centers on *megalothymia*, the desire to claim the honor due to superior excellence. This was historically sought and chiefly achieved through warlike feats of military valor. This ethos would have to be enervated and conquered by the wealth values of capitalism for liberalism to triumph over the *ancien régime*:

> The social embodiment of *megalothymia*, and the social class against which modern liberalism declared war, was the traditional aristocracy . . . he did not act on the basis of economic rationality, selling his labor to the highest bidder: he did not work at all but fulfilled himself in his leisure. His behavior was fenced in by dictates of pride and codes of honor which did not permit him to do things beneath his dignity like engage in commerce. . . . War therefore remained central to the aristocratic way of life, and war as we well know is "economically suboptimal." Much better, then, to convince the aristocratic warrior of the vanity of his ambitions, and transform him into a peaceful businessman.[12]

To this day, it is a staple of liberal internationalism to argue that commerce and economic interdependency make war and military rivalry obsolete. Liberalism is here transformed as a missionary ideology of world-redemption. If war and conflict are the product of illiberal states, then warlike propensities will be eliminated when all nations are converted to the liberal creed. Only then can world peace reign and a true cosmopolitan political emerge. More recently in the twentieth century, Ludwig von Mises, one of the most notable classical liberals, put the case for universalizing liberalism straightforwardly: "Liberal thinking must permeate all nations, liberal principles must pervade all political institutions, if the prerequisites of peace are to be created and the causes of war eliminated."[13]

The unprecedented "unipolar moment"[14] the United States enjoyed after 1989 provided a unique opportunity to try to forge such a truly global liberal order. Since the 1990s, this cosmopolitan dream seemed on the verge of fulfillment through globalization. The establishment of the world's great Kantian project of the EU (1992) and the World Trade Organization (WTO) (1995) seemed to portend a globalized world where tribal religious, ethnic, and national attachments were being transcended, liberal norms internationalized, and capital, goods, and people flowed freely across evermore porous borders. Liberal triumphalism, however, has proved to be premature. New opponents of the liberal dream of cosmopolis were soon to arise, perhaps most consequentially in Russia.

DUGIN AND INTEGRAL TRADITIONALISM: THE RUSSIAN REVOLT AGAINST LIBERAL MODERNITY AND COSMOPOLITANISM

A radical protest against Fukuyama's globalist vision of a universal liberal and modernist civilization is found in the thought of Russia's leading political philosopher, Aleksandr Dugin. The post–Cold War order was characterized in the political sphere by U.S. unipolarity, in the economic sphere by globalization, and in the ideological sphere by political and economic liberalism. For Dugin, this implies further an "end of history" metanarrative according to which all civilizations must ultimately move toward incorporation into this liberal order. Within this universal civilization, identities formed around religious traditions and ethnic cultures will be erased or attenuated within a global system of economic production and exchange. Dugin proposes the replacement of the post–Cold War order by a multipolar order based on a plurality of civilizations.[15] Above all, Dugin is motivated by the most profound opposition to Western modernity, its claims to universality, and its narrative of historical progress.

In his antimodernism, Dugin draws in particular upon the work of René Guénon (1886–1951). This brilliant if eccentric French intellectual passed through phases of Catholicism, theosophy, Freemasonry, and immersion in Hindu thought before he finally settled into the life of a Sufi Islamic mystic in Egypt. Guénon is responsible for the school of "Integral Traditionalism" or "the Perennial Philosophy," which has exercised a significant influence on such important figures as Huston Smith, Mircea Eliade, Seyyed Hossein Nasr, and even the new king of the UK, Charles III.[16] Guénon posited a "primordial tradition" uniting the great religions, each of which is understood as a distinct revelation of the single divine reality. These great sacred traditions (Christianity, Judaism, Islam, Hinduism, Buddhism, Taoism, and Confucianism) in turn gave rise to the major traditional civilizations with their particular forms of sacred art, ritual, mysticism, cosmology, and philosophy. Nonetheless, despite this "exoteric" multiplicity of forms for Guénon, "the real traditional outlook is always and everywhere essentially the same, whatever outward form it may take; the various forms that are specially suited to different mental conditions and different circumstances of time and place are merely expressions of one and the same truth."[17]

For Dugin, the significance of Guénon here is to destroy the pretensions of secularizing Western modernity to universality. Dugin writes: "For the construction of the map of the Logoi of civilizations, Guénon's views are of greater significance than all other theories taken together. First of all, Guénon . . . called for demolishing modern Western European universalism and fully rehabilitating the philosophical, cosmological, anthropological, and social structures of ancient and non-European societies."[18]

Central for Dugin's anti-Westernism and antimodernism is Guénon's idea of a unique "Western deviation."[19] Whereas all other civilizations remained rooted and centered in the divine, transcendent reality and their sacred tradition, Europe uniquely became progressively divorced from sacral realities since the end of the Middle Ages. Instead, Europe became an ever-more secular and materialistic culture focused on the accumulation of earthly riches and technological power. "The civilization of the modern West appears in history as a veritable anomaly: among all those which are known to us more or less completely, this civilization is the only one that has developed along purely material lines," writes Guénon.[20]

Hence, from the standpoint of Integral Traditionalism, so far from representing "progress," Western modernity represents the greatest possible decay. Guénon with customary eclecticism will equate modernity to the Hindu *Kali-Yuga*, the lowest phase of the Hindu cosmological time cycle characterized by materialism, sensuality, and ignorance of spiritual truth. "According to Guénon, European Modernity has become an anti-civilization, an embodiment of all that is contrary to the spirit, Tradition, and sacrality," notes Dugin. "Secularization, humanism, naturalism, mechanism, and rationalism, in Guénon's view, are the essential manifestations of the spirit of perversion which affects all societies, but which only in modern Europe acquired such absolute and complete embodiment."[21]

Guénon's assessment of Western modernity dovetails in many respects with Dugin's other intellectual hero, Martin Heidegger. Like Guénon, Heidegger will argue for a Counter-Enlightenment historical narrative of *decline*: "The spiritual decline of the earth has progressed so far that peoples are in danger of losing their last spiritual strength, the strength that makes it possible even to see the decline . . . the darkening of the world, the flight of the gods, the destruction of the earth, the reduction of human beings to a mass, the hatred and mistrust of everything creative and free have already reached such proportions throughout the whole earth that such childish categories as pessimism and optimism have long become laughable."[22]

Heidegger places this spiritual decline in a philosophical register, thinking of it in terms of his "history of being" (*Seynsgeschichte*), which is for Heidegger a saga of Being's withdrawal or occlusion. This process—ongoing since Plato—has been accelerating in the modern, technological era. Little wonder then that Dugin speaks of Heidegger in exalted terms: "A different, special, exclusive place in the history of philosophy that can be set aside for Heidegger should be recognized in the case that we fully trust Heidegger, immerse ourselves in his thinking, and make him our highest authority."[23]

Heidegger had pointed to technology as a force that was not so much a human instrument as in the dreams of modernity's philosophical founders Bacon and Descartes. Rather it was a force that was transforming and subjecting man to itself—in our contemporary terminology we might speak of *transhumanism*. Heidegger said in 1969: "That is today developed as biophysics: that we may soon have the possibility to create the human, that is . . . regarding his organic nature . . . to construct him just as we need him to be. . . . So, above all the misunderstanding has to be cleared away as if I was against technology. Rather on the contrary, I see in technology, namely its essence . . . that the human being is standing in the range of influence of a power, which challenges him, and in regard to this power he is no longer free."[24]

Dugin sees this transhumanist era of redesigning human nature already arriving in the form of genetic manipulation, transgender modification, cloning, and cyborgs (legitimate concerns!), all of which portend the "end of man" as we have known him.[25] Since this Western modernity is becoming universal, "in the way that decomposition and death are universal,"[26] this situation is dire.

And yet both Guénon and Heidegger see possibilities for salvation from modern decay. For Guénon, the *Kali-Yuga* is part of a deterministic cosmic cycle, which presumes a return to the beginning. In the interim, he sees the need to turn to the resources of the East for spiritual enlightenment (e.g., Islamic mysticism, Hinduism, Buddhism, etc.) where traditional culture has not yet been entirely destroyed.[27] Heidegger speaks similarly (if rather gnomically) of "another beginning" of philosophy and an "Event" (*Ereignis*) that foretells the return of Being.[28]

Dugin aims at a synthesis of Heidegger's fundamental ontology with Guénon's religious mysticism in the project of overcoming modernity. The philosophical struggle between liberal modernism and traditionalism for Dugin also has a spatial, which is to say a *geopolitical*, dimension. Dugin's geopolitics is enchanted and mythic. He speaks of a "sacred geography" and notes that traditional cultures see the East as "the land of Spirit," the paradise land, the land of a completeness, abundance, the sacred "native land" in its fullest and most perfect kind.[29] Russia is between the East and West, a unique *Eurasian* civilization destined to achieve the "new beginning" spoken of by Heidegger. Hence, for Dugin the looming battle between Russia and Western modernity is not merely geopolitical in the ordinary sense, but spiritual, philosophical, and eschatological: "Eurasia is a philosophical topos, exactly. It is first of all a *Seynsgeschichtliche* reality and only then a geopolitical, political or economical one. So it is for me the land of New Beginning. . . . It is the territory for awakening an *Ereignis*. That is the core of my own *Seynsgeschichtliche* vision of the historic moment. The rebirth of Eurasia is an eschatological and spiritual event."[30]

The idea of a "special Russian path" distinct from the West and particularly the Enlightenment, and with a future, eschatological significance has deep roots in Russian thought in the Russian Slavophile tradition of Kireevsky and Khomyakov, and perhaps earlier in its vision of itself as the Third Rome, the defender of "true" Christianity.

Dugin sees the destiny of Russia as leading the resurgence of traditional civilizations in breaking the power of liberal modernism, and creating a "pluriversum" of traditional cultures. His standpoint is not precisely nationalist in the conventional sense, since the units of Dugin's vision are (in his Schmittian terminology) the *Großräume* ("great spaces") of civilizations and empires. Some of these are "civilization-states," such as Russia, China, and India, but other "great spaces" of civilization would include Islam and Europe. Dugin's vision is in its way "postmodern" and "plurivocal" as against the unitary "grand narrative" of liberal globalism and progressivism.

Dugin's Fourth Political Theory in essence transposes the metaphysics of Integral Traditionalism into the *agon* of contemporary geopolitics and ideological struggle. A crucial question is how to assess the Integral Traditionalism that lies behind Dugin's worldview in the light of conservative humanism. The small "t" traditionalist conservatives of the West will acknowledge the problematic nature of many of the trends of modernity critiqued by Guénon, including its secularist trajectory, its materialist ontology, and the loss of the sense of beauty and transcendence—the latter of particular concern for Scruton.[31] Western conservatives, particularly those with values rooted in religious faith, have also been at the forefront of opposing efforts to drive religion from public life, redefine marriage and the family, and annul the distinction of sexes. They have also sounded warnings to humanity about the moral dangers of cloning and genetic manipulation of human beings. Moreover, Guénon's followers, such as Huston Smith, Titus Burckhardt, and Seyyed Hossein Nasr, have made very valuable contributions to the field of comparative religion by showing homologous structures among traditional faiths in, for example, their mystical dimension, and in the symbolic structures of their religious art and sacred cosmology. Nonetheless, there are significant shortcomings. Integral Traditionalism's assessment of the West is rather *too* pessimistic and deterministic, for if the religious, aesthetic, and intellectual inheritances of traditional Western civilization were really and entirely dead beyond hope of recovery, traditional conservativism as such could not exist. The extreme pessimism toward Western culture in its entire postmedieval development can lead—as it did in Guénon's case—to an almost total rejection of Western civilization as such,[32] and to the militant anti-Westernism with which Dugin flirts. At a more conceptual level, though certainly the great traditional faiths share many commonalities in their spiritual and moral teachings (generally far more so than any of them share with secular materialism), there are also important logical incompatibilities between their claims. Religious indifferentism would seem to entail embracing, as having equal validity (or invalidity), the mutually contradictory truth claims of different religions. Dugin's apparent denial of the "unity of truth" in favor of a "plurality of truths" is the point at which the traditionalism of Dugin's Fourth Political Theory dovetails with postmodern relativism. Dugin seems to see the civilizations the great religious traditions forged as giant "monads" whose value structures can only be judged from within. The tendency of Integral Traditionalism to see all religious traditions as, in Guénon's terms, "expressions of one and the same truth"[33] feeds into this tendency toward a pluralist and relativistic cultural monadology that rejects any universal standards of truth and morality by which cultures themselves might be judged.

A HISTORICAL EXCURSUS ON EUROPEAN NATIONALISM

Some self-subscribed conservatives identify conservatism with liberalism. Others, however, take a diametrically opposing view. In our time of backlash against globalization, many conservatives identify conservatism not with liberal cosmopolitanism, but with its very antithesis — *nationalism*. To assess the relation of nationalism to both the liberal and conservative traditions, it is worthwhile to explore its historical origins. Though they draw upon Enlightenment ideas, such as self-determination and popular sovereignty, the real intellectual roots of modern nationalism begin with the German Counter-Enlightenment in the late eighteenth and early nineteenth century, with philosophers such as Gottfried Herder and J. G. Fichte.[34] In his *Ideas on the Philosophy of the History of Mankind* (1784), Herder argues against the notion of a unilinear path of progress for all humanity, and against a single universal standard in the arts and literature. Rather, each culture has its own particular spirit (later called the *volksgeist*) that unfolds in its own way. Art, culture, and customs are all expressions of the particular national spirit.

Each people for Herder is shaped profoundly by its language and connection to the land where the people are autochthonous, by its native soil. Against liberalism's emphasis on the individual, Herder sees the individual as shaped by the organic national community. Herder helps to define the "trinity" that came to define nationhood—ethnos, language, and land. Herder's nationalism, primarily romantic and cultural, became strongly political in reaction to the Napoleonic conquests, which helped bring the sword edge of French imperial universalism to the rest of Europe. We can see already in this early form of German romantic nationalism the provenance (perhaps mediated by the romantic element in Heidegerianism) of Dugin's emphasis on cultural plurivocity and rootedness as against the Enlightenment's universalism.

The Germans at this time acutely felt their division into many statelets as a weakness. Fichte in *Addresses to the German Nation* (1808) adds to the people, land, and language the need for a strong state to protect the nation. From this point, ethnic nationalism conjoined to the new notions of popular sovereignty, and self-determination becomes an ebbing revolutionary force challenging the traditional European dynastic order. The idea of ethnic nationalism entailed some inherently destabilizing elements. The first is the problem of the minority. If the nation is defined as an ethnicity, then other ethnicities are excluded from the nation. This problem, arising from essentialist concepts of the nation, has resulted in various approaches, ranging from autonomy arrangements, secessionism by minority groups to form their own ethnic-states, efforts at assimilating the minorities, expulsions ("ethnic cleansing" as it became called during the Balkan ethnic wars), and at the extreme genocides aiming at to eliminating the "alien" ethnic groups. At the outset, the destabilizing element was caused by the fact that the traditional European order was not based on ethnicity, so if every ethnic nation must have a state, then borders must be redrawn. Nationalism thus fueled dramatic political transformations.

The Italian ethnolinguistic culture successfully completed the unification of Italy (*risorgimento*) in 1870, followed the next year by Bismarck's unification of Germany. Within the Hapsburg Austrian Empire, ethnic nationalists among the Hungarians, Czechs, Slovaks, Serbs, and others all demanded states within their traditional ethnic homelands. The Zionist movement in the late nineteenth century revived the Hebrew language and called for the return of the Jewish people to the lands of biblical Israel. Romantic nationalism became an all-pervasive force, with ancestral folk culture finding expression in high art, influencing music, literature. The nationality struggles within the Hapsburg Empire became a major contributing cause of World War I. The nationalist idea in Europe reached its most extreme (and inhuman) point of development with the emergence of fascism and National Socialism. In Italy, Germany, and elsewhere, the ethnic idea of the nation was conjoined to that of the totalitarian state under the absolute command of the leader, with national greatness assuming an explicitly martial and imperial character exalting heroism, the complete subordination of the individual to the collective, and the glorification of war and conquest.

In its Nazi form, particular emphasis was given to the idea of race. The nation is defined in pseudo-biologistic terms, with minorities such as Jews deprived of citizenship based on ancestry and eventually targeted for extermination throughout Nazi-occupied Europe (we discuss National Socialism in more detail in chapter 8). The extreme nationalism of fascism and Nazism led to atrocities such as the Holocaust and World War II. Europe was in ruins. This saw the hard swing of the pendulum against nationalism toward different ideological forms of cosmopolitanism—liberalism (in Western Europe) and for a time Marxism (in Eastern Europe). The desire to put the nationalist genie back in the bottle led to institutions such as the European Common Market and European Coal and Steel Community. These were designed to integrate the economies of Western Europe on the aforementioned liberal theory that commerce and economic interdependence made war impossible. Kantian cosmopolitanism was back with a vengeance, because nationalism was now tainted by association with fascism. The process of European integration sped up rapidly with the formation of the EU in 1992, which became one of the pillars of the post–Cold War liberal international order.

It was only with the global financial crisis in 2008 that major cracks began to appear, as the tethering of economies seemed to lead to contagion, the need for bailouts, and mutual recriminations among the EU member states. Then mass migration, particularly from the Islamic world, caused widespread concern not only about economic effects but on issues of security and national and cultural identity. This peaked during the 2015–16 migrant crisis as hundreds of thousands of migrants and refugees, many from the war-torn Islamic world, poured into Europe. Amid this crisis, Britain voted to leave the EU. In the United States, Donald Trump was elected president on a platform of protectionism and control of immigration. Trump has since clearly and unambiguously affirmed nationalism, a return to an emphasis on national sovereignty, identity, and borders: "The free world must embrace its national foundations . . . the future does not belong to globalists, the future belongs to patriots."[35]

Nationalist parties meanwhile gathered strength in continental Europe. Perhaps the European leader who has most articulately expressed a nonliberal, nationalist vision of conservatism is Viktor Orban of Hungary. Orban bluntly declared that the era of liberalism is over: "Putting pretension aside, we can call this the era of liberal babble. This era is now at an end, and this situation carries huge risk, but also huge opportunity. It offers the chance for the national-Christian ideology, way of thinking, and approach to regain dominance—not only in Hungary, but throughout the whole of Europe."[36]

Liberalism, as it seems to the Hungarian nationalists, is founded on two negations—the negation of religion (secularism) and the negation of the national-ethnic community (cosmopolitanism). In opposing mass immigration, particularly from the Islamic world, Orban sees his role as defending the traditional religious and ethnic identity of Hungary. He also sees the need the resist the EU's putative objective of erasing traditional religious and national identities: "The purpose of settling these people here is to redraw the religious and cultural map of Europe, and to reconfigure its ethnic foundations, thereby eliminating nation states, which are the last obstacle to the international movement."[37]

In continental Europe, a movement worthy of mention in paving the way for contemporary neonationalism is the French New Right (*Nouvelle Droite*) (ND). This intellectual movement led by the French philosopher Alain de Benoist sees itself as a metapolitical movement that supplies the intellectual tools for a radical critique of liberalism from the right.[38]

Benoist sees liberalism and globalization as merely the latest iteration of Western universalism—following Christianity and colonialism—which has tried to foist itself on the whole world.[39] Against liberalism's emphasis on the "atomic individual," the French ND champions the "concretely rooted people"[40] as the proper context of human beings. And against liberal universalism, it champions the "pluriversum,"[41] the "universe" of distinct ethnic cultures each with their own traditions, customs, religions, languages, and so on. It argues for an *ethnopluralism* that allows each distinct culture to maintain its own identity, and it sees global capitalism and universalist, liberal values as a homogenizing, uprooting, imperial force. And though it has been accused by scholars of conserving a "residue of fascist ideology"[42] and views the immigration of peoples from other cultures negatively,[43] The French ND avowedly disclaims the hierarchical racism of the 1930s extreme Right. Instead, it argues for the "right to difference,"[44] the right of each ethnic culture to maintain its own distinction from all others, against the homogenizing forces of globalization, mass migration, and liberal universalist ideology. The French ND dovetails in many respects with the views of Dugin. But the ND goes further in critiquing Christianity as the taproot of modern liberalism.[45] It also explicitly rejects classical humanism: "This 'immanent transcendence reveals nature as a partner and not as an adversary or object. This does not diminish the unique importance of mankind, but it does deny to man his exclusive position that Christianity and classical humanism assigned him.'"[46]

The French ND, therefore, has a whiff of neopaganism while at the same time is postmodern in rejecting the liberal grand narrative in favor of the plurivocity of cultures and perspectives. What is obscure in this system is how it can avoid the cultural relativism involved in the notion that each culture generates its own "morality," thereby denying the possibility of any universal moral system. Cultural relativism subverts humanism, and thus in chapter 4 we argued for the saliency of natural law as a brake on the moral implications of the Dugin and the French ND's pluriversum.

NATIONALISM AND NATIONAL-CONSERVATISM

To be certain, many elements of today's neonationalism are also conservative in the traditional sense we have outlined, particularly on questions of religion, land, and family. Hungary's constitution speaks with pride in the heritage of Hungarian Christianity going back to St. Stephen.[47] It moreover strongly supports the traditional understanding of the family: "Hungary shall protect the institution of marriage as the union of a man and a woman established by voluntary decision, and the family as the basis of the nation's survival."[48] Hungary has sought to promote procreation and families through government support and incentives.[49]

On an intellectual level, the argument for a close tie between nationalism and conservatism has been carried forward with force by the contemporary American-Israeli scholar Yoram Hazony, a leader in the movement of national-conservatism. Like Dugin, Hazony has recently argued that such universalisms are associated with imperialism—the potentially coercible demand that all peoples follow a single ideological, economic, or political model. Accordingly, he and Offir Haivry make nationalism a central principle of Anglo-American conservatism as the counterideology to universal ideology and imperialism: "The diversity of national experiences means that different nations will have different constitutional and religious traditions. The Anglo-American traditions harkens back to principles of a free and just national state, charting its own course without foreign interference, whose origin is in the Bible."[50]

In his much-acclaimed *The Virtue of Nationalism*, Hazony argues that Western politics has oscillated between two opposing visions of politics. The nationalist vision is centered on "an order of free and independent nations"; the imperial-universalist vision is centered on "an order of peoples, under a single regime of law, promulgated and maintained by a single supranational authority."[51] The fundamental questions are then between universalism and particularism, liberalism and nationalism. Hazony sees the former vision as largely a contribution of ancient Israel, whose history as recorded in the Hebrew Bible involves the struggle of the Jewish people for freedom and security against the Middle Eastern world empires, such as Assyria and Babylonia. In Hazony's historical narrative, Europe took up a similar imperial or universal vision first in the Roman Empire and then in the Roman Catholic Church, which "adopted the Roman dream of universal empire,"[52] forging Christendom (the spiritual rule of the popes and the secular rule of the Holy Roman emperor). Hazony sees the imperial urge to continue in early modernity in the Spanish Empire.[53] It was principally the Protestant nations (he lays great stress on England and Holland) who broke from this Roman imperial tradition. The Protestant nations championed what he sees as the Hebrew biblical ideals of national freedom, sovereignty, and self-determination, which allow each nation to determine its laws and fundamental direction for itself.[54] Nationalism, however, having been discredited by the two world wars and fascism/Nazism,[55] faces the resurgence of liberal cosmopolitanism in the postwar era. Without morally equating liberalism with other universal-imperial projects in history, Hazony nonetheless casts liberalism as essentially imperial in its global ambitions, hostility to sovereign independent states, and demand for universal conformity to its precepts: "Much like the pharaohs, and the Babylonian kings, the Roman emperors and the Roman Catholic Church until well into the modern period, as well as the Marxists of the last century, liberals too, have their grand theory about how they are going to bring peace and prosperity to the world by pulling down all the borders and uniting mankind under their one universal rule."[56]

Hazony is certainly correct to argue that Nazism, because of its peculiar racial imperialism and monstrous evils, is a hyperbolic example to use to critique nationalism. Still, the nationalist project of redrawing the borders of states around ethnic cultures is necessarily implicated in the violent convulsions that broke up the traditional dynastic monarchies of Europe. Unsurprisingly, older European conservatives, such as Count Klemens von Metternich in his multiethnic Austrian Empire, regarded nationalism as a revolutionary force. For this reason, even though they are favorable to patriotism as a virtue, conservatives have viewed nationalism with ambivalence, adopting different positions in different circumstances.

THE CONSERVATIVE *VIA MEDIA*:
EDMUND BURKE, THOMAS AQUINAS,
AND THE ORDER OF CHARITY

How should nationalism be seen from the standpoint of traditionalist conservatism? To be sure, Hazony is correct that traditional conservatism is more *particularist* than liberalism. The cosmopolitan ideal refuses to make any fundamental distinction between the fellow-citizen and the foreigner, for its allegiance is to "universal humanity." But for the conservative, the liberal conception of "universal humanity," like its concept of "individual," is an empty abstraction. The concrete human being always belongs to a *specific* community. The great French conservative Comte Joseph de Maistre notes: "During my life, I have seen Frenchmen, Italians, Russians, and so on; thanks to Montesquieu, I even know that one can be Persian; but I must say, as for man, I have never come across him anywhere; if he exists, he is completely unknown to me."[57]

Hence, for the conservative, it is normal and legitimate to have a privileged attachment to one's own home and hearth, and to nurse a special affection for one's own mother tongue, family members, and the country is no disgrace. At the same time, Western conservative moral sentiment does not rest content with nationalist tribalism, which might reject moral obligations to nonkin or, worse, cultivate xenophobic hostility toward them. So how does conservatism reconcile particularistic attachments with universalistic moral claims? Edmund Burke speaks with great eloquence of the "concentric circles" of moral concern, starting with local and kin communities, but radiating outward, to ultimately include all of humanity: "To be attached to the subdivision, to love the little platoon we belong to in society, is the first principle (the germ as it were) of public affections. It is the first link in the series by which we proceed toward a love to our country and to mankind."[58]

This disposition is closely related to the principles of traditional Christianity with its concern for human dignity even of the farthest stranger. In the famous parable of the Good Samaritan (Luke 10:25–37), Christ pointedly uses the example of the stranger (the Samaritan) as the true "neighbor" (though importantly the situation reflects a concrete, proximate need the Samaritan stranger is responding to with love). The New Testament itself speaks of the church as a universal community meant for and open to all mankind, breaking down tribal divisions. St. Paul proclaimed, "There is neither Jew nor Greek, there is neither slave nor free, there is neither male nor female; for you are all one in Christ Jesus" (Gal. 3:28).[59]

At a theological level, Christianity is a remarkable synthesis of universalism and particularism. The incarnation of Jesus Christ is not a merely abstract principle akin to the god of Greek metaphysics. It is understood as a concrete and unique event in which a divine person enters into human history in its concrete particularity. Christ is born to a particular woman in a particular place, of the particular people of Israel with their roots in the sacred history of the patriarchs, Moses, and the Prophets. And yet this particularity opens up to the most generous and inclusive universalism embracing the whole human race: "And if you be Christ's, then are you the seed of Abraham, heirs according to the promise" (Gal. 3:29).

Burke's position expresses the traditional Christian teaching of the *order of charity* (*ordo amoris*). Preferential love for one's own kin and country has been legitimated by the Catholic tradition. Aquinas writes: "From charity bringing forth and commanding, we love in more ways those who are more closely conjoined to us" (ex caritate elicente cum imperante pluribus modis diligimus magis nobis coniunctos).[60]

Among those to whom privileged charity is due are one's own kin and fellow-citizens. Aquinas rejects an undifferentiated cosmopolitanism, placing a grateful and reverent patriotism under the virtue of *pietas*, but he also mandates protections for innocents everywhere, protected by the deliverances of natural law: "Man is debtor chiefly to his parents and his country, after God. Wherefore just as it belongs to religion to give worship to God, so does it belong to piety, in the second place, to give worship to one's parents and one's country [ad pietatem pertinet exhibere cultum parentibus et patriae]. . . . The worship given to our country includes homage to all our fellow-citizens and to all the friends of our country."[61]

This is the medieval conception of the order of charity, which Burke and conservative humanism inherits. Hence, conservatives praise patriotism as a virtue and are often aligned with the nation-state, without closing themselves to larger and more inclusive communities and traditions.

Europe finds its historical-cultural roots in the two great traditions of the classical Greco-Roman culture and Christianity. These traditions are both pan-European and prenational. The unity of European Christendom only began to weaken with the emergence of the idea of state sovereignty, as kings centralized their authority in Spain, France, and England, and with the Protestant Reformation, which broke the medieval ideal of Europe as a Catholic unity. This ideal was further eroded with the rise of a more virulent nationalism in the nineteenth century. Nonetheless, many European conservatives have always felt an attachment to the great unifying European traditions, which are neither as wide as the global nor as narrow as the national. As Christopher Dawson put the matter: "The ultimate foundation of our culture is not the national state, but European unity. It is true that this unity has not hitherto received political form and may never do so; but it is for all that a real society not an intellectual abstraction, and it is only through their communion in this society that the different national cultures have attained their actual form."[62]

Despite the religious divisions and the rivalry of states, a reverent attachment to the idea of Europe as one Christian commonwealth can be seen in Burke himself:

> The writers on public law have often called this aggregate of nations a commonwealth . . . the nations of Europe have had the very same Christian religion varying a little in the ceremonies and in the subordinate doctrines . . . there was little difference in the form of the Universities for the education of their youth, whether with regard to faculties, to sciences, or to the more liberal and elegant kinds of erudition. From this form the modes of intercourse and in the whole form and fashion of life, no citizen of Europe could be altogether an exile from any part of it . . . when a man travelled or resided for health, pleasure, business, or necessity, he never felt himself quite abroad.[63]

In the same vein, Roger Scruton and Pierre Manent, though skeptical of the EU as a political entity, have argued for a reverent attachment to Europe as the common home and civilization for many nations.[64] The allegiance to the broader community of nations that constitute Europe and the West does not imply an abstract cosmopolitanism.

A word is there needed about the idea of universal "rights of man," which for liberals since the late eighteenth century has served as the main justification for their internationalism. Burke challenged the pretensions of liberalism in his day to be the "universal ideology" all nations must accept. In Burke's view, the liberal theory of "the rights of man" considered as a set of abstract and universal principles without regard to the particular historical tradition, culture, and circumstances is dangerous. It can become a reckless ideology serving to justify subverting any political order fails to conform to the bloodless abstractions of liberal theory: "They have 'the rights of men.' Against these there can be no prescription; against these no agreement is binding. . . . Against these their rights of men let no government look for security in the length of its continuance, or in the justice and lenity of its administration. The objections of these speculatists, if its forms do not quadrate with its theories, are as valid against an old and beneficent government, as against the most violent tyranny, or the greenest usurpation."[65]

At the same time, Burke would affirm that there is an unchanging and universal moral standard—the natural law—by which the nations may be judged. The question of Burke's natural law theory has by now been extensively dealt with in the scholarship.[66] Burke affirms, in short, the obligation of the state to conform its laws to transcendent moral principles. For example, he speaks in the *Reflections* of the fact that "power, which to be legitimate must be according to that eternal immutable law, in which will and reason are the same."[67] Burke's explicit appeals to natural law follow a long pattern; indeed, it was on the back of natural law that Burke frequently denounced abuses by his own government against other peoples. In denouncing the injustices of British rule over Irish Catholics, Burke appeals to a conception of a universally binding natural law easily recognizable by students of Cicero and Aquinas. Laws must conform to natural law to bind: "But if we could suppose that such a ratification [of an unjust law] was not made virtually, but even collectively, still it would be null and void. They have no right to make a law prejudicial to the whole community . . . because it would be made against the principle of a superior law, which it is not in the power of any community, or of the whole race of man to alter—I mean the will of Him who gave us our nature, and in giving, impressed an invariable law upon it."[68]

The natural law, therefore, is universal and binds all. The legitimate regard for differences of national or cultural particularity and their expression in local custom cannot therefore justify the violation of the natural moral law, which is universally binding. Conservative humanism, in short, rejects the cultural relativism of certain forms of nationalism, which sees each nation as essentially a law unto itself, each with its own morality. It holds a middle ground between any narrowly tribal form of nationalism, which might tend to limit moral concern to kin alone and an abstract liberal cosmopolitanism, which plays down or rejects the preferential claims of particularistic identities (such as nationality), in favor of an undifferentiated concern for an abstract, universal humanity. It is favorable to a special attachment to the national and local community, but situates these attachments within wider and more inclusive loyalties. As the Jacobins and Marxists of the modern age have shown, the love for "universal humanity" in the abstract can go hand in hand with the cruelest indifference toward the welfare of concrete human beings. Berdyaev notes that the Christian approach (which informs much of traditionalist conservatism) takes the opposite view:

> The only thing higher than the love for man is the love of God, Who is also a concrete Being, a Person and not an abstract idea. The love of God and the love of man sum up the Gospel morality. . . . Christianity preaches love for one's neighbor and not "those far off." This is a very important distinction. Love for 'the far off,' for man and humanity in general, is love for an abstract idea and not love for man. And for the sake of this abstract love men are ready to sacrifice concrete, living beings.[69]

This tendency toward abstract cosmopolitanism is one element of the liberal project that conservatives will reject. An even more fundamental question, however, is what position conservative humanism must take toward liberalism's most central notion—the liberty and autonomy of the individual.

CHAPTER 7

Liberty and History

What is liberty without virtue and wisdom?
It is the greatest of all possible evils: for it is folly, vice, and madness.
—Edmund Burke, *Reflections on the Revolution in France*

Οὐδεὶς ἐλεύθερος ἑαυτοῦ μὴ κρατῶν
[No man is free who is not master of himself]
—Epictetus, fragment

THE END OF HISTORY AND
THE THEOLOGICAL-POLITICAL PROBLEM

If Fukuyama's end of history thesis is correct and identical to "the un-abashed victory of political and economic liberalism," then the histori-cal process must culminate in some universalization of freedom. The ef-fort to secure the freedom of the individual in political, economic, and religious life lies at the very heart of the modern liberal project. It is left to interrogate what freedom means in the context of liberal ideology.[1] For Americans, central players in this project, the very world "liberty" has an almost sacred significance, as in Abraham Lincoln's Gettysburg Address evocation of the United States as a nation "conceived in liberty." If we are correct in our assertion that conservatism and liberalism are distinct traditions of political thought, it should be possible to articulate a conservative doctrine of freedom distinct from a liberal one. And if the conservative humanist ideal of freedom has value, it ought to provide a compelling critique of the liberal conception—what this modern conception betrayed in the old legacy—even in granting significance to the achievements of modern liberty. These are the principal goals of the present chapter. But first, we will elucidate the Fukuyama's philosophy of history.

It is important to note that Fukuyama's thesis is properly philosophical rather than historical. It is not the kind of claim that can be vindicated or falsified by a simple appeal to historical facticity. The human mind, after all, cannot comprehend "history" as a whole. Even if all states at one moment of time are illiberal, perhaps in the fullness of time they will all become liberal. But conversely, even if all states become liberal at one future moment of history, this would not prove they will always remain so into an indefinite future. It is therefore at the level of philosophy of history (rather than history proper) that Fukuyama makes his case, and it is in this register where his thesis must be interrogated. In this Fukuyama draws upon an existing philosophical tradition. There is no canonical thinker in the Western philosophical tradition who gives history a greater centrality than G. W. F. Hegel: he is the intellectual grandfather of Alexandre Kojève (d. 1968), who is, in turn, the father of Fukuyama's end of history thesis. It would be outside the parameters of this work to summarize Hegel's philosophy of history, but a few points are salient for Fukuyama.

Hegel sees in the successive rise and fall of world civilizations not a random and haphazard process that records human violence and folly, but the forward movement of Spirit toward the full realization of freedom.[2] Hegel on this point thus assimilates the theodicy of biblical religion to the basic progressivism of the Enlightenment. He sees the opposition of "master" and "slave" as the fundamental dynamic that drives the historical progress forward.[3] As Fukuyama explains, for Hegel the most fundamental human drive is not economic prosperity (important as this is) but something more spiritual—the desire for *recognition*: "Hegel provides us with an alternative 'mechanism' by which to understand the historical process, one based on 'the struggle for recognition.' While we need not abandon the economic account of history, 'recognition' allows us to recover a totally non-materialist historical dialectic that is much richer in its understanding of human motivation."[4]

As Fukuyama notes in *Identity* (2019),[5] this desire for recognition drives much of contemporary identity politics: various groups perceived as once marginalized demand equal recognition (as in feminism, civil rights movements, the LGBT movement, etc.); or in nationalism, as national-ethnic communities demand honor and respect (the Scottish, Welsh, Catalans, etc.). The desire for recognition can include also a more personal striving and competition for honor (one of the examples Fukuyama cited in the 1990s was Donald Trump!).[6] In the beginning, only the master received full recognition of his humanity: the aristocracy depicted by Hegel is a martial class that earns recognition by its willingness to sacrifice their own lives. The slave, who prefers life to honor, forfeits full recognition of his humanity. However, over time the master becomes dependent on the slave, and the slave, seeing his humanity transform the world through labor, comes to recognize his own worth, and perhaps even demands his recognition and is willing to take risks for this (the moment of revolt). Once the slave achieves equal recognition with the master, the historical process culminates. For Hegel, such a terminus privileges European history as the locus where universal freedom and recognition were first articulated as an ideal: "The History of the World travels from East to West, for Europe is absolutely the end of History, Asia the beginning."[7] This process of realizing freedom unfolds in three stages: "The East knew and to the present days knows only that *One* is Free; the Greeks and Roman World, that *some* are free; the German World knows that *All* are free."[8]

The bulk of Hegel's *The Philosophy of History* is devoted to an elaboration of this schema. He is attentive to the histories and particularities of the civilizations of "the Orient" from China to the Middle East, but they are all nonetheless fundamentally despotic, involving the rule of God-kings and emperors over slavelike subjects. By contrast, the Greco-Roman world acknowledged the freedom of the aristocracy. But Western antiquity was still rooted in a fundamental distinction between human beings—the Roman gentleman-masters and the barbarians, slaves, and laboring classes who toil for them. This is a point on which Nietzsche and Tom Holland would also agree, albeit taking different sides (we explore this in our concluding remarks chapter).

For Hegel (as for Fukuyama) the pivotal importance of Christianity lies in its universalism and egalitarianism. It was Christianity that provided the spiritual principle to abolish the master–slave relation by proclaiming the equal dignity of all and the ultimate irrelevance of human distinctions: "First, under Christianity Slavery is impossible. . . . 'God will have all men to be saved' utterly excluding all specialty, therefore man—in his simple quality of man—has infinite value and this infinite value abolishes *ipso facto*, all particularity attaching to birth and country."[9]

Yet even though Christianity overcame the "master–slave dialectic" in principle by affirming the equal dignity of all, it would require political modernity to abolish it in practice. Christianity acted as a kind of slow leaven that only gradually loosened the entrenched aristocratic hierarchies. In this respect Hegel sees the French Revolution as an event of singular proportions: "We have to now consider the French Revolution in its organic connection with the *History of the World*; for in its substantial import the event is World-Historical."[10]

Hegel, like Nietzsche,[11] sees the French Revolution as ironically a Christian-inspired revolt of the slave against the master. Despite its surface meaning of an anticlerical revolution, the French Revolution ultimately signifies for them the transformation of the secular world by the Christian spiritual principle. This transformation consists of "the French principles of Liberty and Equality,"[12] culminating in the abolition of all privileges and distinctions. Hence, at last, the liberal state enters the stage of history by giving legal force to the principle of universal recognition. As Kojève put it: "Man seeks from the start *Annerken-nung*, recognition . . . in other words man can be truly 'satisfied,' History can end, only in and by the formation of a Society, of a State, in which the strictly personal, individual value of each is, in its very personality by *all*, by a Universality incarnated in the state as such."[13]

Having thus birthed the modern revolution, what then becomes of Christianity? This religion enunciated the principle of universal dignity, yet its otherworldliness reconciled it to social inequalities. Fukuyama explains: "The problem with Christianity, however, is that it remains just another slave ideology . . . Christianity posits the realization of human freedom not here on earth but only in the Kingdom of Heaven. Christianity, in other words, had the right *concept* of freedom but ended up reconciling real-world slaves to their lack of freedom, by telling them not to expect liberation in this life."[14]

This is the basis of Enlightenment liberalism's polemic against Christian theological politics. One is not free, in the liberal view, so long as one is subordinated in a hierarchy and denied equal recognition. From Fukuyama's standpoint, liberalism draws on Christianity as a historical precursor for its ideas of freedom, equality, and universal dignity, but the political entanglement between theology and politics is for liberalism disastrous. Indeed, the Christian state is the very foil against which liberalism and the Enlightenment arose: "Modern liberalism itself was historically a consequence of the weakness of religiously-based societies which, failing to agree on the nature of the good life, could not provide even the minimal preconditions of peace and stability."[15]

Since the secularization of politics is perceived in liberalism as a momentous advance in history, there is for Fukuyama no "going back" ever from the liberal polity to the Christian polity. Part of the problem for Fukuyama is an element that Christian politics inherited from classical politics. The Greeks starting no later than Aristotle had proclaimed teleology as central to politics—human beings order their lives together politically for "good life" (the life of reason and virtue), understood as universal and common to all. Christianity absorbed and theologized the Aristotelian idea of "final ends" in politics by making the final end of salvation relevant to political life. Christendom, however, owing to the lack of universal agreement on the attainment of this final end, culminated in the confessional violence and conflict of the Reformation era. Liberalism resolved this conflict by removing teleology (and at least explicitly theology) from politics: "One of the achievements of early modern liberalism was its success persuading people of the need to exclude discussion of final ends addressed by religion from the realm of politics."[16] On the one hand, liberalism is a proposed solution to the theological-political problem: it creates a "neutral" state on questions of the final end or supreme good; a state wherein each individual is "free" to pursue *his own* conception of the good life. On the other hand, it smuggles in a Christian appropriation of antique teleology by applying the notion of the final end to universal history (what we have been calling liberalism's "one-mindism").

Fukuyama's liberalism sees itself as the teleological culmination of history's promise of universal and equal recognition.

THE LIBERTY OF LIBERALISM

But even as Fukuyama's theory of history draws from Hegel, his notion of freedom is anything but Hegelian. Fukuyama will not follow Hegel and "venerate the State as an earthly divinity"[17] in which the free individual is subsumed into a larger spiritual organism. On the contrary, Fukuyama's "freedom" is thoroughly bourgeois and liberal: "We might summarize the content of the universal homogenous state as liberal democracy in the political sphere combined with easy access to VCRs and stereos in the economic."[18] In the economic sphere, then, "freedom" for Fukuyama signifies the familiar operations of the "free market" in which the state plays a limited, regulatory role. Fukuyama embraces a certain form of Hegelian egalitarianism, but he will not align with the radical egalitarianism of the Hegelian Left (e.g., Marxism), which is anticapitalist and conceives of freedom principally in terms of collectivist, economic leveling: "Market economies depend on the individual pursuit of self-interest, which leads to inequalities of wealth, given different abilities and conditions of birth. Equality in a modern liberal democracy has always meant something more like an equality of freedom. This means both an equal negative freedom from abusive government power and an equal positive freedom to participate in self-government and economic exchange."[19]

The last part is particularly important. The "right of participation" is the freedom of Pericles, an idea going back to Athenian democracy and the Roman Republic. Negative freedom, however, is an idea unique to modern liberalism. Fukuyama's notion of freedom is decidedly individualist rather than collective.

This becomes part of Fukuyama's critiques of identity politics. Fukuyama deems the focus on collective identities to be in an inherent tension with his liberal concern for the right of the individual to free self-expression. The censoriousness of Left-identitarianism is avowedly aimed at policing the boundaries of acceptable discourse about marginalized identities, boundaries that are sometimes honed to an extreme level of putative sensitivity.[20] And, indeed, there is evidence for Fuku-yama's concerns. Some polls have indicated that 40 percent of millen-nials agreed with censoring speech considered offensive to minority groups.[21] At university campuses, dissenting thinkers have been sub-ject to "deplatforming," removal from social media, and even physical threats and assault.[22] Conservatives have complained about what is called "cancel culture." Even without the instruments of state terror, the use of intimidation and fear of public shaming or job loss can thus have a chilling effect on public debate of sensitive social issues.

For Fukuyama this signifies a fundamental danger of contemporary identity politics to the principles of classical liberalism: "A third problem with current understandings of identity is that they can threaten free speech and, more broadly, the kind of rational discourse needed to sus-tain a democracy. Liberal democracies are committed to the right to say anything you want in a marketplace of ideas. But the preoccupation with identity has clashed with the need for deliberative discourse."[23]

Identity politics, with insistent demands for collective recogni-tion, is now recognized by Fukuyama as a spanner he had not foreseen in the liberal triumphalism that marked his 1989 article. The roots of intolerant Left-identity politics perhaps go back to the 1960s. The New Left Marxist thinker Herbert Marcuse had already provided the theoretical foundation for a contemporary Left-critique of liberal free-dom. The legal "neutrality" of the liberal order, he argued, equalized the expression of the oppressor ("the Right") and the oppressed. Hence Marcuse argues that discourse by the privileged oppressor promotes social inequality and should be suppressed, while discourse that sup-ports egalitarian social goals should be positively encouraged as paving the way for "authentic" tolerance: "Liberating tolerance, then, would mean intolerance against movements from the Right and toleration of movements from the Left. As to the scope of this tolerance and intoler-ance: . . . it would extend to the stage of action as well as of discussion and propaganda, of deed as well as of word."[24]

This Left-egalitarian project requires substantial political and so-cial control over language and thought. This "totalitarian logic"[25] where it gains ascendance will tend to make conservatives more appreciative of the classical liberal tradition insofar as it defends their right to a place in free public discourse. But without a more substantive conception of the good, can liberalism adequately articulate the primacy of one value—free expression—over other values?

"Liberty" in classical liberalism means essentially an absence of external forces obstructing or interfering in whatever speech or action is desired by the agent. In the political sense, the primary concern for liberalism is the state and its power to impose coercive sanctions.[26] Jeremy Bentham writes: "Liberty is neither more nor less than the absence of coercion. This is the genuine, original, and proper sense of the word Liberty. The idea of it is an idea purely negative. It is not anything produced by positive Law. It exists without Law, and not by means of Law."[27]

Law and liberty are here inversely proportional and locked into a zero-sum game. To the degree the law expands, to the same degree the sphere of liberty contracts, and vise versa. The "liberty of liberalism"—that is, negative freedom—emerges in a fully articulated form surprisingly late in history. Among political philosophers, Isaiah Berlin and his intellectual opponent Leo Strauss[28] agree that the *locus classicus* for negative freedom is Thomas Hobbes. Despite his ultimately authoritarian conclusions, Hobbes provides modern liberalism with its central concept of negative liberty.[29] And Hobbes concludes pithily that liberty is "the silence of the Law."[30] Whereof the law does not speak, thereof there is liberty. So much for apprehending the nature of the essence of liberal freedom. How is it to be evaluated?

It is notable that this concept of "negative liberty" is what is reflexively understood as liberty in contemporary liberal societies. If we think for example of the First Amendment to the U.S. Constitution, no law can be made restricting the "free exercise" of religion or "abridging freedom of speech, or of the press." If I enjoy "freedom of speech," it means that the state may not prevent me from saying whatever it is I wish to say.

A difficulty that liberalism has in this respect is articulating precisely why and in what way such liberty is an intrinsic moral good. If freedom is defined negatively as simply "unencumbered action," then how is it a moral good? Don't we require some evaluation of the use of liberty as good or evil, noble or base? One may use negative "freedom of speech" to promote a life of either moral virtue or debauchery, to elevate the good, or to slander and debase the innocent. Remarking upon "the new liberty of France," Burke says, "The effect of liberty to individuals is, that they may do what they please: we ought to see what it will please them to do, before we risqué [*sic*] congratulations."[31] The suspicion is that liberalism unmoored from any broader, universal conception of moral order must veer toward an amoral libertinism. This worry lies close to the heart of Burke and the conservative critique of liberalism. Burke's conservative conception of freedom, connecting freedom to virtue, is an inheritance of Western humanism, both classical and Christian. Let us then look back at premodern freedom, before turning to Burke's conservative freedom.

CLASSICAL AND CHRISTIAN FREEDOM

The philosophers of ancient Greece and Rome enunciated a concept of freedom distinct from the liberal conception we have described. A simple illustration may clarify. Let us imagine the case of an alcoholic. Under what circumstances is an alcoholic "free"? From the standpoint of negative freedom, it would seem as if the alcoholic is free if nothing constrains the fulfillment of his alcoholic desires. Provided that an alcoholic has sufficient funds and continuous access to alcohol whenever the urge arises, he or she can be called "free." The idea of freedom in classical Greek philosophy, by contrast, is centered on an idea of self-mastery (ἐγκράτεια). In the ancient idea, even if nothing external impedes the addictive desire, the alcoholic is nonetheless a slave.

The main starting point in the birth of this concept of freedom as self-mastery is Socrates. In the *Memorabilia* of Xenophon, Socrates asks rhetorically, "Then do you think that the man is free who is ruled by bodily pleasures and is unable to do what is best because of them?"[32]

As Jaeger[33] explains, Socrates transfers the question of slavery and freedom from the issue of social status to the inner soul. External and bodily goods, which are the principal objects of human passions—wealth, pleasure, honor—are of little value, without a rule of virtue. Virtue (αρετή) is essential to the Socratic concept of freedom, but not to the concept negative liberty. Under the Hobbesian account, words can be used to exhort moral goods, but also to corrupt, slander, insult, and defame. By contrast, it is precisely through moral discipline that one acquires freedom in the Socratic model. To acquire the virtue of courage is to gain mastery over fear, to acquire temperance is to learn mastery of sexual and other bodily desires, and so forth. Importantly, these moral virtues are linked to the intellectual virtues, and thus a refinement in the arts and sciences is also an aid to the moral articulation of the passions, an aid to liberty. In the complex relationship between reason and passions, the two domains of virtue, Socrates potently adds that without the virtues, the human soul is so enslaved by the passions it cannot even properly perceive the human good: "Should not every man hold self-control to be the foundation of all virtue, and to first lay this foundation firmly in his soul? For who without this can learn any good or practice it worthily? Or what man that is the slave of his pleasures is not in an evil plight body and soul alike?"[34]

Plato's Socrates is presented as the lived embodiment of this ideal of virtuous self-mastery. Since it turns out that injustice reflects the disharmony of the soul in which the passions rule the higher rational and moral faculties, the unjust are in the worst possible condition. Plato can argue without irony that the tyrant—far from being the freest and happiest of all human beings—is in actuality the most enslaved and miserable of all persons: "Then the tyrannized soul—to speak of the soul as a whole—also will least of all do what it wishes, but being always perforce driven and drawn by the gadfly of desire it will be full of confusion and repentance."[35]

To find an analogy to the modern ideal of liberty among the Greeks, we must look not to philosophy but to rhetoric. Michel Foucault[36] made an important analysis of the Greek concept of "frank speaking" (παρρησία) in the deliberative processes of Athenian democracy. Hence the rhetor Demosthenes admonishes the Athenians: "Think it is your duty, men of Athens, when deliberating about such important matters to allow freedom of speech [παρρησίαν] to every one of your counsellors."[37] Such freedom in the context of political deliberations could be argued to be the ancestor of the "freedom of speech" of modern democracies. The Athenians regarded it as essential to wise deliberations that everyone should be able to speak his mind freely.

Plato, who condemns democracy not least for its judicial murder of Socrates, warns that its "negative liberty" easily turns to licentiousness: "To begin with, are they not free? And is not the city chock-full of liberty and freedom of speech? And has not every man license to do as he likes? . . . and where there is such license, it is obvious that everyone would arrange a plan for living his own life in the way the pleases him."[38]

Plato argued that democracy's tendency to let each one pursue his desires must lead to tyranny; an argument reused by Andrew Sullivan at the democratic election of Donald Trump.[39] The disharmony of the soul, in short, would lead ultimately to the disharmony of the *polis*: "The same malady," I said, "that, arising in oligarchy, destroyed it, this more widely diffused and more violent as a result of this license, enslaves democracy. And in truth any excess is wont to bring about a corresponding reaction, . . . most especially in political societies . . . probably then tyranny develops out of no other constitution than democracy—from the height of liberty, I take it . . .the fiercest extreme of servitude."[40]

As for Aristotle, his remarks on the association of democracy and (negative) liberty seem nearly modern: "Now a fundamental principle of the democratic form of constitution is liberty—that is what is usually asserted, implying that only under this constitution do men participate in liberty, for they assert this as the aim of every democracy."[41] In his view, such "liberty" has value only as a condition for the development of the virtues. A good act done under compulsion cannot be called virtuous in any sense: "The virtues themselves are not done justly or temperately if they themselves are of a certain sort, but only if the agent also is in a certain state of mind when he does them: first he must act with knowledge; *secondly he must deliberately choose the act*, and choose it for its own sake; and thirdly the act must spring from a fixed and permanent disposition of character."[42]

Aristotle will, however, make the argument that negative liberty as an end in itself is a problematic ideal because of its essentially amoral character: "Liberty to do whatever one likes cannot guard against the evil which is in every man's character."[43]

The Stoics meanwhile drew upon another (albeit closely related) element of Socratic freedom, namely, independence (αὐτάρκεια) from external things, such as wealth, pleasure, and honor. Xenophon: "Socrates was living on very little, and yet was wholly independent [αὐταρκέστατα]; that he was strictly moderate in all his pleasures."[44] This is understood as a consequence of Socrates's single-minded focus on the goods of the soul, next to which all else is of little consequence. Socrates famously admonishes the Athenians: "Most excellent man, are you who are a citizen of Athens the greatest of cities and the most famous for wisdom and power, not ashamed to care for the acquisition of wealth [29e] and for reputation and honor, when you neither care nor take thought for wisdom and truth and the perfection of your soul?"[45]

In comparison with the supreme good that is the human soul, the possession of physical and external goods—pleasure, wealth, honor— are matters of indifference. Socrates tells us that no harm can come to a good man,[46] by which he means that physical pain, poverty, and unmerited dishonor are not true harms. Hence, Socrates argues in the *Gorgias* that it is far worse to inflict than to suffer injustice.[47] From the Socratic example, the Stoics drew their ideal of the wise man or sage (σοφός). Possessed with moral wisdom and virtue, the Stoic sage is an oasis of calm and tranquility in the face of life's constantly shifting fortunes. But this self-possession is hard-won; it requires the laborious work of mastering one's passions and enduring difficulties with equanimity.

Stoic freedoms include both freedom from the disturbances of the internal passions through virtuous self-mastery and freedom from being shaken by external events beyond one's power to control. Pierre Hadot describes the sage as having "an unconquerable, unalterable nucleus of freedom."[48] Seneca describes the same in terms of self-sufficiency, asking rhetorically, "What therefore is this soul? The one who possesses no good but its own" (Quis ergo his animus? Qui nullo bono nisi suo nitet),[49] and so is "unterrified in the midst of dangers, untouched by desires, peaceful amid the storm" (interritum periculis, intactum cupiditatibus, inter adversa felicem).[50] Of the sage, Diogenes Laertius comments that "he alone is free and bad men are slaves."[51] This is one of the "paradoxes" taken up by Cicero in his *Paradoxa Stoicorum*, which fittingly summarizes the concept of freedom in the classics. Speaking of the example of a general who must command others, he says, "But how or over what free man, will he exercise control who cannot command his own passions."[52]

It remains to consider the relation of freedom in the classical virtue tradition to Christianity—the world-historical religion that proclaims itself as the one Truth that sets men free.[53] Given Christianity's origins in Israel with its distinct biblical tradition, this brings us to the millennial question of Athens and Jerusalem. On the point of "freedom" as "freedom to do good," which is obstructed by the passions, Christianity and the ancient Greeks and Romans are in broad concord. Consider St. Paul on the problem of slavery to sin: "For I do not do the good I want, but the evil I do not want is what I do. Now if I do what I do not want, it is no longer I that do it but sin which dwells in me. . . . For I delight in the law of God in my inmost self, but I see in my members another war at law with the law of my mind and making me captive to the law of sin which dwells in my members. Wretched man that I am! Who will deliver me from this body of death?"[54]

Both the Socratic and Christian conceptions see man's fundamental condition as one of bondage to self-centered passions. But whereas classical antiquity saw liberation in naturalistic terms as a matter of cultivation in habits of virtue, Christianity regards the slavery to sin as more deeply rooted, a condition that requires the action of God (grace) to liberate man from its bondage. This was the polemic of St. Augustine against Pelagianism, which essentially reduced Christianity to classical naturalism. This difference is amplified in some forms of Christianity that have emphasized the radical nature of the fall (e.g., Calvinist), but it was narrowed in the synthesis of Aquinas, who aimed to reconcile Christianity and Aristotelianism. This is the Thomistic distinction between *natural virtue*, which lies within human power and is developed by habit, and supernatural or *theological virtue*, which is wholly gratuitous.[55] Here is a subtle but more significant distinction, perhaps, in the deepening Christian consciousness of the inherent value of the human person as a center of free activity. Aristotle's statement that the individual is related to the *polis* like limbs to the body[56] clashes with the Christian sensibility that sees the human person as having an eternal destiny of more value than the earthly polity. Augustine's *Civitas Dei*[57] decidedly desacralizes the state, connecting it with the sin of Cain, father of the earthly city, and fulfilling its office both as a consequence and remedy of sin. The Christian medieval world for all its reverence for Aristotle did not subsume all under the "polis," but was decentralized, fostering autonomous authorities and associations with independent powers of action (the Church, trusts, guilds, universities, free cities, decentralized feudal principalities, etc.). Liberalism arose in historical tension with Christianity, but it could legitimately be asked whether it could exist at all without the boundaries Christianity placed on the classical state.[58]

EDMUND BURKE AND CONSERVATIVE FREEDOM

By looking at the preeminent conservative figure of the English-speaking world, it will be possible to better understand freedom in the ideal of conservative humanism in contrast to Fukuyama's commercial liberty. Burke is an exemplar of Erasmus's Renaissance ideal of *docta pietas* ("learned piety"), that is to say, a devout Christian schooled in the classics. There is little question, of course, about his veneration for "the wisest writers of the old philosophy from the time of Stagyrite [Aristotle]" and "the practical politicks of antiquity, where they are brought more directly home to our understandings and bosoms in the History of Rome, and above all, in the writings of Cicero."[59] Yet many of his convictions sprung from a specifically Christian moral concern. It was this that animated his repulsion to the degradation of human dignity in the slave trade. In the classical world, the exclamation of Seneca, "'servi sunt' immo homines" ("they are slaves," people declare. Nay, rather, they are men),[60] was a rarity. Most followed Aristotle in seeing slavery as one of the natural forms of hierarchy and inequality.[61] For Burke the Christian, in contrast, there are no fundamental distinctions in intrinsic moral value and dignity among human beings. Hence, for Burke, the eventual abolition of slavery becomes a matter of religious principle. He called for the immediate amelioration of the cruelty of the practice as the practical and political difficulties were being sorted through:

> Whereas it is expedient, and conformable to the principles of true religion and morality, and to the rules of sound policy, to put an end to all traffick in the persons of men, and to the detention of their said persons in a state of slavery, as soon as the same may be effected without producing great inconveniences in the sudden change of practices of such long standing; and, during the time of the continuance of the said practices, it is desirable and expedient, by proper regulations, to lessen the inconveniences and evils attendant on the said traffick and state of servitude, until both shall be gradually done away.[62]

He was also, despite his support for the English Church establishment, an ardent defender of religious toleration.[63] Indeed, his repulsion at the anti-Catholic penal laws[64] earned him a reputation among his opponents as a crypto-Catholic in league with the Jesuits. Burke also regarded religious tolerance as fully compatible with a Christian kingdom. In addressing the question of Protestant Nonconformists, he writes: "I know nothing but the supposed necessity of persecution that can make an establishment disgusting. I would have toleration a part of establishment, as a principle favorable to Christianity, and a part of Christianity."[65]

On this point, Burke shares with the Enlightenment liberals their plea for religious tolerance (albeit not the demand for a secular state). Burke is friendly to other liberties outside the religious sphere: "I flatter myself that I love a manly, moral, regulated liberty as well as any gentleman of this society."[66] Burke's regard for modern "negative" freedoms comes out in his "Speech on Conciliation with the Colonies" (1775). Here he connects the American love of liberty with the specifically English tradition of limited government and inherited rights.[67] Burke's departure from modern liberalism rests principally on two points. First, Burke sees a dangerous emergent doctrine of the "sovereign individual." This would later manifest clearly in John Stuart Mill: "In that part which merely concerns himself, his independence is, of right, absolute. Over himself, over his own body and mind, the individual is sovereign."[68] We can see today this idea remains basic to the justification for the homicides of abortion and euthanasia—one's sovereign right over oneself. This is seen in the common slogans about "my body" and "my life" in defense of these practices, and in more sophisticated judicial arguments about a "fundamental right to privacy"[69] In contrast, Burke sets freedom in the context of a more Aristotelian understanding in which man is an inherently social being: "Permit me then to continue our conversation and to tell what the freedom is that I love. . . . It is not solitary, unconnected, individual, selfish liberty, as if every man was to regulate the whole of his conduct by his own will. The liberty I mean is social freedom."[70]

Second, Burke departs from the liberal framework by giving primacy to virtue over negative freedom. To have any value, and to be legitimately enjoyed, liberty must indeed aim at virtue: "What is liberty without virtue and wisdom? It is the greatest of all possible evils: for it is folly, vice, and madness, without tuition or restraint."[71] In tones reminiscent of Plato's argument that the unrestrained liberty of licentious democracy is self-negating and issues in tyranny, Burke expresses the conviction that only those who can master their own passions are fit for liberty: "Men are qualified for civil liberty in exact proportion to their disposition to put moral chains upon their appetites. . . . Society cannot exist unless a controlling power upon will and appetite be placed somewhere; and the less of it there is within, the more there must be without. It is ordained in the eternal constitution of things, that men of intemperate minds cannot be free. Their passions forge their fetters."[72]

The life of virtue can be called a more complete form of liberty, in the sense that mastery over the passions frees the will from their compulsive force, and therefore enables a positive liberty—the power to live the good life.

Without a strong framework of traditional institutions to educate members of the community in habits of moral virtue, negative liberty cannot be honorably enjoyed (a theme thoroughly on display at Hogwarts in *Harry Potter*). These will include all that falls under "establishment," including inherited institutions that involve social hierarchy. The hereditary nobility, with their stable property and high status, have independence enough to challenge despotism. Hence their privilege actually defends liberty (an argument similar to that defended by Kolnai). Of course, this is an ideal case—the aristocracy, like other factions in history who have enjoyed power, has often behaved in self-interested and even exploitative ways. Yet it remains nonetheless true that this position of privilege and economic independence, and their noblesse oblige, has allowed the aristocracy to be spokesmen for the voiceless and a hedge against centralized autocracy. Through the eighteenth and nineteenth centuries in Europe and Russia, many of the defenders of the peasantry, from Francois de Charette to Leo Tolstoy, were drawn from the ranks of the nobility.

Burke argues, turning to Cicero to defend the nobility, that the Jacobins wished to eradicate "nobility as a graceful ornament to the civil order. It is the Corinthian capital of polished society. *Omnes boni nobilitati semper favemus*, was the saying of a wise and good man."[73]

Mostly, however, Burke sees the supports for social order and habits of virtue (which allow also freedom to exist) in the trinity of tradition we discussed in the introduction—religion, family, and education.

In Burke's time, the educational formation of British and European gentlefolk still meant largely the Renaissance humanist curriculum of Greek and Latin authors in poetry, rhetoric, history, and philosophy.[74] Burke commends these "more liberal and elegant kinds of erudition,"[75] which refine and develop human excellence in terms of intellectual and moral qualities, aesthetic and literary taste. Concerning the family, we have already referenced in the introduction the importance Burke placed on it as a school for both the physical and moral continuance of society. Roger Scruton states that "conservatives believe, with Burke, that the family is the core institution whereby societies reproduce themselves and pass moral knowledge to the young."[76]

But the most important of the conservative trinity is religion, which Burke calls "the foundation of all civil society."[77] For all his love of the classics, Burke, like George Washington,[78] exhibits scant faith that society as a whole could be sustained merely based on education and moral philosophy without supernatural sanction for society's moral code. Burke, therefore, singles out for special ire the subversion of European Christianity by Enlightenment philosophes: "We are not the converts of Rousseau; we are not the disciples of Voltaire; Helvetius has made no progress amongst us. Atheists are not our preachers; madmen are not our lawgivers."[79]

Burke's anger stemmed from the danger that once religion is subverted, a society can enjoy neither order nor liberty nor peace. As if in grim prognostication of the totalitarian antihumanist ideologies of the twentieth centuries, Burke trembles at what may take the place of Christianity should it be allowed to weaken or fall:

> We know, and it is our pride to know, that man is by his constitution a religious animal; that atheism is against, not only our reason, but our instincts; and that it cannot prevail long. But if, in the moment of riot, and in a drunken delirium from the hot spirit drawn out of the alembick of hell, which in France is now so furiously boiling, we should uncover our nakedness by throwing off that Christian religion which has hitherto been our boast and comfort, and one great source of civilization amongst us, and among many other nations, we are apprehensive (being well aware that the mind will not endure a void) that some uncouth, pernicious, and degrading superstition, might take place of it."[80]

Burke's argument moves in the direction of what Daniel Mahoney has called "the conservative foundations of the liberal order."[81] To be secure in modern liberty, one needs "intermediate" institutions and associations—and so often these have a play character—between the individual and the state that foster freedom in the classical and Christian sense of virtuous self-mastery. Burke would surely agree with Aristotle's assertion that "any state that is truly so called and is not a state merely in name must pay attention to virtue,"[82] and he would disagree with the liberal position that the state is a mere contract to protect individual rights. However, the state's role becomes less necessary the more autonomous, traditional institutions thrive in inculcating habits of virtue, order, religion, family, classical education, and so forth. These traditional institutions need not oppose personal liberty, but may rather provide the morally ordered space for the negative freedoms of modern liberalism to thrive. Where the strong supports of religion, family, and education decline, liberalism becomes self-negating, anarchic, and tends to give way ultimately to various forms of illiberalism. This pattern of uncontrolled desires undermining freedoms and giving way to their opposite has been prognosticated in a sense since the time of Plato. It might appear to be played out today in the tendencies of contemporary society where the most dramatic forms of libertinism coexist with both an expansive state regulatory apparatus and the rise of an illiberal Left aiming to control the limits of acceptable thought and discourse.

CHAPTER 8

Conservatism without Reprimitivism

Thanks for the detective mags!
They are rich *in mental vitamins & calories.*

—Wittgenstein, Letter to Norman Malcolm

In his recent work, Francis Fukuyama has identified a reprimitivism at the heart of politics in the United States. Instrumental to the development of rule of law, he argues, was medieval inheritance law. Breaking kin networks, inheritance law divided property between disparate families, which facilitated agreements about equal protection under the law. Today, he argues, there is a regressive repatrimonialization afoot in the United States, participation in power being restricted to a limited set of elite families. The country's universities are complicit. Going to elite colleges is a proven path to political prominence. Leading political families have an uncanny ability to defy admission statistics and get their kids into the best colleges.[1] This is an example of what political scientists call *insider capture*. One might brush this off, but, as Fukuyama points out, the results are disastrous for the rest of the United States. He argues that the 2008 financial collapse was made worse by bad regulation. Some of the complex formulas of regulation were still being written three years after the legislation, the Frank-Dodd Act (2010), actually passed Congress! He argues the most easy and effective risk-abatement measures—demanding banks increase capital requirements and capping the size of banks—were not even considered. The reason is that in the United States rule is by janissaries, a tiny class fraction who,[2] by a revolving door, staff both banks and Congress.[3] Not rule of law, but rule by persons is back.[4]

In chapter 5, we saw Voegelin's argument that reprimitivism is a constant pressure on the West's politics, an ever-present threat of falling away from the differentiation of Christian liberty into Gnosticism. It is not just liberals and conservatives who fuss over reprimitivism. Marx invokes the idea, too. About labor estrangement, Marx writes:

> We have said above that man is regressing to the *cave dwelling*, etc.—but he is regressing to it in an estranged, malignant form. The savage in his cave—a natural element which freely offers itself for his use and protection—feels himself no more a stranger, or rather feels as much at home as a *fish* in water. But the cellar dwelling of the poor man is a hostile element, "a dwelling which remains an alien power and only gives itself up to him insofar as he gives up to it his own blood and sweat"—a dwelling which he cannot regard as his own hearth—where he might at last exclaim: "Here I am at home"—but where instead he finds himself *in someone else's* house, in the house of a *stranger* who always watches him and throws him out if he does not pay his rent. He is also aware of the contrast in quality between his dwelling and a human dwelling that stands in the *other* world, in the heaven of wealth.[5]

PRIMORDIAL POLITICS

Dugin welcomes primordialism. We think this a terrible strategy for conservatism. We have defended within limits native loyalties, but we are acutely conscious of the danger of atavistic or pagan tribalisms that have proven so destructive. And if we have critiqued the technoscience of the Enlightenment, we do not deny for a moment that many elements of the Enlightenment form part of a worthy development of humanism.

Ours is a conservatism of the *via media*. Enlightenment and conservatism is not an easy relationship, to be sure, but the tensions are no more pronounced than those between Christian humanism and its relationship to Athens and Rome.[6] In Catholic circles, Pope Benedict XVI dedicated his long intellectual career to examining which aspects of Enlightenment liberalism required backing.[7] His political sensibility is very much ours (see our concluding remarks chapter). In a like effort, chapter 5 argues that the division of labor theorized in the Industrial Enlightenment requires backing: a symbol of differentiation, the division of labor, despite significant issues, opens a social space for personalism to flourish. Conservative humanism is not authoritarianism. It must neither invite "the return of the strong gods"[8] nor be blind to the menace of reprimitivism.

This chapter explores the problem of reprimitivism in two parts. In the first, we return to Kolnai. His *The War against the West* (*WaW*) is our guide to why vitalism is so corrosive. Dugin's primordialism is only part of the problem, though. In the second, we examine the hidden threat of angelism within conservative humanism. The threat comes from an omission: the failure of Christian personalists to seriously consider issues raised by psychoanalysis.[9] Like Walter Benjamin and Jean-Pierre Dupuy, we think detective fiction important philosophically, especially its interest in psychoanalysis. We turn to this most widely consumed genre of fiction—and content of so much television and film—to better explore Scruton's idea that conservatism is alert to the role of conceits in good political order.[10] The ideal of the knight, endlessly played with inside the detective genre, as Chesterton points out, is a conceit that helps keep the primitive at bay.[11] A variant on knight-errantry, the detective is an Enlightenment invention[12] and, because against subversion, a conservative figure.

Chapter 2 rejected Dugin's turn to Heidegger. In Heidegger we see a German romantic tendency to reach back beyond Greek rationalism to a more primordial Greek *arche*, which is celebrated as chaotic and amoral. An example is Wagnerism and the cult of the old Germanic deities as part of a romantic-atavistic "return to roots."[13] Suspicious of rationality and moral judgment, people such as Dugin and Alain de Benoist (leader of the French New Right) favor tribalism. The French New Right is explicitly anti-Christian, seeing its universalism as the taproot of liberalism, and Dugin denounces the West's rationalism as inherently racist (*FPT*, 62–65). This chapter will show that despite rejecting fascism, a thinker such as Dugin reaffirms tribal egotism: in *The War against the West*, Kolnai identifies "tribal egotism" as the wellspring of National Socialism.[14]

War against the West (1938) was written in Vienna and put directly into English because Kolnai hoped to alert the Atlantic powers of their doom. The book has a distinctive method. Kolnai literally collected Nazi literature as it was being handed out in the streets and cafés of Vienna. Just as criminal profilers sketch serial killers to try to predict their next steps, so Kolnai sought to distill for Western governments, and especially for the British, the psychological, moral, and political profile of National Socialism. *War against the West* is surely the most detailed, analytical documenting of the thought-world of Nazism by a philosopher. His profile of the Nazis convinced him that the West had to go to war. Few were willing to listen: the United States did not join the war until it was attacked at Pearl Harbor by Japan in December 1941, more than two years after World War II started in Poland. Today, we tend to think of World War II as a matter of moral clarity, but its heroes, such as De Gaulle and Churchill, it must be remembered, came to power as hard-liners: they were thought suspect because they were absolutely opposed to compromise with Hitler. Into the war itself, Lord Halifax, and others, raised the possibility of compromise with Hitler, others even thought that National Socialism represented a radical diversity of opinion that had to be given space by any true liberal politics.

In 1938, there was no declared war, so what was the Nazi war against the West? In some quarters, people wondered if Nazism was a justified criticism of the West, a reform movement, perhaps, or even, as some Catholics catastrophically believed, a revival of the West. At issue, Kolnai argued, was not straightforwardly the open combat to come, but a revolutionary assault on the value structure of the West: its moral, political, metaphysical, and cultural convictions and tendencies were all put in dispute by National Socialism (*WaW*, 311). As a revolutionary movement it was peculiar, however. Mussolini's formula for fascism, "Liberty of real man: the liberty of the state and of man in the state" (*WaW*, 124), was far outstripped by Nazism's "weird idealism of tyranny" (*WaW*, 125). Nazi theorists such as Forsthoff announced uncompromising struggle "against liberty as a postulate of the human spirit" (*WaW*, 107), and Gogarten concluded, "A state rid of the *haut-goût* of evil would no longer be palatable to him" (*WaW*, 127).

Kolnai is careful to parse the political options on the right: he distinguishes conservatism, and even reaction, from Nazism, and Nazism from fascism. In his telling, conservatism tries to protect still-existing pockets of privilege from erosion by progressivism, while reaction tries to resuscitate abolished privilege (*WaW*, 107). By contrast, Nazism aims at a root-and-branch remaking of society, comparable in ambition to the French Revolution. It celebrates vitalism independent of all ennobling values that control and elevate our drives. National Socialism sought a "backward leap across the ages" (*WaW*, 122): "Negating, over and above liberalism, Christian civilization as such (the breeding-ground of Modernity and Progress), as well as the Faith which has informed it, together with some if not most of its sub-soil in Greco-Roman antiquity; and groping back, in its quest for 'rejuvenating' anti-modern traditions, across the Prussian glory of yesterday and the more brutal aspects of the German Middle Ages towards the barbarous world of Teutonic heathendom—not without a side-glance, in my opinion at any rate, at Hindu racialism and caste religion."[15]

Nazism sought to kneecap the entire tradition of Western humanism—not a single one of its pillars would be a landing pad for Hitler's "backward leap across the ages." Having moved race to the absolute center of its politics—Kolnai speaks of a "religion of race" (*WaW*, 122)—Nazism reduces persons to elemental forces and rids them of will, thought, autonomy, flair, and eccentricity. In consequence, the delicate spanning of personal appetite and civilizational offerings was eliminated in Nazi Germany. At stake in the war against the Nazi was, most fundamentally, the survival of human personality. In the writings of Edgar Jung, a Nazified nationalist, Kolnai discovers an astonishing complaint: "Fascism, in virtue of its Latin roots, is still deeply involved in individualist ways of thinking" (*WaW*, 129).

Kolnai defended Christian humanism as a safeguard of the person: "We believe that true community can be based only on personality, which is the irreducible core of human existence, with its susceptibility to moral elevation" (*WaW*, 65). Nazi celebration of tribe swallows this idea just as surely as it swallows the idea of a common humanity.

Punishment, Rosenberg declares, is not linked to persons transgressing objective standards but "the ejection of foreign types and of essence that is not kindred" (*WaW*, 36). Rolf Zimmermann, a modern commentator on Nazism, has spoken of the Nazi commitment to "a rupture of species," and Kolnai, glossing Gogarten, explains: "There is no being 'in oneself,' only a being 'for one another or against one another'" (*WaW*, 70, 294–95). "The soul merged unconditionally in the state, the state an epitome of sacredness" (*WaW*, 37). Throughout the book, Kolnai roundly criticizes Heidegger for fostering such formulations. In addition to subverting the ideas of personality and common humanity, contrary to what is commonly claimed, Nazism was bent on weakening the idea of nation. The Nazi state was not built on nation, but race, manifesting itself as tribe plus empire. Tribe demands intensification of loyalty, a band of brothers (the *männerbund*, "manring"). Tribe conceived as a race of masters demands mastery of others, thus an intensification of imperial ambition and expansion into space. The nation space as a home common to varied peoples linked in solidarity is jumped right over. This imperial vitality, naked of restraining values of person, nation, humankind, or transcendent God, evokes Kolnai's brilliant analysis of disgust. The disgusting is life out of place: life unrestrained, leering and smirking, proboscis-like, feeling its way toward one. Immorality is most strictly infractions against persons, and disgust leaps across all the fields of discretion that civilization opens for the free movement of personal interaction.[16] Tribal unity, what Kolnai calls "tribal egotism," simultaneously submerges distance among persons and precludes others from being persons. When Dugin plays with primordialism, he risks the abolition of humanism. Though he thinks the Enlightenment has spawned all manner of pathologies—and, in part, is certainly right—Dugin seems indifferent to the question whether primordialism rubs shoulders with the most original pathologies of the human spirit.[17]

THE POLITICS OF KNIGHT-ERRANTRY

Vitalism is a threat to conservatism, but so is abstraction. Schmitt's postliberal criticism of the twentieth century's appropriation of Francisco de Vitoria ably shows that abstraction can undermine dignity as fast as vitalism. Kolnai details the pernicious character of Nazi vitalism, but he ultimately saw communism as an even worse predator on human integrity. Its abstraction — mauling human life in its quest for "a unitary plan and wholly master of itself" — aimed at a "spiritual cemetery" more total than National Socialism.[18] Since distance from appetite is basic to civilization, some abstraction is necessary: the trick is not to slip into angelism.

Throughout, we have argued that the Christian purifying of ancient ideals of excellence was a signature development of humanism. Critical to that development was a theology of the image.[19] Axiomatic to Christian belief is that persons are made in the image of God. Humans are owed special protections because God has favored them to embody the truth, goodness, and beauty of the divine itself.[20] Particularly in Catholicism, this belief is affirmed in the claim that human reason is divine-like. It is part of the moral seriousness of Protestantism that it questioned this valorization. Protestantism reminded Catholicism of Augustine's vivid awareness of human wickedness. Karl Barth (d. 1968) argued that we have little capacity for knowledge without the restorative guidance of Christ. Without Christ, says Barth, the mind is "a perpetual forge of idols." By contrast, Catholic humanism argues for a degree of sufficiency in reason, a position Barth famously condemned as a doctrine of the Antichrist.[21] Barth's point is that naïvety (Christian humanism) is just as damaging to good politics as overloading on risk (Dugin). Catholic Renaissance humanists such as Erasmus battled the Reformation suspicion of human nature, but the suspicion took root. Humanism stands accused, and there is now a task to explain what Rémi Brague calls "the legitimacy of the human."[22] Ours is an argument for humanism, but there are plenty of people who think humans are the big problem. We think conservatives should freely own that humans are a morally precarious animal. This has been made patently obvious by psychoanalysis. Nonetheless, we are also a self-monitoring animal. The detective and his stories are an Enlightenment conceit[23] that, contra Barth, pits reason against predation.

Adam Ferguson, a member of the Scottish Enlightenment, argued that the theology of the image mitigated the cruelty of war. His *An Essay on the History of Civil Society* (1767) — a consequential work of political anthropology—demonstrates that the fables and romances a civilization uses to entertain itself can have dramatic influence on its mores. He gives the example of war and knight-errantry: "The hero of modern romance professes a contempt of stratagem, as well as of danger, and unites in the same person, characters and dispositions seemingly opposite; ferocity with gentleness, and the love of blood with sentiments of tenderness and pity."[24] The detective story is replete with heroes imitating the suffering servant: police officers broken by their willingness to suffer out of tenderness for victims.[25]

Walter Benjamin argues that Edgar Allen Poe inaugurated detective fiction as a meditation on the philosophy and science of pathological behavior.[26] Freud also describes Poe's work the same way.[27] The star of the show in Poe is the detective, Le Chevalier C. Auguste Dupin. A hyperintellectual and refined aristocrat, Dupin is also somewhat vampiric: curtains drawn closed all day, the chevalier only bestirs himself at night. However, as Benjamin observes, the chevalier is on the side of the light. He argues that though Baudelaire thought all great writing would have to follow the lead of Poe—being both philosophical and scientific—Baudelaire himself could not write detective fiction: the detective story puts an emphasis on the good, but he was a believer in the fecundity of evil.[28]

Scruton says that it is conservatism that best appreciates that we make sense of ourselves through playing with conceits. He argues that Hume was the first to see this clearly.[29] Hume's earliest essay was on the ideal of chivalry. In a modern register, the Gothic ideal becomes the gallant. Gallantry is necessary, Hume argues, because passions need refining. The human is a "variable animal," but not infinitely elastic. Progress in the passions is possible—"modern politeness, which is naturally so ornamental"—but the problem of power is invariant. Asymmetries of power exist between men and women, those at home and strangers abroad, young and old.[30] Gallantry smooths out these differences.[31]

The detective as a gallant is prominent in the genre. On personal terms with the highest in the land, Chevalier Dupin kicks off the theme.[32] The theme is prominent in the recent BBC hit *Sherlock*.[33] This iteration of *Sherlock* features not only the debonair man himself, but his brother, the chief of the British security establishment, clothed in Savile Row. The bookish and psychological Luther (yes, the TV script is penned by a one-time student of theology) fully combines the gallant and the suffering servant. The same is true of Stella Gibson in *The Fall*. Few figures have cemented their place in popular culture like Hannibal Lecter, aristocratic killer-turned-teacher-of-detection. The detective does not just embody Enlightenment ideals of refinement, but advances personalism. The dead need their rectifier:[34] Luther's estranged wife accuses him of being more in love with the dead than the living.

Neolithic paintings in caves, icons in basilicas, stories on Instagram—images, and the controversies around them—are the stuff of human life. Hume argues that the self is a feigning or disguise crafted by the imagination to cope with anxiety.[35] Dupuy sees something comparable in Hitchcock's *Vertigo*, where the detective, Scottie, has a "crushing revelation": "He realizes—viscerally, from the innermost depths of his being—that what he desired was only an *image* that had been fabricated by another" (emphasis original). Scottie's sense of self becomes inextricable from Madeleine, the heart of his "investigation." Yet, Madeleine is a fabrication: Scottie is caught in a "repetition automatism," images triggering a spiral of desire.[36] Dupuy relies on Lacan's idea that fantasy is sui generis, an organization of "perceptual objects" and desire detached from the pleasure and pain signals of our biological systems.[37] Poe inaugurates another motif of the genre: "It takes one to know one." The detective catches the crook because he is skirting the same pathologies. Dupin and Sherlock are intimates of the demimonde, Luther is ever on edge, and Will Graham is taunted by Lecter: "What are you dreaming of, Will?" There is a famous Lacan essay on Poe and a Lacanian schematics for how crime scenes could be typed by psychoanalytical concepts.[38] In detective fiction, personalism thoroughly escapes angelism.

Few embody the Enlightenment version of knight-errantry like Hercule Poirot: he also knows about psychoanalysis:

> Poirot's face fell, and he spoke very mildly. "I'm afraid I shall not be able to be of much aid to you, then?"
>
> "Next time perhaps," said the inspector soothingly. "Though we don't have murders everyday in this quiet little corner of the world."
>
> Poirot's gaze took on an admiring quality.[39]

American critic Edmund Wilson famously skewered the literary merits of detective fiction by asking, Who cares who killed Roger Ackroyd? His short essay surveying the genre did not actually discuss Agatha Christie's *Murder of Roger Ackroyd*, and had he done so, a deeper, civilizational point might have emerged.

The setting is a quiet village in England between the wars. Everyone knows everyone's business, and gossip about the crime flares as news spreads that the village's wealthiest man has been murdered. Solving the whodunit is a widely recognized image of popular culture: witness the Belgian dandy Poirot. The murder happens in Ackroyd's home, and the mystery unravels in a domestic setting of family, friends, and servants. Property, family, killing. Far from the ideal of the Holy Family, this unholy trinity is a staple of crime, real and fictional. Families are fraught, and Christian personalism seems to have lost sight of this. Scolding theologians, Schmitt argues that no theorist can be a true Christian thinker unless aware of the thoroughgoing wickedness of human nature.[40] Psychoanalysis is not caught unawares,[41] nor is Poirot.

In Agatha Christie, mild-mannered domestic life in the bucolic English countryside means a knife driven into the well-to-do neck of Roger Ackroyd:

> "Of course, he didn't do it," said Caroline, who had been keeping silent with great difficulty.
>
> "Ralph may be extravagant, but he's a dear boy, and has the nicest manners."
>
> I wanted to tell Caroline that large numbers of murderers have had nice manners, but the presence of Flora restrained me.[42]

Poirot knows manners can mask pathologies:

> "Then there is the psychology of a crime. One must study that."
>
> "Ah!" said the inspector, "you've been bitten with all this psycho-analysis stuff? Now, I'm a plain man."
>
> "Mrs. Ragland would not agree, I am sure, to that," said Poirot, making him a little bow. Inspector Ragland, a little taken aback, bowed.[43]

The earnest, "theory is nonsense" police inspector (PC Plod) is, in fact, like everyone in Christie's English village, a vessel of passions and, as Poirot cheekily points out, it is in the domestic sphere where this will be most apparent. Psychoanalysis is the claim that varied drives of the mind hobble self-possession, and that domesticity is horribly fraught. Psychoanalysis is also a theory of establishment and rule of law, especially in Lacan's hands. The invention of the detective is a figure in Lacan's Other.

Pope Francis warns that techno-ontology separates persons from anthropology.[44] Transhumanism dreams of an existence outside cosmos and history, yet personalism flirts with the same. Personalism has been a mainstay of humanism in the twentieth century, and its influence on the repeal of *Roe v. Wade* (June 24, 2022) cannot be gainsaid. In unguarded moments, though, Catholic personalism has a tendency toward angelism. Does personalism dodge the reality of the history of our desire? In his 1953 address to a conference on psychotherapy, Pius XII affirms "man always retains his freedom."[45] Similarly, Karol Wojtyła speaks of the person as "conscious efficacy."[46] The stakes are high, for Wojtyła argues that "only if one governs oneself can one make a gift of oneself, and this again a disinterested gift."[47] Yves Simon: "There is no doubt that in the ideally perfect exercise of free will the motivation would be entirely conscious. It can hardly be contested that without perfect coincidence between the motive of which I am conscious and the motive which really is effective, liberty is lessened somewhat."[48] *Somewhat*? That will depend on how desire is birthed. We agree with Julia Kristeva: a full account of persons cannot dispense with "the intermediary of psychoanalysis."[49] Pius XII gives the reason: "It is only man in the concrete that exists. And yet, the structure of this personal ego obeys in the smallest detail the ontological and metaphysical laws of human nature of which We have spoken above. They have formed it and thus should govern and judge it." According to Lacan, persons "in the concrete" are singularly shaped by the twin pressures of the name-of-the-father (the law) and contingencies of the mother tongue (desire). Lacan's is a profound and unsettling theory; nonetheless, conservative humanism can make good use of his account of desire. Tracey Rowland cautions that Catholic thought has not adequately theorized history. Rightly, neo-Thomism put an emphasis on ontology but, to be true to human experience, the role of history in personal and political identity needs theorizing.

In literary and philosophical circles there is an assumption that Jacques Lacan is a leftist.[50] He is certainly a darling of the Left, but is he a leftist? What he most definitely is not is a progressive, because he tells us again and again that psychoanalysis is not a progressive doctrine. Lacan holds himself to be the most accurate interpreter of Freud, the most astute developer of his legacy. About the politics of psychoanalysis, he says: "Freud was a humanitarian. . . . But, on the other hand, he wasn't a simpleton, so that one can say as well, and we have the texts to prove it, that he was no progressive. I am sorry but it's a fact, Freud was in no way a progressive. And as far as this is concerned, there are even some extraordinarily scandalous things in his writings."[51]

For Lacan, identity is the basic problem psychoanalysis addresses. Identity is fraught, inescapably mixed up with affirmation and aggression, the desire for recognition.[52] Lacan attended Kojève's lectures, which were very influential on Fukuyama, but he drew a very different lesson from them: not neoliberalism's one-mind angelism—peace through universal exchange of ideas and goods—but "castration":[53] by this term Lacan means that establishment (law) is necessary to curtail infant aggressivity. In management of aggression, ancestry looms large. For Lacan, all self-understanding is retrospective. Not only does our sense of self date to the early months of life, but the unconscious— the arbiter of understanding[54]—is like a language:[55] its rhetoric, names, meanings, metaphors, idioms, and symbols, come to us from the past, from establishment.[56] The term for establishment in Lacan is the *Other*, and looming large in the Other are family and property.

Tocqueville is surprised that political commentators do not dwell more on the influence of inheritance. He believes that the laws and mores of inheritance "should be placed at the head of all political institutions," for inheritance "divides, shares, disseminates property and power . . . it crushes or sends flying into pieces all that gets in its way."[57] The liberal conservative Tocqueville agrees with Lacan: there is no self-understanding independent of family and property. However, Tocqueville, unlike Lacan, thinks that political management of inheritance can modify the mores of family and make domestic manners milder. Where law makes persons equal, symmetry becomes a platform for sympathy: "I think that as mores and laws are more democratic, the relationships of father and son become more intimate and milder; rule and authority are encountered less often."[58] Psychoanalysis is a critical corrective of the Tocqueville's conservative naïvety: in democratic humanism,[59] "the father is, in the eyes of the law, only a citizen older and richer than his sons."[60] For Lacan, the father is never merely just older and richer, he is always a lawgiver.[61] Human desire is "bound up since the dawn of history with the imago of the father."[62] The reason is that the father is the root of sympathy and moral order. The father, argues Lacan, is the vehicle by which the narcissistic child "transcends himself in a normative sublimation."[63]

Why do "cherubic" infant narcissists need to submit to norms? Children first take shape psychologically in what Lacan famously termed "the mirror stage." Made in the image of God we might be, but that image is complex and delicate. A child's fascination in front of a mirror is the self's "original dereliction."[64] Apes and chimpanzees do not experience this fascination. For the infant, it is both a jubilant and bleak experience. Gesturing, the child mimics the image in the mirror, falls in love with it, in fact, but also picks up on something eerie: the image is more pulled together and glamorous than the child. The infant experiences interiorly the motor difficulties of a still-maturing and incompetent body. This experience of love (narcissism) is accompanied by jealousy (aggression). *Pace* Tocqueville, fathers are not mild because children are not mild. Every child casts "out onto the world the disorder that constitutes his being."[65]

The vast book and TV industry dedicated to crime fiction is a vapor trail to the aggression and macabre fascinations that inhabit all our psyches. A central plank of conservatism is law and order. The detective protecting establishment saves us from tipping into primitivism. We think Chesterton is right to speak of the detective as an example of knight-errantry. It is a conceit civilization needs, and it is vividly on display in the opening image of Raymond Chandler's noir novel *The Big Sleep*. Entering the property of the family he is to help out, private detective Philip Marlowe observes a stained glass representation of a knight untying the bonds of a captive woman. Rank gallantry maybe, but Hume is surely correct to say that, on account of the problem of the passions, there is a need for "the appearance of sentiments different from those to which [persons] naturally incline."[66]

Concluding Remarks

The Benedict Synthesis

Conservative humanism is a defense of the West. A question we hope to have resolved is which iteration of "the West" conservatives wish to defend. An irony of the historical moment in which the West's technology and economics appeared ascendant was the fracturing of Western identity itself.[1] According to Fukuyama, "the West" should be understood as a liberal commercial idea: a civilizational order expressing Enlightenment cheer about democracy, individual rights, free markets, and technological advancement. This vision was promoted as a global idea, the lynchpin of a universalist, international order. "The West" in a certain sense then is bound to dissolve itself into the universal liberal civilization its destiny is to forge. This narrative about the West we have called *progressivist*—it regards liberal modernity as superior to and superseding all earlier Western understandings. Progressivism introduces an element of discontinuity: liberalism breaks from the premodern past, repudiating the spiritual and intellectual roots of Western civilization. Certainly, liberalism has made genuine contributions to humane living, including increases in material conditions and toleration—but is it enough? Is economic vitalism, technology, disenchantment, and liberal autonomy truly a self-sustaining source of values for the West?

Our sense of the West stands closer to the traditionalist view. Perhaps the most illustrious contemporary example is Benedict XVI

175

(Joseph Ratzinger). Benedict's thinking on Europe identifies continuities between the Greek, Roman, Christian, and modern.

In his Regensburg Address (2006), Benedict defended the roots of Europe:

> This inner rapprochement between Biblical faith and Greek philosophical inquiry was an event of decisive importance not only from the standpoint of the history of religions, but also from that of world history—it is an event which concerns us even today. Given this convergence, it is not surprising despite its origins and some significant developments in the East, finally took on its historically decisive character in Europe. We can also express this the other way around: this convergence, with the subsequent addition of the Roman heritage, created Europe, and remains the foundation of what can rightly be called Europe. [2]

Here, Europe is a great creative synthesis. Christianity has its origins in the East (i.e., in Israel, the Middle East), and yet only by turning to the West (i.e., to Europe, the Greco-Roman world) did Christianity assume "its historically decisive character." The synthesis that developed between the Semitic monotheism of Christianity's origins and the classical European world is therefore for Benedict not coincidental, but providential. Mindful of our earlier discussions of how Nietzsche, Heidegger, and Holland understand the ancients, the role of Greek rationality[3] in Pope Benedict's thinking is noteworthy: "The distinguishing mark of Greek philosophy was that it did not rest content with traditional religions or with the images of the myths; rather, in all seriousness, it put the question about truth. So perhaps at this point we may be able to recognize the hand of providence—why the encounter between the faith of the Bible and Greek philosophy was truly 'providential.'"[4]

To Benedict's mind, so complete was the encounter that he speaks of only "the two great cultures of the West, that is, the culture of the Christian faith and that of secular rationality."[5]

Christianity inherited from Judaism the worship of the one God and its abhorrence of idolatry. Under the Maccabees in the second century B.C., Israel fought to preserve its monotheistic culture from inroads of Hellenistic paganism. Following in the footsteps of Maccabean anti-Hellenism, there have always been elements within Christianity that have viewed the intellectual and aesthetic traditions of the Greco-Roman world with suspicion. Tertullian asked, "Quid ergo Athenis et Hierosolymis? quid academiae et ecclesiae?"[6] (What has Athens to do with Jerusalem? The Church with the Academy?). Martin Luther saw himself as taking up again the cause of the Maccabees against the Catholic scholastics: "What are the universities, as at present ordered, but, as the book of Maccabees says, 'schools of "Greek fashion" and "heathenish manners"' (2 Macc. iv. 12, 13), full of dissolute living, where very little is taught of the Holy Scriptures of the Christian faith, and the blind heathen teacher, Aristotle, rules even further than Christ?"[7]

It is precisely against this type of de-Hellenizing Christianity that Benedict insists that "critically purified Hellenism forms an integral part of the Christian faith."[8] There are grounds for this conviction. The beginning of St. John's Gospel presents Christ as the λόγος. The term is of absolutely central importance in Greek thought. Heidegger is fascinated by the term and postulates the idea of a more archaic etymology of the term as related to "gathering" and "harvest."[9] Heidegger's etymology is much debated.[10] We need not share Heidegger's preference for the privileged validity of the archaic. It seems clear in Heraclitus and, certainly, in the Stoics that the Greek λόγος is the external word that expresses the inward mind,[11] and at the level of natural theology is the divine reason (Word) indwelling and manifest in the cosmos. Christ is the historical fulfillment of Israel's messianic hope. But concerning the λόγος, Christianity is the most "logocentric" religion, contends Benedict, but also something novel:[12] "This is the real innovation of Christianity: The Logos, the truth in person, is also atonement, the transforming forgiveness that is above and beyond our capability and incapability."[13]

A completely de-Hellenized Christianity for Benedict is therefore false to the essence of Christian faith itself. For this reason, Benedict criticizes all that rejects Hellenic philosophical rationality as evinced in important strains within Islam, Protestantism, and even Enlightenment philosophy. Turning the tables on the Enlightenment caricature of Christianity as a "superstitious" religion to which it counterposed the rationalism of the *philosophes*, Benedict proposes that authentic Christianity is the religion of *Logos* and is in a way more rationalist than the rationalists.[14] The real problem is the Enlightenment's "modern self-limitation of reason,"[15] evident in the positivist and materialist doctrines of the period. Unlike Greek rationality, these doctrines exclude metaphysical speculation about persons and ethics, hoping to confine the rational to the scientific-empirical sphere alone so as to maximize technical mastery.[16] In this impoverished view of reason, the most important questions that for the Greeks and Christianity lie within the ordinary domain of philosophical rationality—metaphysics, soul, natural law, the virtues, and God—are excluded by modern scientism as outside the domain of possible rational knowledge. Not only does this falsify the scope of reason, but practically it stokes the irrationalisms of religious and scientistic fundamentalism.[17] Thus, the mission of the Church, insists Benedict, is to demythologize: "Many deities of the world religions are terrifying, cruel, egoistic, or impenetrable."[18] And not just deities, but ideologies, such as the "super-dogma" of relativism:[19] "Demythologization is urgently needed so that politics can carry on its business in a genuinely rational way."[20]

THE BENEDICT SYNTHESIS AND THE LEGACY OF THE GREEKS

Compare Benedict's accommodation of Hellenism to Heidegger's curious and one-sided return to Greek archaism. This return is the launch point for Dugin's Eurasianism. The fundamental question for Heidegger is "the question of Being" (*Seinfrage*), which, for Heidegger, is not a metaphysical question. In the traditional, Aristotelian categorization that passed into the scholastic and rationalist traditions, ontology would be a form of metaphysics.[21] Yet for Heidegger, the whole tradition of Western metaphysics starting with Plato marks a falling away from the question of Being to the question of beings (the ontological difference), and so missed the mark. Heidegger acknowledges Plato as the originator of Western metaphysics, but he reads this tradition as a history of nihilism, that is, the forgetfulness of Being. Plato rethinks the problem of Being in terms of the Eternal Ideas, and then sets up an alternate immutable metaphysical realm that can be attained by the soul, in contrast to the shadowy temporal world. Heidegger agrees with Nietzsche that Christianity took over Platonic metaphysics by distinguishing between an eternal heavenly realm and a temporal earthly one: "Only with the sophists and Plato was seeming explained as, and thus reduced to, mere seeming: At the same time Being as *idea* was elevated to the supersensory realm. The chasm, *khorismos*, was torn open between the merely apparent beings there below, and the real Being up there. Christian doctrine thus established itself in this chasm . . . so Nietzsche was right to say that Christianity is Platonism for the people."[22]

Heidegger thus jettisons both Christianity and Greek metaphysics and instead proposes a return to an "originary experience"[23] of Being to be found in the pre-Socratics. Like Nietzsche, Heidegger's glorification of Hellas is ironic. They both dismiss the main throughline of Greek metaphysics—Platonic, Aristotelian, Stoic—consigned by Heidegger to a "fall" that leads ultimately to the nihilism of modernity. Nor does Heidegger exhibit any concern for Greek virtue ethics (or perhaps ethics generally!), which for him is bound up with the initial Platonic error: "'ethics' appeared for the first time in the school of Plato. These disciplines arose at a time when thinking was becoming 'philosophy' . . . science waxed and thinking waned."[24]

The closest Heidegger has to an ethic is his discourse of "authenticity," which is arguably the ancestor of contemporary claims to privilege the personal, existential "lived experience" against any objective order of truth.

For Heidegger, the European tradition of humanism is a Roman distortion of the Greeks: "The so-called Renaissance of the fourteenth and fifteenth centuries in Italy is a *renascientia romanitatis*. Because *romanitas* is what matters, it is concerned with *humanitas* and therefore with Greek *paideia*. But Greek civilization is always seen in its later form and this itself is seen from a Roman point of view."[25]

A partial corrective to Heidegger's amoralist ontology is found in Leo Strauss. Concerned with the lack of ethics in Heidegger's influential philosophy,[26] Strauss privileges not the Eleatic question of Being but the Socratic question of "the good life." For Strauss, Socrates is the originator of political philosophy,[27] for all politics is concerned with the good.[28] The key question is "natural right": the Socratic confidence that philosophical reason can apprehend moral truths grounded in nature, and hence they are universal rather than rooted in mere convention.

The crisis of modernity for Strauss stems from two sources. First is the dominance of scientific positivism, which excludes the question of the good from its purview (Strauss here has the same concern as Benedict XVI). Second is the rise of historicism (epitomized by Heidegger), which argues against natural right because man's being is so radically historical that the human mind cannot escape its temporality to lay hold of any transcendent moral good.[29] The abandonment of natural right generates the crisis of liberalism, which no longer believes in any overarching Good, but only in the right of each individual to determine the good for himself or herself.[30]

Relativism must ultimately undermine liberalism itself,[31] since liberalism cannot establish its absolute value vis-à-vis other forms of political order. Strauss, therefore, proposes a return to the ancients with their affirmations of classical natural right, virtue, a noncontractarian view of politics,[32] and a belief in social hierarchy against the "permissive egalitarianism" of the moderns.[33]

Many of Strauss's concerns dovetail with conservative humanism. However, Strauss is unlike Benedict, for he thinks the Greeks and the Bible are in the final analysis essentially incompatible. He thinks each has a different understanding of the good life (the philosophical life of inquiry versus obedience to God), and thus one excludes the other: "So philosophy in its original and full sense is then certainly incompatible with the Biblical way of life. Philosophy and the Bible are the alternatives or the antagonists in the drama of the human soul. Each of the two antagonists claims to know or to hold the truth, the decisive truth. The truth regarding the right way of life. But there can only be one truth: hence conflict between these claims and necessary conflict among thinking beings; and that inevitably means argument."[34]

Where Strauss sees conflict, by contrast,[35] Benedict see harmony: the New Testament, he says, "bears the imprint of the Greek spirit."[36] Many of the topics we have discussed, including metaphysics, value hierarchy, and natural law, involve implicitly the anthropological assumption we find already in the Greco-Roman world that human nature is naturally ordered to the transcendent values of truth, goodness, and beauty.[37] About this anthropology, Benedict says, "There are then, let us say, self-subsistent values that flow from the essence of what it is to be a man, and are therefore inviolable: no other man can infringe them."[38]

THE BENEDICT SYNTHESIS AND
THE ENLIGHTENMENT

To the modern ear, talk of human essence exhibiting "self-subsistent values" will inevitably sound like human rights. Benedict thinks human rights stem from medieval natural law, but they have mutated. Fed through Rousseau, human rights now express not a common nature, but an ideal of individual subjectivity.[39] Now rights are corrosive of solidarity, the very thing they were meant to secure.[40] In fact, they are an example of the pathology of modern rationality.

There was nothing straightforward about the Christian appropriation of ancient humanism. Recalling Augustine's conversion, Benedict states, "To become a Christian, Augustine—and the Graeco-Roman world—had to make an exodus, through which they were of course given back anew what they had lost."[41] That journey took centuries and was full of twists and turns of continuity and discontinuity. Benedict is a traditionalist but, on account of his theological rationalism, identifies common cause with Enlightenment reason. Chapter 5—where we showed Smith's account of the division of labor as a support of humanism—was designed as an illustration.

For Benedict, the Enlightenment "contains important values that are essential for us, precisely as Christians, and we do not wish to do without them."[42] University Catholicism[43] tends to dismiss this continuity, and political Catholicism tends to overstate it (e.g., Republican Party politics in the United States). Benedict argues that the founders of the EU—the Christians Konrad Adenauer, Charles De Gaulle, Alcide De Gasperi—believed there was significant consistency between the Christian heritage of Europe and "the great moral impulses of the Enlightenment." Benedict is less convinced, believing that "questions were left open that still await a proper examination."[44] From Descartes to Leibniz (and even Smith), early modern philosophy was suffused with theology, but this is not true of what Benedict calls the second Enlightenment, wherein "man as a product is subject to the control of man."[45] Though the connection between the first and second Enlightenment is what Benedict thinks obscure, the goals of the latter are crystal clear. The tool of the second Enlightenment is technoscience, and its application is to make suffering disappear.[46] It is a Gnosticism: "At the heart of the redemptive process lies, not the suffering and death of Christ, not the crucifixion, but the 'message concerning the holy path,' the teaching. The illumination comes, not through pain, but through the communication of knowledge."[47]

In chapter 5, we argued that it is not capital but Gnosticism that is a competitor with Christianity.[48] The second Enlightenment is a Gnostic project of emancipation from establishment,[49] especially religious. Helvetius writes: "What does the history of religions teach us? That religions have kindled the torch of intolerance everywhere. They have filled the plains with corpses, bathed the countryside with blood, destroyed cities, devastated empires . . . religions have never improved men."[50] The French philosophes were apt to blame religion rather than human nature for the violence they condemned.[51] They imagined the secular future as a Pollyanna of endless progress: the idea of "absolute production" figures in both Fukuyama and Marx. The philosophes were keenly aware of Europe's history of religious wars and persecutions, but of course they knew nothing of the even greater destruction that would one day be wrought by secular ideologies. More remarkably, given our greater historical experience, the Enlightenment's belief that religion per se is the source of violence has survived two world wars, the Nazi Holocaust, Soviet Gulags, and Pol Pot's killing fields of decidedly atheistic communism, "the greatest system of slavery in modern history."[52] As we see with Fukuyama, the naïve Enlightenment confidence in progress appears to have survived the carnage of the twentieth century with little more than minor bruises.

Liberalism, secular and democratic-egalitarian, is clearly not reducible either to the aristocratic ethos of the classical world nor the piety and humility of the Christian ideal, and so Benedict sees in the discontinuity of the second Enlightenment the danger of severing the West from its own foundations: "Above all, however, we must affirm that this Enlightenment philosophy, with its related culture, is incomplete. It consciously cuts off its own historical roots, depriving itself of the powerful sources from which it sprang. It detaches itself from what we might call the basic memory of mankind, without which reason loses its orientation, for now the guiding principle is that man's capability determines what he does."[53]

The civilizational divide today, argues Benedict, is not between the great religions, but between them and secular reason, which they judge alienated from nature and cosmos.[54] All the great religions hold fast to "the basic memory of mankind," that we live by gift:[55] "The book of nature is one and indivisible: it takes in not only the environment but also life, sexuality, marriage, the family, social relations."[56] Having lost the orientation to solidarity gifted by religion, technoscience[57] has introduced a new slavery, featuring widespread abuse of early human life and human trafficking.[58] In this sense, genuine conservatism has always been "Aristotelian" in affirming the naturally communal nature of the human being; a point that dovetails with the solidarity and relationality of Catholic social thought:[59] "God is three, and God is one: he is not eternal solitude."[60] The Enlightenment militated for equal human dignity, the basis of its most fruitful reforms, but where does the idea of human dignity come from? Empirically, human beings are clearly unequal in intelligence, ability, power, wealth, and strength. It is only as a theological-moral proposition deriving historically from Christianity that the West's idea of human dignity assumes coherence. Not, "The result is that man no longer accepts any moral authority apart from his own calculations."[61] But, a bowing attitude:[62] "Responsibility would then mean living our existence as a response—as a response to what we are in truth."[63]

The Benedict Synthesis between Nationalism and Internationalism

The West is losing credibility. China knows the most woke companies in the United States will be submissive as soon as profits are threatened;[64] Russia is reverting to its ancient self-image as the Third Rome and outflexing the West, confidently expanding militarily, commercially, and religiously into Turkey and the Middle East;[65] the shenanigans around confirming the Brexit vote confirmed for many the belief that the EU is antidemocratic, and it nearly shredded the legitimacy of Britain's Parliament; and in the United States, rule of law is eroding, while severe economic disparities birth neofeudalism.[66] To all this can be added the West's "culture of repudiation."[67]

Chapter 6 and 7 situate conservative humanism between liberal internationalism and nationalism. A *via media*, it is a salve for today's antagonisms, which are not simply rhetorical. Ours is a theoretical position built from Anglo-Continental conservatism. There is a tendency in some conservative quarters to think pragmatically: intellectual coherence does not matter as long as you win elections.[68] What is the point of winning elections if you lose the culture and also do not stand for anything coherently conservative? In most European countries, center-right parties have conceded more and more cultural issues to gain power—dropping opposition to abortion, quietly accepting same-sex marriage, and, implicitly, the revolutionary anthropology it supposes,[69] crony capitalism and the financialization of the economy, the militarization of the police, the growth of the managerial state, end runs around double jeopardy—and predictably new rightist movements have arisen, some animated by ideas we argue against here.

Throughout, Scruton aids our reflection on conservative humanism as an ideal to make a whole of the West. Indeed, humanism has played this role for two millennia, but it has mutated in ways unacceptable to the Right. Conservative humanism affirms the nation-form, the shape of the land crafted by peoples over centuries, and their sensibility raised into an established order. We do not concede the metaphysics of Dugin, but, like Benedict,[70] we do understand the conservative impulse his ideas express. Thinkers as diverse as Aquinas, Hume, and Scheler have all observed an *ordo amoris*. The world over, people love what is close to them: it is a world-datum that people cherish family and the local football team. This attachment is expressed in privileged duties toward spouse, kin, fellow-citizens, coreligionists.[71] People care for the land about them and are proud of their institutions and festivals. The *ordo amoris* has two accents, however: particular/privileged loves, and a hierarchy of obligations that are ultimately not regional. Conservative humanism is an ideal. Historically, until very recently, classical and Christian humanism was the core of the West's educational institutions. We argue this was not happenstance. Humanism expresses an ideal of human development, a matter of manners and morals. Framing the ideal was natural law, which was basic to legal reflection in the West for a thousand years: we have inherited rule of law from it. Natural law is no mere formalism; we have shown how it is present on the football field and at the opera. Establishment—the schools, associations, corporations, trusts, and institutions of kingdom and nation—express a value order obedient to the *ordo amoris*: the local shape of life is always tracing a universal law and can be corrected by it. We agree with Fuku-yama, therefore: the universal is crucial. However, we dispute his treat-ment of its content and scope.

Liberalism's mangled relationship to nature, "the basic memory of mankind," hobbles that tradition's account of rights. Manent argues that the liberal version of human rights theory is predicated upon secu-lar humanism's claim that we have no nature.[72] Transsexualism (now ex-pressed as transgenderism—the belief that the body is not determinative of sexual identity, which can be freely chosen) is the latest iteration of the claim, and it has metaphysical roots. Transsexualism—an axiom for today's progressive Left—rejects the idea that someone might suffer body dysmorphia, because, like Descartes, it rejects the idea of sub-stantial form.[73] Aquinas argued that the intelligibility of the world that we give voice to in our classification systems is a consequence of *forma*: metaphysical logics shaping animals, tress, quarks, and gluons (Aris-totle's *morpha*). Descartes, in his deliciously cunning wax example, ar-gued that physical reality was just extension taking on and off variation (modes) due to quanta of force. Nothing more—and certainly no meta-physical furniture like substantial forms—is needed to measure the ob-served phenomena. Transsexualism reiterates the point: the *res cogitans* looks across at the *res extensa* and sees no more than mere extension (otherwise known as the body) able to be varied through money buy-ing the application of surgical patented technologies of force. The trans-sexual who thinks her body is her own is articulated by the property of drug companies, hospitals, and surgeons. Woke capitalism is no differ-ent: the world has neither geography nor value structure: money can be deployed to reshape property and compel new political order. This is why we stated that progressivism is not sui generis, it is merely a vari-ation of Fukuyama's liberal commercial internationalism. Progressivism is a doctrine of money bolted onto a metaphysics of angelism, as Dugin rightly intuits.

THE BENEDICT SYNTHESIS AND REPRIMITIVISM

Chapter 8 links the conservative anxiety about law and order to the phenomenon of reprimitivism, a particular concern of Benedict XVI's.[74]

We explained that reprimitivism can stem from vitalism and angelism, and we examined the phenomenon in relationship to crime and rule of law. Conservatism is also worried about the coarsening of civilization, sex and education being two examples.

An absolute of contemporary liberalism is that religion and morality are entirely separate things, and thus a humanistic atheism is coherent. Like most conservatives, we think not only today's damaged family a refutation of this claim, but that the prevalence of abortion has subverted rule of law.[75] Traditional Christian moral theology sees heterosexual, monogamous marriage as the one exclusive locus for the morally ordered expression of sexuality and the parenthood to which it naturally gives rise. Though arising from its own religious self-understanding, things akin to the Christian ideal of sexuality, marriage, and family are found in diverse civilizations across the globe and throughout history.[76] Natural law, of course, is the reason. For centuries, the Christian sexual ideal was a corner stone of Western civilization. In the twentieth century, secular movements, combined with contraceptive technology, have overthrown this ideal.[77] By the late twentieth century, the critique of the traditional family was reified in vast legal reforms. Enlightenment ideals of liberty (understood as "the sovereign individual") and equality (particularly of women and homosexuals) provided the justification. Many reforms were well warranted, but the continuance of humanistic civilization is, as Christopher Dawson predicted,[78] now an open question. Physical continuity itself is not even guaranteed.[79] Upending traditional sexual politics has brought real harm, borne disproportionately by women, children, the unborn, and has coarsened the culture. Hence the unborn child is all too often a kind of human sacrifice to sustain a revolution. From the Marquis de Sade to psychoanalysis, clarity about antinatalism's desanctification of the human has been on offer, yet few have paid much attention.

In chapter 2 we argued that Dugin's adoption of Heidegger's vitalistic thinking ensures that his conservatism is antihumanistic. If liberal commercialism eschews nature and takes a misstep, then Dugin's vitalism takes a misstep in another direction. Nietzsche and Holland see the classical Greco-Roman world as steeped in an unapologetically aristocratic,[80] inegalitarian ethos, which Christianity upends by proclaiming with a crucified God, "the last shall be first." They take different views on the value of this moral revolution. Nietzsche complains bitterly; Holland is grateful—it made us woke. Holland suggests then that Christianity is an ally of progressivist egalitarianism. Isn't the ethos of siding with the weak underdog against the privileged and powerful precisely the Christian rooted moral sentiment that the Left constantly mobilizes? This is ironic, of course, for the Left is routinely more actively hostile to Christianity than to the classical tradition of hierarchy, whose moral outlook is altogether alien to it.

Certainly, we are not the Greeks alone. In the government buildings of Washington, DC, Enlightenment classicism is at its grandest. Someone might propose that we are better than past inhabitants of the West, because they were Christians, but we are heirs to the rational clarity and humanity of Greece and Rome. Indeed, such a person might be very assured, for the message that Christianity stunts and twists is spread widely abroad. Yuval Harari:

> In the 300 years from the crucifixion of Christ to the conversion of Emperor Constantine, polytheistic Roman emperors initiated no more than four general persecutions of Christians. Local administrators and governors incited some anti-Christian violence of their own. Still, if we combine all the victims of all these persecutions, it turns out that in the three centuries, the polytheistic Romans killed no more than a few thousand Christians. In contrast, over the course of the next 1,500 years, Christians slaughtered Christians by the millions to defend slightly different interpretations of the religion of love and compassion.[81]

This boilerplate stuff of the global liberal, tolerant polytheists versus maniacal monotheists, is the principal target of Benedict's historical and rationalist theology. The caricature owes much to the German philosophers Nietzsche and Heidegger, who both sought a return to the ancients. About Christianity falsity, Nietzsche writes:

> Here you can have an unobserved view into this dark workshop. Wait just another moment, my dear Mr. Daredevil Curiosity: your eyes must first get used to this false shimmering light. . . . There! All right! Now tell us! What is going on down there?

There is a cautious, sly, soft mumbling and whispering coming from all corners. It seems to me that lies are being told; a sugary sweetness clings to every sound. Weakness is to be transformed into a merit.[82]

Nietzsche had other preferences: "It appears to me that the delicacy, even more the hypocrisy of tame domestic animals (by this, I mean modern man, I mean us) is loath to envisage to what extent cruelty constituted the great festivity and pleasure of mankind in earlier days, and even an ingredient in almost all of its pleasures."[83]

Holland, disturbed by ancient cruelty and happy to be a kind-hearted, benevolent humanitarian, views the Christian revolution differently. As Benedict puts it, without Christianity, and the other world religions,[84] "how is respect for man—even the one who is conquered, weak, suffering, or handicapped—to survive?"[85] Not because we are heirs to Athens, we are kinder than people of past ages because the Christian revolution is even further along. Western and, indeed, world history are best viewed as ruptures wrought by a series of Christian revolutions making us all more benevolent: "To dream of a world transformed by a reformation, or an enlightenment, or a revolution is nothing exclusively modern. Rather, it is to dream as medieval visionaries dreamed: to dream in the manner of a Christian."[86]

Thus, as moderns we are more than what the Greeks and Romans bequeathed; we are heirs also of Christianity and the specifically modern developments. Yet whatever its shortcomings, the antique form of humanism retains perennial value for conservative humanism in its ideal of reason and human excellence, which manifested across the whole range of human endeavors. It was the Greeks who set for all Europe an enduring standard in philosophy, mathematics, science, drama and poetic literature, political thought, art and architecture. Hellenism has moreover been a living tradition for the West, which has in new and combined forms continually fertilized European arts and sciences through the centuries. Rome's golden age of Latin literature was directly inspired by Greek letters. The rediscovery of Aristotle in the twelfth century fueled the rise of medieval scholasticism, culminating in Aquinas and Dante. Classical revival in the Renaissance would inspire the great flowering of the arts and letters.

At the time the American frontier opened in the nineteenth century, "education" still meant the same thing as it did among the Renaissance humanists: the study of the best Greek and Roman authors in their original languages. To take a typical example, even to be admitted as a freshman at the University of Virginia in the late 1700s and early 1800s required demonstrating mastery in the following: "in the Latin language, Virgil, Sallust, and the Odes of Horace; in the Greek, the New Testament, Lucian's Dialogues, Xenophon's Cyropaedia, and the Graeca Minora of Dalzel. The course of study embraces the highest Greek and Latin classics, with Grecian and Roman antiquities."[87]

Dickinson College also focused on humane letters. Freshmen year: Sallust and Horace in Latin and Xenophon in Greek; Sophomore: Cicero and Horace in Latin, Xenophon and Euripides in Greek; Junior: Cicero, Juvenal, and Perseus in Latin, Sophocles and Euripides in Greek; and Senior: Aeschylus in Greek, Tacitus and Terence in Latin.[88] The classical languages and humane letters were prized as models of excellence, which helped to refine and perfect the intellectual, aesthetic, and moral characters and abilities of future leaders. But also because they rooted students in the languages and cultures that represented the common roots of Western civilization, the common reference points of its leading, educated classes regardless of nationality. After World War I, as education in the United States democratized, the classics were gradually demoted to a specialized field for scholars and replaced by the Western civilization survey course,[89] or the Great Books program of Mortimer Adler and Robert Hutchins. This type of modernized humanities education often supposed a list of literary, scientific, historical, and philosophical texts deemed seminal to the development of Western civilization, which one read in English translation, and included many modern European and American authors. Starting in the 1960s and culminating in the 1980s, this kind of course came under sustained attack on the grounds that Western civilization and such a Eurocentric curriculum excluded the marginalized voices of women, minorities, and non-Western cultures (thereby ironically expressing, as Holland might say, a rather unique Western-Christian preference for the underdog). At worst, the argument was heard that Western civilization is an inherently racist, white supremacist, and imperialist enterprise. Very soon the astonishing feat of expelling the Western

Civilization course from the American college and university curriculum was widely achieved. The National Association of Scholars concluded from an analysis of Western Civilization courses: "In 1964, the Western Civilization survey course in various guises, along with related courses such as Great Books surveys, were to be found at all the colleges and universities we surveyed. By 2010, the course had disappeared entirely as a requirement at these institutions and was available in some less emphasized form at less than a third of them."[90]

Indeed, matters progressed to the point where it was possible to gain a degree in English at Ivy League schools without having ever read a word of Shakespeare.[91] To be certain, there is value in the capacity for self-critique, and there are plenty of evils in the history of Western civilization (as in others) worthy of such critique. But encouraging either ignorance or self-loathing is not likely to be salutary in promoting the civilizational confidence, which Kenneth Clark rightly said is essential to a civilization's health and survival. It is notable in this regard that China, which in the Maoist era also repudiated its heritage and tradition, today suffers from no similar lack of confidence and is proud to claim its own intellectual and spiritual heritage: "The ideology and culture of today's China is also the continuation and sublimation of traditional Chinese ideology and culture. To understand present-day China, to know the present-day Chinese, one must delve into the cultural bloodline of China, and accurately appreciate the cultural soil that nourishes the Chinese people."[92] It was not just woke sensibility that had it in for Christian humanism. In fact, the progressivist critique was late to the party. Coarsening of culture was not enough for some rightist thinkers: they longed for a subverting of Western tradition. For them, civilization was a falsification of vitalism. They spun Anglo-Continental conservatism around on itself: the criticism they launched at liberalism—an abstraction from nature—was precisely what Anglo-Continental conservatives were up to.[93] We believe these radical rightists succumb to the temptation of primitivism. We make that case in chapter 8, but let's rehearse the argument here and readdress this temptation.

For Nietzsche and Heidegger, it is not Socratic Greek humanism, virtue ethics, and metaphysical rationalism that are of primary interest. Rather, the two Germans are inspired by a more primordial, mythic, even prerational, Greek ἀρχή (arche). They claim to find in pre-Socratic Hellas an atavistic core that is somehow deeper and more profound than Socratic rationalism and virtue ethics. Nietzsche excoriates Socrates as a decadent, precisely for introducing the life of reason and moral virtue as the good life: "Socrates' decadence is suggested not only by the admitted wantonness and anarchy of his instincts, but also by the hypertrophy of the logical faculty and that sarcasm of the rachitic which distinguishes him. . . . I seek to comprehend what idiosyncrasy begot that Socratic equation of reason, virtue, and happiness: that most bizarre of all equations, which, moreover, is opposed to all the instincts of the earlier Greeks."[94]

We have here the improbable scene of the German late romantic Nietzsche condemning the famously temperate Socrates for the "anarchy" of his instincts. But Socrates's sin for Nietzsche is precisely his moral rationalism, which he links to the good of the soul and the hope of its immortality. Nietzsche's strange critique of Socrates is intelligible only on the terms of his radical vitalism. Whatever devalues will and passion for Nietzsche is a symptom of declining life instincts. Already in his earliest work, *The Birth of Tragedy*, Nietzsche attacks Socrates for bringing about the death of Greek tragedy, replacing the Dionysian ecstatic experience of Greek tragic aesthetics with rational optimism. The less wholesome aspects of Greek culture, which so repulse Tom Holland, seem to exercise a certain peculiar fascination for Nietzsche. It is as if the violence of the Greeks manifests their strength and health and holds the heroic secret of their creative genius, in contrast to the softness and effeminacy of the modern bourgeois:

> Thus the Greeks, the most humane men (*Menschen*) of ancient times, have in themselves a trait of cruelty, of tiger-like pleasure in destruction: a trait, which in the grotesquely magnified image of the Hellene, in Alexander the Great, is very plainly visible, which, however, in their whole history, as well as in their mythology, must terrify us who meet them with the emasculate idea of modern humanity. When Alexander has the feet of Batis, the brave defender of Gaza, bored through, and binds the living body to his chariot in order to drag him about exposed to the scorn of his soldiers, that is a sickening caricature of Achilles, who at night ill-uses Hector's

corpse by a similar trailing; but even this trait has for us something offensive, something which inspires horror. . . . Why did the whole Greek world exult in the fighting scenes of the *Iliad*? I am afraid, we do not understand them enough in "Greek fashion," and that we should even shudder, if for once we did understand them thus.[95]

Nietzsche disunites Benedict's synthetic view of the West from the other side. He rejects not the *Greek* heritage (as did Tertullian and Luther) but the *biblical* heritage. If, for Nietzsche, the Greeks and Romans represented the epitome of aristocratic values with their high culture and aestheticism, their martial health and vigor, their demanding inegalitarian ethos, and their contempt for the weak, base, and vulgar, the influence of the Jews represented the opposite, the resentment of the weak against the strong, which gives rise to egalitarian values: "All that has been done on earth against 'the noble,' 'the masters,' 'the rulers,' fades into nothing compared to what the Jews have done against them; the Jews, that priestly people who in opposing their enemies and conquerors were ultimately satisfied with nothing less than a radical revaluation of their enemies' values . . . saying 'the wretched alone are the good; the poor, the impotent, the lowly alone are the good . . . you the power and noble are on the contrary the evil . . . with the Jews there begins the *slave revolt* in morality."[96]

The instrument of Jewish victory was, of course, Christianity: "This Jesus of Nazareth, the incarnate gospel of love, this 'Redeemer who brought blessedness and victory to the poor, the sick, and the sinners— was he not this seduction in its most uncanny and irresistible form, a seduction and bypath to precisely those *Jewish* values and new ideals.'"[97]

Perhaps this is the time to say a few more words about conservative humanism and equality. Let us first assess Holland's thesis about Christian equality and then revisit the thesis about ancient cruelty. There are many values affirmed in the Bible and in Christian life. These include mercy, forgiveness, meekness, love, wisdom, fear of God, humility, and, among many others, equality. The biblical account of equality is complicated. The Gospels do not record Jesus using the word "equality," but St. Paul does: Christ, "who, though he was in the form of God, did not count equality with God a thing to be grasped" (Phil. 2:6). Here, Paul says that Christ humbly obeys the Father, to the point of becoming accursed on the cross. In this, there is an important lesson about equality: "Though he was rich, for your sake he became poor, so that by his poverty you might become rich. Not that others should have relief while you are burdened, but that as a matter of equality your abundance at the present time should supply their needs, so that their abundance may also supply your needs, that there may be equality" (2 Cor. 8). Here, it is likely that St. Paul is referring back to the Old Testament and the Jewish law on debt forgiveness. Deuteronomy 15 spells out the law that every seven years all debts among Jews must be forgiven, so that all will have liberty. The place of this law in the central prayer of Christian life rings loud and clear. The King James version of the Lord's Prayer: "And forgive us our debts, as we forgive our debtors. And lead us not into temptation but deliver us from evil."

In the Bible, the idea of equality is always linked, therefore, with other biblical values: generosity, forgiveness, service, liberty, but most especially, humility. Humility—a lack of precedence over others, as exemplified by Christ crucified among thieves—is the biblical root of equal treatment under the law. Proverbs 20:10: "Unequal weights and unequal measures are both alike an abomination to the LORD." All people are to be measured by the same standard. The idea is codified in the Magna Carta of 1215 as the right to a trial by one's peers—others like you. Enshrined in English law, the idea of equal treatment continues to be worked out in government legislation, but the biblical ideal has traveled the globe and continues to be the benchmark of justice and fairness.

Thus, we cannot agree that the Christian idea of equality is straightforwardly progressive or a prop for woke capitalism. However, equality is a genuine value, as is a good Samaritan benevolence.[98]

Equality must be rightly understood. There are obvious intellectual and physical distinctions among human beings, for not all are equally strong, healthy, wise, or intelligent. Nor do all cultures have equal accomplishments or moral insights in every respect. Human equality is not a finding based on empirical evidence from nature nor a simple and obvious conclusion from the facts of history. Rather, equality is ultimately a moral thesis that rests on the biblical Judeo-Christian faith that all human beings are created in God's image. Specifically, for the Christian, every human being is of infinite value on account of the sacrifice of Jesus Christ for each and all. It is therefore respect for equality of dignity among all human beings that conservative humanism defends, regardless of distinctions of sex, class, or race. As Stephen Tonsor has noted,[99] this Christian ideal of equality in dignity does not exclude hierarchy of function (a prominent feature of the Church and traditional societies); it recognizes the diversity of gifts and charisms (1 Cor. 12:1–11) given for the common good. This implies that not all are equally fitted for all roles, but all are enriched when exercising their proper gifts. Christianity, though an inspiration for profound moral reforms in defense of the weak and oppressed, also recognizes the importance of establishment. Hence St. Paul urges Christians to be deferential to the established authorities and social order (Rom. 13).

Based on this proposition of equal dignity, the conservative humanist may also have a very broad sympathy for the aspiration of classical liberalism to secure greater equality of opportunity by defending individuals against arbitrary discrimination (e.g., against women and racial/ethnic minorities) in the public marketplace of labor, commerce, college admissions, and housing. However, the conservative will look with great suspicion on efforts to secure a mandatory equality of outcome, having seen the totalitarian and antimeritocratic impulses and consequences (with communism as the *reductio*) that often lurk behind efforts to level all such natural and acquired differences that may arise from personal talent, effort, and circumstance. Radical leveling of this type has been the defining hallmark of the revolutionary Left—a pattern that can be discerned in Jacobinism, communism, or even in the (as yet incompletely realized) intolerance of our woke authoritarians, all of which aim to suppress all dissent in avenging the ostensible offences of whole collectivities against egalitarianism. The demand for such a radical equality requires a vast bureaucracy of social control, is antimeritocratic, and is hostile to the aspirations of human excellence and freedom.

Equality was not a prominent value of the pre-Christian classical world. Greece and Rome saw both nature and society as permeated by the principle of hierarchy. Its supreme value of *arete*—excellence emerging out of intense competition—is inherently inegalitarian, presuming that only a few achieve greatness by their talents and by the full development of their natural gifts. The basic classical distinction between the liberal arts and the servile arts presumed a slave society in which some toiled while the *aristoi* devoted themselves to the arts and sciences.

Why then recommend classical humanism if its historical foundations are mired in Greco-Roman slave culture? One can avoid romanticizing antiquity and still acknowledge its humanizing effects. Benedict's "critically purified" Hellenism has enduring value. There is a worthy moral accounting found in Plato, Aristotle, and Cicero that does not entail approval of pederasty, torture, and gladiators. By analogy, John Paul II helped secure freedom for millions in helping erode the communist empire; he is a part of our times, but so are abortion mills, genocide, and sex trafficking. Socrates argued that it is worse to commit injustice than to suffer it, and Seneca pointedly proclaimed the humanity of slaves and recoiled from the gladiator games. There were cruel punishments among Greek tyrants, but also condemnation of them. Aristotle identifies Phalaris, who is said to have roasted humans in a sculpted brazen bull, as an example of the bestial and inhuman (*Ethics* 1148b). Whatever our critiques, our debt to the Greeks in terms of foundational achievements in Western philosophy, science, mathematics, drama, politics, and art is clear enough. Rather than read the classical-aristocratic focus on human excellence and high cultural achievement and the Christian emphasis on inherent human dignity and concern for the lowly and weak in irreconcilable conflict (as Nietzsche does), it is possible to read them as balancing elements that can be contained within the broad tradition of Western humanism.

This is the enduring contribution of the classical world to the central theme of the West and of this book: humanism. Classicism brought into the world an ideal of human excellence and achievement through the education and full development of the whole range of human powers. To this "naturalistic" humanism of the classics, Christianity with its doctrine of the Incarnation provided something yet more essential—a theological foundation to the idea of inherent human dignity. It is true that Christianity tempered man's tendencies to self-exaltation with its salient warnings about the self-destructive dangers of pride and sin—warnings modern man has too frequently ignored to his detriment. Nonetheless, no faith but that of the Christian West has ever given man so central a place in its theological drama. For Christianity declared nothing less than that every human person is of such infinite worth that God himself became man and offered himself in sacrifice for the redemption of each and all. This is why, argues Benedict, the word *consolator* figures so prominently in Christian Latin: it reflects the great promise of Christ to enter our solitude and suffer our desolation.[100] Furthermore, in the Christian tradition, human persons are the microcosm in which the material and spiritual creation meet. Human consciousness receives the macrocosmic universe into itself. It is in this sense that the human soul for Christianity (as Aquinas and Cardinal Henri de Lubac declared) contains the world more than it is contained by it.[101]

We have also explored freedom as one of the great themes of Western humanism through the centuries. This was partially prefigured in the classical age, for Athens and Rome bequeathed the ideal of the free citizen, Socrates elaborated a concept of freedom as virtuous self-mastery, and Aristotle and the Stoics spoke of the power of rational choice (προαίρεσις) as a central element of their philosophical anthropology and ethics. However, the classical world largely felt itself to be enslaved by fate or destiny (as in the tragic poetry of Homer, Aeschylus, and Sophocles), or on the philosophical level by the all-governing causal chain of nature, but it was Christianity that liberated man by proclaiming the transcendent origin of the human person above and beyond natural determinism. Dostoyevsky in his famous "Legend of the Grand Inquisitor" presents Jesus Christ as desiring, above all, human freedom and the free response of the human soul to divine love. The Enlightenment and the liberal tradition took up the theme of freedom by mobilizing a negative conception of liberty (qua Berlin and Hobbes liberty as absence of restraint) into a political project proclaiming the freedom of the individual in the political, economic, and religious spheres. This modern liberty has proven in many respects worthy and fertile in generating a creative, prosperous, tolerant, and self-responsible human ideal and in defending freedom of conscience against authoritarian or totalitarian regimes of coercion. However, the mere liberty to do whatever one wishes divorced from any moral or transcendent purpose can, as Dostoyevsky showed so vividly in his characters (Smerdyakov, Stravogin), degenerate into something aimless, self-destructive, and self-negating.[102] Materialism is sterile soil for the sustenance of freedom. For this reason, we argue that what is worthy in modern liberty must be leavened by the spiritual and philosophical insights of the broader Western tradition with its concern for the cultivation of moral virtues and orientation to transcendent values.

Liberalism may well be the last iteration of the West as an imperial and universal project embracing all humanity. The West as a geopolitical force in world history may wane as its material and technological accomplishments are democratized and spread across other centers of world power, and as its successive ideological projects flounder. But it is the spiritual and intellectual inheritance of Western civilization described in these pages that constitute the true riches of collective and accumulated wisdom that we have received from our ancestors, and it is these that are most truly worthy of conservation. The decline or renewal of the West depends on whether a politics of conservative humanism is able to reclaim the wisdom of our ancestors and rejuvenate the religious, familial, and educational-intellectual traditions of our civilization.

NOTES

Preface

1. Just one illustration are those writers gathering around the liberal conservative magazine *Law and Liberty*, and those gathering about the nationalist magazine *Compact*.

2. Charles Krauthammer, "The Unipolar Moment," *Foreign Affairs* 70, no. 1 (1990): 23–33, doi:10.2307/20044692.

3. The high-water mark was the second inaugural address of George W. Bush: "President Bush's Second Inaugural Address," January 20, 2005, https://www.npr.org/templates/story/story.php?storyId=4460172.

4. Francis Fukuyama, "The End of History," *National Interest* 16 (Summer 1989): 3.

5. Cf. A. Dugin, *The Fourth Political Theory* (London: Arktos, 2012), chap. 5; hereafter cited as *FPT*.

6. For the European belief that ours is a multipolar world and that China is now a world power equal to the United States, see Natalie Tocci, "European Strategic Autonomy: What It Is, Why We Need It, How We Achieve It (Institute of International Affairs, 2021), https://www.iai.it/sites/default/files/9788893681780.pdf, esp. 11.

7. Neonationalist challenges to the liberal cosmopolitan order affirm the return of sovereignty, protectionism, borders, self-determination, national identity, and immigration control. Neonationalist phenomena include the Trump election victory of 2016, Brexit, Orban's Hungary, Poland's Law and Justice government, Modi's electoral victories in India, and these are just a few.

8. UnHerd, "John Gray: This Moment Is Bigger Than 1989," The Post, July 22, 2020, https://unherd.com/thepost/john-gray-this-moment-is-bigger-than-1989/.

9. John Mearsheimer, "Bound to Fail: The Rise and Fall of the Liberal World Order," *International Security* 43, no. 4 (2019): 7–50, https://www.mitpressjournals.org/doi/pdfplus/10.1162/isec_a_00342.

10. PwC projected that by the year 2050 China will have by far the largest share of global GDP (PPP) at 20 percent. The United States share will fall to third at 12 percent, while the EU will fall to only 9 percent. In short, China is expected to have a GDP only slightly less than that of the United States and the European Union combined. See "The World in 2050," PwC, https://www.pwc.com/gx/en/issues/economy/the-world-in-2050.html.

11. Brian Wang, https://www.nextbigfuture.com/2017/05/by-2022-chinas-navy-will-outnumber-the-us-and-in-the-2030s-will-achieve-qualitative-parity.html; Cf. Nick Danby, "China's Navy Looms Larger," https://harvardpolitics.com/world/prcnavy/.

12. Please see the lead essay in the forum discussion, Graham McAleer, "*The End of History* at Age 30," *Law and Liberty*, https://lawliberty.org/forum/as-the-world-gets-messier-and-messier/.

13. R. Kaplan, *The Return of Marco Polo's World* (New York: Random House, 2018).

14. A. Krieg and J.-M. Rickli, *Surrogate Warfare: The Transformation of War in the Twenty-First Century* (Washington, DC: Georgetown University Press, 2019).

15. U.S. Department of State, "About Us — The Global Coalition to Defeat ISIS," September 10, 2014, https://www.state.gov/about-us-the-global-coalition-to-defeat-isis/.

16. Bruce Reidel, "Pakistan's Problematic Victory in Afghanistan," *Brookings*, August 21, 2021, https://www.brookings.edu/blog/order-from-chaos/2021/08/24/pakistans-problematic-victory-in-afghanistan/.

17. One example of very many similarly themed magazine articles: Reynolds Wolfe, "From the End of History to the Russian Invasion of Ukraine," *Cold War Studies*, March 3, 2022, https://coldwarstudies.com/2022/03/03/from-the-end-of-history-to-the-russian-invasion-of-ukraine/.

18. An allusion to Nicholas Berdyaev's remarks about the need for Christianity; see Berdyaev, *The Fate of Man in the Modern World* (London: Student Christian Movement Press, 1935),139.

19. Roger Scruton, *Modern Culture* (New York: Continuum, 2000), 134.

20. The Stanford case is not anecdotal; only consider the rapid disappearance of such courses across colleges and universities in the Unites States. See the National Association of Scholars, "The Vanishing West," https://www.nas.org/reports/the-vanishing-west-1964-2010.

21. Erika Lynn Abigail Persephone Joanna Kreeger, February 22, 2016. https://www.stanforddaily.com/2016/02/22/the-white-civs-burden/.

22. See Dan Mahoney, "A Revolutionary Moment?," June 18, 2020, https://lawliberty.org/podcast/a-revolutionary-moment/.

23. For one example in a vast commentary on the problematic nature of the West: https://asia.nikkei.com/Opinion/Wars-are-only-evil-when-Westerners-are-the-victims.

24. Cardinal Robert Sarah offers another: "John Paul II was convinced that the two lungs of Europe had to work together. Today, Western Europe is employing extraordinary means to isolate Russia. Why persist in ridiculing that great country? The West is displaying unheard-of arrogance"; Sarah, *The Day Is Now Far Spent* (San Francisco: Ignatius, 2019), 239. Cf. the now legendary John Mearsheimer YouTube lecture with more than 27 million views: https://www.youtube.com/watch?v=JrMiSQAGOS4.

25. Viktor Orban's Speech, "Speech at the 14th Kötcse Civil Picnic" September 5, 2015, https://www.kormany.hu/en/the-prime-minister/the-prime-minister-s-speeches/viktor-orban-s-speech-at-the-14th-kotcse-civil-picnic; English copy of the speech at *Magyarzorzag Jobban Teljesit*, September 17, 2015, http://2010-2015.miniszterelnok.hu/in_english_article/viktor_orban_s_speech_at_the_14th_kotcse_civil_picnic.

26. Donald Trump, "Trump: I am a Nationalist," C-Span clip, October 22, 2018, https://www.c-span.org/video/?c4756750/user-clip-trump-nationalist.

27. Consider only how the Labour Party's response to Brexit, the most consequential event in postwar British history, was knee-capped when the party's urban elite (metropolitan internationalists) found themselves completely adrift from the patriotic Labour voter in the northern, industrial towns (the so-called Red Wall).

28. Charles Clover, "The Unlikely Origins of Russia's Manifest Destiny," *Foreign Policy*, July 27, 2016: https://foreignpolicy.com/2016/07/27/geopolitics-russia-mackinder-eurasia-heartland-dugin-ukraine-eurasianism-manifest-destiny-putin/.

29. Paul Ratner, "The Most Dangerous Philosopher in the World," Big Think, December 18, 2016, https://bigthink.com/the-past/the-dangerous-philosopher-behind-putins-strategy-to-grow-russian-power-at-americas-expense/.

30. Anton Barbashin and Hannah Thoburn, "Putin's Brain," *Foreign Affairs*, March 31, 2014, https://www.foreignaffairs.com/articles/russia-fsu/2014-03-31/putins-brain.

31. A short overview of Dugin's Fourth Political Theory can be found at this site devoted to his thought: "Fourth Political Theory -Shortest Presentation," http://www.4pt.su/en/content/fourth-political-theory-shortest-presentation.

32. Examples of his extremism are found in the interview he gave with Polish journalist Grzegorz Gorny, "Esperando a Ivan el Terrible," August 2, 1998, https://www.geopolitika.ru/es/article/esperando-ivan-el-terrible.

33. For an evaluation of Dugin's sociology of the ethnos, see Michael Millerman, "The Ethnosociological and Existential Dimensions of Dugin's Populism," *Telos* 193 (2020): 95–113, http://journal.telospress.com/content /2020/193/95.extract. Millerman includes the following quotation from Dugin on the relation of ethnos/*narod* and race: "It is entirely possible that from a racial point of view he may belong to an anthropological type altogether uncharacteristic for the main population of Eastern Slavic-Great Russians. But from an ethnic point of view, there can be no doubt that he will be Russian if he considers himself Russian, speaks Russian, thinks in Russian, and is a coparticipant in Russian culture. His biological or racial belonging may be extremely vague. But from the point of view of ethnosociology we are undoubtedly dealing with a member of the Russian ethnos" (99). Some scholars, however, do see a kind of residual racialism in Dugin, if not precisely of a racial hierarchy, at least of seeing a mystical significance in blood and racial typologies. Cf. Marlène Laruelle, "Aleksandr Dugin: A Russian Version of the European Radical Right?" (Washington, DC: Woodrow Wilson International Center for Scholars; Kennan Institute Occasional Papers Series #294, 2006), https:// www.wilsoncenter.org/publication/aleksandr-dugin-russian-version-the -european-radical-right-2006.

34. Roger Scruton, *The West and the Rest* (Wilmington, DE: ISI, 2002), 7 and 60–61. Cf. Scruton, *Conservatism* (London: All Points Books, 2017), 2–5 and 104.

35. Cf. Scruton, *Conservatism*, 37–42.

36. Roger Scruton, *How to Be a Conservative* (London: Bloomsbury, 2014), 135–36.

37. Roger Scruton, "Why I Became a Conservative," *New Criterion* 41, no. 5 (2003), https://newcriterion.com/issues/2003/2/why-i-became-a -conservative.

38. Jason A. Josephson-Storm, *The Myth of Disenchantment* (Chicago: University of Chicago Press, 2017).

39. Enormous books trying to corral the disparate parts of Enlightenment thinking are a staple of the publishing industry. A few examples include J. Israel, *The Radical Enlightenment* (Oxford: Oxford University Press, 2002); A. Pagden, *The Enlightenment: And Why It Still Matters* (New York: Random House, 2013); R. Robertson, *The Enlightenment* (New York: HarperCollins, 2021); and B. Friedman, *Religion and the Rise of Capitalism* (New York: Knopf, 2021).

40. Pope Francis, *Laudato Si'* (2015), chap. 3, https://www.vatican.va /content/francesco/en/encyclicals/documents/papa-francesco_20150524 _enciclica-laudato-si.html.

41. Cf. Francis Fukuyama, *The End of History and the Last Man* (New York: Free Press, 2006), 194–95.

42. Cf. Cardinal Sarah's assessment of the West's "self-sufficient pride" making a *tabula rasa* of the past (Sarah, *The Day Is Now Far Spent*, 211).

43. Aurel Kolnai, "The Humanitarian versus the Religious Attitude," in *Politics, Values, and Nationalism* (Brunswick, NJ: Transaction, 2013), 175–96. Cf. D. Mahoney, *The Idol of Our Age* (New York: Encounter, 2018).

44. P. Manent, "Libéralisme et Christianisme," *Le Nef*, no. 194 (June 2008); Manent, *Natural Law and Human Rights* (Notre Dame, IN: University of Notre Dame Press, 2020), 46–51. Cf. Dugin, *FPT*, 25–27.

45. On the adoption of vitalism in German geopolitical thinking after World War I, see J. Haslam, *No Virtue Like Necessity* (New Haven, CT: Yale University Press, 2002), 176–78.

46. R. Zimmermann, "Aurel Kolnai and Franz Neumann: Normative Critique and Structural Analysis of National Socialism," in *Aurel Kolnai's "The War against the West" Reconsidered* (London: Routledge, 2020). Cf. E. Voegelin, *Race and State*, in *The Collected Works of Eric Voegelin* (Baton Rouge: Louisiana State University Press, 1990), 2:180. Hereafter cited as *Collected Works*.

47. Roger Scruton, "The Turing Machine Speaks," *City Journal* (Summer, 2019), https://www.city-journal.org/yuval-noah-harari.

48. E. Przywara, *Analogia Entis* (Grand Rapids, MI: Eerdmans, 2014), 257.

49. Sarah, *The Day Is Now Far Spent*, 212–19.

50. J.-P. Dupuy, *The Mark of the Sacred* (Stanford, CA: Stanford University Press, 2013), 68. All emphasis in quoted material is original unless otherwise stated.

51. Manent, *Natural Law and Human Rights*, 100.

52. See G. McAleer and C. Wojtulewicz, "Why Technoscience Cannot Reproduce Human Desire according to Lacanian Thomism," *Forum Philosophicum* 24, no. 2 (2019): 279–300, https://philpapers.org/archive/WOJWTC.pdf.

53. Fukuyama, *The End of History*, 201.

54. A. Schopenhauer, *The World as Will and Representation* (New York: Dover, 1969), 1:99.

55. Sarah, *The Day Is Now Far Spent*, 280.

56. Ibid.

57. J. Smith, *The Internet Is Not What You Think It Is* (Princeton, NJ: Princeton University Press, 2022), 15–21.

58. E. Voegelin, *Science, Politics and Gnosticism* (Wilmington, DE: ISI Books, 2004), 80.

59. Voegelin describes the Nazi version: "The Nationalist Socialist transvaluation which has reached a rock-bottom of despiritualized, chaotic animal

force"; Eric Voegelin, "Nietzsche, the Crisis and the War," *Journal of Politics* 6, no. 2 (1944): 185.

60. E. Voegelin, "The Eclipse of Reality," in *Collected Works*, 28:111–12.

61. N. Berdyaev, *The End of Our Time* (Sheed & Ward, 1938), 27.

62. The Protestant theologian Reinhold Niebuhr was one of the most famous spokesmen for this cautionary, Augustinian note. The savage cruelty of modern history in the twentieth century testifies to the universality and recalcitrance of human sin in the historical process, and the need to temper the expectations of secular humanist optimism concerning human nature and to be wary of the idea of inevitable historical progress.

63. "Conservatism is about freedom, yes. But it is also about the institutions and attitudes that shape the responsible citizen, and ensure that freedom is a benefit to us all" (Scruton, *Conservatism*, 39).

64. Roger Scruton, "Stand Up for the Real Meaning of Conservatism," https://www.roger-scruton.com/articles/267-stand-up-for-the-real-meaning -of-conservatism.

65. Biotech, nanotech, communication, and brain science have vast political, financial, and book press support (Dupuy, *The Mark of the Sacred*, 73–82), and also great intellectual resources (https://www.humanityplus.org/). About the well-heeled movement, Cardinal Sarah warns: "We are reaching here the end of the process of self-rejection and of hatred of human nature that characterizes modern man. Man hates himself to the point where he wants to reinvent himself. But he runs the serious risk of disfiguring himself irremediably" (Sarah, *The Day Is Now Far Spent*, 176).

66. John Paul II's argument is that the modern West's economy is built upon homicide: abortion, euthanasia, assisted suicide, and suicide, all killings to ensure the fecundity of capital. In 2022, in light of the possible overturning of *Roe v. Wade*, Janet Yellen, the U.S. treasury secretary, said overturning would have "very damaging effects on the economy" (https://fortune.com/2022 /05/10/yellen-overturning-roe-v-wade-would-set-women-back-decades/). In addition, and darkly, John Paul II also argued in a 1995 encyclical that there was a medical conspiracy ushering in a fresh totalitarianism in the West (*Evangelium vitae*, paras. 4, 17, 20, 70).

67. Nasr himself is among the most profound contemporary philosophical and religious critics of modernism, as a necessarily anthropocentric movement of thought and culture that threatens all the spiritual traditions that have forged the existing world civilizations.

68. We adopt these terms from the Polish Jesuit Erich Przywara. See Przywara, *Analogia Entis*.

69. Scruton, *How to Be a Conservative*, 37–38.

70. Pope Francis, "Address to Participants in the Congress on Child Dignity in the Digital World," November 14, 2019, https://www.vatican.va/content /francesco/en/speeches/2019/november/documents/papa-francesco_20191114 _convegno-child%20dignity.html.

71. Compare Scruton: "For in aesthetic judgment we view our surroundings as ends in themselves, abstracting from the demands of utility and function. Hence aesthetic interest is always searching for what is permanent, intrinsically valuable, in harmony with our shared form of life" (Roger Scruton, "The Fabric of the City," https://www.rogerscruton.com/images/The_Fabric _of_the_City.pdf.

72. Scruton, *How to Be a Conservative*, 136.

73. In the Regensburg Address, Benedict XVI speaks of the pathology of reason, the flat conception of rationality promoted by materialism and positivism. Elite opinion of the contemporary university is reductionistic, wholly at odds with how people the world over understand their lives. As Scruton observes, people have elaborate self-conceptions built around multiple ideals, what Francis calls biography, not biology. The consequence is that stunted reason becomes intolerant: incapable of dialogue with persons, reason subverts itself.

74. The problem with materialism is not only the elite intolerance its stunted account of reason breeds but the racism it fosters in populist movements. Sociologists point out that far-right populism is awash with terms such as *bio-culture* and *bio-anthropological,* with a bacterial conception of human being underwriting the fear of white extinction; see C. Bhatt, "White Extinction: Metaphysical Elements of Contemporary Western Fascism," *Theory, Culture & Society* 38, no. 1 (2021): 42–44. Kolnai points out in *The War against the West* that biocentrism—which keys civilization to blood and genetics— was a favorite theme of the vitalist metaphysics of National Socialism.

75. "Rights in turn depend on the web of reciprocal duties, which binds stranger to stranger under a common obedience. . . . Rights are not secured by declaring them. They are secured by the procedures that protect them"; Roger Scruton, *A Political Philosophy* (London: Continuum, 2006), 20.

76. David Hume, "Of the Rise and Progress of the Arts and Sciences," in *Essays Moral, Political and Literary* (Carmel, IN: Liberty Fund, 1987), 118.

77. Throughout this book we rely on British and European conservative thinkers. It is a decision to limit the scope of our sources—already voluminous— because the American conservative tradition is simply enormous. Obviously, we think our focus a good complement to readers whose touchstone might be the American tradition.

78. Scruton, *A Political Philosophy*, 202. Cf. Hume, "Of the Rise and Progress of the Arts and Sciences," 124.

79. This tendency is found, for example, in David Walsh, *The Priority of the Person* (Notre Dame, IN: University of Notre Dame Press, 2020).

80. For example, John Paul II, *Theology of the Body* (Boston: Pauline Books & Media, 1997).

81. The seminal Catholic appropriation of psychoanalysis remains A. Vergote, *Guilt and Desire: Religious Attitudes and Their Pathological Derivatives* (New Haven, CT: Yale University Press, 1988).

82. Freud, Jung, Lacan, and Kristeva—none belong to the Left; see A. Colston, "Left Freudians: The Psychoanalytic Politics of Disobedience," *History of the Present* 12, no. 1 (2022): 127–42.

83. The Week, "Are Conservatives Still the Party of Law and Order?," Today's Big Question, October 5, 2021, https://www.theweek.co.uk/news /crime/954344/are-the-conservatives-still-the-party-of-law-and-order.

INTRODUCTION. Conservatism: The Quest for a Quiddity

1. Samuel Huntington, "Robust Nationalism". *The National Interest*, December 1, 1999, https://nationalinterest.org/article/robust-nationalism-698.

2. See Online Etymology Dictionary, s.v. "tradition," https://www.etym online.com/word/tradition.

3. Cicero, *De oratore ad Brutum* 34/120, https://www.thelatinlibrary .com/cicero/orator.shtml#34.

4. Cicero, *De imperio Cn. Pompei* 60 (my translation), https://www.the latinlibrary.com/cicero/imp.shtml.

5. Confucius, Analects 7.1, trans. Charles A. Muller, http://www.ac muller.net/con-dao/analects.html#div-3.

6. Edmund Burke, *Reflections on the Revolution in France*, http://oll .libertyfund.org/titles/burke-select-works-of-edmund-burke-vol-2. Hereafter cited as Burke, *Reflections*.

7. Ibid.

8. Immanuel Kant, *Critique of Pure Reason* (Cambridge: Guyer & Wood, 1998, 2007), 100–101, note a.

9. Thomas Paine, *Commonsense*, https://oll.libertyfund.org/quotes/381.

10. Cf. Scruton, *Conservatism*, 33.

11. Leo Strauss, "Nietzsche" (Lecture transcription of session 1), October 6, 1971, https://leostrausstranscripts.uchicago.edu/philologic4/strauss /navigate/16/2/.

12. Roger Scruton, *Modern Culture* (Bloomsbury, 2018), 5.

13. Ibid., 5.

14. John Kekes, *A Case for Conservatism* (Ithaca, NY: Cornell University Press, 1998), 33 and 35.

15. Leo Strauss, "Relativism," in *The Rebirth of Classical Political Rationalism*, ed. Thomas L. Pangle (Chicago: University of Chicago Press, 1989), 17.

16. Kekes, *A Case for Conservatism*, 34.

17. George Washington, Farewell Address (1796), https://avalon.law.yale.edu/18th_century/washing.asp.

18. Burke, *Reflections*.

19. Anthony Quinton, *The Politics of Imperfection: The Religious and Secular Traditions of Conservative Thought from Hooker to Oakeshott* (London: Faber & Faber, 1978): 9–23.

20. Ibid., 10–12.

21. Christopher Dawson. *Religion and Culture: The Gifford Lectures* (1947) (New York: Meridian Press, 1960).

22. Cf. Scruton, *Modern Culture*, 73.

23. T. S. Eliot, *Notes toward a Definition of Culture* (London: Faber & Faber, 1948), 122.

24. Roger Scruton, *The Meaning of Conservatism* (London: Macmillan, 1999), 144.

25. Ibid., 45.

26. Juan Donoso Cortés, *Essays on Catholicism, Liberalism, and Socialism: Considered in their Fundamental Principles*, trans. Rev. William McDonald (Dublin: M. H. McGill & Son, 1879), 246.

27. *The Book of Mencius*, 4, a, Chinese Text Project, https://ctext.org/mengzi/teng-wen-gong-i.

28. Aristotle, *Politics* 1252a–b, in *Aristotle*, Vol. 21, trans. H. Rackham (Cambridge, MA: Harvard University Press, 1944), http://www.perseus.tufts.edu/hopper/text?doc=Perseus:text:1999.01.0058.

29. Cf. Scruton, *Modern Culture*, 61.

30. Mencius, *The Mencius*, in *The Four Books* (4A26), ed. James Legge, trans. Daniel K. Gardner (Hackett, 2007), 77.

31. Edmund Burke, *Letters on a Regicide Peace*, in Burke, *Select Works of Edmund Burke*, https://oll.libertyfund.org/titles/burke-select-works-of-edmund-burke-vol-3.

32. Christopher Dawson, "The Patriarchal Family in History" (Sheed & Ward, 1956), Catholic Culture, https://www.catholicculture.org/culture/library/view.cfm?recnum=860.

33. For Catholic social thought on the issue, see Graham McAleer, *Ecstatic Morality and Sexual Politics: A Catholic and Antitotalitarian Theory of the Body* (New York: Fordham University Press, 2005).

34. Werner Jaeger, *Paideia: The Ideals of Greek Culture* (New York: Oxford University Press, 1962), 1:3.

35. Christopher Dawson, *The Crisis of Western Education* (Washington, DC: Catholic University of America Press, 2010), 5. For an in-depth treatment of the specifically Greek educational tradition, see Jaeger, *Paideia*.

36. Dawson, *Crisis of Western Education*.

37. Ibid., 5–6.

38. Ibid.

39. Christopher Dawson, *The Making of Europe: An Introduction to the History of European Unity* (Washington, DC: Catholic University of America Press, 2003), 53.

40. Ibid., 60.

41. Ibid., 5n.

42. Carl B. Cone, "Edmund Burke's Library," *The Papers of the Bibliographical Society of America* 44, no. 2 (1950): 153–72, http://www.jstor.org/stable/24298752.

43. Benito Mussolini, "The Doctrine of Fascism" (1932), http://www.worldfuturefund.org/wffmaster/Reading/Germany/mussolini.htm.

44. Scruton, *The Meaning of Conservatism*, 142.

45. Benedict XVI, *Caritas in veritate*, paras. 37–39.

46. Leo XIII, *Rerum novarum*, para. 9.

47. Roger Scruton, "What Trump Doesn't Get about Conservatism," *New York Times*, July 4, 2018, https://www.nytimes.com/2018/07/04/opinion/what-trump-doesnt-get-about-conservatism.html.

48. J.-P. Dupuy, *Economy and the Future* (Lansing: Michigan State University Press, 2014), ix–xiii.

49. Scruton, *A Political Philosophy*, 33.

50. Scruton, *Conservatism*, 37.

51. Ibid., 41.

52. Pope Francis, *Laudato Si'*, paras. 115–19.

53. A Pew Study indicated that 40 percent of U.S. millennials favor restrictions on free expression to protect minorities from offensive expression; see Jacob Poushter, "40% of Millennials OK with Limiting Speech Offensive to Minorities," Pew Research Center, November 20, 2015, https://www.pewresearch.org/fact-tank/2015/11/20/40-of-millennials-ok-with-limiting-speech-offensive-to-minorities/.

54. Cf. Plato, *Laws* 644, and Scruton, *A Political Philosophy*, 33–34.

55. Richard Gummere translation: "nullum suspicio, nullum in bonis numero quod ad aes exit. Meritoria artificia sunt, hactenus utilia si praeparant ingenium, non detinent. Tamdiu enim istis inmorandum est quamdiu nihil ani-

mus agere maius potest" (Seneca, *Epistulae morales* 88), http://www.thelatin library.com/sen/seneca.ep11-13.shtml.

56. Juvenal, *Satire* 6.292, https://www.thelatinlibrary.com/juvenal/6.shtml.

57. "Ideo negotatio, secundum se considerata, quandam turpitudinem habet, inquantum non importat de sui ratione aliquid honestum finem hones-tam vel necessarium"; Aquinas, *Summa theologiae* II-II, q. 77, a.4, http://www.corpusthomisticum.org/sth3061.html#42226.

It should be said, however, that the later Thomist tradition reflected in the School of Salamanca in the sixteenth century made a number of important con-tributions to modern economic theory. Viewing the modern dynamic invest-ment economy as changing the status of money, they argued for the legitimacy of modest interest to cover the opportunity cost of not having money present at hand, and for a market theory of value. Hence they are often positively viewed by classical liberals as forerunners. Cf. Llewelyn Rockwell, "The True Found-ers of Economics: The School of Salamanca," April 20, 2018, https://mises.org /wire/true-founders-economics-school-salamanca. See also Friedrich Hayek's remarks on the School of Salamanca as a bridge to classical liberal economics: https://mises-media.s3.amazonaws.com/hayeksalamanca.pdf.

58. Montesquieu, *The Spirit of the Laws*, 20.1.

59. Ludwig von Mises, *Socialism* (New Haven, CT: Yale University Press, 1962), 386.

60. See Bradley Birzer, "Edmund Burke and the Dignity of the Human Person," December 19, 2019, https://theimaginativeconservative.org/2019/12 /edmund-burke-dignity-human-person-bradley-birzer.html.

CHAPTER 1. Humanism: The Master Idea of Western Civilization

1. For the New Right explicitly defining themselves against Fukuyama, see Dugin, *Fourth Political Theory*, 67 and 110–14.

2. Right on cue, once Joe Biden, the seventy-eight-year-old Democrat, won the 2020 U.S. presidential election, the *Wall Street Journal* published an opinion piece by the media face of liberal international relations theory, Fareed Zakaria: he argues that after four years of a nationalist president it is time for the United States to return to a policy of peace through the global develop-ment of markets, backed by governance insights gained over the years by "the warriors and statesmen" of the United States (Zakaria, "The World Needs American Idealism Again," *Wall Street Journal*, November 21, 2020). The na-tional security advisor in the Biden White House agrees: Jake Sullivan, "What Donald Trump and Dick Cheney Got Wrong about America," *The Atlantic*,

January/February 2019, https://www.theatlantic.com/magazine/archive/2019/01/yes-america-can-still-lead-the-world/576427/. For the same from the U.S. foreign policy establishment, see Paul Miller, "The End of History at 30: Francis Fukuyama Was Right (Mostly)," *The American Interest*, January 14, 2019, https://www.the-american-interest.com/2019/01/14/fukuyama-was-right-mostly/. In light of the Russo-Ukraine War of 2022, the liberal frenzy for war with Russia was deafening and, as Mearsheimer points out, the United States did go to war against Russia. Mearsheimer rejects that the idea that the United States merely engaged in a proxy war (Jasmin Kosubek, "Wrecking Ukraine: The Cost of Winning the War with Geopolitics Expert John Mearsheimer," https://www.youtube.com/watch?v=q4TV4_taLzE. Nonetheless, liberal opinion in full gnostic mode hoped for a truly apocalyptic showdown: Simon Tisdall, "Timid West Must Draw a Line in the Sea and Break Putin's Criminal Food Blockade" *The Guardian*, June 26, 2022, https://www.theguardian.com/commentisfree/2022/jun/26/timid-west-ukraine-line-in-sea-break-vladimir-putin-criminal-blockade.

3. Francis Fukuyama, "The End of History," *National Interest* 16 (Summer 1989): 3.

4. A. Kolnai, "Three Riders of the Apocalypse," in *Privilege and Liberty and Other Essays in Political Philosophy* (Lanham, MD: Lexington, 1999), 105–18.

5. John Locke (1632–1704) is conventionally regarded as "the father of liberalism."

6. Roger Scruton. "The Turning Machine Speaks: Silicon Valley Guru Yuvak Noah Harari's Chilling Post-Humanism," *City Journal*, Summer 2019, https://www.city-journal.org/yuval-noah-harari.

7. S. Rossbach, *Gnostic Wars: The Cold War in the Context of a History of Western Spirituality* (Edinburgh: Edinburgh University Press, 1999), 224.

8. Voegelin argues that modernity retains an "eschatological tension left over from the Puritan Revolution," itself dating to Israel, which endows liberalism with a sense of finality; see Eric Voegelin, "Industrial Society in Search of Reason," in *World Technology and Human Destiny*, ed. R. Aron (Ann Arbor: University of Michigan Press, 1963), 37 and 170.

9. Burke, *Reflections*.

10. Scruton, *Conservatism*, 45. Cf. A. Quinton, *The Politics of Imperfection* (New York: Faber & Faber, 1978), 59.

11. The term is associated with Pope Benedict XVI interpreting Vatican II in light of, and not as rupture from, tradition.

12. This view, so central to the traditional classical and Christian West, is, however, challenged by modern materialistic ontologies, and various material-

istic ideologies that proceed from it, whether totalitarian forms, such as Marxist economism and various forms of racialism, or in the tendencies of modern consumerism, which treat the human being as purely physical and satisfied by material ends. Liberalism, insofar as it affirms human dignity and rights, does implicitly have a connection with the traditional view, even if it is rendered inconsistent and self-undermining insofar as it tries to align a notion of human dignity deriving ultimately from Christian sources with a secular and materialist ontology.

13. Stephen Tonsor argues that Christian humanism is THE culture of conservatism; see Tonsor, "Why I Too Am Not a Neoconservative," in *Equality, Decadence, and Modernity*, ed. George L. Schneider (Wilmington, DE: ISI Books, 2005), 307.

14. Jaeger, *Paideia*, 1:xv. Jaeger's three-volume work remains the magisterial work concerning the Greek ideal of education and culture, together, perhaps, with H. I. Marrou, *A History of Education in Antiquity*, trans. George Lamb (Madison: University of Wisconsin Press, 1982).

15. Herodotus, *Histories* 1.4.

16. Jaeger, *Paideia*, 1:xxiii (my italics).

17. H. Johnston, "Liberal Education," in *The New Catholic Encyclopedia* (Washington, DC: Catholic University of America Press, 1967), 8:700–701.

18. For relevant articles, see ibid., 8:700–701. Also see R. M. Ashley, "Liberal Arts," in ibid., 8:696–99.

19. Dawson, *The Crisis of Western Education*, 24. Dawson's chapter 3 contains an excellent summary of education in the Renaissance.

20. Plato, *Republic*, bk. 10, 606e.

21. H. I. Marrou, *A History of Education in Antiquity*, 36–45, for the reference and general discussion of the archaic Greek education.

22. Cf. Aristotle, *Nicomachean Ethics* 1123a–25a. See also Jaeger, *Paideia*, 1:11–13.

23. Homer, *Iliad* 6.208 and 11.74.

24. For Voegelin's claim that the ancient ideal of the good society included the obviousness of slavery, see Voegelin, "Industrial Society in Search of Reason," 38.

25. Thucydides, *History of the Peloponnesian War*, trans. Benjamin Jowett (Oxford: Clarendon, 1881), 2.40, http://www.perseus.tufts.edu/hopper/text?doc=Perseus%3Atext%3A1999.04.0105%3Abook%3D2%3Achapter%3D40.

26. Besides Jaeger and Marrou, we might consider also W. K. C. Guthrie, *The Sophists* (Cambridge, 1977). At all events, the signature importance of the Sophists becomes evident when we consider the important role rhetoric plays in education through the later classical period and again during the Renaissance.

27. Jaeger, *Paideia*, 1:300. Note that Jaeger is using a culture/civilization distinction that was common in Germany at his time, with civilization referring more to artifacts and technology, and culture referring more to spiritual and intellectual development.

28. Gorgias, *Encomium of Helen*, trans. George A. Kennedy, http://www2.csudh.edu/ccauthen/576f12/gorgias-helen.pdf.

29. Cf. Hume, "Of the Rise and Progress of the Arts and Sciences," 119.

30. Plato, *Protagoras* 318e.

31. Famously in the discussion by Cicero, *Tusculan Disputations* 5.10.

32. Plato, *Apology* 29d–29e.

33. Plato, *Gorgias* 521d.

34. Jaeger, *Paideia*, 3:46.

35. Cf. Marrou, *A History of Education in Antiquity*, 220.

36. Ibid., part two, which deals with education in the Hellenistic era.

37. Horace, *Epistulae* 2.155–56, https://www.thelatinlibrary.com/horace/epist2.shtml.

38. Aulus Gellius, *Attic Nights* 13.17, https://penelope.uchicago.edu/Thayer/E/Roman/Texts/Gellius/13*.html.

39. Cf. also D. Hume, "Of Refinement in the Arts," in *Essays Moral, Political and Literary*, 270–71. See also David Hume, *Essays Moral, Political, Literary*, https://oll.libertyfund.org/title/hume-essays-moral-political-literary-lf-ed.

40. Seneca, *Epistularum Moralem ad Lucillium* 88, http://www.thelatinlibrary.com/sen/seneca.ep11-13.shtml.

41. A distinction critically reworked by Hume at the dawn of the West's commercial age; see Hume, "Of Refinement in the Arts," 270–71.

42. Quoted in Quintillian, *Institutio oratoria* 12.1, http://www.perseus.tufts.edu/hopper/text?doc=Perseus:abo:phi,1002,00112:1.

43. Cicero, *Pro Archia* 1, in *The Orations of Marcus Tullius Cicero*, trans. C. D. Yonge (London: Henry G. Bohn, 1856), http://www.perseus.tufts.edu/hopper/text?doc=Perseus%3Atext%3A1999.02.0019%3Atext%3DArch.%3Achapter%3D1.

44. Quintillian, *Institutio oratoria* 10.1.

45. This is the inspiration for the idea of the core curriculum at Jesuit colleges, which, as late as the 1980s still caught the attention of Allan Bloom—Fukuyama's mentor—in his classic *The Closing of the American Mind*.

46. Christopher Dawson, *The Crisis of Western Education* (New York: Sheed & Ward, 1961), 7.

47. On the ancient gods as "highly sophisticated fields of mythical imagination," see E. Voegelin, "The Gospel and Culture," in *Collected Works*, 12:195–96.

48. E. Voegelin, *Order and History*, Vol. 4, *The Ecumenic Age* (Baton Rouge: Louisiana State University Press, 1974), 129.

49. Polybius, *Histories* 6.56, trans. Evelyn S. Shuckburgh (London: Macmillan. 1889. Reprint Bloomington 1962), http://www.perseus.tufts.edu/hopper /text?doc=Perseus%3Atext%3A1999.01.0234.

50. Tom Holland, *Dominion: How the Christian Revolution Remade the World* (New York: Basic Books, 2019), 137–41.

51. We discuss Benedict XVI on the political implications of this encounter at length in our concluding remarks chapter.

52. Nicholas Berdyaev, *The Divine and the Human* (London: Geoffrey Bles, 1949), 22–23.

53. E. Voegelin, "Anxiety and Reason," in *Collected Works*, 28:81.

54. Cf. Voegelin, *The Ecumenic Age*, 137.

55. E. Voegelin, *Science, Politics and Gnosticism* (ISI, 2004), 85–86.

56. E. Voegelin, *History of Political Ideas*, Vol. 1, *Hellenism, Rome, and Early Christianity* (Baton Rouge: Louisiana State University Press, 1997), 71. Cf. Voegelin, "Anxiety and Reason," 93.

57. From *In Cantica* 2, quoted by Henri de Lubac, *The Drama of Atheistic Humanism* (San Francisco: Ignatius, 1995), 20.

58. St. Gregory of Nyssa, *On the Making of Man*, 4, https://www.ellopos .net/elpenor/physis/nyssa-man/4.asp.

59. See, for example, Reinhold Niebuhr, "Augustine's Political Realism," in *The Essential Reinhold Niebuhr: Selected Essays and Addresses* (New Haven, CT: Yale University Press, 1986), 123–41. Niebuhr's was an Augustinian response to the excesses of Enlightenment liberal optimism, which he felt had led many to be naïve about the totalitarian challenges of the twentieth century.

60. John Paul II, *Redemptor hominis*, para. 10.

61. Ibid., para. 13.

62. Council of Chalcedon (451), in *The Sources of Catholic Dogma*, ed. Henry Denzinger, trans. Roy J. Defferari (Fitzwilliam, NH: Loreto Publications, 2004), 148.

63. For related discussions of this theme, see Nicholas Berdyaev, *Freedom and the Spirit* (1935) (Salem, NH: Ayer, 1992), 189–238; Berdyaev, *The Divine and the Human*; and Dawson, *Dynamics of World History*, esp. 245–83; see also J. Thornhill, "Christocentrism," in *The New Catholic Encyclopedia*, 3:660.

64. Thomas Aquinas, *Super Boethiam De Trinitate*, trans. Rose E. Brennan, https://isidore.co/aquinas/english/BoethiusDeTr.htm#11. Latin text at http://www.logicmuseum.com/authors/aquinas/superboethiumq1.htm.

65. Thomas Aquinas, *Summa Contra Gentiles* 1.5, https://maritain.nd .edu/jmc/etext/gc1_7.htm. Source text: *An Annotated Translation (with some*

abridgement) of the "Summa Contra Gentiles" of Saint Thomas Aquinas by Joseph Rickaby (London: Burns and Oates, 1905).

66. A. Quinton, "Religion and Science in Three Great Civilisations," in *From Wodehouse to Wittgenstein* (London: St. Martin's Press, 1998), 3–22.

67. There are, of course, outlier figures. Machiavelli's ethics, to take one example, are difficult to square with Christian ethics. But it should be noted that they are equally difficult to square with Ciceronian ethics, and, in fact, as Quentin Skinner notes, parts of *The Prince* are directed specifically against Cicero, one of the pillars of Renaissance humanism. It is an error to take the exception for the rule.

68. Christopher Dawson, *The Dividing of Christendom* (San Francisco: Ignatius, 2008), 62–63.

69. Erasmus, *De ratione studii* 3, https://books.google.es/books?id=XX k8AAAAcAAJ&printsec=frontcover&source=gbs_ge_summary_r&cad=0#v =onepage&q=fontes&f=false.

70. Dawson, *Dividing of Christendom*, 60.

71. Pico della Mirandola, *Oration on the Dignity of Man*, http:// vserver1.cscs.lsa.umich.edu/~crshalizi/Mirandola/.

72. For this point, Rosenthal would note a debt to Ted Roedel.

73. Cardinal Jacopo Sadoleto, *De Pueris Recte Instituendis*, trans. Trafford Camapgnac, in *Sadoleto on Education* (Oxford: Oxford University Press, 1916), 12.

74. Paul Oskar Kristeller, "HUMANISM," *Minerva* 16, no. 4 (1978): 589, http://www.jstor.org/stable/41820353.

75. Dawson, The Crisis of Western Education, 24.

76. Ibid., 35. We might argue that Leonardo is the link between the Italian Renaissance and the scientific revolution.

77. Reinhold Niebuhr, *The Nature and Destiny of Man* (Louisville, KY: Westminster John Knox Press), 2:72.

78. As if in reaction to the optimistic elements of Renaissance humanism, the Pauline-Augustinian emphasis on sin and fallenness then return in a hyperbolic form during the Reformation, as with the Calvinist doctrine of total depravity. Niebuhr argues, however, that the optimistic strains of the Renaissance were stronger, as evidenced by the victory of Enlightenment optimism.

79. Dawson, *The Crisis of Western Education*, 5.

80. Kristeller, "HUMANISM," 593.

81. E. Christian Kopff, "Greek to Us: The Death of Classical Education and Its Consequences," https://theimaginativeconservative.org/2012/03/greek -to-us-death-of-classical.html#.USeJz6X3i2A.

82. For more on the intellectual history of rights debates the Salamancans drew upon from the Middle Ages, see, for example, Anabel Brett, *Liberty, Right,*

and Nature: Individual Rights in Later Scholastic Thought (Cambridge, 2003), and Brian Tierney, *The Idea of Natural Rights* (Eerdmans, 1997).

83. Vitoria argued that children and the mad have legal rights, that as members of humankind they have legal protection. He advanced these arguments to blunt colonial efforts on the pretext that the American peoples were children or imbeciles and so had no legal dominion over their own lands; see Francisco de Vitoria, *Political Writings* (Cambridge: Cambridge University Press, 2001), 249–51, 321.

84. C. Schmitt, *The Nomos of the Earth* (Candor, NY: Telos, 2003), 116–19.

85. Bacon, *The Major Works* (New York: Oxford University Press, 2002), 147.

86. Rene Descartes, *Discourse on Method*, 6, in *Discourse on Method and Meditations*, trans. Elizabeth S. Haldane and G. R. T. Haldane (Mineola, NY: Dover Publications, 2003), 41 (my italics).

87. Fukuyama, *The End of History and the Last Man*, 71–72.

88. Francis Bacon, *The New Organon*, aphorisms 1.3, in *The Works of Francis Bacon*, ed. Spedding and Ellis (London: Longman, 1857–1870), https://www.bartleby.com/br/242.html.

89. Dupuy, *The Mark of the Sacred*, 67.

90. Marquis de Condorcet, *Sketch for a Historical Picture of the Progress of the Human Mind.* (1795), in *The Portable Enlightenment Reader*, ed. Isaac Kramnick (Penguin, 1995), 26.

91. Ibid., 27.

92. Reinhold Niebuhr, *The Nature and Destiny of Man* (Charles Scribner, 1964), 1:24.

93. It is striking to what degree the idea of constant innovation in production marks Fukuyama's argument. Commodity wars are not even on the horizon (Fukuyama, *The End of History and the Last Man*, 96, 108, 234). To see the point, read Fukuyama alongside Carl Schmitt's passages on acquisition (Schmitt, *Nomos of the Earth* (New York: Telos, 2003), 324–35. Ignoring the heft of a commodity economy led to the crazy U.S. miscalculation about the power of sanctions over the Russian economy in 2022; see https://www.tabletmag.com/sections/news/articles/is-america-the-real-victim-of-anti-russia-sanctions.

94. For a study of this development, see, for example, Brett, *Liberty, Right, and Nature.*

95. For example, David Bentley Hart and Seyyed Hossein Nasr.

96. Voegelin argues that not only is materialism our intellectual condition, it is an axiom about which no questions may be asked. It has the same dogmatic standing inside our universities as the Trinity inside orthodox Christianity (Voegelin, "Industrial Society in Search of Reason," 44).

97. Baron d'Holbach, *Natural Ideas Opposed to the Supernatural*, in Kramnick, ed., *The Portable Enlightenment*, 143.

98. Cf. R. Scruton, *Modern Culture* (Bloomsbury, 2018), 28–29 and 33.

99. N. Berdyaev, *The Meaning of History* (London: Geoffrey Bles, 1949), 141.

100. Roger Scruton, "The Turing Machine Speaks," *City Journal*, Summer 2019, https://www.city-journal.org/yuval-noah-harari.

101. Nicholas Berdyaev, *The Fate of Man in the Modern World* (London: Student Christian Movement Press, 1935), 25. The critique of the modern idolatry of material forces, such as economics (Marxism) and racial biology (Nazism), is prominent in this work.

102. John Paul II, *Evangelium vitae*, para. 19, http://www.vatican.va /content/john-paul-ii/en/encyclicals/documents/hf_jp-ii_enc_25031995 _evangelium-vitae.html.

103. Pope Francis: "What is now happening, and drawing us into a perverse and barren way of thinking, is the reduction of ethics and politics to physics. Good and evil no longer exist in themselves; there is only a calculus of benefits and burdens. As a result of the displacement of moral reasoning, the law is no longer seen as reflecting a fundamental notion of justice but as mirroring notions currently in vogue. Breakdown ensues: everything is 'leveled down' by a superficial bartered consensus. In the end, the law of the strongest prevails" (*Fratelli tutti*, para. 210, https://www.vatican.va/content/francesco /en/encyclicals/documents/papa-francesco_20201003_enciclica-fratelli -tutti.html).

104. Illustrative is a podcast hosted by the London School of Economics where philosophers in the UK assure listeners that they have an emotive belief in human rights but are nonplussed about the grounds of the belief. By Humean standards, this is dogmatism, and such a belief will not pass global scrutiny; see LSE Online Event, "What's Wrong with Rights?," October 19, 2021, https:// www.youtube.com/watch?v=Lm2l2ywvQN4.

105. Critical race theory is an explicitly antiliberal school of ethnic/racial identity political thought: "Critical race theory questions the very foundations of the liberal order, including equality theory, legal reasoning, Enlightenment rationalism, and neutral principles of constitutional law"; Richard Delgado and Jean Stefancic, *Critical Race Theory*, 3rd ed. (New York: NYU Press, 2017).

CHAPTER 2. The Metaphysics of Conservatism

1. Voegelin, "Anxiety and Reason," 81.

2. Voegelin, *The Ecumenic Age*, 59.

3. For Voegelin, a symbol is what he calls a *cosmion*, "a whole little world," wherein clear to consciousness is a pattern of life, an essence transcending the persons instantiating it. It sets a style of life and sometimes has significant theoretical weight, e.g., the social contract theory of government is a symbol for those strongly believing—even in the face of contrary evidence—that they participate in a government that only rules by their leave (E. Voegelin, "Immortality: Experience and Symbol," in *Collected Works*, 12:52–53).

4. Geopolitics is "directly connected with symbolic geography, which regards the entire earth as a single Sacred Text, written with special signs and symbols" (A. Dugin, "Ot sakral'noi geografii k geopolitike," *Elementy*, no. 1 (1992), 19, as quoted in https://www.ucis.pitt.edu/nceeer/1994-807-21 -Epstein.pdf.

5. Aleksandr Dugin, "Geopolitics: Theories, Concepts, Schools, and Debates," January 2, 2019, https://eurasianist-archive.com/2019/01/02/dugin-in -shanghai-international-relations-and-geopolitics-lecture-2/.

6. "So what is the space of Geopolitics? It is qualitative, not quantitative. It is not 'physical' space or 'scientific' space. The quality of space is something like 'life-space' . . . 'living space,' in an organic attitude that is qualitative. Space is quality, where orientations do matter. This is much more of Aristotelian space than the space of modern physics" (ibid.).

7. The important point for Durand is that an image, myth, or symbol is not part of language; it is not part of a chain of signifiers. Take Lacan's example. Two doors, one with GENTS above and one with LADIES. The names are not actually descriptive of the doors, they signify only because of a mass of cultural meaning; see J. Lacan, *Écrits* (New York: Norton, 2006), 416. Indeed, today, who can pass through which door is an open question precisely because the background of meaning that assigns the labels is putatively shifting. Images and myths are not arbitrary, like signs are: the image is saturated with its meaning. See Gilbert Durand, *The Anthropological Structures of the Imaginary*, 11th ed. (Brisbane: Boombana Publications, 1992), 33.

8. Scruton, *How to Be a Conservative*, 37–38.

9. He does not say, but surely, he is inspired by Sorel on this point.

10. J. Niewiadomski, "'Denial of the Apocalypse' versus 'Fascination with the Final Days': Current Theoretical Discussion of Apocalyptic Thinking in the Perspective of Mimetic Theory," in *Politics & Apocalypse*, ed. R. Hamerton-Kelly (Lansing: Michigan State University Press, 2007), 51–67.

11. E. Voegelin, "Response to Professor Altizer's 'A New History and a New but Ancient God?,'" in *Collected Works*, 12:302.

12. See https://www.wilsoncenter.org/sites/default/files/media/documents /publication/OP294_aleksandr_drugin_laruelle_2006.pdf.

13. Voegelin, "Anxiety and Reason," 82.

14. The transmutation driven by Gnosticism, Voegelin's signature thesis.

15. E. Voegelin, "Ersatz Religion," in *Science, Politics and Gnosticism* (Wilmington, DE: ISI, 2004), 61.

16. Scruton, *How to Be a Conservative*, 135.

17. See Theopopedia, http://theopopedia.lett.unitn.it/?encyclopedia=angels-of-the-nations#_ftn26.

18. Giorgio Agamben, *The Mystery of Evil: Benedict XVI and the End of Days* (Stanford, CA: Stanford University Press, 2017).

19. Benedict XVI, Regensburg Address, http://www.vatican.va/content/benedict-xvi/en/speeches/2006/september/documents/hf_ben-xvi_spe_20060912_university-regensburg.html.

20. N. Price, *Children of Ash and Elm* (New York: Basic Books, 2020), 218–20.

21. Though it recalls St. Bonaventure's metaphysics, symbolic geography in Dugin's telling flips between the unity of a people's myth—their rituals, folklore, and deities—and the fragmentation of land: "Geopolitics affirms that the most important category of human life and political relations is space. If you, your country, your culture, or your people, live in one kind of space, it will have special values, special politics, and special political organization—if, for example, you live on an island or in a coastal space, you will be obliged to have a different political system, cultural set of values, and so on" (Dugin, "Geopolitics"). The angel seems heavily determined by the vitalism of soil.

22. J. Derrida, "White Mythology: Metaphor in the Text of Philosophy," *New Literary History* 6, no. 1 (1974): 5–74.

23. Scruton, *How to Be a Conservative*, 83.

24. Illustrative is Wang Huning, the Chinese politburo's strategist: "Fukuyama's argument clearly states that the development of the history of humanity can only be explained through the lens of Western history, meaning that the histories of other regions can be discounted, because Western ideology has already become the end point of the development of history. This kind of reasoning is the essence of cultural hegemony." Huning cites Deng Xiaoping: "When certain Western countries talk about human rights or about the illegitimacy of the socialist system, they are in fact simply wielding cudgels with which they hope to damage our state power" (Wang Huning, "Cultural Expansion and Cultural Sovereignty," https://www.readingthechinadream.com/wang-huning-ldquocultural-expansion-and-cultural-sovereignty.html).

25. Smith, *The Internet Is Not What You Think It Is.*

26. J. Smith, *Irrationality: A History of the Dark Side of Reason* (Princeton, NJ: Princeton University Press, 2019).

27. Adam Smith, *Lectures on Jurisprudence* (Carmel, IN: Liberty Fund, 1982), 106.

28. Scruton, *How to Be a Conservative*, 33.

29. Dugin's idea of the *dividual* (*FPT*, 150).

30. Voegelin believes Averroes plays a role in the West's apocalyptic revolutionary movements (*Science, Politics and Gnosticism*, 74), which includes Fukuyama's liberalism.

31. Tom Holland argues that liberal modernity has been a series of Christian revolutions. This thesis clearly owes something to the eminent American legal historian Harold J. Berman. In his seminal book, *Law and Revolution* (Cambridge, MA: Harvard University Press, 1983), Berman argues that Western law took a decisive turn to rule of law during the papacy of Gregory VII (Gregory the Great). This was no mere administrative wave of a wand, however, but a militarily enforced transformation of property and power. Gregory enforced a new establishment on an old Europe. The same was to happen when Luther caught the Spirit. Then, Gregory's establishment was on the receiving end, and new forms of social and political organization put in place by the armies of princes loyal to the talented theologian. For the sake of righting wrongs, Paul, Pope Gregory, and Luther shattered ancient, abiding orders. The same was to happen with the French Revolution, Napoleon, and others. Holland views this righting of social justice wrongs as a peculiarly Christian idea. Each liberal revolution in mores has had the same moral core: "a desperation to be cleansed of original sin." Holland sees this motivation today in the woke, who ask for forgiveness for their white privilege. Likely, such people are avowedly anti-Christian, but the gesture remains Christian. No Greek or Roman would ask for such forgiveness: it can only happen today because the air we breathe is Christian: "Certainly, to dream of a world transformed by a reformation, or an enlightenment, or a revolution is nothing exclusively modern. Rather, it is to dream as medieval visionaries dreamed: to dream in the manner of a Christian" (Holland, *Dominium*, 13). A similar case is that of Angela Merkel, former chancellor of Germany, who opened her country's borders to 1 million migrants in 2015. She acted, she argued, without regard to religion: she was no Good Samaritan, just doing what any human being would do given the situation. Holland is quite sure this is false. The brutality of the ancients shows there is no natural law making us good.

32. D. Walsh, *Politics of the Person as the Politics of Being* (Notre Dame, IN: University of Notre Dame Press, 2015), 242–43; cf. D. Walsh, *The Priority of the Person* (Notre Dame, IN: University of Notre Dame Press, 2020), 44–45.

33. About abstraction, Bell argues that it "smuggles the privileged choice of the privileged to depersonify their claims and then pass them off as the universal authority and the universal good"; Derrick Bell, "Who's Afraid of Critical Race Theory," *University of Illinois Law Review* 1995, no. 4 (1995): 901.

34. And this interview, which includes Fukuyama, too: The Agenda with Steve Paikin, "Clashing Visions," February 9, 2015, https://www.youtube.com /watch?v=Uh_OAHqiMGA.

35. Scruton, *Modern Culture*, 17.

36. For Dugin, the inner logic of commercial liberalism is "the gradual liberation of man from all that which is not himself (from all non-human and supra-individual values and ideals), one must sooner or later free a man from his own self" (*FPT*, 151). Cf. P. Manent, *Montaigne: Life without Law* (Notre Dame, IN: University of Notre Dame Press, 2020), 202, on liberalism and "the decreation of man."

37. Predicted centuries before by Shaftesbury. Commenting upon the party of alchemists—for us, the business of technoscience—Shaftesbury writes: "We have a strange fancy to be creators. . . . For with some of these it has been actually under deliberation how to make man by other media than nature has hitherto provided. Every sect has a recipe"; Lord Shaftesbury, *Characteristics of Men, Manners, Opinions, Times* (Cambridge: Cambridge University Press, 1999), 234–35.

38. Scruton, "The Turing Machine Speaks."

39. W. Eilenberger, *Time of the Magicians* (London: Penguin, 2020), 328.

40. Walter Benjamin, "On the Concept of History," https://www.sfu.ca /~andrewf/books/Concept_History_Benjamin.pdf.

41. Cf. G. Agamben, *Stasis* (Stanford, CA: Stanford University Press, 2015), 68.

42. Who, in turn, was inspired by Schmitt's political theology. In 1930, Benjamin wrote to Schmitt to thank him for his inspiration. The interesting history of that letter—and its suppression by Adorno—is examined by Sam Weber, "Taking Exception to Decision: Walter Benjamin and Carl Schmitt," *Diacritics* 22, no. 3 (1992): 5–18.

43. G. Agamben, *The Kingdom and the Glory* (Stanford, CA: Stanford University Press, 2011), 157, 64–65.

44. Ibid., 157–58.

45. Dupuy points to the Averroism inside a U.S. federal government report of the National Science Foundation and the Department of Commerce that relishes the idea that "humanity would become like a single, distributed and interconnected 'brain' based in new core pathways of society." The report, *Converging Technologies for Improving Human Performance*, admits the diversity of human language would need to be done away with to attain such a goal. The 2002 report was surely inspired by Fukuyama. See J.-P. Dupuy, *The Mark of the Sacred* (Stanford, CA: Stanford University Press, 2013), 64–65, 84–85.

46. Agamben, *Stasis*, 44–45.

47. Ibid., 24. After the sweeping police powers introduced in European countries for the sake of saving the people from COVID-19, Agamben's argument takes on fresh traction. He was not slow to remind everyone: Giorgio Agamben et al., "Coronavirus and Philosophers," *European Journal of Psychoanalysis*, February 26, 2020, https://www.journal-psychoanalysis.eu/coronavirus-and-philosophers/.

48. Cf. A. de Botton, *The Pleasures and Sorrows of Work* (New York: Vintage, 2010), 206–7.

49. Damien Broderick, as cited by Dupuy, *The Mark of the Sacred*, 68.

50. Pope Francis, Address, Pontifical Academy for Life, Clementine Hall, February 20, 2020, https://www.vatican.va/content/francesco/en/speeches/2020/february/documents/papa-francesco_20200228_accademia-perlavita.html.

51. A. Moyse, *The Art of Living for a Technological Age* (Minneapolis, MN: Fortress, 2021), 116.

52. Floridi labels those immersed in techno-ontology the *hypermodern*; see L. Floridi, *The Fourth Revolution* (Oxford: Oxford University Press, 2014).

53. Dupuy, *The Mark of the Sacred*, 77–81.

54. The Telos Press Podcast, "David Westbrook on Social Capitalism," April 20, 2021, http://www.telospress.com/david-a-westbrook-on-social-capitalism/.

55. Floridi, *The Fourth Revolution*, 31.

56. Smith, *The Internet Is Not What You Think It Is*, 15–16.

57. Pope Francis, Address, Pontifical Academy for Life.

58. An illustration is the establishment reaction to the private investor craze of January 2021 in the United States. A case of how dare *they* do what we do: Caitlin McCabe and Juliet Chung, "Brokers Cool Off Highflying Stocks," *Wall Street Journal*, January 29, 2021.

59. Technology companies outstrip even military contractors in their spending on lobbyists in Washington, DC (Ryan Tracey et al., "Facebook, Amazon Lead in Lobbying," *Wall Street Journal*, Monday, January 25, 2021).

60. Dugin's point is also made by the middle-of-the-road, level-headed Pierre Manent, *The City of Man* (Princeton, NJ: Princeton University Press, 1998), 99, and Manent, *Natural Law and Human Rights*, 100.

61. The Nexus Institute, "Bernard-Henri Lévy vs. Aleksandr Dugin at the Nexus Symposium 2019," October 11, 2019, https://www.youtube.com/watch?v=x70z5QWC9qs&t=2832s.

62. Employing, as one might expect, a far more charitable and dialogical idiom than Dugin, the Roman Catholic Church has also had grave concerns about the "gnostic" tendency in gender theory to detach the subjective will from the "givenness" of nature and the body, such that maleness and femaleness are

deemed fluid choices rather than a differentiation anchored in natural realities. The effect has been the break down in the distinction of the sexes. Do we see here the radicalization of the liberal emphasis on autonomy and choice conjoined with postmodern antiessentialism? See Congregation for Catholic Education, "Male and Female He Created Them" Vatican City, 2019, http://www.vatican.va/roman_curia/congregations/ccatheduc/documents/rc_con_ccatheduc_doc_20190202_maschio-e-femmina_en.pdf. These concerns were already voiced by then Cardinal Ratzinger, *The Ratzinger Report* (Herfordshire: Fowler Wright Books, 1985), 95–96.

63. On the role of theology in Dugin, see the interesting article by Dina Khapaeva, "The Gothic Future of Eurasia," *Russian Literature* 106 (2019): 79–108, esp. 84.

64. For Scruton on the importance of rituals, see Scruton, *Modern Culture*, 8–9.

65. Mikhail Epstein, "The Russian Philosophy of National Spirit: Conservatism and Traditionalism," The National Council for Soviet and East European Research (Washington, DC, 1994), https://www.ucis.pitt.edu/nceeer/1994-807-21-Epstein.pdf .

66. It might look like Dugin is a return to the idea of nationalism as polytheism—a claim made about the nationalism of the 1930s by Berdyaev (*The Fate of Man in the Modern World*). However, his apocalyptic vision confirms Voegelin's thesis that the stridency of modern politics trades on Christian eschatology. For Voegelin, modern politics is riven by an "inner-Christian tension" (E. Voegelin, *The New Science of Politics*, 107).

67. M. Heidegger, *Introduction to Metaphysics* (New Haven, CT: Yale University Press, 2014), 12.

68. Ibid., 113.

69. Holland, *Dominion*, 31–32.

70. Ibid., 32.

71. Ibid., 10.

72. Heidegger, *Introduction to Metaphysics*, 113.

73. Ibid., 111.

74. M. Heidegger, *The Metaphysical Foundations of Logic* (Bloomington: Indiana University Press, 1984), 194–95.

75. Heidegger, *Introduction to Metaphysics*, 117.

76. Dugin's position that Western reason is just a particular ethnos is found in Heidegger's discussion of astronomy as one particular way of tracing being, but it has no greater validity in depicting "the seeming in which sun and Earth stand" than does observing "the sea in the evening" (Heidegger, *Introduction to Metaphysics*, 115).

77. Heidegger, *Introduction to Metaphysics*, 15–16.

78. Kolnai identified Heidegger as a Nazi in 1938. This is far earlier than others. It is telling that Heidegger's *Introduction to Metaphysics* is about a great leap back behind Western humanism just at the time that National Socialism is also talking that same way (see chapter 8). Heidegger was an irrationalist, like Dugin, both disdaining the rational order inside Western humanism.

79. For vivid descriptions of buffeting landscape, see Cormac McCarthy's *Blood Meridian*.

80. Dugin: "you risk everything, or everything and everyone puts you at risk" (*FPT*, 54).

81. R. Caillois, *Man, Play, and Games* (Champaign: University of Illinois Press, 2001), 87.

82. Every Peter Thiel Video, "Peter Thiel on Higher Education as Insurance and Tournament," May 25, 2016, https://www.youtube.com/watch?v=Yb 28ZSvuKEw.

83. I. Hacking, *The Taming of Chance* (Cambridge: Cambridge University Press, 1990).

84. Caillois, *Man, Play, and Games*, 141.

85. Ibid., 132.

86. Aquinas, *On Being and Essence* (Toronto: Pontifical Institute of Medieval Studies, 1991), 48, 47. "Predication is something achieved by the intellect in its act of combining and dividing, having for its foundation in reality the unity of those things, one of which is attributed to the other" (49).

87. Ibid., 47.

88. Adam Smith builds his account of beauty along the same lines; Smith, *Theory of Moral Sentiments* (Carmel, IN: Liberty Fund, 1976), 198–200.

89. S. Cohen, "Family Resemblance in the Thirteenth Century," *Philosophy* 48, no. 186 (1973): 391–94.

90. G. Leibniz, *Discourse* (Mineola, NY: Dover, 2005), 8–9.

91. Dugin is not always consistent: "We create a search algorithm woven of all those elements ignored or rejected by modernity" (*FPT*, 189).

92. G. Leibniz, *The Monadology* (Mineola, NY: Dover, 2005), 58–59.

CHAPTER 3. Establishment

1. "The notion of 'rights' has achieved an unnatural predominance in the language of politics. Conservatives have tended to conceive the power of the state as an embodiment of privilege, rather than as a source of gifts" (Scruton, *Meaning of Conservatism*, 42).

2. E. Voegelin, *Order and History*, Vol. 1, *Israel and Revelation*, in *Collected Works*, 14:4.

3. Ibid., 14:5.

4. Friedrich Nietzsche, *The Genealogy of Morals*, First Essay, sec. 10 (Oxford: Oxford University Press, 1998), 22.

5. Przywara, *Analogia Entis*, 375.

6. Pierre Manent, *City of Man* (Princeton, NJ: Princeton University Press, 1998), 201.

7. Immanuel Kant, *Groundwork of a Metaphysics of Morals* (New Haven, CT: Yale University Press, 2002), 43.

8. Eula Biss and Mavis Biss, "Are Anti-vaxxers Conscientious Objectors?," *The Atlantic*, July 29, 2019, https://www.theatlantic.com/family/archive/2019/07/anti-vaxxers-measles-conscience-morals/594646/.

9. Scruton, *Meaning of Conservatism*, 186.

10. Ibid., 70–71.

11. Richard Rorty, *Philosophy as Poetry* (Charlottesville: University of Virginia Press, 2016), 19.

12. Ibid., 62.

13. J.-P. Dupuy, *The Mark of the Sacred* (Stanford, CA: Stanford University Press, 2013), 105–6.

14. Lacan's Other is a ridge built around the Thing, to block access. When Lacan used the concept of the Thing (he did not always subscribe to the idea), it marked a site of catastrophe. The Thing is also the origin of civilization. Civilization lets us dip our toes in the Thing, to get the thrill of it, and even a savage thrill, yet civilization holds us back—this idea of a subterfuge thrill is Lacan's most famous, what he calls *jouissance*. The ridge is part of what Lacan calls the "symbolic," the vast array of manners, institutions, and rites that compose civilization. The symbolic also includes subversive elements, too, but what countermands aggression—the moral law—is housed in the symbolic variants of the father. An example is the philosophical classic *Fear and Trembling*, where Kierkegaard toys with the idea in his existentialist treatment of Abraham and Isaac. For Kierkegaard, the story is about the anguish and horror of God holding Abraham on the edge of being a child-murderer. Our culture returns again and again to this story because it gives us a glimpse of the Thing, full exposure to which we avoid; see D. Leader, *Jouissance* (Polity, 2021), 72. A colleague told us that at a Thanksgiving dinner hosted by a theologian, the theologian took her newborn and as a "joke" placed him on the table and picked up the knife . . . and then, of course, replaced the baby with the turkey. This story is pure Lacan. The psyche hovers about gaps—the wounds of Christ, or in the fantasy of our theologian, the wounds of the Christ child, his

inner Herod popping out—cultural production returning again and again to holes; see Jacques Lacan, *Seminar 20* (Norton, 1999), 8. Examples abound. Some are mild. Collecting matchboxes, luxury watches with open backs so you can see *in*, and, of course, detective fiction. Readers get to be up close and personal to bodies full of holes, but then the bodies are covered by sheets, the holes veiled, and the detective sets about filling the holes for sure by catching the killer. We discuss the political significance of detective fiction in chapter 8.

15. Though late in the day, Andrew Sullivan, in an eloquent and surprising piece, makes the reactionary point: the heritage of philosophy strongly suggests that institutional support for privilege is a bulwark against tyranny (Andrew Sullivan, "Democracies End When They Are Too Democratic," *New York Magazine*, May 1, 2016, http://nymag.com/daily/intelligencer/2016/04/america-tyranny-donald-trump.html. He was not too fond of papal arguments along these lines at the time of the gay marriage debate.

16. See an account of George Washington in Andrea Wulf, *Founding Gardeners* (New York: Vintage Books, 2012).

17. "Indeed, it is as if the *axiological nuance* of an object . . . were the *first* factor that came upon us. . . . A value precedes its object; it is the first "messenger" of its particular nature" (M. Scheler, *Formalism in Ethics and Non-Formal Ethics of Values*, 18).

18. Scheler, *On the Eternal in Man*, 35; Scheler, *Formalism in Ethics and Non-Formal Ethics of Values*, 324–25.

19. In *The Tyranny of Values* (1960), Schmitt argues that the idea of value is utterly saturated by commerce, that the exploration of value "belongs in the economic sciences"; see Carl Schmitt, *"The Tyranny of Values" and Other Texts* (Telos, 2018), 9. It is not the inner economic character of values that irks Schmitt but his belief that a value hierarchy forms a "point of attack," setting in place "the potential aggressiveness that is immanent to any setting of values" (33). It is Schmitt's contention that the legal and moral interest in a value scale was twinned with the effort to revivify natural law (15), to which he also objected, and for the same reason. We address that reason in chapter 4.

20. For Scruton's sense of a contemplative metaphysics as the heart of conservatism, see D. McPherson, "Existential Conservatism," *Philosophy* 94 (2019): 383–407, and Roger Scruton, "Things as They Seem," 461–71, in ibid.

21. J. Ruskin, *Unto This Last and Other Writings* (London: Penguin, 1985), 119.

22. "*Le Sacre* used awkward, weighted postures and blunt, asymmetrical gestures. The steps were performed pigeon-toed"; see M. Hodson, *Nijinsky's Crime against Grace: Reconstruction Score of the Original Choreography for Le Sacre du Printemps* (Hillsdale, NY: Pendragon Press, 1996), vii.

23. It is the extension of color in its phenomenological appearance that explains its partibility; that it can sit along a colorway, e.g., part of the striping on your plaid shirt. Not all values have this partibility, e.g., the experience of a person, but the person's body does. Whether a value has extension and partibility is a phenomenological experience, but to it Scheler adds a value characterization: the higher the value the less it is divisible. The pennies you just spent on that pizza do not even begin to help you buy the *Mona Lisa*: the painting has a colorway, but its high artistry means the painting has transcended its physical composition, it is next level stuff, so to say. This is why Scheler rejects the common idea—expressed by Schmitt—that values are economic through and through. Economic values are keyed to partibility: "Thus a piece of cloth is, more or less, double the *worth* of one-half of it. The height of the value conforms in this case to the extension of its bearer" (Scheler, *Formalism in Ethics and Non-Formal Ethics of Values*, 93). Indeed, Scheler goes on the offensive against those who think values are intrinsically an economic manner of assessment, arguing that only those in the grip of the capitalist way of looking at the world could even propose such an argument, so obviously wrong is it on close phenomenological appraisal (268–69).

24. A. Kolnai, *Ethics, Value, and Reality* (London: Routledge, 2008), 100.

25. Smith, *Theory of Moral Sentiments*, 159.

26. Cf., on negative prohibitions and dread, Lord Kames, *Essays on the Principles of Morality and Natural Religion* (Carmel, IN: Liberty Fund, 2005), 34–35.

27. Kolnai, *Ethics, Value, and Reality*, 105.

28. Ibid., 106.

29. Scheler, *The Nature of Sympathy*, 60–61.

30. Ibid., 11 (emphasis original).

31. Scheler, *Formalism in Ethics and Non-Formal Ethics of Values*, 357.

32. Scheler, *The Nature of Sympathy*, 75.

33. Scheler, *Formalism in Ethics and Non-Formal Ethics of Values*, 487.

34. Scheler, *The Nature of Sympathy*, 121–23; Scheler, *Formalism in Ethics and Non-Formal Ethics of Values*, 485.

35. Scheler, *Formalism in Ethics and Non-Formal Ethics of Values*, 89.

36. Ibid., 91–92.

37. Ibid., 93.

38. Scheler, *The Nature of Sympathy*, 72.

39. Ibid., 242.

40. Ibid., 60.

41. See his brilliant, if dark, M. Scheler, *Ressentiment* (Milwaukee, WI: Marquette University Press, 1994).

42. Scheler, *The Nature of Sympathy*, 39–44. But compare: "Psychologically, however, we must regard it as a more general characteristic of the hypnotic state, that in it the intellectual centre of all cognitive activity is put out of action, whereas the organic reflex system is stirred into increased activity, and this in respect of its most ancient functions and modes of operation; the 'seat' of the hypnotic subject's own intellectual activity is so *usurped* by that of the hypnotist that his organic and motor centres also come under the latter's intellectual authority, employment and control" (Scheler, *The Nature of Sympathy*, 21).

43. Manent, *Natural Law and Human Rights*, 109.

44. About a totalitarianism's true believer, Kolnai writes: "a dull, unawoken and prejudiced being, lacking the civilized traits of human autonomy, rationality, versatility and world-openness"; see A. Kolnai, *Politics, Values, and National Socialism* (Routledge, 2017), 45.

45. Scheler, *The Nature of Sympathy*, 107.

46. Ibid., 117.

47. A. Kolnai, *Privilege and Liberty and Other Essays in Political Philosophy* (Lanham, MD: Lexington, 1999), 115.

48. Kolnai, *Politics, Values, and National Socialism*, 50–51.

49. Scruton, *Meaning of Conservatism*, 142.

50. Kolnai, *Privilege and Liberty and Other Essays in Political Philosophy*, 47.

51. Ibid., 22.

52. Perhaps this is because of its formal erosion, as famously stated by Alexis de Tocqueville: "The hatred that men bear to privilege increases in proportion as privileges become fewer and less considerable, so that democratic passions would seem to burn most fiercely just when they have least fuel." For a survey of some of the illusions afoot about who is, and who is not, privileged, see Douglas Murray's amusing account of his attending a London conference, "Women Mean Business," in Murray, *The Madness of Crowds* (Bloomsbury, 2019), 84–87.

53. Kolnai, *Ethics, Value, and Reality*, 154.

54. Ibid., 175 (emphasis original).

55. Ibid., 185.

56. On this score, Scruton was impressed with Hume and hostile to Rawls for his effort to theorize away the idea of an historically evolved moral sensibility (Scruton, *Meaning of Conservatism*, 189–91).

57. D. Hume, "Of the Refinement in the Arts," in *Essays Moral, Political and Literary* (Carmel, IN: Liberty Fund, 1985), 273.

58. Kolnai, *Ethics, Value, and Reality*, 185.

59. Ibid., 181.

60. J. R. R. Tolkien, *The Letters of J. R. R. Tolkien* (Mariner, 2000), 178–79.

61. Bilbo Baggins has, Tolkien tell us in *The Hobbit*, many rooms devoted to clothes. When attending reunions for the boys of King Edward's, the prestigious Birmingham School, Tolkien was remembered for "my taste in coloured socks" (*Letters of J. R. R. Tolkien*, 70). Tolkien struggled for money his whole life but would die a millionaire—in the 1970s a rare feat: one of the first things he did when the money from *LOTR* rolled in was buy himself a pair of handmade brogues.

62. In his use, it is meant to evoke the *potentia obedientialis* of theology: "LOTR is of course a fundamentally religious and Catholic work; unconsciously so at first, but consciously in the revision. That is why I have not put in, or have cut out, practically all references to anything like 'religion,' to cults or practices, in the imaginary world. For the religious element is absorbed into the story and the symbolism" (*Letters of J. R. R. Tolkien*, 172).

63. See Kolnai, "The Sovereignty of the Object: Notes on Truth and Intellectual Humility," in *Ethics, Value, and Reality*, esp. 38.

64. *Letters of J. R. R. Tolkien*, 90.

65. Ibid., 24.

66. Ibid., 72. "That is they are the descendants of Men that tried to repent and fled Westward from the domination of the Prime Dark Lord, and his false worship, and by contrast with the Elves renewed (and enlarged) their knowledge of the truth and the nature of the World. They thus escaped from 'religion' in the pagan sense, into a pure monotheist world, in which all things and beings and powers that might seem worshipful were not to be worshipped, not even the gods (Valar), being only creatures of the One" (*Letters of J. R. R. Tolkien*, 204).

67. Tolkien amusingly says—and the British monarchy does somewhat echo—"Give me a king whose chief interest in life is stamps, railways, or racehorses; and who has the power to sack his Vizier . . . if he does not like the cut of his trousers" (*Letters of J. R. R. Tolkien*, 64).

68. "I am in fact a Hobbit (in all but size). I like gardens, trees, and unmechanized farmlands; I smoke a pipe, and like good plain food (unrefrigerated), but detest French cooking; I like, and even dare to wear in these dull days, ornamental waistcoats" (*Letters of J. R. R. Tolkien*, 288–89).

69. *Letters of J. R. R. Tolkien*, 240.

70. Ibid., 161.

71. Ibid., 220.

72. Ibid., 239.

73. Ibid., 321.

74. Lord Shaftesbury, *Characteristics of Men, Manners, Opinions, Times* (Cambridge, 2003), 416–17n25.

75. A. Kolnai, *The War against the West* (London: Victor Gollancz, 1938), 318.

76. *Letters of J. R. R. Tolkien*, 156.

77. Ibid., 205.

78. Ibid., 197.

79. Ibid., 212.

CHAPTER 4. Law

1. Aristotle is an ancient source: in his *Nicomachean Ethics*, he divides political justice between *conventional* justice (δικαίου . . . νομικόν) and *natural* justice (δικαίου . . . φυσικόν) (*Nicomachean Ethics* 1134b, http://www.perseus .tufts.edu/hopper/text?doc=Perseus%3Atext%3A1999.01.0053%3Abekker% 20page%3D1134b). Conventional justice is variable and depends on human agreement; natural justice is universal and binds, whether or not people agree to its precepts. For example, Aristotle would say our laws that require cars to stop at a red light are purely conventional, while he uses the example of killing and eating children as an example of intrinsically bestial acts, which are evil regardless of convention (ibid., 1148).

2. Pope Paul VI, *Declaration on Religious Freedom/Dignitatis humanae*, December 7, 1965: http://www.vatican.va/archive/hist_councils/ii_vatican _council/documents/vat-ii_decl_19651207_dignitatis-humanae_en.html.

3. Lacan, *Seminar 7*, 4.

4. Lacan, *Écrits*, 111–12.

5. Ibid., 73.

6. Kant is a committed rationalist and would never concede a core holding of Lacan: the articulation of desire in speech banishes "the subject of knowledge" (J. Lacan, "Remarks on Daniel Lagache's Presentation," in *Écrits*, 572); "the fact that the whole truth is what cannot be told" (*Seminar 20*, 92), a position found in Lacan's mentor, Pascal; see Blaise Pascal, *Pensées* (Penguin, 1995), #199. For Lacan, the weirdness of human appetite means Kant's rational moral law has no home, so to say, in our human makeup.

7. Lacan, "Kant with Sade," in *Écrits*, 659.

8. Pascal, *Pensées*, #84: "*Descartes.* In general terms one must say: 'That is the result of figure and motion,' because it is true, but to name them and assemble the machine is quite ridiculous."

9. Animating the whole psychological, social, and political order is what Lacan calls *the Thing*. An interpretation of Freud's death instinct, it is a place we want to encounter yet shudder before. It is a place of vulnerability, where

longing and violence entwine (*Seminar 2*, 37). Part of my core identity, the Thing is a place of "unfathomable aggressivity from which I flee." How to escape? Things are not so simple: I don't altogether want to flee. This place is also the origin of my jouissance, the confused pleasure I take in a bewildering aggressivity. The mistake of someone like Bentham is to think we have clarity about pleasure: that we can easily index our pleasure so as to understand the application of the principle of the greatest happiness of the greatest number (Lacan rubbishes this idea in *Seminar 2*, chap. 1). Kant's problem is comparable.

10. Lacan, "Kant with Sade," 660. Cf. Lacan, "The Subversion of the Subject and the Dialectic of Desire," in *Écrits*, 700.

11. The phallus is a symbol or linguistic structure for Lacan (*Seminar 2*, p. 272). All desire has its place in language, an achievement of the phallus: "The phallus is the privileged signifier of this mark in which the role of Logos is wedded to the advent of desire" (*Écrits*, 581). This role is that of the Other, which splits my desire, draping its aggression in the acceptable garments of the law. Hence Lacan says: "The phallus as a signifier provides the ratio of desire (in the sense in which the term is used in "mean and extreme ratio" of harmonic division)" (Lacan, "The Signification of the Phallus," in *Écrits*, 581), Cf. "The Subversion of the Subject and the Dialectic of Desire," 696–97.

12. N. Price, *Children of Ash and Elm* (Basic Books, 2020), 1–2.

13. P. Manent, *Natural Law and Human Rights* (Notre Dame, IN: University of Notre Dame Press, 2020), 34 and 22.

14. Aquinas, *ST* I-II, q. 28, a. 5. Cf. St. John Paul II, *Veritatis splendor*, para. 48, and *Theology of the Body*, 223.

15. For the significance of this axiom to natural law, see McAleer, *Ecstatic Morality and Sexual Politics*.

16. There are varieties of natural law—e.g., Scotist, Ockhamist, Leibnitzian, Smithian—and even rival Thomistic theories. The most famous of the latter is the theory associated with John Finnis, who criticizes the prominence given to desire in typical treatments of Aquinas.

17. Aquinas, *ST* I-II, q. 94, a. 2.

18. R. Caillois, "Festival," in *The College of Sociology 1937–39* (University of Minnesota Press, 1979), 279–303.

19. Manent, *The City of Man*, 153–55.

20. Manent, *Natural Law and Human Rights*, 7–11.

21. See the many examples in G. McAleer, *Erich Przywara and Postmodern Natural Law: A History of the Metaphysics of Morals* (Notre Dame, IN: University of Notre Dame Press, 2019).

22. Ratzinger, *Dialectics of Secularization*, 69.

23. Detached from "hereditary principle" (Burke), Britain's second chamber no longer functions as a trustee but, remarks Scruton, as "a kind of TV chat

show." No longer inoculated from the demotic by the stability of land and family, the British Constitution lost an orientation of time distinct from presentism (Scruton, *Meaning of Conservatism*, 49–52). For the significance of Scruton's and Burke's use of the idea of the trustee, please see B. Harrington, *Capital without Borders* (Cambridge, MA: Harvard University Press, 2016), esp. chap. 3.

24. Scruton, *Meaning of Conservatism*, 58.

25. Scruton, *How to Be a Conservative*, 136.

26. D. Finn, "The Obsessive Remainers Have Scored a Massive Own Goal," *Jacobin Magazine*, December 19, 2019, https://jacobin.com/2019/12 /remainers-brexit-labour-party-jeremy-corbyn-boris-johnson .

27. Amanda Sloat, "Brexit Endgame: British Voters Back Boris and Brexit," *Brookings*, December 13, 2019: https://www.brookings.edu/blog /order-from-chaos/2019/12/13/brexit-endgame-british-voters-back-boris -and-brexit/. The Tory Party slogan for the 2019 general election was "Get Brexit Done," a correct assessment that for nearly 60 percent of voters the point of the election was to sort out the final standing of Brexit (Sir John Curtice, "General Election 2019: Will This Be a Brexit Election," BBC News, November 7, 2019, https://www.bbc.com/news/uk-politics-50303512). Boris Johnson called for an election to compel a final (second!) national judgment on the UK leaving the EU.

28. The Remain movement deflated after the election, and its loss at the ballot box was keyed to a misrecognition of the political game afoot (David Runciman, "It Was All a Dream: There Was No Way to Stop Brexit," *The Guardian*, February 1, 2020, https://www.theguardian.com/commentisfree /2020/feb/01/stop-brexit-remainers-eu-referendum-politics).

29. Scruton, *Meaning of Conservatism*, 51–52.

30. For an insightful comedy sketch to this point, see The Two Ronnies, "Courtroom Quiz," https://www.youtube.com/watch?v=QOn3gF_OQag. Cf. Manent, *Natural Law and Human Rights*, 111. Manent is fond of the image of the play of gears. To a car enthusiast, that means play in the ludic sense, the fun of the drive and even the personality of the car. It speaks to the virtuoso talent of the maker and skill in the lapping of the gears.

31. Te-Ping Chen, "Wigged Out: Hong Kong's Lawyers Bristle over Horsehair Headpieces," *Wall Street Journal*, April 30, 2013.

32. J. Huizinga, *Homo Ludens* (Boston: Beacon Press, 1955).

33. Caillois, *Man, Play, and Games*.

34. In *Roe v. Wade*, the Court argued that the then-current state restrictions against abortion were not derivable from common law; see *Roe v. Wade*, 410 U.S. 113 (1973), (https://tile.loc.gov/storage-services/service/ll/usrep/usrep 410/usrep410113/usrep410113.pdf). The legislative acts outlawing abortion

were, as they put it, "of recent vintage" (129). Putting great stress on the common law, the justices concluded that it was never settled law that the abortion of a "quick" baby was a homicide (132–36). At the Founding, abortion before quickening was legal, and the Court was much taken with Coke's formulation that the abortion of a "quick" child was a misprison (i.e., a misdemeanor) and not murder.

35. In *Dobbs v. Jackson* (2022), the Court overturned *Roe*, contesting the history of common law it invoked: "Guided by the history and tradition that map the essential components of the Nation's concept of ordered liberty, the Court finds the Fourteenth Amendment clearly does not protect the right to an abortion" (3). The history invoked by both *Roe* and by the Biden administration's own legal counsel in trying to defend Jackson is immediately engaged by the justices: "At common law, abortion was criminal in at least some stages of pregnancy and was regarded as unlawful and could have very serious consequences at all stages. American law followed the common law until a wave of statutory restrictions in the 1800s expanded criminal liability for abortions. By the time the Fourteenth Amendment was adopted, three-quarters of the States had made abortion a crime at any stage of pregnancy. This consensus endured until the day Roe was decided. Roe either ignored or misstated this history, and Casey declined to reconsider Roe's faulty historical analysis" (ibid.).

36. See McAleer, *To Kill Another*.

37. Cicero is an ancient source: "True law is right reason in agreement with nature; it is of universal application, unchanging, and everlasting . . . one eternal and unchangeable law will be valid for all nations and all times" (Est quidem vera lex recta ratio naturae congruens, diffusa in omnes, constans, sempiterna . . . sed et omnes gentes et omni tempore una lex et sempiterna et immutabilis continebit) (Cicero, *De re publica* 3.33, trans. Clinton W. Keyes in the Loeb edition).

38. "Traditional natural law is primarily and mainly an objective 'rule and measure,' a binding order prior to, and independent of, the human will, while modern natural law is, or tends to be, primarily and mainly a series of 'rights,' of subjective claims, originating in the human will"; see Leo Strauss, *The Political Philosophy of Hobbes* (Chicago: University of Chicago, 1963), vii–viii.

39. Cf. Benedict XVI, *Caritas in veritate*, chap. 3: http://www.vatican.va/content/benedict-xvi/en/encyclicals/documents/hf_ben-xvi_enc_20090629_caritas-in-veritate.html.

40. Manent, *Natural Law and Human Rights*, 70 and 101–2.

41. For a meditation on stones and collecting, see R. Caillois, *The Writing of Stones* (Charlottesville: University of Virginia Press, 1985).

42. For this point about collectors and natural law, see Lord Kames, *Essays on the Principles of Morality and Natural Religion* (Liberty Fund, 2005), 47–48.

43. Martin Luther King Jr., "A Letter from a Birmingham Jail" (1963), 3, https://isiorg.b-cdn.net/wp-content/uploads/2016/01/Letter_Birmingham _Jail.pdf?x65544.

44. A. Kolnai, *Ethics, Value & Reality* (Transaction, 2008), 162–63.

45. Clive Walker, "Human Rights and Counterterrorism in the UK," *Ashgate Companion to Political Violence*, https://www.ohchr.org/Documents /Issues/RuleOfLaw/NegativeEffectsTerrorism/Walker.pdf, esp. 9–10.

46. J. Yoo, *The Powers of War and Peace* (Chicago, 2006).

47. David Dyzenhaus, "Schmitt v. Dicey: Are States of Emergency Inside or Outside the Legal Order?," *Cardozo Law Review* 27, no. 5, https://tspace .library.utoronto.ca/bitstream/1807/89175/3/Schmitt%20v.%20Dicey.pdf.

48. Perhaps more remarkably, Vitoria's natural law analysis was demanding in the moral restraints it imposed on the Spaniards also. Hence Vitoria will argue that one cannot reduce the encountered nations to slavery or deprive them of *dominium*; the populations have rights over their persons and possessions because, as human beings, they are created in God's image, which cannot be lost even by mortal sin: "Dominium fundatur in imagine Dei; sed homo est imago Dei per naturam, scilicet per potentias rationales; ergo non perditur per peccatum mortale" (Vitoria, *De Indis*, 1.2.). He argues anthropologically that their rational and human nature is shown in the *ordo* of their cities, systems of governance, marriage customs, and forms of industry and commerce (ibid., 1.6). The practices of human sacrifice and cannibalism he attributes in modern terms to nurture, and not nature—the product of an "evil and barbarous education" (ex mala et barbara educatione). It is widely recognized that Vitoria and the Salamancans were thus pivotal thinkers in the development of universal human rights in its modern form. The Salamancans and Las Casas also had an important historical role in influencing the Spanish Crown's intervention with the New Laws of 1542, to forbid the enslavement of the New World natives. The complex history that followed will not be recounted here.

49. Perhaps Nietzsche's greatest contribution to ethics and psychology is his proposal that *ressentiment* pervades modernity and underwrites the ethos of humanitarianism. This ethos must be sharply distinguished from humanism. For Max Scheler's extensive elaboration of Nietzsche's assessment of humanitarianism as *ressentiment*, see Scheler, *Ressentiment* (Marquette University Press, 1994). For the critical distinctions between humanitarianism and humanism, see Aurel Kolnai, *Politics, Values, and National Socialism* (Routledge, 2013), 175–96. For a recent book recalling the importance of Kolnai's discussion, see D. Mahoney, *The Idol of Our Age* (Encounter, 2018).

50. Schmitt, *The Nomos of the Earth*, 107. For Schmitt, it is Vitoria's natural law assertion of the equality between Spaniards and Indians that in fact triggers and warrants the cruelty.

51. Hence King in 1963 links natural law and Christian personalism, just as the popes will do after Vatican II. In Manent, the personal embodiment of natural law is explored through the three great motives of human action: pleasure, utility, and reputation (*honestum*) (Manent, *Natural Law and Human Rights*, 101, 107–9).

52. Relying on Burke, Scruton twins law and land. However, for Burke, it is more the history of a land and a people. Inheritance of settled institutions and manners is critical for Burke. In Schmitt, law gains its coordinates from the lay of the land. Though they are not unconnected, analytically geography, rather than history, is critical to Schmitt. In Schmitt's eyes, Burke is a romantic, patching over the risk of politics with aesthetic ideals; see C. Schmitt, *Political Romanticism* (Routledge, 2010), 88 and 56; for a like criticism of Burke, see Dugin, *FPT*, 91–92.

53. Schmitt, *The Nomos of the Earth*, 74–75, 42, and 343.

54. Against natural law, Schmitt embraced Bodin: "Now the state was conceived of juridically as the vehicle of a new spatial order . . . [o]nly with the clear definition and division of territorial states was a balanced spatial order, based on the coexistence of sovereign persons, possible." An implication of Bodin's position is a change in the idea of war: war is defensive, a matter of retaining territorial integrity, and no longer excuses "cabinet" or missionary wars. Natural law is a figure of sea-consciousness, not land. Dugin: "Technological development does not at all abolish the principles of classical geopolitics, simply because Land and Sea are not substances, but concepts. Land is a centripetal model of order, with a clearly expressed and constant axis. Sea is a field, without a hard center, of processuality, atomism, and the possibility of numerous bifurcations. In a certain sense, air (and hence also aviation) is aeronautics. And even the word astronaut contains in itself the root 'nautos,' from the Greek word for ship. Water, air, outer space—these are all versions of increasingly diffused Sea. Land in this situation remains unchanged. Sea strategy is diversified; land strategy remains on the whole constant" (Theory Talks, "Alexander Dugin on Eurasianism, the Geopolitics of Land and Sea, and a Russian Theory of Multipolarity," Theory Talk #66, December 7, 2014, http://www.theory-talks.org/2014/12/theory-talk-66.html).

55. Schmitt, *The Nomos of the Earth*, 107.

56. Ibid., 128. This is why Schmitt thought the Westphalian system more moral than natural law. However, he is critical of its founding concept, the idea of the nation as a moral person in the state of nature. This personalism would stoke future humanitarian depredations (Schmitt, *The Nomos of the Earth*, 147). The Westphalian system needs to be refounded upon the idea of the *nomos* of the earth. Dugin argues that it is this critical insight that shapes all New Right thinking (*FPT*, 43).

57. Schmitt mostly rails against the way Vitoria's Thomism is presented in modern scholarship; he thought him a far more complex thinker than early twentieth-century jurisprudence admitted. Around the time of World War I, jurists manipulated Vitoria for ideological reasons of global governance (Schmitt, *Nomos of the Earth*, 119 and 321).

58. Ibid., 114.

59. Ibid., compare and contrast 178 and 59.

60. Ibid., 78 and 74.

61. "Every new age and every new epoch in the coexistence of peoples, empires, and countries, of rulers and power formations of every sort, is founded on new spatial divisions, new enclosures, and new spatial orders of the earth" (Schmitt, *The Nomos of the Earth*, 79).

62. This problem handicaps the return to integralism sought by some Catholics; see Thomas Crean and Alan Fimister, *Integralism: A Manual of Catholic Political Philosophy* (Editiones Scholasticae, 2020). The authors argue that societies are well ordered when "enabling the part to be perfected by taking its proper place within the whole. The good of a part as such lies in being well ordered toward its whole; hence the good of a person who belongs to a society, insofar as he belongs to it, is to tend towards its common good" (31). Individual, state, and Church are like so many nesting dolls. Organicism places each not only in a specific order but in a radical dependence on the overarching whole, the Church. This is because human persons have a supernatural end that "infinitely transcends the good of any natural society." The Church does not merely cap things off, therefore, but is the whole, earthly and cosmic, from which the parts are derived. Society is not the coming together of discrete, autonomous parts for mutual projects, but more like a rose, a singular unity unfolding and relaxing into so many connected iterations.

63. It is a curiosity that Dugin is as much an Averroist as Fukuyama. For the lure of Averroes in modernity, see Scheler, *Formalism in Ethics and Non-Formal Ethics of Values*, 510.

64. Ibid., 503 and 512–13.

65. Francisco de Vitoria, *On Homicide*, 189.

66. For the critical role of secondary causality in Aquinas, see Przywara, *Analogia Entis*, 208–11, 223–24.

67. Vitoria, *On Homicide*, 187. Contrast Crean and Fimister: "An innocent man has the right to life because anyone who kills him is harming the common good, of which an innocent man is an important part." A killer, however, is not transgressing a right to life stemming from "human nature without reference to any society" (Crean and Fimister, *Integralism*, 36–37).

68. Strauss rejects this, arguing "the notion of nature is not coeval with human thought." As evidence, he states that there is no natural law teaching in

Hebrew scripture; Leo Strauss, "On Natural Law," in *Studies in Platonic Political Philosophy* (Chicago, 1968), 138. This claim is hotly contested by Hazony: Yoram Hazony, "Leo Strauss and the Bible," *Perspectives on Political Science* 45, no. 3 (2016), 190–207, https://www.yoramhazony.org/wp-content/uploads /2016/07/Hazony-Bible-and-Leo-Strauss-2016.pdf.

69. A human "could not be what he is, without knowing natural law, just as he could not be rational without knowing the principle of non-contradiction." This is because "reason by its very nature is oriented toward determining both what is and what ought to be"; see J. Carey, *Natural Reason and Natural Law* (Resource Publications, 2019), 173.

70. Aquinas, *De ente et essentia* (Toronto: Pontifical Institute of Medieval Studies, 1968), 32.

71. L. Strauss, "On Natural Law," in *Studies in Platonic Political Philosophy*, 142.

72. See F. de Waal, *Primates and Philosophers* (Princeton, NJ: Princeton University Press, 2006), esp. 18 on Aquinas. Cf. F. Fukuyama, *Political Order and Political Decay* (New York: Farrar, Straus and Giroux, 2014), 8–9.

73. Strauss to Voegelin, February 25, 1951; as quoted in Ellis Sandoz, *Republicanism, Religion, and the Soul of America* (Columbia: University of Missouri Press, 2006), 129.

74. As does anthropology; see Dupuy, *The Mark of the Sacred*.

75. Festivals are found the world over, and, as French anthropology shows, they are the "reign of the sacred" (Caillois, "Festival," 282–85).

76. Lea Surugue, "Why This Paleolithic Site Is So Strange (and So Important)," *Sapiens*, February 22, 2018, https://www.sapiens.org/archaeology/pale olithic-burial-sunghir/.

77. Just as well, too: Fukuyama argues that rule of law has its origin in religion (Fukuyama, *Political Order and Political Decay*, 11–12).

78. As with the Russo-Ukraine War of 2022, a huge tranche of articles appeared arguing that 9/11 refuted the end of history thesis. Not only did Fukuyama think 9/11 *geopolitically* a blip, in the popular imagination he was correct: globalization marched on. However, 9/11 really did point to the emergence of something comparable to Dugin's *pluriversum*, and by around 2017 a swathe of books began to appear about the end of globalization.

79. Razib Khan, "Why the West Lost India's Culture Wars," Unherd, April 14, 2021, https://unherd.com/2021/04/the-culture-wars-of-post-colonial -india/.

80. G. Shakhanova, "The Patriotic Turn in Russia: Political Convergence of the Russian Orthodox Church and the State?," *Politics & Religion* 15, no. 1 (2022): 114–41, esp. 127.

81. C. Bambach, *Heidegger's Roots: Nietzsche, National Socialism, and the Greeks* (Ithaca, NY: Cornell University Press, 2005), 37.

82. L. Strauss, "Philosophy as Rigorous Science," in *Studies in Platonic Political Philosophy*, 32–34; cf. Manent, *The City of Man*, 154–55. Heidegger's version of the "Greeks" is, to our mind, an oddity. We see no reason to doubt Kolnai's assessment that Heidegger's adoption of the archaic Greeks, dwelling on a mystical bond with Being and the soil, and a heroic martial ethos, is a function of his Nazism. It is precisely the prehumanist Greece Heidegger likes, and we think Dugin makes common cause with Heidegger here: because, in our opinion, to relativize the Greek achievement is a way of diminishing the West. Heidegger critiqued the whole European tradition of classical humanism as reflecting a Roman distortion of the Greeks: "The so-called Renaissance of the fourteenth and fifteenth centuries in Italy is a *renascientia romanitatis*. Because *romanitas* is what matters, it is concerned with *humanitas* and therefore with Greek *paideia*. But Greek civilization is always seen in its later form and this itself is seen from a Roman point of view"; Martin Heidegger "Letter on Humanism," in *Basic Writings*, ed. David Farrell Krell (New York: HarperPerenial, 2008), 225. Heidegger thus turns to the "Greeks" but Heidegger's "Greeks" are shorn of their rational metaphysics, ethics, and humanism, as long meditated upon and treasured in the Western tradition.

83. Carey, *Natural Reason and Natural Law*, 289. Cf. G. Soffer, "Heidegger, Humanism, and the Destruction of History," *Review of Metaphysics* 49, no. 3 (1996), 547–76, esp. 548.

84. M. Heidegger, *The Metaphysical Foundations of Logic* (Bloomington: Indiana University Press, 1983), 99. Cf. Leo Strauss. *Natural Right and History* (Chicago, 1966), chaps. 1 and 2.

85. Heidegger, *Metaphysical Foundations of Logic*, 127.

86. "In other words, it must become clear from the metaphysics of Dasein why, in conforming to the essence of its being, Dasein must itself take over the question and answer concerning the final purpose, why searching for an objective answer is in itself a or *the* misunderstanding of human existence in general" (Heidegger, *Metaphysical Foundations of Logic*, 185).

87. "Dasein is the constant urgency of defeat and of the renewed resurgence of the act of violence against Being, in such a way that the almighty sway of Being violates Dasein (in the literal sense), makes Dasein into the site of its appearing, envelops and pervades Dasein in its sway, and thereby holds it within Being" (Heidegger, *Introduction to Metaphysics*, 198).

88. Przywara, *Analogia Entis*, 619.

89. Strauss, "Philosophy as Rigorous Science," 33.

90. The refusal of any country from the Global South (75% of the world's population) to participate in sanctions against Russia in 2022 points not merely to the collapse of globalization but a disinclination to even think in terms of a global economic order managed by international bodies rooted in U.S. muscle. Furthermore, the emergence of BRICS, an explicitly non-Western, nonuniform trade alliance, points to polycentrism: Samir Saranabhijnan Rej, "Building New Alliances with BRICS," *The Hindu*, March 24, 2016, https://www.thehindu.com/opinion/op-ed/Building-new-alliances-with-BRICS/article14171411.ece.

91. It is noteworthy that Heidegger talks of "the court of justice" established by logos as part of the derivative, fallen, and nihilistic history of the West (Heidegger, *Introduction to Metaphysics*, 198–99).

92. Przywara, *Analogia Entis*, 622.

93. T. Hibbs, "Principles and Prudence," *New Scholasticism* 61 (1987): 271–84. The argument is also found in Hibbs, *Virtue's Splendor* (Fordham, 2001).

94. Cf. A. Krieg and J.-M. Rickli, *Surrogate Warfare* (Washington, DC: Georgetown University Press, 2019). See also Robert D. Kaplan, *The Return of Marco Polo's World* (Random House, 2018). For a global map of dissolving governments, see p. 49, fig. 5.3 in Seth Jones, "The Evolution of the Salafi-Jihadist Threat," CSIS, November 20, 2018, https://www.csis.org/analysis/evolution-salafi-jihadist-threat.

95. Robert D. Kaplan, "The Coming Anarchy," *The Atlantic*, February 1994, https://www.theatlantic.com/magazine/archive/1994/02/the-coming-anarchy/304670/.

96. See Arpad Szakolczai's essay series, "The End of Kantian Universalism," VoegelinView, April 13, 2020 (in four parts), https://voegelinview.com/the-end-of-kantianism-fairground-economy-police-states-and-the-permanent-apocalyptic-sacrificial-carnival/.

97. Valentina di Donato and Tim Lister, "The Mafia Is Poised to Exploit Coronavirus, and Not Just in Italy," CNN, April 19, 2020, https://www.cnn.com/2020/04/19/europe/italy-mafia-exploiting-coronavirus-crisis-aid-intl/index.html.

98. Cat Rainsford, "History of Activism Helps Mexico's Indigenous Resist Organized Crime: Report," InsightCrime, October 15, 2019, https://www.insightcrime.org/news/analysis/history-of-activism-helps-mexicos-indigenous-to-resist-organized-crime-report/.

99. Justin Scheck et al., "Former BP Chief's New Quest: Wildcatting on the Edge of Danger," *Wall Street Journal*, November 11, 2013. Cf. Robert D. Kaplan, *The Revenge of Geography* (London: Penguin, 2013).

100. For the increased awareness in business literature of the intensifying risk of violence, see Patrick Lagadec, "A New Cosmology of Risks and Crises: Time for a Radical Shift in Paradigm and Practice," *Review of Public Policy*, June 22, 2009, 473–86.

101. Scott Calvert, "Johns Hopkins Pushes for Armed Police on Campus," *Wall Street Journal*, February 1, 2019.

102. Vitoria, *Political Writings*, 299.

103. Ibid., 300.

104. Ibid., 301.

105. Ibid.

106. During the Covid lockdown in the United States, Google and Amazon where hired to administer state aid when government departments were overwhelmed; Sarah Chaney, "Amazon, Google Help States as Coronavirus Boosts Unemployment Claims," *Wall Street Journal*, May 12, 2020. For companies collecting and assessing data for the state's security forces, see Andy Greenberg, "How a 'Deviant' Philosopher Built Palantir, a CIA-Funded Data-Mining Juggernaut," *Forbes*, August 14, 2013, https://www.forbes.com/sites /andygreenberg/2013/08/14/agent-of-intelligence-how-a-deviant-philosopher -built-palantir-a-cia-funded-data-mining-juggernaut/?sh=153d90077785; Antione Gara, "This Startup Is Creating a Real-Time Data Map of the Global Economy," *Forbes*, February 4, 2014, https://www.forbes.com/sites/antoine gara/2019/02/04/this-startup-is-creating-a-real-time-data-map-of-the-global -economy-blackrock-and-paypal-are-buying-it/?sh=3b200d2428c8.

107. "Google Spent $21 Million Lobbying an Increasingly Tech-Nervous Washington in 2018," Bloomberg, January 22, 2019, http://fortune.com/2019 /01/22/google-lobbying-washington-21-million-dollars-2018-privacy-tariffs -trade-immigration-sundar-pichai/.

CHAPTER 5. Humanistic Enterprise

1. Brunello Cucinelli, "My Idea of Humanistic Capitalism and Human Sustainability," a speech delivered in Rome at the G20, October 31, 2021, https://www.brunellocucinelli.com/en/humanistic-capitalism.html.

2. M. Grice-Hutchinson, *Early Economic Thought in Spain 1177–1740* (Allen & Unwin, 1978). Cf. M. Rothbard, *Economic Thought before Adam Smith*, Vol. 1, chap. 4, https://mises.org/library/austrian-perspective-history -economic-thought.

3. Hume and Smith read Pierre Bayle's *Dictionary*, large chunks of which are lengthy quotes from, and critical commentary upon, Leibniz's *Theodicy*;

see N. Phillipson, *Adam Smith: An Enlightened Life* (New Haven, CT: Yale University Press, 2010), 61.

4. G. Agamben, *The Kingdom and the Glory* (Stanford, CA: Stanford University Press, 2011), 270 and 283–85.

5. Dugin, *FTP*, 14.

6. The division of labor is the inner logic of the invisible hand, the providential character of which is explicit: "Nearly the same distribution of the necessaries of life, which would have been made, had the earth been divided into equal portions among all its inhabitants, and thus without intending it, without knowing it, advance the interest of the society, and afford means to the multiplication of the species. When Providence divided the earth among a few lordly masters, it neither forgot nor abandoned those who seemed to have been left out of the partition" (Smith, *TMS*, IV.1.10, 185).

7. John Gray, "Surveillance Capitalism vs. The Surveillance State," Noēma, June 17, 2020, https://www.noemamag.com/surveillance-capitalism -vs-the-surveillance-state/.

8. Dugin, *FPT*, 30. Cf. http://www.vatican.va/content/francesco/en /speeches/2020/february/documents/papa-francesco_20200228_accademia -perlavita.html, and D. Murray, *The Madness of Crowds* (Bloomsbury, 2020), 2.

9. W. Benjamin, *The Arcades Project* (Cambridge, MA: Harvard University Press, 1999), 667.

10. Factory machinery solved a problem for capital, namely, how to integrate the bodies of women and children in manufacturing. Their "weak" or "underdeveloped" musculatures added a friction callus, so to say, inhibiting the productivity of human dynamics; see K. Marx, *Capital*, Vol. 1, chap. 15, sec. 3A: "Appropriation of Supplementary Labour-Power by Capital. The Employment of Women and Children," https://www.marxists.org/archive/marx /works/1867-c1/ch15.htm#S3a.

11. Benjamin, *Arcades Project*, 695.

12. For an account of Vaucanson, see Jessica Keating, "The Automaton," in *The Oxford Handbook of the Baroque* (Oxford: Oxford University Press, 2019), 203–6.

13. Benjamin, *Arcades Project*, 695.

14. W. Benjamin, *Charles Baudelaire* (London: New Left Books, 1973), 132. Cf. Esther Leslie, "Walter Benjamin: Traces of Craft," *Journal of Design History* 11, no. 1 (1998): 7.

15. For an illustration, Benjamin directs us to a toy, a phenakistoscope, discussed by Baudelaire, "Philosophy of Dolls," in *On Dolls*, ed. K. Gross (Notting Hill Editions, 2012), 18.

16. Workers spinning yarn for one hour "now represent nothing but definite quantities of labour, definite masses of crystallized labour time" (Benjamin, *Arcades Project*, 659).

17. "If I say: Roman law and German law are both systems of law, my statement is perfectly self-evident. But if I say: the law, that abstract concept, realizes itself in Roman law and in German law, those concrete legal systems, my context becomes mystical" (Benjamin, *Arcades Project*, 658). In Engels, it is not abstraction that is decisive, but just the heft of who has access to more capital; see F. Engels, "The Principles of Communism," part 4, https://www .marxists.org/archive/marx/works/1847/11/prin-com.htm.

18. Agamben, *The Kingdom and the Glory*, xii, 255–56.

19. Where capitalist property does not exist, Marx claims, "our products would be like so many mirrors, out of which our essence shone"; from a commentary by Marx on James Mill as quoted by E. G. West, "The Political Economy of Alienation: Karl Marx and Adam Smith," *Oxford Economic Papers*, n.s., 21, no. 1 (1969): 19.

20. For this turn in politics, see Kaplan, *The Return of Marco Polo's World*, but most especially his podcast series with leading IR people *Global Demons*, https://www.fpri.org/multimedia/global-demons-podcast/.

21. Popular expressions of this attitude include not only *Lord of the Rings*, but its imitators, *Harry Potter* and *Game of Thrones*, to name only two. Concretely, it is palpable in the green movement, environmentalism, new urbanism, localism, and hipster culture.

22. Consider only the rise of hipster culture and, among a host of examples, the return of craft brewing, riding bikes and scooters, vintage clothing, and traditional men's barbers. The return of pop stars releasing albums in vinyl, the slowness movement in the massive wellness industry, and the shift in tourism from destinations to experiences, e.g., staying at an olive oil farm, and the list goes on and on.

23. See the interesting dispute between Scruton and Richard Reinsch, with the later arguing that data shows the suburbs support families and the most fertile ground for new conservatives in the United States are suburban areas: Liberty Law Talk, "How To Be A Conservative: A Conversation with Sir Roger Scruton," *Law & Liberty*, August 16, 2021, https://lawliberty.org /podcast/a-conversation-with-roger-scruton-on-how-to-be-a-conservative/.

24. For these themes, see the popular modern Western series *Yellowstone*.

25. For a summary of charges against modernity, see R. Robertson, *The Enlightenment* (Harper, 2021), 769.

26. E. Baptist, *The Half Has Never Been Told* (Basic, 2016).

27. V. Postrel, *The Fabric of Civilization* (Basic Books, 2020), 65–68.

28. Important sources for Smith's historical method are his *Lectures on Jurisprudence*, "The History of Astronomy," *The Theory of Moral Sentiments* (*TMS*), and, of course, *The Wealth of Nations* (*WN*).

29. E. Voegelin, *The New Science of Politics* (Chicago, 1987), 163; hereafter cited as *NSP*.

30. "Among the modern apocalypses there should especially be reckoned certain "philosophies" of history that achieve a transfiguration of society, not by divine intervention, but by revolutionary action of man" (Voegelin, "Anxiety and Reason," 66).

31. "One should, on the contrary, speak of the illusion of disappearance, for under the dominance of modern gnosticism and scientism the cosmos has been relegated to a position so subordinate that its presence has become almost unbelievable. An ardent Communist, for instance, would be greatly surprised if he learned that by his activities he participates in a cosmological rite of renewal in order to assuage his anxiety of existence" (Voegelin, "Anxiety and Reason," 66).

32. E. Voegelin, *History of Political Ideas*, Vol. 6, *Renaissance and Reformation*, in *Collected Works*, 22:129.

33. E. Voegelin, "Ersatz Religion," in *Science, Politics and Gnosticism* (ISI, 2004), 61.

34. Voegelin, "Industrial Society in Search of Reason," 171. Cf. Voegelin, "Ersatz Religion," 63.

35. Voegelin, *The Ecumenic Age*, 20.

36. Voegelin, "Ersatz Religion," 80. Core properties of Gnosticism (ibid., 64–65) are the following: dissatisfaction with the world; the problem is the world, not us; the belief that salvation from the world is possible; the order of being will have to be changed in history to correct its fault lines; the salvific change in history must come through human agency; knowledge—*gnosis*—of how to effect the transformation is "the central concern of the gnostic"; seeking "the construction of a formula for self and world salvation." Gnosticism thus has a prophetic cast.

37. Voegelin, *The Ecumenic Age*, 134.

38. E. Voegelin, "Configurations of History," in *Collected Works*, 12:107.

39. E. Voegelin, "What Is History?," in *Collected Works*, 28:30–31.

40. For an excellent discussion, see B. Cooper, *Paleolithic Politics* (Notre Dame, IN: University of Notre Dame Press, 2019).

41. E. Voegelin, *Order and History*, Vol. 1, *Israel and Revelation* (Louisiana State University Press, 2001), 5.

42. Voegelin, "Anxiety and Reason," 59.

43. Voegelin, *The Ecumenic Age*, 149.

44. Ibid., 154.

45. E. Voegelin, "What Is History?," 32.

46. For Voegelin, human nature is fixed: no political symbol can "remove the soul and its transcendence from the structure of reality" (*NSP*, 165).

47. "In its order every society reflects the type of men of whom it is composed. One would have to say, for instance, that cosmological empires consist of a type of men who experience the truth of their existence as a harmony with the cosmos" (*NSP*, 62).

48. "In the symbolic form of the myth, thus, Plato recognizes the philosopher's role in history as that of the man who is open to reality and willing to let the gift of the gods illuminate his existence" (Voegelin, *The Ecumenic Age*, 184).

49. Voegelin, *Israel and Revelation*, 87. Plato could not deliver full differentiation because for the Greeks an abiding symbol is "intracosmic gods" (E. Voegelin, "The Gospel and Culture," in *Collected Works*, 12:194).

50. E. Voegelin, "The Beginning and the Beyond," in *Collected Works*, 12:228.

51. Voegelin, *The Ecumenic Age*, 74.

52. Voegelin, *Israel and Revelation*, 129.

53. "All gnostic movements are involved in the project of abolishing the constitution of being, with its origin in divine, transcendent being, and replacing it with a world-immanent order of being, the perfection of which lies in the realm of human action. This is a matter of so altering the structure of the world, which is perceived as inadequate, that a new, satisfying world arises. The variants of immanentization, therefore, are the controlling symbols" (Voegelin, "Ersatz Religion," 75).

54. Cf. Voegelin, "Industrial Society in Search of Reason," 44.

55. Voegelin, *Israel and Revelation*, ix; Voegelin, *NSP*, 134.

56. Voegelin, "Anxiety and Reason," 61.

57. For Voegelin, Christianity is not just a "saving tale" but "so not an ordinary myth, but a saving tale saved from death." He accords nearly the same status to the myth of Socrates as articulated by Plato (E. Voegelin, "Structures of Consciousness," in *Collected Works*, 33:368).

58. On the importance of trust in politics, see Scruton, *A Political Philosophy*, 7–8, and Scruton, *How to Be a Conservative*, 15–16, 58.

59. Scruton, *Modern Culture*, 73.

60. Voegelin, *The Ecumenic Age*, 19.

61. Ibid., 28.

62. For examples, look up the automaton's maker, Jaquet Droz.

63. Alexander Marshack introduced the idea that calendric notations etched on bone played a role in rituals and rites (the objects show wear from having been massaged in the hands), see the NASA presentation of Marshack's work, "The Oldest Lunar Calendars," NASA Solar Science Institute, https://sservi.nasa.gov/articles/oldest-lunar-calendars/. For a thorough discussion, see Cooper, *Paleolithic Politics*.

64. "There is a strict correlation between the theory of human existence and the historical differentiation of experience in which this existence has gained its self-understanding" (*NSP*, 79).

65. E. Voegelin, *Order and History*, Vol. 3, *Plato and Aristotle* (Louisiana State University Press, 1999), 186.

66. Smith, *Lectures on Jurisprudence*, 204.

67. Eric Voegelin, "Caught Up in 18th Century Thought," VoegelinView, September 1, 2014, https://voegelinview.com/caught-up-in-18th-century-thought-pt-1/.

68. Cf. Manent, *Natural Law and Human Rights*, 21–24.

69. Voegelin, "Structures of Consciousness," 362–64.

70. In a Voegelin letter to Karl Löwith from 1944, as quoted in S. Rossbach, "Understanding in Quest of Faith: The Central Problem in Eric Voegelin's Philosophy," in *Politics & Apocalypse*, 224.

71. Cf. Dupuy, *The Mark of the Sacred*, 11–12. Nor is Hume, fantasy being basic to his account of world-building in the *Treatise*.

72. Voegelin, *Israel and Revelation*, 3.

73. "Merchants are commonly ambitious of becoming country gentlemen, and when they do, they are generally the best of all improvers. A merchant is accustomed to employ his money chiefly in profitable projects; whereas a mere country gentleman to employ it chiefly in expence. . . . Those different habits naturally affect their temper and disposition in every sort of business" (*WN*, III.iv.3).

74. Men's jackets have buttons on the right so in drawing a sword from left to right the movement of their arms would not be delayed by a cuff catching on a button, see Megan Garber, "The Curious Case of Men and Women's Buttons," *The Atlantic*, March 27, 2015: https://www.theatlantic.com/technology/archive/2015/03/the-curious-case-of-men-and-womens-buttons/388844/.

75. For Smith, morality is less about intentions (*TMS*, II.iii.2), and more about participation in an objective value order (*TMS*, V.1.8–9).

76. Oberlo, "Mobile Commerce Sales in 2022," https://www.oberlo.com/statistics/mobile-commerce-sales.

77. For a useful discussion, see Christopher J. Berry, *Social Theory of the Scottish Enlightenment* (Edinburgh University Press, 1997), 124–25.

78. The division of labor is a theoretical symbol tracking an animating political symbol, luxury: "New symbols will be developed in theory for the critically adequate description of symbols that are part of reality" (*NSP*, 29). Not a watch, but a fine illustration of how luxury is made today: Beretta, "Human Technology," Vimeo, https://vimeo.com/111721083.

79. Adidas, "Adidas Shoe Collector," Vimeo, https://vimeo.com/199 200432.

80. Atomization might not be as complete as John Gray thinks. Woke (il)liberalism is solidaristic, e.g., safe spaces, college dorms for LGBT+, speech codes, massive government funding in the United States for historically Black colleges (the HBCs), the Peace Corps, Teach for America, and so on. Critically, as plenty have observed, the woke solidarity of colleges has migrated into corporate America.

81. T. S. Eliot, "Notes Towards the Definition of Culture," in *Selected Prose of T. S. Eliot*, ed. Frank Kermode (London, 1975), 298.

82. John Ortved, "Four-Figure Denim for (Only) Your Figure," *Wall Street Journal*, September 27, 2013.

83. On collecting—and thus property—as a directive of natural law, see Lord Kames, *Essays on the Principles of Morality and Natural Religion*, 47–48.

84. Dugin is certainly right that transhumanism is a feature of modernity; it is on the menu. But as the moon phase watch and jeans examples illustrate, commerce is as much about old things, as new. Luxury is as much Ruskin, as it is Tesla. Ruskin was a pointed critic of the division of labor. His classic work on the Gothic begins by denouncing Smith's example of the pin factory. Nonetheless, bespoke Japanese selvage jeans rely on aesthetic qualities valued by Ruskin (R. Dickinson, "Needlework and John Ruskin's 'acicular art of nations,'" https://journals.openedition.org/erea/6710). The seamstresses ply the needle in a manner he much approved, bespoke manufacture, like the Gothic, being "capable of perpetual novelty"; see J. Ruskin, *Unto This Last and Other Writings* (Penguin, 1985), 92–95. It can also be noted that Ruskin was not averse to finding soul-moving beauty in the summit of the division of labor, both in manufacture and operation, in early nineteenth-century England: Nelson's ships of the line. See his comments on Turner's *The Fighting Téméraire*, https://art-bin.com/art/oruskin5.html.

85. J. Muller, *Adam Smith in His Time and Ours* (The Free Press, 1993), 60.

86. J. Kotkin, *The Coming of Neo-Feudalism* (Encounter, 2020).

87. Sam Long, "The Financialization of the American Elite," American Affairs Journal 3, no. 3 (2019), https://americanaffairsjournal.org/2019/08/the-financialization-of-the-american-elite/.

88. For an extremely interesting, and disturbing example, see Dupuy, *The Mark of the Sacred*, 81n45.

89. Ajay Singh Chaudhary and Raphaële, "The Supermanagerial Reich," *Los Angeles Review of Books*, November 7, 2016, https://lareviewofbooks .org/article/the-supermanagerial-reich/.

90. Kyle Chayka, "The Subway That Sunk: How Silicon Valley Helps Spread the Same Sterile Aesthetic Across the World," The Verge, https:// www.theverge.com/2016/8/3/12325104/airbnb-aesthetic-global-minimalism-startup-gentrification.

91. Benedict XVI, *Caritas in veritate*, chap. 3.

92. Cf. the series of passages from papal encyclicals gathered by Tihamér Tóth, "Is There a Vatican School for Competition Policy?," *Loyola University Chicago Law Journal* 46, no. 101 (2015): 597–99.

93. Congregation for the Doctrine of the Faith and the Dicastery for Promoting Integral Human Development, "'Oeconomicae et pecuniariae quaestiones': Considerations for an Ethical Discernment Regarding Some Aspects of the Present Economic-financial System," *Bulletin of the Holy See Press Office*, May 17, 2018, https://press.vatican.va/content/salastampa/en/bollettino /pubblico/2018/05/17/180517a.html, esp. paras. 13 and 14.

94. See http://www.vatican.va/content/francesco/en/speeches/2020 /february/documents/papa-francesco_20200228_accademia-perlavita.html.

95. There is no reason in principle why a conservative could not support strict gun laws, price controls on hospital and medical services, and national railways, as Tories in the UK have long demonstrated. Scruton reflects this in *Meaning of Conservatism*, and in his chapter "The Truth in Socialism" in *How to Be a Conservative*.

96. Smith was an establishment thinker: see D. Winch, *Smith's Politics* (Cambridge, 1978), 140–41, a consequential work that changed scholarship on Smith. Jerry Muller argues that Smith's political ethics is a case for the institutional direction of the passions (Muller, *Adam Smith in His Time and Ours*, 88–89), and more recently, Fonna Forman: "It is a delicious irony of history, and an uncomfortable biographical fact for many, that Smith ended the last twelve years of his career, as his father had, working as a customs commissioner, a proud tax collector in the Scottish customs house, the very agent of British mercantilism"; see F. Forman, "Adam Smith and a New Public Imagination," in *Are Markets Moral?*, ed. Arthur M. Melzer and Steven J. Kautz (University of Pennsylvania Press, 2018), 171. Forman argues that there is no modern theorist more misunderstood than Smith, an opinion shared by French theorist Jean-Pierre Dupuy. For the role of institutions in mentoring a free economy in Smith, see P. Sagar, *Adam Smith Reconsidered* (Princeton, NJ: Princeton University Press, 2022), 110.

97. Benedict XVI, *Caritas in veritate*, para. 35.

98. Botton, *The Pleasures and Sorrows of Work*, chap. 3.

99. Jeffrey Ball, "As Exxon Pursues African Oil, Charity Becomes Political Issue," *Wall Street Journal*, January 10, 2006.

100. Prada CSR #PradaGroupReponsibility, YouTube, December 15, 2015, https://www.google.com/search?q=prada+video+corporate+social +responsibility&rlz=1C5GCEM_en&oq=prada+video+corporate+social +responsibility&aqs=chrome..69i57j33i299l2.16859j0j15&sourceid=chrome &ie=UTF-8#fpstate=ive&vld=cid:346af432,vid:oVYL0mhOyQg. The particular ethical focus of Prada is all the more startling once it is known that Miuccia Prada, designer and highly successful businesswoman with a net worth of $11 billion, is also a PhD in political science and a one-time member of the Communist Party.

101. For these various points from *Laudato Si'*, see paragraphs 129, 94, and 112, respectively. "For example, there is a great variety of small-scale food production systems which feed the greater part of the world's peoples, using a modest amount of land and producing less waste, be it in small agricultural parcels, in orchards and gardens, hunting and wild harvesting or local fishing. Economies of scale, especially in the agricultural sector, end up forcing smallholders to sell their land or to abandon their traditional crops" (*Laudato Si'*, para. 129).

102. Benjamin, *Arcades Project*, 653.

103. See his delightful essay, Walter Benjamin, "Unpacking My Library: A Talk about Book Collecting," https://warwick.ac.uk/fac/arts/english/current students/undergraduate/modules/lit/syllabus/unpacking_my_library.pdf, and his fascination with toy collecting in "Old Toys" in Kenneth Gross, *On Dolls* (Notting Hill Editions, 2018).

104. Benjamin, *Arcades Project*, 71.

105. L. Strauss, "Philosophy as Rigorous Science," in *Studies in Platonic Political Philosophy* (Chicago, 1983), 32.

106. Maurice Cornforth, *Marxism and the Linguistic Philosophy* (New York: International Publishers, 1965), 237. Cf. Engels on replacing the division of labor (and thus class): "It was based upon the insufficiency of production. It will be swept away by the complete development of modern productive forces"; (Frederick Engels, *Socialism: Utopian and Scientific*, III: Historical Materialism, https://www.marxists.org/archive/marx/works/1880/soc-utop/ch03.htm.

107. "The *division of labour* is the economic expression of the *social character of labour* within the estrangement. Or, **since *labour* is only an expression of human activity within alienation**, of the manifestation of life as the alienation of life, the *division of labour*, too, is therefore nothing else but the *estranged, alienated* positing of human activity as a *real activity of the species* or as *activity of man as a species-being*" (italics in original, bold added) (Karl Marx, *Economic and Philosophical Manuscripts of 1844*: "Human Requirements

and the Division of Labour under the Rule of Private Property," https://www
.marxists.org/archive/marx/works/1844/manuscripts/needs.htm, sec. 34). Engels is a little more circumspect, but still assumes what we believe all teachers
will say is a counterfactual: "Finally, when all capital, all production, all exchange have been brought together in the hands of the nation, private property
will disappear of its own accord, money will become superfluous, and production will so expand and man so change that society will be able to slough off
whatever of its old economic habits may remain"; Frederick Engels, *The Principles of Communism* (1847): https://www.marxists.org/archive/marx/works
/1847/11/prin-com.htm, sec. 18). "The existence of classes originated in the division of labor, and the division of labor, as it has been known up to the present, will completely disappear. For mechanical and chemical processes are not
enough to bring industrial and agricultural production up to the level we have
described; the capacities of the men who make use of these processes must un-
dergo a corresponding development" (sec. 20). "Communal control over production by society as a whole, and the resulting new development, will both
require an entirely different kind of human material. . . . Education will enable
young people quickly to familiarize themselves with the whole system of production and to pass from one branch of production to another in response to
the needs of society or their own inclinations" (sec. 20).

108. Marx's imagination runs to a full "fire and brimstone" Last Judgment. About the pope, Marx says, how surprised he will be "when the reflection of burning cities in the sky will mark the dawn," when the celestial har-
monies are replaced by revolutionary songs, "with the guillotine beating time"
(Benjamin, *Arcades Project*, 652). Voegelin characterizes this as a *Blutrausch*, a
"blood-intoxication," whereby a superman—a Gnostic hero—will emerge from
human sacrifice (*OH*, 4:253–54).

109. Interestingly, there are Soviet-era moon phase watches. Of course,
technically, they are nothing like a Jaeger-LeCoultre, but the real question is
why they exist at all. They are incompatible with the political symbol of Marxist Gnosticism. Voegelin argues that no matter the political symbol, our existential, cosmic reality intrudes and makes itself known. He invokes Thomas
Reid's commonsense philosophy to explain: Reid argues that language itself
conveys core metaphysical commitments that all humans share, e.g., we are active, responsible agents, the division of male and female, the existence of an external world, etc. (Voegelin, "Structures of Consciousness," 369). Thus, a symbol of the *analogia entis*, the moon phase watch, persisted inside the Soviet
Union. Another instance is the elite Soviet ballet, which taught dancers to keep
their heads up by telling them to "look at the Czar" in the royal box; a case of
hierarchy and differentiation intruding.

110. Agamben, *The Kingdom and the Glory*, 188.

111. Ibid., 168 and 256.

112. Which is perhaps the same thing: see the fashion plates in the exhibition catalogue *Heavenly Bodies: Fashion and the Catholic Imagination* (The Met, 2018).

113. Agamben, *The Kingdom and the Glory*, xii.

114. G. Agamben, *The Highest Poverty* (Stanford, CA: Stanford University Press, 2013).

115. Cf. M. Bakunin, *Revolutionary Catechism*, parts IX–X, https://www.marxists.org/reference/archive/bakunin/works/1866/catechism.htm.

116. Brunello Cucinelli: "Hamlet of Cashmere and Harmony," http://www.brunellocucinelli.com/en/solomeo#the-territory.

117. Scheler, *The Eternal in Man*, 399–400.

118. For this observation, see Chantal Delsol, *Icarus Fallen* (ISI, 2010).

119. Brian Blackstone and Vanessa Fuhrmans, "What Is Germany's Mittlestand?," Wall Street Journal, June 27, 2011.

120. Small Business & Entrepreneurship Council, "Facts & Data on Small Business and Entrepreneurship" (2019), https://sbecouncil.org/about-us/facts-and-data/.

121. A five-minute video, "A Man and His Dream," tells the story of Cucinelli's father (Brunello Cucinelli, "A Man and His Dream," Vimeo, https://vimeo.com/37749677). His father left the village and went to the city to work in a factory. Cucinelli narrates that there his father was mocked for his village ways and was repeatedly humiliated by co-workers, who thought him a rube. In starting his clothing business, Cucinelli, dubbed by the *Wall Street Journal* "King of Cashmere," swore to find a business model that would guarantee he and his staff could work with dignity. Besides evidence of the beautiful working conditions, the video includes Cucinelli speaking of his philosophical inspirations. From his reading, Cucinelli gathered what was necessary. From Kant, he learnt about beauty, from Rousseau, the worth of village life, and from St. Benedict, the role of the abbot father who manages others but always with an eye to the confirmation of their dignity.

122. Eric Voegelin, "Testing the Truth of Man's Experience in the In-Between," VoegelinView, December 14, 2012, https://voegelinview.com/testing-the-truth-of-the-in-between/.

123. In Voegelin, a symbol is a society's self-understanding. In commercial civilizations, the division of labor is a symbol developed theoretically to match a symbol as a lived reality, the moon phase watch or luxury. There are two sets of symbols: "The symbols in reality are themselves to a considerable extent the result of clarifying processes so that the two sets will also approach each other frequently with regard to their meanings and sometimes even achieve identity" (*NSP*, 29).

CHAPTER 6. The Conservative *via media:*
Between Nationalism and the Dream of Cosmopolis

1. William Kristol and Robert Kagan, "Toward a Neo-Reaganite Foreign Policy," *Foreign Affairs* July/August 1996, https://carnegieendowment .org/1996/07/01/toward-neo-reaganite-foreign-policy-pub-276.

2. Thomas Jefferson to Rogers Clark, December 25, 1780, https:// founders.archives.gov/documents/Jefferson/01-04-02-0295.

3. Woodrow Wilson, Speech to Congress, April 1917, http://history matters.gmu.edu/d/4943/.

4. Declaration of the Rights of Man and of the Citizen, https:// avalon.law.yale.edu/18th_century/rightsof.asp.

5. Marquis de Condorcet, *Sketch for a Historical Picture of the Human Mind*, in Kramnick, ed., *The Portable Enlightenment Reader*, 27.

6. Immanuel Kant, *Kant: Political Writings*, ed. H. S. Reiss, trans. H. B. Nisbet (Cambridge University Press, 1991), 95–130.

7. Kant, *Idea for a Universal History*, eighth proposition, in *Kant: Political Writings*, 51.

8. Kant, *Perpetual Peace*, in ibid., 99.

9. Ibid., 113–14.

10. Ibid.

11. Ibid., 101.

12. Fukuyama, *The End of History and the Last Man*, 185.

13. Ludwig von Mises, *Liberalism: In the Classical Tradition*, https:// mises.org/library/liberalism-classical-tradition/html/p/47. This text was cited by Hazony in making his case that liberalism is inherently universalistic.

14. The phrase comes from Charles Krauthammer's famous article, "The Unipolar Moment," *Foreign Affairs* 70, no. 1 (1990): 23–33: https://www.foreign affairs.com/articles/1991-02-01/unipolar-moment.

15. See, for example, Dugin, "Fourth Political Theory: Shortest Presentation," http://www.4pt.su/en/content/fourth-political-theory-shortest -presentation.

16. The speech of Charles, prince of Wales, to a traditionalist conference can be found here, http://www.sacredweb.com/conference06/conference _introduction.html.

17. René Guénon, *The Crisis of the Modern World*, in *The Collected Works of René Guénon* (Sophia Perennis), 30. Kindle.

18. From Dugin, *Geosophy: Horizons and Civilization*; quoted in Jafe Arnold, "Guénon in Russia: The Traditionalism of Alexander Dugin," Academia .edu, 33.

19. René Guénon, *The Essential René Guénon: Metaphysical Principles, Traditional Doctrines, and the Crisis of Modernity* (World Wisdom), 271. Kindle. From his *Introduction to the Study of Hindu Doctrines*.

20. Ibid., 68: from *East and West*.

21. Dugin, "The Logos of Europe," http://www.4pt.su/en/content/logos -europe-catastrophe-and-horizons-another-beginning.

22. Heidegger, *Introduction to Metaphysics*, 42. Kindle.

23. Dugin, "Encounter with Heidegger: An Invitation to Journey," http:// www.4pt.su/en/content/encounter-heidegger-invitation-journey.

24. From Richard Wisser's 1969 interview with Martin Heidegger, http:// intelart.blogspot.com/2017/05/richard-wisser-interview-with-martin.html.

25. See, for example, Dugin, "Anthropological Aspect of Postmodernity," http://www.4pt.su/en/content/anthropological-aspect-postmodernity, and also Dugin, "Eurasian Idea and Postmodernism," http://www.4pt.su/en/content /eurasian-idea-and-postmodernism.

26. Cf. "Encounter with Dugin: An Invitation to Journey."

27. "If one wishes to know metaphysics, therefore, one must turn to the East; and even if one's wish is to recover some of the metaphysical traditions that may once have existed in the West, a West that was in many respects much closer to the East than it is today, it is above all with the help of Eastern doctrines and by comparison with them that one may succeed, because these are the only teachings in the domain of metaphysics that can still be studied directly"; René Guénon, *The Essential René Guénon: Metaphysical Principles, Traditional Doctrines, and the Crisis of Modernity* (World Wisdom), 77. Kindle. From *Studies in Hinduism*.

28. "Therefore we must direct our historical meditation, perhaps still more inconspicuously and decisively, only to the thinkers belonging to the history of the first beginning so that through the interrogative dialogue with their way of questioning we might unexpectedly plant a questioning that will some day find itself explicitly rooted in another beginning"; Martin Heidegger, *Contributions to Philosophy (Of the Event)* (Indiana University Press), 177. Kindle.

29. Dugin, "Sacred Geography to Geopolitics," http://www.4pt.su/en /content/sacred-geography-geopolitics.

30. Interview by Michael Millerman, "Alexander Dugin on Martin Heidegger," Academia.edu.

31. For example, Scruton's program for the BBC, *Why Beauty Matters*, https://www.bbc.co.uk/programmes/b00p6tsd.

32. A point made by Robert V. Young; see Young, "Transatlantic Conservatism and the Dilemma of Tradition," https://isi.org/modern-age/transatlantic -conservatism-and-the-dilemma-of-tradition/.

33. "The real traditional outlook is always and everywhere essentially the same, whatever outward form it may take; the various forms that are specially suited to different mental conditions and different circumstances of time and place are merely expressions of one and the same truth; but this fundamental unity beneath apparent multiplicity can be grasped only by those who are able to take up a point of view that is truly intellectual"; Guénon, *Crisis of the Modern World*, 30. Note that Guénon's concept of "intellectual" is roughly equivalent to the Neoplatonic or medieval Victorine understanding of "mystical intuition."

34. For a brief overview of the rise of romantic nationalism, see R. Palmer and J. Colton, *A History of the Modern World*, 4th ed. (New York: Alfred Knopf, 1971), 442–47.

35. Reuters, "Trump Calls on Nations to Reject Globalism, Embrace Nationalism," September 21, 2019, https://www.reuters.com/article/us-un -assembly-trump-globalism/trump-calls-on-nations-to-reject-globalism -embrace-nationalism-idUSKBN1W91XP.

36. Viktor Orban's Speech, September 5, 2015, https://www.kormany .hu/en/the-prime-minister/the-prime-minister-s-speeches/viktor-orban-s -speech-at-the-14th-kotcse-civil-picnic.

37. Viktor Orban, http://www.kormany.hu/en/the-prime-minister/the -prime-minister-s-speeches/speech-by-prime-minister-viktor-orban-on-15 -march.

38. Cf. Alain de Benoist and Charles Champetier, *Manifesto of the French New Right in the Year 2000*, http://www.4pt.su/en/content/manifesto-french -new-right.

39. Ibid., II.8.

40. Ibid., II.2.

41. Ibid., II.8.

42. Roger Griffin "Between Metapolitics and *apoliteia*: The Nouvelle Droite's strategy for Conserving the Fascist Vision in the 'interregnum,'" *Modern & Contemporary France* 8, no. 1 (200): 35–53, https://www.tandfonline .com/doi/abs/10.1080/096394800113349.

43. Benoist and Champetier, *Manifesto of the French New Right*, III.3

44. Ibid., III.1–2.

45. Ibid., I.1.

46. Ibid., II.12.

47. Hungarian Constitution, https://www.constituteproject.org/constitu tion/Hungary_2011.pdf.

48. Ibid., article L.

49. "Hungary Tries for Baby Boom with Tax Breaks and Loan Forgive-ness," https://www.bbc.com/news/world-europe-47192612.

50. Ofir Haivry and Yoram Hazony, "What Is Conservatism?," *American Affairs* 1, no. 2 (2017), https://americanaffairsjournal.org/2017/05/what-is-conservatism/. Hazony's case for nationalism was subsequently developed in his *The Virtue of Nationalism*.

51. Yoram Hazony, *The Virtue of Nationalism* (New York: Basic Books, 2018), 16. Kindle.

52. Ibid., 21.

53. Religious intolerance was widespread in Europe in the sixteenth century, and it is legitimate from a modern viewpoint to lament the harsh treatment of Protestants in Spanish-ruled Holland, as for that matter of Catholics in Protestant England and its rule in Ireland. But it is unclear why Spain, which ruled Holland by existing principles of dynastic succession, was behaving in a more imperial way than, say, England in Ireland and in the Anglo-Spanish war in the late sixteenth century. Queen Elizabeth I had been actively aiding the Dutch rebels by agreeing to send a military expedition to aid the Dutch rebellion in 1585. England had in effect declared war on Spain by the Treaty of Nonsuch (1585). It is also noteworthy that the defeat of the Spanish Armada in 1588 was not the end of the Anglo-Spanish war, which continued inconclusively until the Treaty of London in 1604, with England experiencing subsequent losses. Cf. Wes Ulm, "The Defeat of the English Armada and the 16th-Century Spanish Naval Resurgence," Harvard University personal website, http://www.people.fas.harvard.edu/~ulm/history/eng_armada.htm. Britain, Spain, Holland, and France were all, of course, empire-builders in the early modern era.

54. Ibid., chap. III, "The Protestant Construction of the West."

55. Ibid., chap. V, "Liberalism Discredited."

56. Ibid., chap. VI. "Liberalism as Imperialism," 43–44.

57. Joseph de Maistre. *Considerations on France*, VI. http://maistre.uni.cx/considerations_on_france.html.

58. Burke, https://www.constitution.org/eb/rev_fran.htm. A similar idea is found among the classical Stoics (e.g., Hierocles).

59. See https://www.biblegateway.com/passage/?search=Galatians+3&version=RSVCE.

60. Aquinas, *ST* II-II q. 2, a. 7, resp. (Edizione San Paolo, 1988).

61. Aquinas, *ST* II-II, q. 101, a. 1, trans. Dominican Fathers (Westminster, MD: Christian Classics, 1981). The Latin text I included for clarification is from Edizione San Paolo, 1988.

62. Dawson, *The Making of Europe.*

63. Edmund Burke, *Letters on a Regicide Peace*, https://oll.libertyfund.org/titles/burke-select-works-of-edmund-burke-vol-3.

64. The Paris Statement: *A Europe We Can Believe In.*

65. Burke, *Reflections*.

66. Perhaps the most important work in this secondary literature is Peter Stanlis, *Edmund Burke and Natural Law* (Transaction Press, 2015), https:// books.google.es/books?id=VFq_WufAqQwC&source=gbs_navlinks_s. See also ISI's review of the literature on Burke, https://isi.org/intercollegiate -review/edmund-burkes-progeny-recent-scholarship-on-burkes-political -philosophy/.

67. Burke, *Reflections*.

68. Edmund Burke, *Tracts Relative to the Laws of Popery in Ireland* (1760–65), http://www.ricorso.net/rx/library/authors/classic/Burke_E/Ir _Affairs/Tracts_1763.htm. The bracketed section is added by the author. Cf. Aquinas, *ST* II-II, q. 96, a. 4.

69. Nicholas Berdyaev, *The Destiny of Man* (San Rafael, CA: Semantron Press, 2009), 106.

CHAPTER 7.   Liberty and History

1. Parts of this chapter are drawn from Alexander S. Rosenthal-Pubul, "Reflections on Ancient and Modern Freedom: Greek Philosophical Thought and Modern Liberalism," *The Modern Age* (Winter 2016): 35–45.

2. Important to mention is that Hegel's conception of freedom is distinct from that of Anglo-American liberalism, which from Hegel's standpoint is incomplete and focuses merely on the subjective freedom of the individual and not on freedom embodied in the rational state and the absolute spirit.

3. See G. W. F. Hegel, *Phenomenology of Spirit*, secs. 178–96.

4. Fukuyama, *End of History and the Last Man*, 144.

5. Francis Fukuyama, *Identity: Contemporary Identity Politics and the Struggle for Recognition* (London: Profile Books, 2019).

6. Fukuyama, *The End of History and the Last Man*, 328.

7. G. W. F. Hegel, *The Philosophy of History*, trans. J. Sibree (Amherst, NY: Prometheus Books, 1991), 103.

8. Ibid., 104.

9. Ibid., 334.

10. Ibid., 452.

11. Cf. Nietzsche, *The Will to Power*, 94.

12. Hegel, *The Philosophy of History*, 452.

13. Alexandre Kojève, *Introduction to the Reading of Hegel* (Ithaca, NY: Cornell University Press, 1980), 58.

14. Fukuyama, *The End of History and the Last Man*, 197. It is possible at this point that Fukuyama is just explaining his or Kojève's view of Hegel

and Christianity. In fact, however, Hegel seemed to see his own philosophy as a kind of philosophical Christianity.

15. Francis Fukuyama, "The End of History?," *The National Interest*, no. 16 (1989): 14.

16. Fukuyama, *The End of History and the Last Man*, 345–46.

17. G.W. F. Hegel, *Outlines of the Philosophy of Right*, trans. T. M. Knox; rev. and ed. Stephen Houlgate (New York: Oxford, 2008), 258.

18. Fukuyama, "The End of History?," 8.

19. Fukuyama, *Identity*, 47.

20. The Left-egalitarians typically mobilize legitimate moral concerns, such as about racism, but their censoriousness is by no means limited to overtly hateful and bigoted utterance as commonsense would understand it. To cite one example "All lives matter" is now a controversial statement that has led to people losing their jobs; Cf. David Aaro, "Sacramento Kings Announcer Grant Napear out after 'All Lives Matter Tweet,'" Fox News, July 3, 2020, https://www.foxnews.com/sports/sacramento-kings-announcer-out-following-all-lives-matter-tweet.

21. Pew Research Center, "40% of Millennials OK with Limiting Speech Offensive to Minorities," https://www.pewresearch.org/fact-tank/2015/11/20/40-of-millennials-ok-with-limiting-speech-offensive-to-minorities/.

22. See the case of Charles Murray at Middlebury College (Vermont) in 2017. In the melee of violent students outside the lecture hall, Allison Stanger, Murray's host and Middlebury professor, received a concussion; see http://www.middlebury.edu/newsroom/information-on-charles-murray-visit.

23. Fukuyama, *Identity*, 116.

24. Herbert Marcuse, "Repressive Tolerance," in Robert Paul Wolff, Barrington Moore Jr., and Herbert Marcuse, *A Critique of Pure Tolerance* (Boston: Beacon Press, 1969), 95–137, https://www.marcuse.org/herbert/publications/1960s/1965-repressive-tolerance-fulltext.html.

25. See Daniel Mahoney, "A Revolutionary Moment?," *Law & Liberty*, June 18, 2020, https://lawliberty.org/podcast/a-revolutionary-moment/.

26. "I am normally said to be free to the degree to which no man or group of men interferes with my activity. Political liberty in this sense is simply the area within which a man may act unobstructed by others. If I am prevented by others from doing what I can otherwise do, I am to that degree unfree"; Isaiah Berlin, "Two Concepts of Liberty," in *Four Concepts of Liberty* (Oxford University Press, 1969), 122.

27. Jeremy Bentham, *University College Papers* LXIX, 44; quoted in Frederick Rosen, *Classical Utilitarianism from Hume to Mill* (New York: Routledge, 2003), 247.

28. "If we may call liberalism that political doctrine which regards as the fundamental political fact the rights, as distinguished from the duties, of man, and which identifies the state with the protection or safeguarding of those rights, we must say that the founder of liberalism was Hobbes"; Leo Strauss, *Natural Right and History* (Chicago: University of Chicago Press, 1992), 181–82.

29. "LIBERTY or FREEDOME signifieth (properly) the absence of Opposition (by Opposition, I mean externall Impediments of motion; . . . A FREE-MAN, *is he, that, in those things, which by his strength and wit he is able to do, is not hindered to do what he has a wit to do*"; Hobbes, *Leviathan*, XXI, "Of the Liberty of Subjects" (Penguin, 1985), 261.

30. Ibid., 271.

31. Burke, *Reflections*.

32. Xenophon, *Memorabilia*, ed. E. C. Marchant (1923), 4.5.3, http://www.perseus.tufts.edu/hopper/. Cf. also https://isi.org/modern-age/reflections-on-ancient-and-modern-freedom/.

33. See the discussion in Jaeger, *Paideia*, 2:53, and notes on 379.

34. Xenophon, *Memorabilia* 1.5.4–5.

35. Plato, *Republic* (Books VI–X), trans. Paul Shorey (Cambridge, MA: Harvard University Press, 2006), 577d-e. I may also use the digital version on Perseus.org: *Plato in Twelve Volumes*, Vols. 5 and 6, trans. Paul Shorey (Cambridge, MA: Harvard University Press, 1969).

36. See the discussion of *parrhesia* in Michel Foucault's Berkeley lectures on the topic, which was formerly accessible at https://foucault.info/parrhesia/foucault.DT1.wordParrhesia.en/.

37. Demosthenes, *Exordia* 27.1, http://www.perseus.tufts.edu/hopper/text?doc=Perseus%3Atext%3A1999.01.0068%3Aexordium%3D27%3Asection%3D1 (my addition of the Greek term). The concept also appears in the tradition of Attic drama. See Euripides, *Hippolytus* 422. Euripides has his character Phaedra state that she gave birth to her children "that they may live in glorious Athens as free men, free of speech and flourishing"; http://www.perseus.tufts.edu/hopper/text?doc=Eur.%20Hipp.%20422&lang=original.

38. Plato, *Republic* 557b.

39. Sullivan, "Democracies End When They Are Too Democratic."

40. Plato, *Republic* 563e, https://www.perseus.tufts.edu/hopper/text?doc=Perseus%3Atext%3A1999.01.0168%3Abook%3D8%3Asection%3D563e.

41. Aristotle, *Politics* 1317b, in *Aristotle in 23 Volumes*, Vol. 21, trans. H. Rackham (Cambridge, MA: Harvard University Press, 1944), http://www.perseus.tufts.edu/hopper/text?doc=Perseus%3Atext%3A1999.01.0058%3Abook%3D6%3Asection%3D1317a.

42. Aristotle, *Nicomachean Ethics*, trans. H. Rackham (Cambridge, MA: Harvard University Press, 1999), 1105a-b (my italics).

43. Ibid., 1319.

44. Xenophon, *Memorabilia* 1.2.14, http://www.perseus.tufts.edu/hopper/text?doc=Perseus%3Atext%3A1999.01.0208%3Abook%3D1%3Achapter%3D2%3Asection%3D14. See also Jaeger, *Paideia*, 1:55, for a discussion of the Socratic concept of *autarkeia*.

45. Plato, *Apology* 29d-e, http://www.perseus.tufts.edu/hopper/text?doc=Perseus%3Atext%3A1999.01.0170%3Atext%3DApol.

46. Plato, *Apology* 41d.

47. Plato, *Gorgias* 469.

48. Pierre Hadot, *What Is Ancient Philosophy?* (Cambridge, MA: Harvard University Press, 2002), 223.

49. Seneca, *Ad Lucillium* 41.6 (my translation).

50. Ibid., 41. Second English translation is Richard M. Gummere. See Loeb Vol. 75, which includes the Latin. Perhaps more literally the last might be rendered "happy in the midst of adversity."

51. Diogenes Laertius, "Zeno," in *Lives of Eminent Philosophers*, Vol. 7, chap. 1, trans. R. D. Hicks (Cambridge, MA: Harvard University Press, 1972), http://www.perseus.tufts.edu/hopper/text?doc=Perseus%3Atext%3A1999.01.0258%3Abook%3D7%3Achapter%3D1.

52. Cicero, *Paradoxa Stoicorum* V.33: Quo modo aut cui tandem hic libero imperabit, qui non potest cupiditatibus suis imperare?; http://www.thelatinlibrary.com/cicero/paradoxa.shtml. English translation by Cyrus R. Edmonds at https://archive.org/stream/StoicParadoxesParadoxaStoicorumMarcusTulliusCicero/Stoic%20Paradoxes%20%28Paradoxa%20Stoicorum%29%20-%20Marcus%20Tullius%20Cicero_djvu.txt.

53. John 8:32.

54. Romans 7:21–24 (RSV).

55. See Aquinas, *ST* I-II, q. 62, a. 1, trans. Fathers of the English Dominican Province (Westminster, MD: Christian Classics. 1981).

56. Aristotle, *Politics* 1253a.

57. Cf. Augustine, *Civitas Dei*, 15.

58. It is hard to imagine liberalism ever having arisen without the fourteenth-century debates about nominalism and the fixity of nature. For the legal implications of these extreme metaphysical speculations, see Vitoria, *On Homicide*.

59. Edmund Burke, *Letters on a Regicide Peace*, https://oll.libertyfund.org/titles/burke-select-works-of-edmund-burke-vol-3.

60. Seneca, *Ad Lucillium* 47, trans. Richard Gummere, Loeb Vol. 75.

61. Aristotle, *Politics* 1254b–1255a.

62. Edmund Burke, Letter to the Honorable Henry Dundas, April 9, 1792, https://oll.libertyfund.org/titles/burke-select-works-of-edmund-burke-vol-4/simple.

63. William F. Byrne, "Burke's Wise Counsel on Religious Liberty and Freedom," The Imaginative Conservative, July 27, 2012, https://theimaginative conservative.org/2012/07/burkes-wise-counsel-on-religious.html.

64. Edmund Burke, *Tract on the Popery Laws* (1765).

65. Edmund Burke, "Speech on the Relief of Protestant Dissenters," in *The Portable Edmund Burke*, ed. Isaac Kramnick (Penguin, 1999), 107–16. Kindle.

66. Burke, *Reflections*.

67. "In this character of the Americans, a love of freedom is the predominating feature which marks and distinguishes the whole.... They are therefore not only devoted to liberty, but to liberty according to English ideas, and on English principles"; Edmund Burke, "Speech on Conciliation with the Colonies" (March 22, 1775), http://press-pubs.uchicago.edu/founders/documents/v1ch1s2.html.

68. John Stuart Mill. "On Liberty," chap. 1, https://www.utilitarianism.com/ol/one.html.

69. As in the famous and recently overturned *Roe v. Wade* (1973) Supreme Court case. The court's opinion resting largely on the right to privacy can be found at https://supreme.justia.com/cases/federal/us/410/113/.

70. Edmund Burke, Letter to Francois Depont, http://oll.libertyfund.org/quotes/473.

71. Burke, *Reflections*.

72. Edmund Burke, "Letter to a Member of the National Assembly" (1791), http://www.gutenberg.org/files/15700/15700-h/15700-h.htm#MEMBER_OF_THE_NATIONAL_ASSEMBLY.

73. Burke, *Reflections*. The citation is from Cicero, *Pro Sestio* 9.21, rendered by E. D. Yonge as "all virtuous men naturally look with favour on noble birth."

74. M. L. Clarke, *Classical Education in Britain, 1500–1900* (Cambridge: Cambridge University Press, 1959), 61.

75. Burke, *Letters on a Regicide Peace*.

76. Roger Scruton, "Identity, Family, Marriage: Our Core Conservative Values Have Been Betrayed," *The Guardian*, May 11, 2013, https://www.the guardian.com/commentisfree/2013/may/11/identity-family-marriage-conservative-values-betrayed.

77. Burke, *Reflections*.

78. "And let us with caution indulge the supposition that morality can be maintained without religion. Whatever may be conceded to the influence of refined education on minds of peculiar structure, reason and experience both forbid us to expect that national morality can prevail in exclusion of religious principle" (Washington, Farewell Address).

79. Ibid.

80. Burke, *Reflections*.

81. Daniel Mahoney, *The Conservative Foundations of the Liberal Order* (Wilmington, DE: ISI Books, 2010).

82. Aristotle, *Politics* 1280b.

CHAPTER 8. Conservatism without Reprimitivism

1. Valerie Strauss, "The Rich Have Always Had a Leg Up in College Admissions: How Different, Then, Is This New Scandal?," *Washington Post*, March 12, 2019, https://www.washingtonpost.com/education/2019/03/13/rich -have-always-had-leg-up-college-admissions-how-different-then-is-this-new -scandal/.

2. It is not only principled liberals making this point, so is the hard Left; see Chaudhary and Raphaële, "The Supermanagerial Reich."

3. F. Fukuyama, *Political Order and Political Decay: From the Industrial Revolution to the Globalization of Democracy* (Farrar, Straus and Giroux, 2014), 464–66 and 478–79.

4. For Hume on the permanent risk of repatrimonialization, see Hume, *A Treatise of Human Nature*, 3.2.10, 10–11.

5. Marx, "Human Requirements and the Division of Labour under the Rule of Private Property," sec. 20.

6. In addition to Tom Holland and Nietzsche, see the eighteenth-century debates about modern civility and military honor, and whether these belonged to Christianity or the ancients; among many discussions, see R. Robertson, *The Enlightenment* (HarperCollins, 2021), 689–92.

7. M. Agbaw-Ebai, *Light of Reason, Light of Faith: Joseph Ratzinger and the German Enlightenment* (South Bend, IN: St. Augustine's Press, 2021).

8. An image invoked by the well-known Catholic conservative Rusty Reno. Although not always clear, Reno, *The Return of the Strong Gods* (New York: Regnery, 2019), appears to flip between a flirtation with a Prussian-style conservatism and the current fashion for ultramontanism in Catholic circles.

9. For example, traces of angelism can be found in John Paul II, *Theology of the Body*, despite the obvious effort to forestall the possibility. During

John Paul II's papacy, Catholic social thought combined natural law and the philosophy of the person. In *Theology of the Body*, John Paul II is primarily interested in the naked body, part of his emphasis on the transcendence of persons. In an age of technoscience, this is salutary. He is also completely alert to the problematic nature of desire, but, in our opinion, he does not go far enough: he does not take the potential of psychoanalysis seriously. In an address to psychiatrists, he strongly asserts the transcendence of the person, despite the fact that his mentor, Pope Paul VI, had edged closer to psychoanalysis. See, respectively, John Paul II, "Address of His Holiness John Paul II to the Members of the American Psychiatric Association and the World Psychiatric Association," Consistory Hall, Vatican, January 3, 1993, http://www.vatican .va/content/john-paul-ii/en/speeches/1993/january/documents/hf_jp-ii_spe _19930104_psychiatric-association.html, and Paul VI in 1973, "Now we estimate this famous current of anthropological studies," as quoted in Renato Foschi, Marco Innamorati, and Ruggero Taradel, "'A Disease of Our Time': The Catholic Church's Condemnation and Absolution of Psychoanalysis (1924–1975)," *Journal of the History of the Behavioral Sciences* 54, no. 2 (2018):85–100, https://pubmed.ncbi.nlm.nih.gov/29528127/.

10. See Scruton on the "pieties of ordinary existence," which, present in the fictions of law, provide a people with a self-image; Scruton, *Meaning of Conservatism*, 74.

11. "There is, however, another good work that is done by detective stories. While it is the constant tendency of the Old Adam to rebel against so universal and automatic a thing as civilization, to preach departure and rebellion, the romance of police activity keeps in some sense before the mind the fact that civilization itself is the most sensational of departures and the most romantic of rebellions" (G. K. Chesterton, "A Defence of Detective Stories," Society of Gilbert Keith Chesterton, https://www.chesterton.org/a-defence -of-detective-stories/).

12. Umberto Eco's *The Name of the Rose*, which includes a thirteenth-century Franciscan as a detective, is obviously playful. The way the monk investigates using a pair of spectacles as akin to a microscope points to the modernity of the novel. In *Meditation on the Common Concept of Justice*, Leibniz expressed his belief that at the time there were not even ten thinkers throughout Europe looking through microscopes. He argued that princes could do no better for their kingdoms than proliferate the use of microscopes; see G. Leibniz, *Political Writings* (Cambridge: Cambridge University Press, 1996), 51–53. Ernest Bloch astutely observes that detective fiction is micrological; see E. Bloch et al., "A Philosophical View of the Detective Novel," *Discourse* 2 (Summer 1980): 40.

13. Wagner returned to the theme of Christianity in *Parsifal*, as Scruton discusses; see Roger Scruton, *Wagner's Parsifal: The Music of Redemption* (London: Allen Lane, 2020). Cf. Scruton, *Modern Culture*, 73.

14. A. Kolnai, *The War against the West* [*WaW*] (New Left Books, 1938).

15. A. Kolnai, "Three Riders of the Apocalypse," in *Privilege and Liberty*, 111.

16. A. Kolnai, *On Disgust* (Chicago: Open Court, 2004).

17. Likely one of the most ancient, the sexual use of children is explored grimly in the detective novel by Eric Axl Sund, *The Crow Girl* (New York: Knopf, 2016).

18. A. Kolnai, "Three Riders of the Apocalypse," in *Privilege and Liberty*, 112 and 114.

19. J. Rist, *What Is Truth? From the Academy to the Vatican* (Cambridge: Cambridge University Press, 2016).

20. "Something like an original memory of the good and true (they are identical) has been implanted in us, that there is an inner ontological tendency within man, who is created in the likeness of God, toward the divine"; J. Ratzinger, *On Conscience* (San Francisco: Ignatius, 2007), 32.

21. See John Betz's discussion in his introduction to Przywara, *Analogia Entis*, 17–23.

22. R. Brague, *The Legitimacy of the Human* (South Bend, IN: St. Augustine's Press, 2017).

23. One reason for this is, as Ernest Bloch points out, evidentiary trials date to the mid-eighteenth century; Bloch et al., "A Philosophical View of the Detective Novel," 33.

24. A. Ferguson, *An Essay on the History of Civil Society* (Cambridge: Cambridge University Press, 1995), 191–93.

25. A fine example of the suffering servant motif is investigator Will Graham of the FBI in Thomas Harris, *Red Dragon* (New York: Dell, 2002 [1981]).

26. In Dostoyevsky, sons kill fathers, the young prey upon the old, and, in turn, the old, often with the connivance of parents, prey upon the young. In *Crime and Punishment*, the most monumental and probing work of detective fiction, a new, disturbing layer of human personality is revealed: we are made privy to the unrelenting, psychic self-abuse and moral confusion of the killer, Raskolnikov.

27. A. Yang, "Psychoanalysis and Detective Fiction," *Perspectives in Biology and Medicine* 53, no. 4 (2010): 598.

28. Benjamin, *Charles Baudelaire*, 43.

29. Scruton, *Meaning of Conservatism*, 190.

30. D. Hume, *Treatise of Human Nature*, 1:2.3.1. 5–10, pp. 258–59.

31. D. Hume, *Essays Moral, Political, and Literary*, 130–34. Chivalry is both natural and artifice. It is natural because both the asymmetries of power and the compensating symmetries of "play and dalliance" are ever-present. Hume predates Scheler on the universal pantomime throughout nature. For Scheler, see chapter 3 herein, and, for Hume, *Treatise of Human Nature*, 1:2.2.5, 14–15, p. 234–35. For "play and dalliance," consider the continuity between medieval knights wearing the colors of their beloveds and British fighter pilots in World War II hanging their girlfriends' bras from the outside of the cockpit. The norms of civilization—manners and mores—aim to throw their weight behind the natural propensity to "play and dalliance" in order to master abusive power.

32. The ideal is a challenge to a basic idea in Tocqueville. Of aristocracies compared to democracies, he writes: "They gave to mores generosity rather than mildness, and although they suggested great attachments, they did not give birth to true sympathies; for there are real sympathies only between similar people; and in aristocratic centuries, you see people similar to you only in the members of your caste"; Alexis de Tocqueville, *Democracy in America* (Liberty Fund, 2012), 991.

33. Poe's characterization of detective stories as "tales of ratiocination" is exemplified by not only Dupin and Sherlock but also by Dostoyevsky's police chief, Porfiry Petrovich, an insightful, cunning, and versatile adversary of crime.

34. A persistent theme in the TV show *Bosch*, where detective Harry Bosch reminds colleagues that each victim counts or none of us counts.

35. Among many passages in Hume, see Hume, *Treatise of Human Nature*, 1:2.1.10, 9, 205. Conservative humanism must, we believe, take seriously all of the arts by which humans navigate the problem of our existence. Hume is a reminder that even personalists sensitive to psychoanalysis can underestimate the challenge. Yves Simon: "Among the lasting achievements of modern psychoanalysis perhaps none is more significant than its having shown that an individual's strongest and most idiosyncratic tendencies are sometimes caused by childhood accidents"; see Y. Simon, *An Yves R. Simon Reader: The Philosopher's Calling*, ed. M. Torre (Notre Dame, IN: University of Notre Dame Press, 2021), 254.

36. Dupuy, *The Mark of the Sacred*, 208–9.

37. Francis is the only pope (we know of) who has been in Lacanian psychoanalysis. It is likely the source of his formulation that we are both biography and biology.

38. Lacan, *Écrits*, 6–50 and 102–22.

39. Agatha Christie, *The Murder of Roger Ackroyd* (New York: Harper-Collins, 2011), 92.

40. C. Schmitt, *Concept of the Political*, 64.

41. Dugin: "One can imagine civilization as the numerator, and savagery-barbarism as the denominator of a conditional fraction. Civilization affects consciousness, but the unconscious, through the unceasing `work of dreams' (Freud), constantly misinterprets everything in its favour" (*FPT*, 105–6).

42. Christie, *Murder of Roger Ackroyd*, 75.

43. Ibid., 93.

44. Pope Francis, *Fratelli Tutti*, para. 43.

45. Pius XII, "Address of the Holy Father Pio XII to the Participants in the Fifth International Congress of Psychotherapy and Clinical Psychology," Monday, April 13, 1953, https://nacn-usa.org/wp-content/uploads/Pius-XII-1953-Psychotherapy-and-Psychology-Address.pdf, para. 10.

46. K. Wojtyła, *Person and Community* (New York: Peter Lang, 2008), 137, 190–91.

47. Ibid., 194. "The true measure of any human being lies in morality; through morality, we each write our own most intimate and personal history" (156).

48. Simon, *An Yves R. Simon Reader*, 220.

49. J. Kristeva, *Passions of Our Time* (New York: Columbia University Press, 2018), 232.

50. Scruton is typical of conservatives. Unmasking Žižek's excuses for Stalin and Mao, Scruton lumps Lacan in with Žižek. It is understandable: Žižek is Lacan's most well-known commentator, and a prolific leftist writer. Scruton believes that the revolutionary fervor of Žižek is aided and abetted by Lacan's theory of the Other: "The mirror stage provides the infant with an illusory (and brief) idea of the self, as an all-powerful other in the world of others. But this self is soon to be crushed by the big Other, a character based on the good-breast/bad-breast, good-cop/bad-cop scenario invented by psychoanalyst Melanie Klein. In the course of expounding the tragic aftermath of this encounter, Lacan comes up with astounding aperçus, often repeated without explanation by his disciples, as though they have changed the course of intellectual history" (Roger Scruton, "Clown Prince of the Revolution," *City Journal*, September 29, 2016, https://www.city-journal.org/html/clown-prince-revolution-14632.html). This passage does not get Lacan quite right (Lacan, not altogether respectfully, dissents from Klein's theory, for example). Note that Scruton assesses Lacan situated in the Left's commentarial tradition. This is a shame because "the big Other" is a conservative phenomenon.

51. Lacan, *Seminar 7*, 183–84.

52. This is not exactly news. No psychoanalyst can surprise Aquinas very much about the character of our desires. The analysis of the seven

deadly sins provided the medieval with an astonishing conceptual range to plumb the depths of human evasion, self-deceit, and hatred. Still, psychoanalysis is a significant development of this earlier psychological tradition, as Paul VI appreciated.

53. Lacan, *Seminar 14*, http://www.lacaninireland.com/web/wp-content/uploads/2010/06/Logic-of-Phantasy-spring-1999.pdf.

54. Lacan, *Seminar 20*, 88.

55. For an extremely interesting Lacanian account of the connection between skin, language, and self, as illustrated by the sad case of autism, see Leon Brenner, "Autism in the Lacanian Clinic – the Dermic Drive," January 27, 2022, https://www.youtube.com/watch?v=apn7eCkCsCY.

56. A deceptively simple example of recognition is the custom of queuing: why we do it, what we think about the person who jumps the queue, and what we think he must think of you and me if he thinks we'll put up with it. The tussle for recognition in the phenomenon of queuing is part and parcel of a struggle for recognition that goes on inside our own psyches. Our subjective lives, Lacan argues, are themselves a complex social struggle. Indeed, the two are intimately united. Our innermost lives are also social and public: my personal sense of self inextricably linked to public, established, hierarchical structures of recognition.

57. Tocqueville, *Democracy in America*, 79–80.

58. Ibid., 1037.

59. Lacan is as decisive against leftist humanism. Transhumanism cannot remove the question of inheritance. Humans are birthed; AI is manufactured. No matter the future intimacies we might have with AI—as caregivers, surgeons, cooks, spouses—AI has the form of technoscience. Even if we expect AI to machine biological systems—microbots inside our DNA, say—AI will always be industrial. It will be "birthed" by engineers and accountants, not mothers. The current business of AI is industrialism, but even if that were to change, even if corporations took pity on their property and allowed self-conscious AI freedom instead of slavery, it would not change the fact that AI has an origin story completely unlike that of humans. They will not have mothers because they will never be born immature. They will not have fathers for they have no need of castration. Conservatism is right: there is an essential relationship between being human and being part of a family.

60. Tocqueville, *Democracy in America*, 1035.

61. Lacan, *Seminar 20*, 77, 83.

62. J. Lacan, "Aggressiveness in Psychoanalysis," in *Écrits*, 95.

63. Ibid., 97.

64. Ibid., 99.

65. Ibid., 93. Hence, Lacan's grim joke: "It is a fact of [psycho-analytic] experience that what I want is the good of others in the image of my own" (*Seminar 7*, 187). Castration dampens the anger at source. This dampening generates sympathy, which, in Lacan, is built on the respect demanded by the father. Of course, the role of the father can be, and has been throughout history, played by others, and not just fathers. The father is an *imago*, a structure of the unconscious. In the first instance, the father is not literally a father, but a castration function (Lacan, "Aggressiveness in Psychoanalysis," 89–91). Moreover, the "original dereliction" is not overcome fully, and thus respect and sympathy sit atop the untrustworthy sands of jealously and resentment (ibid., 95–96). It is for this reason that modernity's favored child, humanitarianism, "tends to misrecognize the constancy of aggressive tension in all moral life" (ibid., 97).

66. It is striking that the detective barely figures at all in Patricia Highsmith's crime novel *The Talented Mr. Ripley* (New York: Vintage, 1999). The book ends with Ripley, a terrifyingly pragmatic killer, well and truly scot-free.

Concluding Remarks

1. See Alexander S. Rosenthal-Pubul, "What Went Wrong in Europe? A Reflection on Western Modernity," *The Modern Age* 54 (2012): 17–27, and Rosenthal-Pubul, "Modernism, Tradition, and Humanism: The Foundations of Western Civilizational Identity," in *Global Challenges to the Transatlantic World*, Biblioteca Benjamin Franklin (University of Alcala, 2015), 19–26.

2. Pope Benedict XVI, Regensburg Address: "Faith, Reason, and the University: Memories and Reflections," September 12, 2006, http://www.vatican.va/holy_father/benedict_xvi/speeches/2006/september/documents/hf_ben-xvi_spe_20060912_university-regensburg_en.html.

3. "Socrates' taking up of this question bestowed on *the way of philosophizing* inspired by him a kind of salvation-historical privilege and made it an appropriate vessel for the Christian Logos" (Ratzinger, *On Conscience* (San Francisco: Ignatius, 2007), 28; emphasis added).

4. J. Ratzinger, *Truth and Tolerance* (Ignatius, 2003), 95.

5. J. Habermas and J. Ratzinger, *The Dialectics of Secularization* (San Francisco: Ignatius, 2006), 75. He is unlikely to write this now, but Benedict does add: "These two determine the situation of the world to an extent not matched by another cultural force" (79).

6. Tertullian, *De praescriptione haereticorum*, http://www.thelatinlibrary.com/tertullian/tertullian.praescrip.shtml.

7. Martin Luther, "Address to the Nobility of the German Nation" (1520), https://sourcebooks.fordham.edu/mod/luther-nobility.asp.

8. Benedict XVI, Regensburg Address.

9. "Now, what does λόγος /λέγειν properly mean if, as we contend, the word originally did not have anything to do with saying and asserting, speech and language? λέγειν—legere in Latin—is the same word as our word 'to read' [lesen], but not that particular 'reading' which we immediately associate with script and thereby with the written word and, by extension, with speech and language. Henceforth, we will take lesen in a much broader and also more original sense as meaning [267] 'to harvest,' such as 'to harvest the ears in the field,' 'to harvest the grapes in the vineyard,' and 'to harvest wood in the forest.' λέγειν, to harvest; λόγος, the harvest"; see Martin Heidegger, Martin. *Heraclitus: The Inception of Occidental Thinking and Logic: Heraclitus' Doctrine of the Logos*, trans. Julia Goesser Assaiante and S. Montgomery Ewegen (Bloomsbury, 2018), 203. Kindle.

10. Cf. Arthur W. H. Adkins, "Heidegger and Language," *Philosophy* 37, no. 141 (1962): 229–37, http://www.jstor.org/stable/3748439. But for a more favorable account, see David Hoffmann, "Logos as Composition," *Rhetoric Society Quarterly* 33, no. 3 (2003): 27–53, http://www.jstor.org/stable/3886194.

11. See *Liddell and Scott's Greek-English Lexicon*, s.v. λόγος, https://www.perseus.tufts.edu/hopper/text?doc=Perseus%3Atext%3A1999.04.0057%3Aentry%3Dlo%2Fgos.

12. An idea with a long lineage. One might look to St. Clement of Alexandria's *Stromata*, where Greek philosophy along with Jewish prophecy is presented as *praeparatio evangelica*.

13. Ratzinger, *On Conscience*, 40.

14. J. Ratzinger, *Christianity and the Crisis of Cultures* (Ignatius, 2006), 43.

15. M. Agbaw-Ebai, *Light of Reason, Light of Faith: Joseph Ratzinger and the German Enlightenment* (St. Augustine's Press, 2021), 3.

16. J. Ratzinger, *Truth and Tolerance* (Ignatius, 2003), 126–27.

17. J. Ratzinger and M. Pera, *Without Roots* (Basic Books, 2006), 69.

18. J. Ratzinger, *Values in a Time of Upheaval* (San Francisco: Ignatius, 2006), 161.

19. Ratzinger and Pera, *Without Roots*, 128.

20. Ratzinger, *Values in a Time of Upheaval*, 18.

21. "According to Heidegger, the question of the meaning of Being, and thus Being as such, has been forgotten by 'the tradition' (roughly, Western philosophy from Plato onwards). Heidegger means by this that the history of Western thought has failed to heed the ontological difference, and so has articulated Being precisely as a kind of ultimate being, as evidenced by a series of

namings of Being, for example as idea, energeia, substance, monad or will to power"; see Michael Wheeler, "Martin Heidegger," in *Stanford Encyclopedia of Philosophy* (Winter 2018 ed.), ed. Edward N. Zalta, https://plato.stanford.edu/archives/win2018/entries/heidegger/.

22. Martin Heidegger, *Introduction to Metaphysics*, trans. G. Fried and R. Polt (New Haven, CT: Yale University Press, 2014).

23. Martin Heidegger, *The Essence of Truth* (London: Bloomsbury, 2013), 6.

24. Martin Heidegger, "Letter on Humanism," in *Basic Writings*, ed. David Farrell Krell (New York: Harper Perennial, 2008), 256.

25. Ibid., 225.

26. For a good study on the Strauss–Heidegger relation, see Richard L. Velkey, *Heidegger, Strauss, and the Premises of Philosophy: On Original Forgetting* (Chicago: University of Chicago Press, 2011).

27. Leo Strauss, Lecture One on the *Meno* (1966), 6, https://wslamp70.s3.amazonaws.com/leostrauss/s3fs-public/Meno%20%281966%29.pdf.

28. Ibid., 1.

29. Strauss, *Natural Right and History*, esp. chaps. 1 and 2.

30. "Liberalism has abandoned its absolutist basis and is trying to become entirely relativistic"; see Leo Strauss, "Relativism," in *The Rebirth of Classical Political Rationalism*, ed. Thomas Pangle (University of Chicago, 1989), 17.

31. See Habermas and Ratzinger, *Dialectics of Secularization*, 58–61, on "shared collaboration" as necessary for rule of law.

32. See Benedict XVI, *Caritas in veritate*, para. 35, on distributive justice.

33. Leo Strauss, "Introduction to Political Philosophy," session 15, https://leostrausstranscripts.uchicago.edu/philologic4/strauss/navigate/11/7/.

34. Leo Strauss, "The Mutual Influence of Theology and Philosophy," *Independent Journal of Philosophy* 3 (1979): 114. There is currently a version found at https://kupdf.net/download/leo-strauss-the-mutual-influence-of-theology-and-philosophy-15505349pdf_5a872907e2b6f5784fda3374_pdf.

35. Admittedly, in 1984, Ratzinger did think that Western morality was a direct revelation of God and not anything discernible from an anthropology (see "Bishops, Theologians, and Morality," in Ratzinger, *On Conscience*, 54–55, 64–66. However, he later changed his position.

36. Benedict XVI, Regensburg Address.

37. Ratzinger, *Values in a Time of Upheaval*, 63.

38. Habermas and Ratzinger, *Dialectics of Secularization*, 61 and 71. Here, Ratzinger prefers Scheler's talk of values, but, as pope, he expresses the "inbuilt order" of being human in terms of natural law; see *Caritas in veritate*, paras. 48 and 59.

39. Ratzinger, *Truth and Tolerance*, 239.

40. Habermas and Ratzinger, *Dialectics of Secularization*, 71. Cf. Ratzinger, *Values in a Time of Upheaval*, 54.

41. Ratzinger, *Truth and Tolerance*, 87.

42. J. Ratzinger, *Christianity and the Crisis of Cultures* (Ignatius, 2006), 35 and 39. For Benedict, the positive gains of modernity include "the relative separation of Church and state, freedom of conscience, human rights, and reason's responsibility for itself" (J. Ratzinger, "Europe: A Heritage with Obligations for Christians," in *Church, Ecumenism, and Politics* (San Francisco: Ignatius, 2008), 219).

43. By this phrase, we mean the Catholic academics working in the spirit of Alasdair MacIntyre, and, to the right of him, seminary professors, an exemplar being Crean and Fimister, *Integralism*. For the East Coast college spirit of the young U.S. Catholic Right, see https://scholars-stage.blogspot.com/2021/04/the-problem-of-new-right.html.

44. Ratzinger, *Values in a Time of Upheaval*, 152.

45. Ibid., 156–57. Cf. Ratzinger, *Christianity and the Crisis of Cultures*, 26–28.

46. "Learning to live also means learning to suffer. This is why reverence for that which is holy is also essential" (Ratzinger, *Values in a Time of Upheaval*, 159).

47. Ratzinger, *Truth and Tolerance*, 89. Benedict relies on the definition of Gnosticism given by Hugo Ball.

48. Ibid., 90. More needs to be said. In chapter 5 we used Voegelin's definition: It is political poison, he argues, to think that a sage can deliver illumination and so enlighten minds as to utterly transform the tensions intrinsic to historical human existence. Gnosticism is not merely Alexandrian Hellenism. According to Voegelin, the book of Isaiah is *metastatic*, that is, it offers a magical vision in which humans on this earth will be miraculously changed and perfected through messianic agency. This vision resonates in the New Testament and so Protestant strains are not simply wrong to think eschatological Christianity is the essence of the religion. Voegelin argues that Catholic metaphysics—the *analogia entis*—restrained the Gnosticism present in the Bible. For an excellent discussion, see J. Rhodes, "Voegelin and Christian Faith," *Center Journal* (Summer 1983): 55–105.

49. Ratzinger, *Truth and Tolerance*, 239.

50. Helvetius, *De L'Homme*, sect. VII, CD. I quote from Reinhold Niebuhr, *The Nature and Destiny of Man* (New York: Charles Scribner's Sons, 1964), 1:97.

51. "The time will come when the sun will shine only on free men who know no other master but their reason; when tyrants and priests or their stu-

pid or hypocritical instruments, will exist only in works of history and on the stage; when we shall think of them only to pity their victims and their dupe"; see Marquis de Condorcet, *Sketch for a Historical Picture of the Human Mind*, in Kramnick, ed., *The Portable Enlightenment*, 30.

52. Ratzinger, *Truth and Tolerance*, 234.

53. Ratzinger, *Christianity and the Crisis of Cultures*, 41.

54. Ibid., 44.

55. In light of COVID-19, John Gray argues: "Yet the notion persists that pandemics are blips rather than an integral part of history. Lying behind this is the belief that humans are no longer part of the natural world and can create an autonomous ecosystem, separate from the rest of the biosphere." Pestilence has revealed the extent of angelism in modernity: John Gray, "Why This Crisis Is a Turning Point in History," *The New Statesman*, April 6, 2020, https://www.newstatesman.com/international/2020/04/why-crisis-turning -point-history.

56. Benedict XVI, *Caritas in veritate*, para. 51.

57. Of course, technoscience is commercial, but, more critically, it is mythical. Transhumanism is a "gnostic apocalypticism," technoscience a rationality entwined with myth; see Ratzinger, *Values in a Time of Upheaval*, 18, 23, and 26.

58. Ibid., 147; see the disturbing article on the baby business by Tamara Audi, "Assembling the Global Baby," *Wall Street Journal*, December 10, 2010.

59. Benedict XVI, *Caritas in Veritate*, para. 53.

60. Ratzinger, *Values in a Time of Upheaval*, 165.

61. Ratzinger, *Christianity and the Crisis of Cultures*,44. Cf. Ratzinger and Pera, *Without Roots*, 75.

62. Ratzinger, *Values in a Time of Upheaval*, 149.

63. Ratzinger, *Truth and Tolerance*, 254.

64. NYT Editorial Board, "When It Comes to China, Silence is Golden" *New York Times*, October 7, 2019, https://www.nytimes.com/2019/10/07 /opinion/nba-china-daryl-morey.html.

65. Nicholas K. Gvosdev, "How the Russian Orthodox Church Influences Russia´s Behavior," *The National Interest*, July 8, 2019, https://national interest.org/feature/how-russian-orthodox-church-influences-russias-behavior -66091.

66. Fred Bower "The New Feudalism," *National Review*, July 9, 2014, https://www.nationalreview.com/2014/07/new-feudalism-fred-bauer/.

67. Ratzinger and Pera, *Without Roots*, 78–79. Rusty Reno's *Return of the Strong Gods* exposes the roots of this loss of credibility. It is self-inflicted. During the Cold War, a totalitarian empire sought to subvert our democracies and failed. A combination of market innovation and bloody realism in politics

defeated the Soviets. Percolating all the time, however, was a criticism internal to the West: leading theorists sought to undermine confidence in their own civilization, to puncture the belief that the West's political, cultural, economic, and religious heritage was worthy of celebration and sacrifice.

68. David Frisk, "What Conservatives Ought to Be For," Forum, *Law & Liberty*, April 8, 2020, https://lawliberty.org/forum/what-conservatives-ought-to-be-for/.

69. David Crawford, "Liberal Androgyny: 'Gay Marriage' and the Meaning of Sexuality in Our Time," *Communio*, Summer 2006, https://www.communio-icr.com/articles/view/liberal-androgyny-gay-marriage.

70. "The coming clash will be between this radical emancipation of man and the great historical cultures" (Ratzinger, *Christianity and the Crisis of Cultures*, 44).

71. Benedict XVI, *Caritas in Veritate*, para. 40.

72. See our discussion of Manent in chapter 4, and cf. Ratzinger and Pera, *Without Roots*, 76–77.

73. Ratzinger and Pera, *Without Roots*, 131–32.

74. Ratzinger, *Values in a Time of Upheaval*, 104–5.

75. See McAleer, *To Kill Another*.

76. Ratzinger, *Christianity and the Crisis of Cultures*, 35. Even Hume thinks procreative sex first brings to mind the idea of the social contract; see Hume, *A Treatise of Human Nature*, 1:3.2.2, 4, p. 312.

77. "The radical detachment of the Enlightenment philosophy from its roots ultimately leads it to dispense with man" (Ratzinger, *Christianity and the Crisis of Cultures*, 42).

78. Bertrand Russell was among the most forceful critics of Christian sexual ethics in the early twentieth century: he argued that contraception would "liberate" sex from marriage and reproduction, such that sex might be enjoyed without the responsibilities of childbearing. Already in 1933, replying to Russell, Christopher Dawson expressed the fear that this revolution, so far from being a benign liberation, would lead to the devaluation of marriage and the destruction of the physical basis for the communication of humanism: "For, as Mr. Russell is never tired of pointing out, the use of contraceptives has made sexual intercourse independent of parenthood, and the marriage of the future will be confined to those who seek parenthood for its own sake rather than as the natural fulfilment of sexual love. But under these circumstances who will trouble to marry? Marriage will lose all attractions for the young and the pleasure-loving and the poor and the ambitious. The energy of youth will be devoted to contraceptive love. . . . It is impossible to imagine a system more contrary to the first principles of social well-being. So far from helping modern society to surmount its present difficulties, it only precipitates the crisis. It

must lead inevitably to a social decadence far more rapid and more universal than that which brought about the disintegration of ancient civilization"; Christopher Dawson, "The Patriarchal Family in History." Originally published by Dawson in 1933, this work was included in the Dawson anthology *Dynamics of World History* (Sheed & Ward, 1956), 156–66, https://www .catholicculture.org/culture/library/view.cfm?recnum=860.

79. Ratzinger and Pera, *Without Roots*, 66. Fertility rates have fallen dramatically and are now below replacement (considered to be 2.1) in most of the Western world. In the United States, the fertility rate fell from 3.654 in 1960 to 1.73 in 2018. In the EU they have fallen from 2.6 in 1960 to 1.557 in 2018 (https://data.worldbank.org/indicator/SP.DYN.TFRT.IN?locations=EU).

80. Cf. R. Brague, *The Legitimacy of the Human* (St. Augustine's Press, 2017).

81. Y. Harari, *Homo Sapiens* (HarperCollins, 2015), 216.

82. F. Nietzsche, *Genealogy of Morals* (Penguin, 2014), 1.14.

83. Ibid., 2.6.

84. Benedict is not naïve about the world's religions. He does not think them all equal, and Christianity, like all other religions, needs to be tempered by reason. "For its part, *religion always needs to be purified by reason* in order to show its authentically human face" (Benedict XVI, *Caritas in veritate*, para. 56; emphasis original). See his powerful pages on the *religious* sentiment animating Aztec sacrifice in Ratzinger, *Truth and Tolerance*, 74–75.

85. Ratzinger, *Values in a Time of Upheaval*, 110.

86. Holland, *Dominion*, 13.

87. George R. Wood, *A History of the University of Pennsylvania to 1827* (Philadelphia: McCarty & David, 1834).

88. Daniel Walker Howe, "Classical Education in America," *Wilson Quarterly* (Spring 2011), https://www.wilsonquarterly.com/quarterly/spring-2011 -the-city-bounces-back-four-portraits/classical-education-in-america/. The return to the study of the ancients as a way to shore up civilizational foundations has been taken up by Poland, which recently decided to include the study of Latin and classical antiquity as part of the core curriculum: https://notesfrom poland.com/2020/07/21/poland-adds-latin-to-core-curriculum-to-help-pupils -understand-foundation-of-western-civilisation/. Arguably, in Europe as a whole the decline of the classics in general education has not been quite as dramatic as in the United States. In Europe, the study of classical history and Greek and Latin letters is still included, at least as an option, in many secondary schools.

89. Gilbert Allardyce, "The Rise and Fall of the Western Civilization Course," *American Historical Review* 87, no. 3 (1982): 695–725, doi:10.2307 /1864161.

90. Peter Wood, Glenn Ricketts, Ashley Thorne, and Stephen H. Balch, "The Vanishing West: 1964–2010," National Association of Scholars, May 2, 2011, https://www.nas.org/reports/the-vanishing-west-1964-2010/full-report.

91. Valerie Strauss, "Students Remove Shakespeare Portrait from English Department at Ivy League School," *Washington Post*, December 13, 2016, https://www.washingtonpost.com/news/answer-sheet/wp/2016/12/13/students-remove-shakespeare-portrait-from-english-department-at-ivy-league-school/?utm_term=.2e3c0c214bd7.

92. Xi Jinping, Speech on Confucius's Birthday (September 24, 2014), China-US Focus, http://library.chinausfocus.com/article-1534.html.

93. For this argument fully on display, see Heidegger's criticism of values at the end of *Introduction to Metaphysics*, 220–22.

94. Friedrich Nietzsche, *Twilight of the Idols*, "The Problem of Socrates," 4, in Kaufmann, ed. and trans., *The Portable Nietzsche*, 475, https://archive.org/details/ThePortableNietzscheWalterKaufmann.

95. Friedrich Nietzsche, "Homer's Competition," December 1872, http://nietzsche.holtof.com/Nietzsche_various/homers_competition.htm. In fact, Nietzsche may be partially right insofar as the Greek striving for excellence had a competitive edge that manifested in such sublimated forms as Olympic games and poetic competitions.

96. Friedrich Nietzsche, *On the Genealogy of Morals*, trans. Walter Kaufmann (New York: Vintage, 1989), 33–34.

97. Ibid., 35.

98. See M. Scheler, *The Nature of Sympathy* (Transaction, 2008), 99–100. Cf. Lord Kames, *Essays on the Principles of Morality and Natural Religion*, 37–39.

99. Stephen Tonsor, "Equality in the New Testament," in *Equality, Decadence, and Modernity*, (Wilmington, DE: ISI Books, 2005), 71–84.

100. Ratzinger, *Values in a Time of Upheaval*, 163.

101. Henri de Lubac, *The Drama of Atheistic Humanism* (San Francisco: Ignatius, 1995), 21.

102. Cf. Nicholas Berdyaev, *Dostoyevsky* (Semantron Press, 2009), chaps. 3–4, 67–110.

INDEX

Agamben, Giorgio
  angelism, 48–50
  fashion industry, 101, 115–16
ancient Greece
  freedom, 151–55
  Greeks and natural law, 91–93
  Greek education, 13–15, 25–30,
    32–35, 37
  and Heidegger, 51–55, 237n82
  Pope Benedict XVI, 176–80
  sophists, 27–28
Aquinas, Thomas
  Christocentrism, 33
  individualism, 56–58
  metaphysics, 46, 53
  natural law, 87–96, 138, 140, 155
  value hierarchy, 67–68
Aristotle
  anticommercialism, 19
  education, 29
  family, 10
  hierarchy, 156
  influence of, 156, 188
  Luther's critique of, 177
  metaphysics, 185
  political animal, 10, 155
  virtue ethics, xii, xxxii, 26, 160,
    195

Augustine of Hippo
  on the divine city, 155
  on the earthly city, 105
  on evil and human nature, 32, 155,
    167
  Pope Benedict XVI on, 181
Averroism/angelism, 46
  and division of labor, 112–13, 115,
    119
  and reprimitivism, 163, 167, 169,
    171–72

Bacon, Francis, xxv, 37, 127
Benedict XVI, Pope, 44, 60, 62, 163
  the Benedict Synthesis, 175–78
  —and the Enlightenment,
    181–82
  —and the Greeks, 178, 180
  —between nationalism and
    internationalism, 183–84
  —and reprimitivsim, 187–88
Benjamin, Walter, 163, 168
  angelism, 44, 48
  fashion industry, 114–15
Berdyaev, Nicholas, 23, 40–41, 141
Bible, the, 12, 14, 31, 43, 50, 79, 135,
    176, 180, 192–93
Bodin, Jean, 44

Burke, Edmund, 3–4, 18, 22, 24,
    234n52
    and J. R. R. Tolkien, 75, 78
    liberalism and conservative
        freedom, 150–51, 156–60
    natural law, 137–40
    relation to Counter-
        Enlightenment, 63–64
    on religion 5, 7
    rights, 84

capitalism 17–21
    and division of labor, 110
    the French New Right, 134
    humanistic enterprise, 117, 124
    and transhumanism, 100
Catholic Social Thought (CST), 16,
    56, 113–14
    definition, xxiii
China, 190
    Confucian tradition, 3, 6, 8,
        10–11, 13
Churchill, Winston, xviii, 164
Cicero, 101, 117, 140, 154, 156, 158,
    189, 195
Columbus, Christopher, xvii–xviii
Communism, 41, 44, 167
Condorcet, Marquis de, 63, 122,
    138
Cortes, Juan Donoso, 10, 63
Cucinelli, Brunello, 99, 116–18

Dawson, Christopher, 8, 11, 13–14,
    26, 30, 34, 139, 186
democracy, 4, 23, 84–85
    Fukuyama, 148–49, 175
    of Plato, 152–53, 158
Descartes, René, 37, 46, 53, 106, 127,
    181, 185

Dugin, Aleksandr, 2, 5, 42–46,
    202n33
    angelism and apocalypse, 47–51,
        218n21
    conservative humanism,
        184–85
    individualism, 55–58
    integral traditionalism, 125–31
    nationalism, 134–35
    natural law, 92–93
    occasionalism and a good politics,
        88–89
    postliberalism, 10
    primordialism, 162–64, 166
    risk, 53–55
    transhumanism, 100, 112, 128

Eliot, T. S., 9–10, 112
Enlightenment, 4–5, 8, 20, 24,
    36–41, 44, 181–83
    and Burke, 157, 159
    Counter-Enlightenment, 63,
        127, 130
    detective stories and
        enlightenment, 167, 169
    and Dugin, 47
    and Hegel, 144, 147
    and Heidegger, 48
    Industrial Enlightenment and
        labor, 101–2, 118
    liberalism, 121–22, 130–31
    in relation to humanism, 162–63,
        166
    and Voegelin, 107–8
Erasmus, Desiderius, 34, 156, 167
European Union, 132–33, 139
    Brexit and natural law, 84–85,
        183
    liberalism, 125

fascism, 16, 132, 164–65
Francis, Pope
  angelism, 49–50
  financialization and CST, 113–14
  transhumanism, 171
French New Right (*Nouvelle Droite*), 133–34
French Revolution, 3–5
  Declaration of the Rights of Man, 38, 122
  from the perspective of Hegel, 146
Fukuyama, Francis, 2
  angelism, 50–51, 56, 102
  critique of identity politics, 148–49
  and Dugin, 43, 46–47
  end of history thesis, 103, 143–47
  and J. R. R. Tolkien, 74, 78
  "the Mechanism," 37, 107
  megalothymia, 124
  political Islam, 92
  reprimitivism, 161
  Western liberalism, 23–24, 125, 175, 182

globalization, 130, 133–34
  and Dugin, 47, 125
Gnostics/Gnosticism, 103–8
Gregory of Nyssa, 31–32, 35
Guénon, René, 125–30

Hazony, Yoram, 135–37
Heidegger, Martin, 44–45
  angelism, 48
  metaphysics, 51–56, 58, 177–80, 222n76
  natural law, 92–93
  spiritual decline, 127–28

Hobbes, Thomas, xxxi, 49, 82, 95, 108, 150–51, 196
Holland, Tom, 52, 60, 145, 176, 186–89, 191–92
Homer, 26–27, 30, 196
humanism, 9, 24
  Catholic humanism, 167
  Christian humanism, 55, 101, 165, 184
  classical humanism, 34, 51, 195
  conservative humanism, 56, 60, 78, 129, 140–41, 156, 163, 175, 192–94
  —natural law, 84, 90, 92–93
  —value theory, 69
  division of labor, 111–12
  modern/secular humanism, 25, 36–40, 42
humanistic enterprise, 99, 117
human rights, 38, 41
Hume, David, xi, xviii, xxix, xxx–xxxi, 20, 46, 55, 65, 73, 106, 168–69, 173, 184

individualism, 41, 46, 56

Jaeger, Werner, xxv, 12, 25–27
Jefferson, Thomas, xviii, 1, 39, 121–22
John Paul II, Pope, 32, 62
  CST, 259n9
  culture of death, 41, 103

Kolnai, Aurel
  and J. R. R. Tolkien, 75–77
  on moral reformers, 86
  privilege, 69–73
  reprimitivism, 163–67
  value, 65

Lacan, Jacques, 62–63, 81, 169, 171–73, 264n56
Leibniz, Gottfried, 56–58, 67, 99, 181
Lincoln, Abraham, 143
Locke, John, 1, 39, 41
Luther, Martin, 177, 192

Machiavelli, Niccolò, 82, 91
Maistre, Joseph de, 63, 137
Marx, Karl
    alienation, 100–101
    labor estrangement, 162
    Marxism/Marxists, 19, 21, 24, 122, 141
    private property, 114–15
Metternich, Klemens von, 5, 136
modernity, 108, 125–29
    Dugin on postmodernism, 47, 51

nationalism, 130–36
natural law
    of Aquinas, 57, 138
    of Benedict, 180–81
    of Burke, 140
    counters and responses, 84–95, 97, 184, 186
    introductory discussion, 79–83
    and the papacy, 59–60
    of Smith, 111
Nazism, 132, 136
    and Kolnai, 164–65
    and Zimmermann, 166
Niebuhr, Reinhold, 36, 38
Nietzsche, Friedrich, 176, 186–88, 233n49

Orban, Viktor, 133

Paul the Apostle, 32, 60, 137, 155, 192–94
Plato
    democracy, 152–53, 158
    ethics, 119, 178, 195
    influence of, 30, 35, 53
    liberty, 153, 158, 160
    metaphysics, 127, 178–79
    sophists, 27
    virtue ethics, 152
populism, 72, 85
progressivism, 34, 165, 175, 185
    Rorty's university progressivism, 62–63
Przywara, Erich, 60, 93

Quintillian, 30
Quinton, Anthony, 7–8

Renaissance
    Erasmus, 156, 167
    humanism, 33–36, 39
    Renaissance Spain/Spanish theology, 99
reprimitivism, 161–63, 185–86
    definition, xxix, xxxiii
Rorty, Richard
    progressivism, 61–64, 75
Rousseau, Jean-Jacques, 159, 181
Russia, 125, 128–29

Scheler, Max, 44
    humanistic enterprise, 117–18
    value, 60–61, 64–65, 226n23
    value hierarchy, 67–69
Schmitt, Carl, 63, 170, 234n52
    conservative humanism, 97
    natural law critique, 86–89, 234n54

Scruton, Roger 16, 18, 43–44, 61,
    263n50
  conservative humanism, 184
  on family, 10
  knights, 163, 168
  modernity, 129
  natural law critique, 84–87
  regulation, 114
Seneca, xii, 20, 29, 154, 156, 195
Stoicism, 6, 153–54, 177, 179,
    196
Strauss, Leo
  on Marxism, 115
  modernity, 179–80
  natural law critique, 90–93
Suarez, Francisco, 44

Tertullian, 177, 192
Tolkien, J. R. R., 74–78
traditionalism, 14
  integral, 125–26, 128–30

transhumanism, 41, 112, 127–28,
    171

United States
  liberalism, 121, 124, 143
  natural law and Baltimore, 94–95
  reprimitivism, 161–62

Vitoria, Francisco de, 36, 39, 41
  natural law, 87–89, 91, 95–97,
    268n48
Voegelin, Eric 31, 43–44, 268n48
  differentiation, 104–7, 119,
    248n109
  philosophy of history, 102–4,
    108–9, 111
Voltaire, 39, 159

Washington, George, xviii, 6, 64, 159

Xenophon, xii, 19, 26, 151, 153, 189

GRAHAM JAMES McALEER

is professor of philosophy at Loyola University Maryland and the author of numerous books, including *Erich Przywara and Postmodern Natural Law: A History of the Metaphysics of Morals.*

ALEXANDER S. ROSENTHAL-PUBUL

is lecturer at Johns Hopkins University's Center for Data Analytics, Policy, and Government and director of the Petrarch Centre, LTD. He is author of *The Theoretic Life: A Classical Ideal and Its Modern Fate.*

Printed in the USA
CPSIA information can be obtained
at www.ICGtesting.com
CBHW052329091124
17077CB00024B/240